POWER AND POVERTY

Recent Titles in
Contributions to the Study of Aging

POWER AND POVERTY

Old Age in the Pre-Industrial Past

Edited by Susannah R. Ottaway,
L. A. Botelho, and Katharine Kittredge

Foreword by W. A. Achenbaum

Contributions to the Study of Aging, Number 27

GREENWOOD PRESS
Westport, Connecticut • London

Library of Congress Cataloging-in-Publication Data

Power and poverty : old age in the pre-industrial past / edited by Susannah R. Ottaway,
   L.A. Botelho, and Katharine Kittredge; foreword by W.A. Achenbaum.
         p.   cm.—(Contributions to the study of aging, ISSN 0732–085X ; no. 27)
      Includes bibliographical references (p.   ) and index.
      ISBN 0–313–31128–5 (alk. paper)
      1. Old age—Europe—History.   2. Old age—United States—History.   3.
   Aged—Europe—Social conditions.   4. Aged—United States—Social conditions.   I. Ottaway,
   Susannah R., 1967–   II. Botelho, L.A. (Lynn A.)   III. Kittredge, Katharine.   IV. Series.
   HQ1064.E8P69   2002
   305.26'094—dc21   2002021623

British Library Cataloguing in Publication Data is available.

Library of Congress Catalog Card Number: 2002021623
ISBN: 0–313–31128–5
ISSN: 0732–085X

First published in 2002

Greenwood Press, 88 Post Road West, Westport, CT 06881
An imprint of Greenwood Publishing Group, Inc.
www.greenwood.com

Printed in the United States of America

The paper used in this book complies with the
Permanent Paper Standard issued by the National
Information Standards Organization (Z39.48–1984).

10 9 8 7 6 5 4 3 2 1

Copyright Acknowledgments

The editors and publisher gratefully acknowledge permission for use of the following material:

From Jack Resch. *Suffering Soldiers: Revolutionary War Veterans, Moral Sentiment, and Political
Culture in the Early Republic.* Amherst: University of Massachusetts Press, 1999.

From Kirk Combe and Kenneth Schmader. "Naturalizing Myths of Aging: Reading Popular
Culture." *Journal of Aging and Identity* 4, no. 2 (June 1999): 79–109.

This volume is dedicated to the memory of Peter Laslett (1916–2001) in deepest appreciation for his encouragement and inspiration.

Contents

Illustrations

TABLES

FIGURES

Foreword

W. A. Achenbaum

This wonderful collection of essays began as a set of conference working papers. Fifteen mostly young and midcareer scholars gathered at Ithaca College to analyze various dimensions of how people in past times perceived and experienced advanced age. In the course of discussing one another's work and revising drafts for publication, the participants built on previous efforts to reconstruct the history of old age in Western civilization. They challenged prevailing wisdom, added fresh insights and data to our knowledge, and invited others to do more work on illuminating the interconnected themes of authority, autonomy, and responsibility among the aged in the pre-industrial past. In so doing, the authors' collective efforts replicate an important step in historical gerontology's pattern of development over the past thirty years.

In the early 1970s, the late David D. Van Tassel, rightly perceiving that biomedical researchers, psychologists, and social scientists dominated gerontology, wondered how scholars from the humanities might enhance "scientific" research on old age. With support from the National Endowment for the Humanities (NEH), in 1975 he asked three dozen luminaries and rising stars in art criticism, history, literature, philosophy, and religion to join him in envisioning possible lines of inquiry. (Van Tassel also invited a few graduate students like me to attend.) After listening to addresses by Erik Erikson, economist Juanita Kreps, several physicians, and Leon Edel, among others, participants returned home to write essays on topics of their choice, which were critiqued at the 1976 meetings of the Gerontological Society.

From this NEH project emerged two volumes, *Aging and the Elderly: Humanistic Perspectives in Gerontology* (1978) and *Aging, Death, and the Com-*

pletion of Being (1979). Neither collection set a research agenda. The "humanities," after all, cover a lot of ground. Besides, contributors were understandably reluctant to claim too much authority in a nascent field of inquiry in which they had little expertise. Van Tassel accomplished his objective, however. All the participants wrote at least one more essay on aging. David Hackett Fisher gained much from the project while he put the finishing touches on *Growing Old in America* (1977); my *Old Age in the New Land* (1978) was richer for insights I gained from the symposium.

In 1984 Van Tassel invited a group of scholars to Case Western Reserve University for another symposium. The guest list this time mainly included historians, political scientists, and sociologists interested in the connections between policymaking and the elderly. Those who contributed to *Old Age in a Bureaucratic Society* (1986) generally had already published in the field, and they went on to write other articles and monographs. Such continuing commitment to niche building is commendable, to be sure, but I was struck by the absence of many eager graduate students who might have been enticed to do work in gerontology or untenured professors from the humanities who might have represented the next scholarly cohort.

Indeed, I remain dismayed by the relative paucity of new talent willing and able to enrich the field of historical gerontology. The ideological, conceptual, and methodological styles associated with the so-called "new social history" made it possible to reconstruct the meanings and experiences of hitherto "invisible" segments of society. Historians now play key roles in the intellectual life of African American studies and women's studies programs, interdisciplinary ventures that have helped to shift scholarly paradigms on most U.S. campuses. Graduate students are far more likely to write dissertations in gay or lesbian history than to pursue research in historical gerontology. It may be that the data on elders in past times are too hard to extract. It is more likely that most men and women in their twenties or thirties do not find the subject matter attractive or cannot imagine how to connect issues such as widowhood or wisdom with the experiences they have had or the professional ambitions to which they aspire.

Susannah Ottaway is correct when she writes in her introduction that "the history of old age has reached something of an impasse." My cohort of scholars has helped to lay the foundations for good work in this area, but historical gerontology desperately needs a fresh infusion of men and women who are willing to work at the interstices of several disciplines while they craft scholarship that will help us to refine old questions as we address new problems. So I welcome this volume not just for its contents but also for its roster of contributors. I hope that *Power and Poverty: Old Age in the Pre-Industrial Past* has the same salutary effect on advancing historical gerontology as did David Van Tassel's works in showing the value of historical perspectives in probing the opportunities, challenges, and mysteries of late life.

Acknowledgments

The editors would like to thank the Huntington Library for permission to reproduce the image of Mother Shipton in Chapter 12. We would also like to thank the University of Massachusetts Press for permission to reproduce parts of Jack Resch's 1999 publication *Suffering Soldiers: Revolutionary War Veterans, Moral Sentiment, and Political Culture in the Early Republic* in Chapter 2. Finally, we gratefully acknowledge the editors of the *Journal of Aging and Identity* for their permission to reprint a revised version of Kirk Combe and Kenneth Schmader's article, "Naturalizing Myths of Aging: Reading Popular Culture," *Journal of Aging and Identity* 4, no. 2 (June 1999): 79–109, as Chapter 10.

In addition, we would like to thank John Krout, the director of the Ithaca College Gerontology Institute, and his staff, especially Terry Beckley, for their support of the September 1999 conference from which this volume emerged. Indiana University of Pennsylvania helped to cosponsor this event, and the staff of Carleton College's Information Technology Services provided crucial support. Several participants in that conference, notably Lisa Dillon, Jim Oeppen, and Jim Smith, whose work is not represented here, were a vital part of that symposium. Individual contributors have noted their intellectual debts in their separate chapters, but the editors would like to thank W. A. Achenbaum for reading the entire manuscript.

Introduction: Authority, Autonomy, and Responsibility Among the Aged in the Pre-Industrial Past

Susannah R. Ottaway

Many physical signs of old age are universal, and people all over the world and through history have shared certain experiences of aging, such as growing gray-haired, or, for women, going through menopause. At the same time, cultural attitudes toward old age vary, and individuals move along unique paths through the life-course. Writing a history of old age in a specific historical context requires the historian to acknowledge both the universalistic and the individualized aspects of aging, while creating a narrative that speaks to the common experiences and expectations of old age in the place and period studied. The essays in this volume do not try to homogenize the highly variable experiences and images of old age that characterized pre-industrial Western societies; each author, for example, defines "old age" in the way that best accords with their subject of study. Nonetheless, this book demonstrates that there were strong commonalties in attitudes toward old age and in the lived experiences of the elderly of Europe and America from the sixteenth through the early nineteenth centuries. Despite facing deep poverty in old age (the connection of aging with impoverishment emerges as a common theme in many of these essays), elderly men and women in the pre-industrial West sought to retain their economic and residential independence, while participating in the reciprocal responsibilities that tied the elderly into networks of familial and community support. At the same time, although negative images of old people were common in literature and popular print, old women and especially old men often exercised authority within the family and wider social circles. These three themes of autonomy, responsibility, and authority in old age are central to this volume.

When historians first became interested in the history of old age in the 1970s

and early 1980s, their discussion focused primarily on the apparently straightforward questions: Did old people in the past command more respect than they
do in contemporary societies? Did care for the elderly take place within the
family or in broader social institutions such as local or state-sponsored welfare
and charities?[1] Several decades on, although these questions remain central to
many studies, they have also metamorphosed into a much more complex set of
queries. Indeed, at this time, our recognition of the need to account for gender,
class, ethnicity, health, and stages of old age as variables within the experience
of old age in any given culture makes it very difficult for historians of aging to
make broader generalizations about old age in former times.[2]

Especially in regard to the pre-industrial period, the history of old age has
thus reached something of an impasse, and sometimes seems to have lost its
initial sense of urgency.[3] Determined not to make the mistake of early historians
of the family like Lawrence Stone and Philippe Ariès, whose sweeping narratives of change in the pre-modern past have been attacked relentlessly, those
who study the elderly in the early modern era have exercised caution, stuck
closely to the evidence of their archival sources, and so created a subfield of
history characterized by an acute awareness of the need to differentiate among
its subjects of study. When David Vassberg acknowledges, in his essay for this
volume, the difficulty of drawing generalizations from the "kaleidoscopic diversity" of experiences and images of old age in early modern Castile, he identifies a central problem for historians of old age more generally.[4] There is good
reason for this: Many historians have learned from gerontologists and social
scientists to regard old age as "a function of the life that the person has lived."[5]
Many of those who emphasize the diversity of experiences and images of old
age, including many of the contributors to this volume, do so to validate the
human experiences of older people in the past and challenge overarching stereotypes concerning the elderly. In effect, the insistence on the individuality of
the experience of aging—its specificity not only in time and place, but also
according to gender, social class, and even individual life experience—successfully challenges ageism, and allows us to overcome the "enormous condescension of posterity" toward the elderly.[6] Unfortunately, the result is that although
historians of old age have created works of admirable sensitivity, it can be
difficult to see how such studies can be connected into a broader analysis of old
age in past time. Moreover, cultural histories of old age that have traced broad
changes in attitudes toward the elderly have been constructed using small sub-
sets of the elderly or a narrow range of documents. Attempts to create master
narratives have thereby themselves rested precariously on fragments of the history of old age.[7]

We have only to look at some of the fine recent publications on aging in
order to demonstrate how fractured is our current view of older people in the
past. In their introduction to the collection of essays *Women and Ageing in
British Society Since 1500*, Lynn Botelho and Pat Thane concluded: "These
essays have uncovered the diverse nature of female old age over a long span of

time and, at any one time, a diversity that shares the experiences of the larger society."[8] Paul Johnson and Pat Thane's volume, *Old Age from Antiquity to Post-Modernity*, probably goes further than any other publication to relaunch old-age studies for historians with its focus on the three issues of participation, well-being, and status. All the same, it is not clear how far these essays go to address the "problems of incoherence and inconsistency" that Johnson identifies as facing historians of aging as they cope with "changes in intellectual fashion." Johnson himself concludes that "Perhaps we should resist the attempt to integrate, to construct a meta-narrative of old age."[9] Johnson suggests that historical gerontologists can focus productively on smaller questions in national (or even local) contexts.

Early modern historians have already shown the utility of this approach.[10] The detailed local studies that have been so characteristic of inquiries on the history of old age have also contributed remarkably to our arsenal of methodologies and source materials. Such studies are indeed valuable, but there is an urgent need to bring their results to bear on the greater issues of old age in the past. How can early modern historians create some broader generalizations about the history of old age while continuing to utilize the local and microhistorical approach that has proven so fruitful to this field?

The symposium for which the essays in this collection were prepared was convened in an effort to address such questions; what follows in this introduction reflects some of the stimulating conversation and tentative conclusions that were expressed during discussions at Ithaca College in 1999. Rather than merely summarizing the contents of the volume, or providing a historiographical overview, this introduction suggests a lens through which to view this book and seeks to clarify how these essays collectively contribute to a greater understanding of old age in pre-industrial Western societies. As we will see below, this lens is constructed primarily around the themes of authority, autonomy, and responsibility. This focus has not been forced on the contributors, nor should it be assumed that the authors share the view of this editor. This volume does not propose a metanarrative of old age from the past to the present, and it certainly should not be taken as supporting a reversion to modernization theory, which was the focus of much research by sociologists and some social historians in the 1970s.[11] In a sense, these essays offer a continuation of the subtle and narrowly focused work that has so characterized the history of old age and aging.[12] When the essays in this collection are viewed together, however, they demonstrate that the examination of the nature and sources of old people's authority—and sometimes the loss of that authority—can create a connective tissue within the body of work on old age in this period. The societies examined here include England, France, Germany, Italy, Spain, and the United States from the sixteenth through the early nineteenth centuries. (It should be noted that this volume's coverage of "only" six countries, and "only" roughly 300 years, actually makes it one of the most focused of the collections of essays to emerge on the history of old age.)

Examining older people's authority can go beyond questions about whether there was a gerontocracy in the past, or whether the elderly were valued,[13] because it can help us to evaluate the social experience of aging. The emphasis throughout this collection is on older people's ability to achieve a "good" old age—an *independent* old age—as defined by the social and cultural world of pre-industrial Western societies. Many recent works have highlighted the importance of independence to older men and women, and analyzing their struggle for self-sufficiency is a fruitful line of enquiry, closely related to the study of authority in old age.[14] In examining the lives of the elderly to determine whether and how older individuals preserved their autonomy, we see that in familial relationships, interaction with state and local institutions, and even portrayals in literary and artistic sources, old age as a stage of life was endowed with certain characteristics of power, especially for the well-off, in pre-industrial times.[15] At the same time, old women and men experienced continued and reciprocal obligations to kin and community. Naturally, there were significant differences in experience according to the sex, economic class, and geographical location of the elderly person, and, with dire poverty a common experience of the aged, this was no "golden age of aging" in the pre-industrial West.[16]

The three interconnected themes of (1) the nature of the association between aging and authority, (2) the degree and type of autonomy achieved in old age, and (3) the responsibilities felt by and toward older men and women each emerges clearly in this collection of essays. This particular articulation of the themes seems most resonant and helpful in regard to the essays here. However, it must be noted that each of these topics bears a close resemblance to the main themes expressed in Johnson and Thane's *Old Age from Antiquity to Post-Modernity*. That work focused on the issues of status, well-being, and participation, which closely connect to the questions of (respectively) authority, autonomy, and responsibilities discussed here. Thus, this book builds on the Johnson and Thane collection, while its tighter focus allows for a clearer picture of how these themes converge in a given period of time.

Part I of this volume, which focuses on experiences of old age among men and women in France, America, and Britain, highlights especially clearly the importance that older individuals placed on retaining their self-sufficiency. This point is demonstrated in David Troyansky's analysis of early-nineteenth-century French magistrates, as well as in Jack Resch's study of American Revolutionary War pensioners, who seem obsessed with maintaining their self-reliance. Independence is also a recurrent motif among the determinedly "useful" women in Britain and Colonial America depicted in the essay by Anne Kugler. At the same time, the autonomy desired and experienced by pre-industrial aged people must not be mistaken for isolation; for the independent old age sought by these men and women was to be shared by well-maintained networks of family and friends. Sherri Klassen's study of friendship among old women in eighteenth-century Toulouse even suggests that age could bring with it a greater attachment to close friends. The ability to craft a "good old age" depended not merely on economic security, but also on nurturing connections within the family and community.

Indeed, the first part in this collection reveals the importance of viewing the authority and autonomy exercised by aging individuals through the lens of both familial and societal interactions. Old people in these pre-industrial societies derived much of their considerable economic and moral power from their position as heads of households and families—when they could keep such positions. Resch demonstrates that elderly Revolutionary War veterans retained a great deal of control over their children through the exercise of their patriarchal roles. In both England and America, Anne Kugler shows, the power older women gained from their family position could even extend beyond the kin network into the exercise of considerable political and religious influence. Such power, however, came with an awareness of the older person's sense of responsibility for helping their families, even while they recognized the reciprocal obligations of younger kin toward them. Thus, for example, even though some of the eighteenth-century French wills studied by Sherri Klassen showed evidence of "patronage, coercion, or manipulation" of the younger generation, the testators are most notable for their attention to the future needs of their families and family estates. Yet these relationships were made more complicated and uncertain by the physical debilities associated with old age. While acknowledging the clear connection between old age and infirmity, these chapters differentiate among different stages of old age and show that sickness and infirmity impaired rather than ended the older person's interactions with and responsibilities to their families, at least until the last stage of "decrepit" old age.

Not all of an older person's authority came from his or her family position, for older people had complex relationships with both state and society. David Troyansky's French magistrates emphasized that their pensions were not a handout, but a social right that they had earned through a lifetime of professional service. In other words, their claim to the money that would allow them continued residential and economic autonomy was based on their earlier exercise of authority, just as the American veterans' pensions were forms of recognition for revolutionary service, not simply a type of charity. It is striking that many French magistrates wished to continue in their duties even after they were pensioned, which suggests the continued importance of sociopolitical authority and responsibility to these older men. Although unable to act as professional servants of the state, elite old women from England and America, Kugler shows, could exercise a parallel form of social power derived from their religious authority; their well-known piety allowed them at times to "speak to, advise, and reprove" their kin and wider community. Old men and old women took considerable pride in their ability both to influence and to assist others, for it is within their own personal narratives—their exercises in self-fashioning—that these themes emerge so clearly.

When elderly people were faced with dire poverty, as so many were in pre-industrial societies, the nature of their authority, their quest for autonomy, and the reciprocal responsibilities of the older person to his or her wider network of kin and neighbors faced additional challenges. The chapters in Part II of this volume each recognize the connection between aging and impoverishment and utilize sources that stem from the respective societies' attempts to alleviate this poverty.[17] However, the essays go beyond the portrayal of the elderly as needy victims of the passage of time. Angela Groppi's essay on the flow of resources between generations in papal Rome finds that "the first duty of every individual was to support himself or herself by his or her own labor." Autonomy in early modern Rome was thus a responsibility rather than merely a goal of the aged. When such independence proved impossible, the authority of an older person to demand support from family members (especially sons) was enforced not merely by moral strictures but by the power of the law courts. Groppi demonstrates that there was a complex interplay of "reciprocal influences and manipulations" that took place among individuals, families, and official institutions like law courts and hospitals.

Louise Gray's exploration of Hessians who petitioned for admission to hospitals also uncovers the continued expectation among the elderly that they would work and that they could and would adjust their employment and lifestyle to accommodate the physical challenges of old age. It was only once complete immobility was reached that the older person abandoned attempts at self-help and applied for a place in the hospital. Even at their most reduced state, Gray notes, older men and women "believed themselves capable of making their own decisions" and were never reduced to the status of minors; they maintained authority at the very least over their own lives. At the same time, Gray's work, like Groppi's, demonstrates the strength of community obligation toward the elderly. This is revealed most intriguingly in attitudes toward old people who beg, which appeared to be widely tolerated by authorities, supported by neighbors, and even regarded as a form of work (ironically, even as self-help) by older people themselves. Among the poor in Rome and Hesse, it seems, the type of "power" exercised by the aged (in marked contrast to the authority of the better-off studied in Part I) was less an authority over others than an entitlement to claim assistance once desperate need and physical debility rendered independence impossible.[18]

Gray and Groppi are both attuned to the importance of gender in determining experiences of aging, but the focus on differences in male and female old age is even more explicit in Jane Pearson's examination of the effect of an economic crisis on the living situations of the elderly in the English town of Bocking. Pearson pays special attention to differences in household status and economic abilities between old men and women. While both the autonomy and authority (reflected, for example, in the ability to head an economically viable household) of wealthier old men withstood a severe economic downturn, poorer men and aged women were more severely affected. Even so, Pearson suggests that the exodus of families from the town allowed older women to exercise their preference for solitary living, demonstrating the likelihood that elderly women placed a high priority on residential independence even in difficult times.

Each of these three essays portrays the experience of old age as characterized by considerable self-sufficiency (at least until the last stage of decrepit old age). It is important nevertheless to note that these essays do not lead to an idealized picture of the lives of independent, old, poor people in the pre-industrial period; such people were undoubtedly patching together lives of independent misery. Still, most histories of old age have described the ways in which the elderly were helped, and these essays show the importance of combining such descriptions with an analysis of the ways in which old women and old men worked to help themselves. Here, the struggle for autonomy takes its place at the center of the social history of old age.

Was this lived experience reflected, however, in the cultural ideals and images of old age in the pre-industrial period? One of the weaknesses of historical studies of old age has been the well-documented failure to mesh cultural and social histories of aging.[19] Most evident in this regard has been an inability to account adequately for the nature of depictions of the elderly in print—both images and text. In both popular and elite representations, as the essays in the second half of the book demonstrate, there is a tendency to portray the elderly in highly exaggerated terms. These images can be ones of tremendous respect, especially for powerful old men, and they can be viciously demeaning, particularly for old women. Such extremes of representation of old age seem to be a far cry from the crafting of an independent yet socially connected old age that so many of the essays in Part I of this volume revealed.

The essays by David Vassberg, Alison Rowlands, and Kirk Combe and Kenneth Schmader serve as a bridge between the chapters that are concerned primarily with the experiences of old age and those that focus on images of the elderly in visual and literary sources. Part III thus sheds light on the disjunction between cultural and social histories of old age. Vassberg pairs a survey of depictions of the aged in proverbs, folklore, and Golden Age Spanish literature with a detailed analysis of the aspects of older Castilians' lives that is evident from surviving early modern census material. In the Spanish case, image and reality are shown not to be in tension. Vassberg juxtaposes exceedingly positive and negative representations of old age in a way that "cancels out" the extreme images (both extremes are shown to be mere caricatures). Vassberg shows that the heterogeneity of the proverbial and literary depictions of the aged mirrors the diversity of social and economic situations among the elderly of Castile, but in both, physical infirmity and economic disability are common themes. In Spain, dependence appears to have been a common and accepted experience of the elderly, especially old widows. But even here, old men and women used their economic power as property owners and their moral authority as parents and community elders actively to ensure that they received good care in their advanced old age. Vassberg's approach is one useful way of reconciling the literary and economic history of old age.

In contrast, Alison Rowlands emphasizes the degree of disjuncture between representation and reality in the case of early modern witch trials. She shows that the stereotype of witches as old women is not fully borne out in the reality of witchcraft accusations; males and females of all ages might find themselves accused of witchcraft in early modern Europe. Her essay is thus a forceful reminder of the need to consider representations of the elderly within their wider social context. Here, too, the utility of examining the connection between old age and power is evident, as Rowlands finds that "one general clue to the greater vulnerability of women aged forty to sixty to accusations of witchcraft may be found in contemporary ways of thinking about power and its exercise."

Combe and Schmader analyze viciously ageist early modern drama and contrast modern ageist assumptions with gerontological reality. Their essay is explicitly designed as a word of caution to historians of aging, emphasizing that "the perceptions, depictions, and ways people might speak about elders and aging is often likely to be quite distinct from the reality of those things in any given historical period." At the level of the deep structure of language, the authors explain, everyday speech is biased against elders. Following the insights of Roland Barthes, they show that such ageism must be seen as part of the "cultural and political realm of human power relations." In other words, while this essay focuses exclusively on negative stereotypes of elderly men and women, it, too, is centrally concerned with the degree of power exercised by the aged. In seventeenth- and eighteenth-century comedy, the elderly who failed to use their authority to meet their obligations to their children (denying their sons or daughters their due rights) were portrayed as tyrants. In drama, as in life, authority had to be tempered with the proper exercise of responsibility, or it caused generational conflict in the pre-industrial period.

Finally, each of the essays in Part IV of the volume seeks to describe and explain the attitudes toward aging that are revealed in representations of the elderly in England. Despite her emphasis on the individuality and the variety of aged characters drawn by Shakespeare in his plays, Janice Rossen contends that the "exemplary model for aging in Shakespeare's universe is Adam in *As You Like It*." The reason is that Adam combines an independence of spirit and a desire to continue to be useful to his employer with a degree of authority that is specifically connected to his age. There are, in other words, strong echoes of the experiences of early modern aged people in the literary depictions of old age from the Bard himself. Older characters in Shakespeare's works combine a concern over their waning power with a desire to stay connected to their communities and especially their kin. As Rossen comments, "Abandonment is, perhaps, the most deeply rooted fear harbored by aging characters." The multidimensional old characters in Shakespeare's plays obviously contrast with the caricaturized old men and women (indeed, all the characters) in the later comedies discussed by Combe and Schmader, and remind us of the remarkable depth and nuance of Shakespeare's work.

The early modern plays studied by Combe and Schmader lampooned both male and female elderly, and in Shakespeare, both old men and old women were portrayed as complex characters; but, as the final essays in this volume show, aging women generally received more negative treatment than old men in both popular and elite representations. Indeed, L. A. Botelho finds that in cheap prints in seventeenth-century England, old men were almost universally portrayed as dignified figures of authority. This society's apparent comfort with the figure of the aged male exercising his patriarchal power (which mirrors the view from Part I that older individuals placed importance on their continued exercise of such authority) stands in marked contrast to the depiction of old women as witches or as witchlike. Botelho sees these images as reflective of the inherently transgressive—and therefore potentially powerful and subversive—nature of old women who were without male control and without the female responsibility of childbearing and housekeeping. Botelho's analysis receives further support from Katharine Kittredge's essay, which focuses on more elite images from the eighteenth century. In part, Kittredge shows, negative images of aging spinsters and widows stemmed from older women's real knowledge and social autonomy, which was perceived as "deeply threatening" during that period. At the same time, societal discomfort with the social responsibility of assisting single women, old and economically disadvantaged as they tended to be, probably also contributed to their negative portrayals in contemporary works.

In each of the essays in this volume, the themes of authority, autonomy, and responsibility permeate the analysis of old age in the pre-industrial past. Older people, both male and female, could effectively draw on their roles as heads of families, their service to the community, and their accumulated years of experience—including their acknowledged role as keepers of public and individual memory—to justify and perpetuate their authority. That such power varied markedly according to gender, status, place, and individual life experience does not render the exploration of age's authority ineffective. On the contrary, we can use topics like power or autonomy as ways to measure the effects of status or gender on one's experience of aging. As in nearly all fields of history, it is different relationships to power that have defined the divergent experiences of rich and poor, man and woman. As Botelho's and Pearson's essays demonstrate with especial vividness, older men and women shared neither stereotyped images nor household status. Older men differed from older women in their social and work activities, their networks of kin and friends, and their self-fashioning. Similarly, while all the essays reveal that there were *reciprocal* responsibilities between children and parents, on one hand, and between older residents (especially superannuated public servants) and their communities, on the other hand, the exact nature and enforcement of these responsibilities varied according to geographical location and social class.

The essays in this volume make it clear that in crafting a "successful" old age for themselves—a *dignified* old age—older people in pre-industrial societies sought independence and self-sufficiency. At the same time, however, these men and women as a group were economically disadvantaged and were beset by ill health. The ubiquity of poverty among the aged is a recurrent theme in these essays, and this is clearly signaled by our decision to juxtapose power with poverty in the title of this volume. Still, older people's sense of responsibility—of the reciprocal obligations that existed among the generations—tied them into kin and community networks, keeping them at the very center of pre-industrial social life, just as the history of old age belongs at the very center of social history.

Readers of this book will undoubtedly be tempted to read individual essays rather than reading this volume as a whole—such is the fate of any "conference volume." It has been the goal of this introduction to urge that these essays be read together, just as they were created together, to replicate the stimulating and fruitful discussion enjoyed by those who participated in the conference from which they emerged.

NOTES

1. Pioneerwork in the field includes Peter Laslett, "The History of Ageing and the Aged," in his *Family Life and Illicit Love in Earlier Generations: Essays in Historical Sociology* (Cambridge, Eng.: Cambridge University Press, 1977); David Hackett Fischer, *Growing Old in America* (New York: Oxford University Press, 1978); Peter Stearns, ed., *Old Age in Pre-industrial Society* (London: Holmes and Meier, 1982); Keith Thomas, "Age and Authority in Early Modern England," *Proceedings of the British Academy* 62 (1976): 3–46.

2. The inability of historians to find a "master narrative" of the history of old age has been noted, with varied levels of concern, in recent surveys of the field. David Troyansky, "Historical Research into Ageing, Old Age and Older People," in *Critical Approaches to Ageing and Later Life*, ed. Anne Jamieson, Sarah Harper, and Christina Victor (Buckingham, Eng.: Open University Press, 1997), 49–61; Paul Johnson, "Historical Readings of Old Age and Ageing," in *Old Age from Antiquity to Post-Modernity*, ed. Paul Johnson and Pat Thane (London: Routledge, 1998), 1–17; and Pat Thane, "Aging in the West," in *Handbook of the Humanities and Aging*, ed. T. Cole, R. Kastenbaum, and R. Ray (New York: Springer Verlag, 2000), 3–24. For another useful overview of the historical literature on old age in Western society, see Margaret Pelling and Richard M. Smith, Introduction to *Life, Death and the Elderly: Historical Perspectives*, ed. Margaret Pelling and Richard M. Smith (London: Routledge, 1991), 1–39.

3. This sense of urgency is perhaps most clearly reflected in Peter Laslett's claim that the history of old age is "necessary knowledge," but it can also be seen in Margaret Pelling and Richard M. Smith's (both of whom work on the early modern period) view of old-age studies as "timely and fresh" in the 1980s, and in Peter Stearns's characterization of old age as a field of history that was "shockingly untended" in 1982. Peter Laslett, "Introduction: Necessary Knowledge: Age and Aging in Societies of the Past," in *Aging in the Past: Demography, Society and Old Age*, ed. David Kertzer and Peter Laslett (Berkeley: University of California Press, 1995); Pelling and Smith, Introduction, 1; Stearns, Introduction to *Old Age in Pre-industrial Society*, 1.

4. One symptom of this has been the relative dearth of monographs, especially on the early modern period, compared to collections of essays in the field.

5. The phrase is from David D. Van Tassel, Introduction to *Aging, Death and the Completion of Being*, ed. David D. Van Tassel (Philadelphia: University of Pennsylvania Press, 1979), x.

6. E. P. Thompson's call to rescue the working class from the condescension of posterity remains a clarion call to all social historians of any historical group that is generally seen as disempowered by historical studies. E. P. Thompson, *The Making of the English Working Class* (New York: Vintage Books, 1963), 12. Paul Johnson also used this quote in his essay cited above.

7. This point was raised by Pat Thane, "The Cultural History of Old Age," *Australian Cultural History* 14 (1995): 26. This is not to deny the importance of such excellent works of cultural history as Terri Premo, *Winter Friends: Women Growing Old in the New Republic 1785–1835* (Urbana: University of Illinois Press, 1990) and Thomas Cole, *Journey of Life: A Cultural History of Aging in America* (Cambridge, Eng.: Cambridge University Press, 1992). And there are a few works that attempt to treat old age more holistically, such as W. Andrew Achenbaum, *Old Age in the New Land: The American Experience Since 1790* (Baltimore, MD: Johns Hopkins University Press, 1978); Peter Borscheid, *Geschichte des Alters: Vom Spätmittelalter zum 18. Jahrhundert* (Münster: Deutscher Taschenbuch Verlag, 1987); and Pat Thane, *Old Age in English History: Past Experiences, Present Issues* (Oxford, Eng.: Oxford University Press, 2000).

8. Lynn Botelho and Pat Thane, Introduction to *Women and Ageing in British Society Since 1500*, ed. Lynn Botelho and Pat Thane (London: Longman, 2001), 11.

9. Paul Johnson, "Historical Readings of Old Age," 1, 17. Pat Thane makes much the same point in *Old Age in English History: Past Experiences, Present Issues* (London: Oxford University Press, 2000), 16.

10. Good examples of this approach include not only essays in both the Botelho and Thane and Thane and Johnson volumes cited above, but also M. Pelling, "Old Age, Poverty and Disability in Early Modern Norwich: Work, Remarriage and Other Expedients," in *Life, Death and the Elderly: Historical Perspectives*, ed. Margaret Pelling and Richard M. Smith (London: Routledge, 1991), 74–101; S. J. Wright, "The Elderly and Bereaved in Eighteenth-Century Ludlow," ibid., 102–133; Sherri Klassen, "Aging Gracefully in the Eighteenth Century: A Study of Elderly Women in Old Regime Toulouse," Ph.D. diss., Syracuse University, 1996.

11. Pelling and Smith (Introduction, 4) note the seeming connection between modernization theory and a history of aging that paints broad generalizations about the place of the elderly in premodern societies, and Pat Thane's *Old Age in English History* (passim) effectively negates any kind of narrative of declining status among the elderly from the medieval to the modern world. Cf. Donald Cowgill and Lowell Holmes, eds., *Aging and Modernization* (New York: Appleton-Century-Crofts, 1972).

12. Paul Johnson draws a useful distinction between old age and aging in "Historical Readings of Old Age," 3–5. I will not repeat his conclusions here, but his discussion encompasses much of the conversation had by participants in the conference from which this volume emerges.

13. An example of a work that focuses on the question of whether or not the aged were valued is Georges Minois, *History of Old Age: From Antiquity to the Renaissance*, trans. Sarah Hanbury Tenison (Chicago: University of Chicago Press, 1989). In their unwillingness to create sweeping generalizations about the respect for the aged in past societies, historians can be seen to have taken very much to heart Pat Thane's warning that the existence of competing representations of old age makes it tricky to pinpoint a

dominant discourse about old age in any one society, let alone within a concept as general as "preindustrial societies." See "The Cultural History of Old Age," 23–29; also see Thane, *Old Age*, 6–7. There has also been a widespread acknowledgment of the difficulty of finding old women and men in the historical record.

14. See especially Thane, *Old Age*, passim; Richard Smith, "Ageing and Well-Being in Early Modern England: Pension Trends and Gender Preferences under the Old Poor Law c. 1650–1800," in Johnson and Thane, *Old Age*, 64–95; Amy Froide, "Old Maids: The Lifecycle of Single Women in Early Modern England," in Botelho and Thane, *Women and Ageing*, 89–110; and Anne Kugler, "I Feel Myself Decay Apace," in Botelho and Thane, *Women and Ageing*, 66–88.

15. Authority has been usefully defined in the context of early modern England as "the power or right to define and regulate the legitimate behaviour of others" (Paul Griffiths, Adam Fox, and Steve Hindle, Introduction to their *Experience of Authority in Early Modern England* [New York: St. Martin's Press, 1996], 1). Here I am using *authority* in a somewhat broader sense, and closer to a more general definition of power, as in the *Oxford English Dictionary* definition of authority as the possession of power over others. From the online version of the O.E.D., http://dictionary.oed.com/entrance.dtl, accessed 2 May 2002.

16. The focus on authority may seem to contradict Pat Thane's recent comment (in Thane, *Old Age*, 7) that "It is difficult to find in historical or anthropological studies of any place or time unambiguous respect for old age as such." This introduction is not trying to claim that old men and women's power was straightforward or uniform in nature. Rather, the authority that accompanied old age can be revealingly studied to identify both universalities and differences among older populations of the past. The theme of reciprocity among generations is also effectively highlighted in Thane, *Old Age*, passim.

17. These chapters thus build on the work done on the importance of bureaucracies in determining the experience of old age. See, for example, David Van Tassel and Peter Stearns, eds., *Old Age in a Bureaucratic Society* (Westport, CT: Greenwood Press, 1986).

18. On the issue of entitlement, see also Smith, "Ageing and Well-Being." My own research also supports this conclusion: Susannah R. Ottaway, *The Decline of Life: Old Age in Eighteenth-Century England* (Cambridge, Eng.: Cambridge University Press, forthcoming). But cf. Jeremy Boulton, "Going on the Parish: The Parish Pension and Its Meaning in the London Suburbs, 1640–1724," in *Chronicling Poverty: The Voices and Strategies of the English Poor, 1640–1840*, ed. Tim Hitchcock, Peter King, and Pamela Sharpe (London: Macmillan, 1997), 19–46.

19. This has been noted in many studies of old age, such as Stearn, Introduction, 14, and David Troyansky, "Balancing Social and Cultural Approaches to the History of Old Age and Ageing in Europe," in Johnson and Thane, *Old Age*, 96–109.

Crafting a Good Old Age

PART I

Crafting a Good Old Age

Aging and Memory in a Bureaucratizing World: A French Historical Experience

David G. Troyansky

A common point of departure for historical investigations into old age has been the observation of a split between social and cultural approaches to the past. The idea runs through the recent collection of essays edited by Paul Johnson and Pat Thane, and Carole Haber, in a review of the book, declares "the need to take the next step in aging history: to form the bridge between cultural perceptions and social realities."[1] Pat Thane has demonstrated one way of doing so, looking at a great variety of sources and eschewing any grand narrative, whether of decline or of progress.[2] Another solution is to find a particular source that might permit the historian's equivalent of a deep ethnographic reading.[3] What is needed is a source that identifies a population of the aged and allows them to speak—no easy matter for the pre-industrial world, for both social and cultural historians often fail to take us inside the minds of historical actors. We are left on the outside, reconstituting households, studying social policies, or examining cultural representations. Even in the post-industrial world it is considered innovative when the aging speak for themselves, theorizing about aging and telling their own stories outside the categories of gerontological science.[4]

In my own contribution to the Johnson and Thane book I described how a particular group of individuals, retiring magistrates in early-nineteenth-century France, presented themselves as aged in order to demand pensions for their public service. Here I will continue looking at that population but will develop the idea that historians of old age might hold together social experience and cultural representation by examining the theme of history and memory. Individual and collective memory link the experience of aging with historical time; life histories and historical narratives are interwoven. For almost a generation now, historians have explored the workings of memory, the multiple retellings of historical events, the reinterpretations that became fixed not only in historical writings but in public commemorations, monuments, and museums. Collective memories came to define social or cultural groups, from regional, religious, and ethnic to national and transnational. Scholars have examined ceremonies of commemoration and the design of monuments and museums to understand the reach of reconfigured pasts into the present.[5]

Some memories became official, but alternative memories survived, some finding expression in writings associated with emerging bureaucratic institutions. In this chapter I want to insist on the importance of bureaucracy not only for the survival of appropriate historical documents but also for their creation. In composing demands that met with bureaucratic approval, individuals deployed their memories to construct aging identities. Collectively pension dossiers represent the creation of a social group; materials within the dossiers permit the recognition of individuals' perspectives. In this chapter I demonstrate how a particular group of post-Revolutionary French magistrates reconstructed their own career trajectories and linked personal histories to national history.

Event history has rarely been the province of historians of aging and the aged, but the history of events provides us with an opportunity to examine the workings of memory. Alan Spitzer has recently shown how political memory was deployed by politicians of the Bourbon Restoration.[6] Memory and forgetting played important roles in political careers spanning various regimes, but they also shed light on the aging self. People told stories to justify their behavior and career choices; how they did so tells us something about aging in the past. Already in the late eighteenth and early nineteenth centuries, some individuals were constructing aging identities by looking back across a turbulent era and trying to make sense of it all.

The occasion for all this memory work was the process of change set in motion by the French Revolution, the event that brought a largely pre-industrial France into the modern political world, initiated important social welfare legislation, contributed to the development of ideas of career and retirement in the public sector, and provided rich and dramatic material to be remembered and refashioned as even relatively minor political actors survived and aged. One might assume it was a revolt by youth against age, as it has sometimes been described as the work of a band of brothers overthrowing fathers (there were sisters and mothers too, but they seem to have been pushed aside).[7] Nevertheless, the Revolution used the image of the old man and old woman to give itself a certain permanence, an anchor, and politicians pioneered social legislation, elaborating a right to a good old age and retirement. In part, the concern for old age grew out of rhetoric itself. In part, it grew out of social need. The mass mobilization for war left soldiers' dependents in difficult circumstances. Aging veterans and their widows had already posed a challenge in the Old Regime. The Revolutionary and Napoleonic periods only added to the problem, and more and more people began speaking a language of social rights. Later in the nineteenth and twentieth centuries, those who sought pensions and social welfare spoke of a promise made in the Revolution but never fully redeemed.[8]

Another way in which the Revolution represented an important step in the shaping of old age as a stage of life, and retirement as a way of managing that stage, is in the development of a civil service. Revolutionary-era bureaucrats gained civil-service status and an expectation of a full career and retirement.[9] Formal career dossiers and bureaucratic methods of acquiring rights to pensions made their way onto the scene. France and other European countries had awarded pensions as recompense for state service in the pre-Revolutionary era, but Old Regime pensions, most thoroughly studied from their moment of Revolutionary elimination, had largely been based upon individual favor. Then, too, people who owned their offices, as was often the practice in the Old Regime, could simply sell them.[10] Some pensions were based upon need and merit, but there was certainly some degree of truth in the Revolutionary characterization of Old Regime pensions as wasteful.[11] Revolutionary pensions were to be different. They were to be public rewards for exceptional service to France. They would go to inventors, artists, and others who made sacrifices for France, to dependents of soldiers, and to the worthy poor. At first, they had little to do with careers. Soon enough, bureaucratic systems were set up within government ministries. Rules were uneven, so ministries wrote other ministries, asking advice. In an atmosphere of great uncertainty, prospective retirees made up arguments and employed a variety of rhetorical devices. They demanded personal intervention, recounted heroic and pathetic tales, and spoke of illness, family responsibilities, and key political moments. In short, they made sense of their careers and complained about inequities.

In the Napoleonic era, postulants designed charts to represent their careers, with references to documentation of particular offices and accomplishments. Decrees of 1806 and 1807 spelled out procedures for claiming rights to pensions and for forcing the retirement of infirm magistrates, but they built upon the practices of such institutions as the Old Regime army and the Ferme Générale and upon Revolutionary notions of social debt.[12] The Napoleonic period saw the emergence of individual pension schemes for employees of the Ponts-et-Chaussées, Mines, Relations Extérieures, Préfecture de Police, and Ministère du Commmerce.[13] Cartons of pension demands sent to the Ministry of Justice in the Napoleonic period reveal claims of entitlement.[14] Eventually, in the Bourbon Restoration of 1814 and 1815, the Ministry of Justice came up with a systematic way of handling claims. Royal *ordonnances* of 23 September 1814 and 9 January 1815 set conditions of thirty years of service and sixty years of age, or ten years of service with infirmity caused by the work, to permit magistrates to claim a pension.[15]

Demands poured in, but it took time to get some postulants to adhere to the rules. In 1819 a circular was sent to courts throughout France restating official requirements but reminding potential retirees to make formal requests. The circular included a model form for would-be pensioners to fill out and a list of required documents. Legislative, administrative, and judicial services were to be totaled in printed columns. Demands, blending the language of favor and right, would be summarized in reports made by the bureaucracy. Formulas used the average of the last three years' salary and the total years served. Those who failed to get what they wanted wrote again and again. If they lived until the next revolution (a generational phenomenon in nineteenth-century France), they assumed they would get a fairer hearing, but in fact it often made no difference, as the bureaucracy was becoming entrenched—the same Monsieur Romer headed the accounting department of the ministry from the Napoleonic era into the 1830s—and its functioning transcended regimes. Unhappy ex-magistrates wrote multiple letters, and some paid to have their complaints printed and circulated in public.

Many careers cut across the Revolutionary divide. Magistrates, like other Frenchmen, had to deal with a fundamental shift from a society of privilege to a nation of citizens. People learned the new rules of the game by participating.[16] Along with a new civic order came a democratization of honor.[17] Magistrates' sense of being derived also from belonging to what has been described as a "themistocracy," an aristocracy of lawyers deserving of their own order separate from the classic three estates, and from the historical experience of making careers in an increasingly bureaucratic world.[18] As men of the law, they spoke the Revolutionary language of human rights and the careerist language of entitlement. Their values were formed in both Old Regime and Revolution. Their pension demands referred to the appropriate legislation and revealed personal expectations. As "themistocratic" professionals, they presented themselves as respectable and honorable; as postulants, they dramatized their life experiences and pleaded for sympathy.[19]

Before guidelines were standardized, the postulant created his own genre, a narrative of self-presentation that combined years of service with lost health and performance of duties with acts of political courage. A great deal of self-fashioning was called into play. Letters that accumulated in a magistrate's dossier reveal changing strategies. Comparisons are made with colleagues, friends, and rivals. A composite portrait of the aging magistrate emerges. He asks for a retirement pension in his mid-sixties. He describes the challenge of living in interesting times. He claims to embody qualities of stability and competence; he writes of his family's history and honor. He recounts heroic actions. He speaks of health and wealth sacrificed, of honor besmirched, of the public served. He may have contributed to the Revolution, but the safest strategy appears to be the claim of serving France and the magistracy. The rules held out the possibility of counting some Old Regime service as national service; magisterial tradition itself transcended regime.

For magistrates whose careers began in the Old Regime, post-Revolutionary memories expressed nostalgia and sometimes resentment. They rooted individual narratives in family, regional, and national histories. They wrote of multiple generations of public service. For some, the Revolution was a great interruption;

for others, it provided new challenges and continued service. For some, particular events stand out and provide the drama of a lifetime; for others, events flatten out. Some began their accounts generations back; others began with their own education. They applied different rhetorical modes: heroism, pathos, simple expectation, special pleading. Some presented the Old Regime as a paradise lost; others recognized how their destinies were linked to the Revolution. In interesting ways, they juxtaposed individual experiences and public events.

Arguments about justice, paternal kindness, right, equity, welfare, humanity, and need depended upon a subjective understanding of the historical moment, but much depended also upon the circumstances of retirement. Was it forced? Was it the result of warfare, institutional infighting, political conflict, purge, personal enmities, or cutbacks in the ministry? Was it the result of physical or mental decline? Was it desired or resisted? In some cases, judges presented the decision to retire as part of a plan for the rest of their lives. Some described decisions resulting from months or even years of planning. Others described emergencies.

All such matters have come to characterize the process of retirement in the modern world to one extent or another, but Revolutionary-era magistrates faced those questions in an extreme form. Whereas in the Old Regime they either decided on their own or under pressure of family or colleagues to pass on or sell their offices, now they were dealing with paid positions in a period of rapid change. Under what circumstances would they give up? Their demands communicated memories of professional careers and family responsibilities. Their narratives recounted professional accomplishments as the natural course of following a traditional calling and accepting tasks thrust upon them.

At the very least, many postulants asked to be named honorary judges in their former jurisdictions. This would allow them to maintain a certain status, expressed both in a formal role in civic functions and in still being listed in the imperial or royal *Almanac*. They made themselves the heroes of their time, standing up to terrorists and fighting brigands and draft resisters. But they also sought sympathy, describing disabilities, misfortunes, and poverty. They claimed that poverty itself brought no shame—losing wealth while serving the public suggested virtuous behavior—but described a shame that might redound to the magistracy and public service if their misery were widely known. Personal and family honor were tied to the honor of the magistracy. While some judges wrote generally of a time of repose, others described a classical return to the country and a humanist retirement to the study.

The Ciceronian model of a respectable and honorable retirement was a theme that had become common in Enlightenment France. Some pension applications evoked Cicero's classic text on old age, *De Senectute*. Such was the case of Gilles Joseph Deligné, a judge in Rennes who in September 1810 used lines from Cicero's text to give meaning to his own life.[20] In this way the high culture of the period made its way into bureaucratic correspondence. It is worth noting that Deligné was deploying personal and political memory to achieve his goal, not just making a philosophical case. At first he wanted to avoid retirement, even in his eighties, but then he embraced the idea and provided a range of justifications for an honorable retirement. He particularly wanted to avoid the shame of being thought to have been fired and the recriminations of families desirous of revenge for his judgments. From there he moved to a discussion of physical ailments and his inability to collect a financial debt. Without a position or an honorable retirement, he claimed, he would simply die.

Three months later, having received neither a new post nor a retirement pension, Deligné tried another strategy, emphasizing an infirmity that dated back twenty-one years. Recognizing that physical disability might result in an entitlement, he told a story of an icy New Year's Day 1789 in Rennes, when he fell and broke his right leg, the setting of which resulted in the loss of two and a half inches of bone and a need for crutches. This was not just any break. It was occasioned by patriotic activity, as he braved the weather at 6:00 P.M. to observe a secret "antipatriotic" meeting of deputies of the Third Estate. "It is evidently to my patriotic zeal for the success of our revolution that . . . I owe the unfortunate fracture of my leg." Refusal of a pension would constitute another misfortune. He ended the letter with an accounting of his income, his dependence upon his wife, and the fact that his son-in-law had received a military pension. His last claim described a diet of bread and water, but the key feature of the account was the memory of 1789, and one imagines Deligné's repeating it whenever possible.

Repetition of the narrative, whether written or oral, gave the author a chance to shape it into compelling form. It constituted more than a cry for help, for it accompanied that cry with a sense of a long career, following a centuries-old model, veering off course, and meeting new expectations, punctuated by moments of drama and emergency. Deligné's series of memoirs covers the range that characterized a great many bureaucrats' demands. It is difficult to separate their themes, for they were interrelated, but time and again memories featured three: professional service, with its moral, economic, and domestic components; participation in formal politics; and the aging of the body. Memories of the Revolution itself and the negotiation between magistrates and the ministry over interpreting the law provided a kind of narrative punch.

The Revolutionary and Napoleonic divide had a fundamental impact on individual lives and careers, but aging magistrates looked back and tried to create coherence. When Augustin Loubers (de Cordes) discovered in August 1810 that his position was going to be eliminated, he began his letter to the ministry by recounting his calling to the law, both by birth and by taste, his teaching in the law faculty of Toulouse before the Revolution, and his service in a series of judicial posts ever since. In principle he would have preferred staying active, "but his advanced age and the infirmities he has contracted in the painful exercise of his functions put him (to his great regret) out of condition to continue his services."[21] He remembered a particular case in the winter of 1805 (Pluviôse, Year 13) when he had to travel to the town of Grenade, in the *arrondissement* of Toulouse, to track a criminal. He fell, hurting his right leg severely and forcing him to stay in bed for twenty months. The pain and the remedies applied deprived him of the greater part of his "physical and moral faculties," so that he could not undertake another career. The immediate cause of Loubers's inactivity was the suppression of his post. As he told it, however, in his demand for support, it was his life story, not an institutional reform, that merited attention. In his narrative, destiny had shaped his career until the combination of accident and aging brought it to an end.

The government's interpretation of the law provoked some challenges. During the Restoration, François Marie Perret presented his career as one of almost constant judicial service but demanded that his period of imprisonment during the Terror count as well.[22] The bureaucracy recognized that he did not have enough time of service, but the circumstances led the ministry to offer him a temporary stipend. He continued to protest. He would have done well not to quibble with his reward because ministerial investigations in 1816 revealed an overly enthusiastic revolutionary. Still, that enthusiasm was expressed in a self-justifying document written during the Terror. Such self-presentation is difficult to assess, but it indicates the need to shape one's memory to the time. When revolution came again, in 1830, he tried again, but regardless of regime, the state was the state, and the rules were the rules.

The working out of the rules and the correspondence over their implementation became a common theme in magistrates' life stories. Former regicide Charles François Oudot spent the entire Bourbon Restoration in exile in Belgium. In making his case with the new regime over the period 1830–1840, he protested that his mistreatment by the Bourbons should be undone. Not only should he be paid as of 1830—the ministry agreed—but he should be provided back pay for his years in exile, years that had ruined him financially. The ministry interpreted laws of the Napoleonic and Restoration periods as preventing such largesse. Oudot's memoirs analyzed the appropriate laws and recounted case after case of other individuals who had been exiled, stripped of pensions, and then reinstated. His own story consisted of long-term service—thirty-seven years—and what he saw as one great injustice, but its telling involved comparisons with other situations.[23]

Those careers were obviously marked by political decisions, and often the retired magistrates chose to be discreet. A very common strategy in reconstructing careers was to blend the life history with public events. Consider the end of Pierre Chiniac's career.[24] He had made serious enemies during the Terror. A cover letter of 24 January 1811 accompanied a twenty-four-page printed justification of his political behavior and a four-page handwritten plea, which began, "When I asked your Excellency's permission last year to go to the waters for the reestablishment of my health, I took the liberty of saying that if my infirmities would no longer permit me to exercise my functions, I would hope that out of his goodness he would procure for me an honorable retirement. I see with pain that my forces diminish each day, that there remains for me very little time to live and that it is time to put an interval between life and death." He then went on to present "the picture of my life" and his works as a man of letters and as a magistrate.

"I was born the 5th of May 1741 of a family that for more than three centuries occupied places in the magistrature at the Sénéchaussée Présidiale of Périgueux." He recounted his studies at the University of Paris, his reception to the bar by the Paris Parlement, and his naming in the town of Uzerches to major offices, which he held until the Revolution. Then, as he told it, he was "forced" by the inhabitants of the city of Uzerches to accept the command of the National Guard "to maintain among them good order and union," and, in January 1790, he was unanimously elected mayor of the city. Administrative and judicial appointments and elections followed. In sum, he presented his political life as honorable service forced upon him. Selfless performance became part of the remembered self.

By the fall of 1793, he had moved to Agen and married, but people he described as "disorganizers of society" denounced him as an "enemy of the people." He told of arrest and imprisonment, of the involvement in his case of a variety of local and national political figures, and of his survival in the face of death threats. He claimed that "duty" was always his compass and that he preferred his conscience to material wealth. He returned to judicial service. He followed the political survey with the intellectual itinerary of a "man of letters." He wrote that he had published a history of the Celts in two volumes in 1771 and listed a variety of other publications, on Church politics, on moral philosophy, and on tolerance. He tied together his various activities in a plea for help.

"These literary works and what I have suffered in the Revolution, especially during the year 1794 when I was in irons, have altered my health, which was very robust. I have had an attack of paralysis, and its effects warn me every day that I have little time to live. My fortune was reduced almost to zero by the diverse losses that I suffered in the Revolution and the expenses that they've occasioned. I have sold the little property that remained to a relative who, after having promised to pay me only when money will have regained its value, had the indignity to pay me when a thousand francs of assignats only were worth 24 livres. My wife has a mediocre fortune." He claimed it would pain "the generous heart of his Imperial and Royal Majesty" to let him suffer at seventy years of age and asserted, "I have so little time to live that the payment which his Majesty will deign to give me can't be a burden for the state."

The printed memoir detailed his political career and reproduced an assortment of documents demonstrating Chiniac's political and moral virtues. It described his enemies and his respect for the law. It began with a claim that he has been persecuted and that he owed it to the public to provide his side of the story. It recounted cruelties and kindnesses during his ordeal. In describing his arrest and transfer from Toulouse to Agen, he recalled the cruelty of the authorities who would not allow his wife to ride with him, forcing her to hire another coach. When the committee of the commune of Agen planned to take him to Brive, he feared he would be killed, but he had a happy memory of the officers who escorted him and allowed him to spend the night at home, giving his wife a chance to launch a successful appeal.

The handwritten account used some of that material but weaved together a political, professional, and medical history. It constituted a demand and a memoir, which featured the high and low points of his career and how it had ended up. The French Revolution might have set precedent in the history of civil service, the magistracy, and public pensions, but it was also an occasion for heroic activity that avoided the "excesses" of the Revolution or for painful loss of property. Memory of that activity formed a kind of life review.

Another magistrate who supplied a political self-portrait was Roussel-Bouret, who wrote the minister of justice on 16 June 1810.[25] Roussel claimed to have been owed a pension that dated back to the Old Regime. He described being in decline. "My multiple infirmities warn me that I'm reaching the last steps of my long and sad career." He lamented his destiny, wondering how it could be that after a "life devoted to so many works as useful as they were painful," after a youth of ease and then so much misfortune, described in his self-portrait, "would it be my fatal destiny that I end my days in the greatest distress, in poverty, in the denial of the things most necessary in old age?" He evoked the themes of justice, equity, welfare, and humanity and interjected that the minister had invited him personally to write.

His next written demand came in August and began with a physical accounting, including colic and fever that prevented him from pleading in person. He claimed he had been the victim of calumny and quoted the Bible, Richelieu, and La Fontaine about how good men always have their detractors. He claimed he was really not importunate by nature, that he was naturally timid and, thus, slow to ask. He wished he could still work, but he had grown old, and his health forbade. He signed off as "the very humble, very devoted and very humble servant Roussel-Bouret, more than octogenarian, former magistrate of the sovereign courts, as much before as since the Revolution, pensioner of the state, originally of 2,000 livres, now reduced to 166 francs!!" Another letter repeated the essentials in January 1811. It added a comparison with the success of mere copyists in obtaining greater pensions, and it complained that the printing of his political life cost more than three years of his little pension. He repeated the minister's own words, that "you can count on my justice," that "the intention of the Emperor is to accord to public functionaries pensions proportioned to the importance and duration of their services." How to interpret the law became part of the story.

The combination of present misery and historic service is obvious in the dossier of François Anne Louis-Phelippes de Coatgoureden de Tronjolly, a judge in Brittany, who recounted his sacrifices for the republic and the defense of humanity, and complained that "the air of Napoléonville is killing me and that 1,250 francs, which comprises my salary, are insufficient to support me in this city even alone." He described his family's discomfort in Rennes.[26] Born 15 February 1751, and thus fifty-seven years old when he tried to obtain a new post or a pension, he wrote about thirty-five manuscript letters, including one across which he scrawled, "I await justice!" He assured the minister that he was neither mad nor infirm, but that the region's climate was killing him and that he didn't understand the local dialect. He said he had been happier imprisoned in the Conciergerie of Paris during the Terror. In one of his printed demands, he wrote in the third person, "Yes, SIRE, his sorrows and his name belong to history; he will declare until death, his wife and children will claim, when he is no longer, he sacrificed his fortune for the State."

He claimed to have rendered thirty-six years of service, following in a 500-year tradition of his family in Brittany. He went back fourteen generations to a great battle in which an ancestor had distinguished himself, and then linked his own service in the magistracy to the military service that was more routinely rewarded. He saw himself as performing on an even bigger stage, however. "Christopher Columbus was treated as a visionary and as a madman, after having rendered great services for the Spanish and posterity: he had discovered America. But, SIRE, what haven't I done for the French?" He recalled the drownings, shootings, and brigandage of the Terror in the Loire region and declared himself an avenger on a Europe-wide stage. In other words, at the time of the greatest internal conflict in Revolutionary France, he saved the country. Thinking ahead to posterity, he even provided verses to be placed beneath his portrait.

The pattern for many magistrates was to recount memories of resisting radicals at the height of the Revolution. Others expressed considerable pride in their Revolutionary contributions and credentials. Napoleonic magistrates, like politicians of the era, came from virtually all ideological backgrounds, but they naturally attempted to refashion themselves as essentially moderate. When the Bourbon Restoration came in 1814–1815 (with the 100-day Napoleonic interlude), it became practical to present oneself as counterrevolutionary and more dangerous to feature revolutionary service. Thus, Jacques Alexis Thuriot de la Rosière, a regicide, a member of the Committee of Public Safety, and the man who presided over the Convention on 9 Thermidor, tried to claim that he had been maligned and was really a defender of the royal family.[27] His letter of 6 March 1815 responded to an ordinance of 15 February concerning his eligibility for a retirement pension. He launched into his life history: born in Sézanne, Marne, 1 May 1753, lawyer in the Parlement de Paris since 9 July 1778, judge in the district tribunal, service in the Legislative Assembly, Convention, and so on. Laws and ordinances, he claimed, assured him a pension. He also explained that his property had been devastated by the allies' invasion of France. He claimed his intention was to reside in the country but that he would have to return to Paris to support his wife and son. In 1814 he had received assurances that the new king, Louis XVI's brother, would not hold a grudge, but he was still sent into exile in 1816.

Then came his great exercise in self-fashioning. In January 1824, at age 71 and in ill health, he wrote King Louis XVIII himself from Liège: "Justice is the principal attribute of Royalty, the right of claiming it is sacred and inviolable." He recalled saving the riches housed in the Tuileries during the great insurrection of 10 August 1792, which overthrew the monarchy. He headed a deputation of the Legislative Assembly that faced the Paris crowd in the courtyard of the Tuileries. "The scenes were frightful, the crowd was enormous, the most horrible vociferations made themselves heard, everything was braved by the deputation.

"By force of perseverance I managed to make myself heard and to make them promise to respect the two palaces and the riches that were there." He went on to recall his protecting the queen by advising her through the intermediary of a tall brown-haired employee of the royal household, his attempting to delay a 16 December 1792 decree banishing members of the royal family from France, and his arguing for the queen in the Committee of Public Safety in July 1793. For all this, he said, he was denounced. Furthermore, he recovered some royal property and participated in the downfall of Robespierre, an event he narrated in great detail, painting a portrait of the horrors he had prevented. He claimed to have protected the king's daughter, saved the National Library, and negotiated the safety of six fellow magistrates who had been members of the Convention. The last two pages focused on the pension itself, his claim that his right to it was "incontestable," and his desire to return to France.

His memories of 1792–1794 were vivid, his situation that of the moderate squeezed from both extremes. His old age was one of remembering and interpreting. The shape of that memory depended in part on his perception of the law and current political circumstances, but he could always claim it was a patriotic memory.

Even a man who had served as a spy for the English—we only know this in retrospect and from other sources—turned himself into a patriot. His public face was similar to Thuriot's, but he spoke in a sense for an entire generation. François Joseph Gamon justified his pension demand by recounting his services and explained his decision to retire by saying that he couldn't help it that he came of age during the Revolution and reached old age in a very different era.[28] Born 6 April 1767 in the Ardèche, he was only forty-seven years old when he retired in 1814. He claimed the infirmities of old age had led him to try to retire three years earlier. The ministry asked him to hang on. He narrated his political career by referring to particular acts, events, and speeches. He had opposed the execution of the king, and he was proscribed with the Girondins and denounced by Jean-Paul Marat, fled the country, and returned after the fall of Robespierre. He recounted the "deluge of maledictions" and "violent murmurs" that accompanied his moderate proposals in the Convention. He explained his desire to retreat from public life. He was tired of political battles, suffering from "this fatigue of the soul that one suffers when one has known the men and profound perversity of our century." He deserved a pension, he said, because of twenty-four years of legislative, judicial, and administrative service, the mediocrity of his fortune, and "because if a fatal destiny has thrown me onto a theater of crimes and revolutions, I have resisted the torrent of public corruption, and I braved death, I dare say, to save the life of the king, and also to save France from anarchy: nevertheless, I was one of the youngest among the passengers embarked on the vessel of the revolution." His sense of historical time and his political memory forged his identity: "I am French: and if I have the regret that in the time I have lived, all my services were rendered to the *patrie*, and not at the same time to the Bourbons, the illustrious head of that family will recognize that having come, so to say, into the world in 1791, being born in the cradle of the republic I had to be by force of circumstances as well as by my principles one of the defenders of this republic which declared itself the enemy of the Bourbons, that this separation of France and her former kings was from the origin of the revolution the will of my century, and that to obey the general will was my duty." Like Thuriot, he suffered exile, but his return was authorized in 1818, and, like Thuriot, he was persecuted by revolutionaries for being a royalist and by royalists for being a revolutionary. His clandestine service to England only compounded the complication of his identity.

What counted as public life was not limited to formal politics. Public history has its proper shape. Individual lives intersect it in unpredictable ways. Richard François Chaix d'Estanges, a prosecutor who found himself without a position when his court was suppressed, characterized his own career as having political and historical importance.[29] For us, his storytelling was most striking. The dossier remarked that he was guilty of some sort of "immorality," but his own testimony suggested he was in trouble only because he was a married former priest. Whatever the truth, he recounted several events in which he had distinguished himself in local history and found himself at odds with religious officials. One dispute concerned whether one need obey a sovereign who encourages injustice. Another was considerably less philosophical, a murder case in which, he claimed, two priests, both administrators at a Reims secondary school, encouraged a jury to acquit a guilty defendant.

Chaix d'Estanges wanted a pension, but in his demands he repeatedly recounted a seemingly irrelevant case. According to him, Marie Catherine Sarré, 28-year-old wife of Christophe Gatier, a coachman in Delville, department of the Ardennes, was having an affair with an older man named Gervaise, who was killed on 6 March 1809. He surmised that she was also having an affair with Gervaise's eldest son. Three weeks before the murder, Gervaise the son and Mme. Gatier were alleged to have formed the plot to assault the father. She would arrange a rendezvous and lead him into the woods, where the son and two other men, paid with the victim's money, would beat him. In a scene worthy of comic opera treatment, she dined on the appointed evening with the son and the two coconspirators in one cabaret and in another cabaret with the father. She went from one to the other and set up the tryst/ambush in the woods. Chaix d'Estanges noted that the jury might have made a distinction between plotting to beat up and rob the father and intending to kill him. He was convinced that it was the priests who worked to get her acquitted, that they wanted to prove how powerful the protection of priests could be.

What does all of this have to do with the demand for a pension? He was convinced that his reputation had been sullied and so called to mind his enemies, explained their hostility, and tried to put his own actions in a favorable light. We are not dealing with a simple formula leading to the awarding of a pension. Memory of past actions was marshaled. Who he was derived from what he had done and how he could represent himself.

Who one was also derived from bodily experience. Magistrates wrote easily of physical ailments: fevers, blindness, paralysis, gout, incontinence, and the like. Medical certification became part of the process, as the ministry required letters from two practitioners. While some postulants claimed that age itself should be proof of deterioration, a medical discourse about the particular hazards of the magistracy and of the aging of the magistrate evolved. Falling off a horse or cart while on judicial business had immediate consequences, but the more sedentary labors of judges also could be life-threatening. Doctors and surgeons described the strokes and heart attacks, gout and asthma, blindness, deafness, and paralysis, the difficulty urinating that caused pain, or the incontinence that kept a judge at home. They went beyond describing illness or disability and argued that the job itself caused the disability. Long hours of work in unhealthy environments, the emotional strain of the court, and the need to learn new law codes took their toll. The medical language of the aging body made its way into magistrates' demands.

Pierre-François Anfrye, who had risen to be presiding judge of the Civil Tribunal of Versailles before resigning in April 1819 because of "grave infirmities," concluded his career short of thirty years—he served only twenty-five years, seven months, and twenty-seven days but argued for twenty-nine.[30] He mentioned poor eyesight, kidney stones, bladder problems, and gout. That he had resigned before being granted a pension was the sticking point. The themes that recur in his correspondence are service, illness, and lack of resources. He called the law Machiavellian and jesuitical and claimed a proprietary right, as salaries had been subject to withholding for the creation of a ministerial pension fund. His career history involved an earlier resignation from a judgeship in the wake of Louis XVI's execution on 21 January 1793. He found it hard to accept that the government of Louis's brother would mistreat him. He ended his account with a description of an operation for stones.

Complaints of physical infirmity humanize accounts of aging magistrates and contribute to a portrait of the aging body. Parliamentary debates over 1824 legislation encouraging forced retirement for infirm judges explored the vocabulary of "permanent" or "incurable" disease. Justice Minister Peyronnet described magistrates unwilling or unable to recognize their disabilities,[31] but many first-person accounts displayed both acute and chronic ailments without shame. Throughout the first half of the nineteenth century, medical documentation formed only one part of the dossier, but it was the one supported by scientific expertise. Nonetheless, the political might still trump the medical. When 66-year-old Jean De Sèze missed his thirty years by a few months in 1830, he claimed a ten-year illness, but his colleagues doubted its severity and announced that he had made it known that he did not want to serve the new regime.[32]

When Revolution came again in 1848, the problem of workers' retirement reappeared, and in the early 1850s mandatory retirement at seventy or seventy-five (depending upon the office) was instituted in the judicial system. Is it possible that magistrates were becoming less inclined to employ the medical language of the aging body? Or was the government simply searching for an easier procedure by avoiding having to judge individual accounts? Only further research will tell. Until midcentury, however, those seeking pensions reconstructed life histories by recounting memories of professional activities, family histories, economic and political challenges, and physical decline.

We think of bureaucracy as impersonal, but a developing bureaucracy encouraged the communication of remarkably intimate details as aging magistrates made sense of their lives. Industrialization, the modern labor market, and the welfare state will have their roles in the construction of the aging self, but an early experience came in the development of public sector employment and the concomitant elaboration by individuals of their life histories, the shaping of political and personal memories into something to be cashed out.

NOTES

The archival research on which this chapter is based was undertaken thanks to a Faculty Development Leave from Texas Tech University and a Senior Fulbright Research Fellowship at the Ecole des Hautes Etudes en Sciences Sociales (Paris) in 1996–1997.

1. *American Historical Review* 105, no. 5 (December 2000): 1699. The book is Paul Johnson and Pat Thane, eds., *Old Age from Antiquity to Post-Modernity* (London: Routledge, 1998).

2. Pat Thane, *Old Age in English History: Past Experiences, Present Issues* (Oxford, Eng.: Oxford University Press, 2000).

3. For a model ethnographic study of aging, see Lawrence Cohen, *No Aging in India: Alzheimer's, the Bad Family, and Other Modern Things* (Berkeley: University of California Press, 1998).

4. Jaber Gubrium, *Speaking of Life: Horizons of Meaning for Nursing Home Residents* (Hawthorne, NY: Aldine de Gruyter, 1993); for a more theoretical and more wide-ranging discussion of identity, see James A. Holstein and Jaber F. Gubrium, *The Self We Live By: Narrative Identity in a Postmodern World* (New York: Oxford University Press, 2000).

5. The most influential work has been Pierre Nora's seven volumes, *Les Lieux de mémoire* (Paris: Gallimard, 1984–1993), but also important is John R. Gillis, ed., *Commemorations: The Politics of National Identity* (Princeton, NJ: Princeton University Press, 1994). On the impact of Nora, see the recent review by Hue-Tam Ho Tai, "Remembered Realms: Pierre Nora and French National Memory," *American Historical Review* 106, no. 3 (June 2001): 906–922.

6. Alan B. Spitzer, "Malicious Memories: Restoration Politics and a Prosopography of Turncoats," *French Historical Studies* 24, no. 1 (Winter 2001): 37–61.

7. Lynn Hunt, *The Family Romance of the French Revolution* (Berkeley: University of California Press, 1992).

8. Gilles Pollet and Bruno Dumons, *L'État et les retraites: genèse d'une politique* (Paris: Belin, 1994); Elise Feller, "La Construction sociale de la vieillesse (au cours du premier XXe siècle)," in *Histoire sociale de l'Europe: industrialisation et société en Europe occidentale, 1880–1970*, ed. François Guedj and Stéphane Sirot (Paris: Seli Arslan, 1997).

9. Catherine Kawa, *Les Ronds-de-cuir en révolution: Les employés du ministère de l'Intérieur sous la Première République (1792–1800)* (Paris: Comité des travaux historiques et scientifiques, 1997).

10. William Doyle, *Venality: The Sale of Offices in Eighteenth-Century France* (Oxford, Eng.: Clarendon Press, 1996).

11. T.J.A. Le Goff, "Essai sur les pensions royales," in *État, marine et société*, ed. M. Acerra et al. (Paris: Presses de l'Université de Paris-Sorbonne, 1995).

12. For the army, see Jean-Pierre Bois, *Les Anciens Soldats dans la société française au XVIIIe siècle* (Paris: Economica, 1990). For civil pensions, see Vida Azimi, "Les Pensions de retraite sous l'Ancien Régime," in *Mémoires de la Société pour l'Histoire du Droit et des Institutions des anciens pays bourguignons, comtois et romands*, 43e fascicule (1986): 77–103. More generally on old age, see Jean-Pierre Bois, *Les Vieux: de Montaigne aux premières retraites* (Paris: Fayard, 1989); Jean-Pierre Gutton, *Naissance du vieillard: Essai sur l'histoire des rapports entre les vieillards et la société en France* (Paris: Aubier, 1988); David G. Troyansky, *Old Age in the Old Regime: Image and Experience in Eighteenth-Century France* (Ithaca, NY: Cornell University Press, 1989).

13. On retirement in particular, see Guy Thuillier, *Les Pensions de retraite des fonctionnaires au XIXe siècle* (Paris: Comité d'Histoire de la Sécurité Sociale, 1994), and Bernd Wunder, "Die Einführung des staatlichen Pensionssystems in Frankreich (1760–1850)," *Francia* 11 (1983): 417–474. On the state more generally, see Pierre Rosanvallon, *L'État en France de 1789 à nos jours* (Paris: Seuil, 1990), and André Gueslin, *L'État, l'économie et la société française XIXe–XXe siècle* (Paris: Hachette, 1992).

14. Napoleonic-era demands are found in the Archives Nationales (AN) first twenty cartons of BB25 and in BB2 10. Hundreds more cartons in series BB25 contain subsequent dossiers down to the middle of the nineteenth century.

15. *Bulletin des lois*, 5e série, f.2, no. 40 (1814): 225–229; 5e série, f.3, no. 70 (1815): 1–3. For policy debates over the retirement of civil servants, see Guy Thuillier, *Les Retraites des fonctionnaires: débats et doctrines (1790–1914)*, 2 vols. (Paris: Comité d'Histoire de la Sécurité Sociale, 1996).

16. Isser Woloch, *The New Regime: Transformations of the French Civic Order, 1789–1820s* (New York: Norton, 1994).

17. William Reddy, *The Invisible Code: Honor and Sentiment in Postrevolutionary France, 1814–1848* (Berkeley: University of California Press, 1997).

18. The notion of themistocracy is used in Richard Mowery Andrews, *Law, Magistracy, and Crime in Old Regime Paris, 1735–1789*, vol. 1 (Cambridge, Eng.: Cambridge University Press, 1994). Among the works on French bureaucracy are Clive H. Church, *Revolution and Red Tape: The French Ministerial Bureaucracy 1770–1850* (Oxford, Eng.: Clarendon Press, 1981), and Guy Thuillier, *La Bureaucratie en France aux XIXe et XXe siècles* (Paris: Economica, 1987).

19. A social historian's treatment of the magistracy is found in Christophe Charle,

"Les Magistrats en France au XIXe siècle: Les fondements sociaux et politiques d'une crise prolongée," in *El tercer poder: Hacia una comprensión histórica de la justicia contemporánea en España*, ed. Johannes-Michael Scholz (Frankfurt-am-Main: Vittorio Klostermann, 1992). For the perspective of historians of law, see Jean-Pierre Royer, *La Société judiciaire depuis le XVIIIe siècle* (Paris: PUF, 1979); Jean-Pierre Royer, Renée Martinage, et Pierre Lecocq, *Juges et notables au XIXe siècle* (Paris: PUF, 1982); and Marcel Rousselet, *La Magistrature sous la monarchie de juillet* (Paris: Sirey, 1937). The most ambitious treatment of the judiciary across the Revolution covers one department of France and avoids general conclusions: Jean-Claude Gégot, "Le Personnel judiciaire de l'Hérault (1790–1830)," Thèse, Université Paul Valéry de Montpellier, 1974. For a more current approach to comparable figures, see Robert Descimon, Jean-Frédéric Schaub, and Bernard Vincent, *Les Figures de l'administrateur: institutions, réseaux, pouvoirs en Espagne, en France et au Portugal 16e–19e siècle* (Paris: EHESS, 1997).

20. David G. Troyansky, "Balancing Social and Cultural Approaches to the History of Old Age and Ageing in Europe: A Review and an Example from Post-Revolutionary France," in Johnson and Thane, *Old Age*, 100–102. Where appropriate, I have borrowed a few passages from that chapter.

21. AN BB2 10.

22. AN BB25 33.

23. AN BB25 36.

24. AN BB2 10.

25. Ibid.

26. AN BB25 18.

27. AN BB25 36.

28. AN BB25 33.

29. AN BB2 10.

30. AN BB25 252.

31. The debates can be followed from 17 April to 12 June in *Archives Parlementaires*, edited by J. Mavidal and E. Laurent, 2e série, vols. 40 and 41 (Paris: Librairie administrative de P. Dupont, 1878).

32. AN BB25 272.

2

Poverty, Patriarchy, and Old Age: The Households of American Revolutionary War Veterans, 1820– 1830

Jack Resch

The passage of the 1818 Revolutionary War Pension Act created the first program of relief for elderly American veterans who claimed to be poor. Because veterans were required to pass a means test to continue on the pension rolls after 1820, their claims provide a unique view of the wealth and family positions of a large group of elderly men and their households. Applicants were required to report their real and personal property and the composition of their households; many claimants volunteered assessments of their health, the afflictions suffered by spouses and members of their households, and in some instances accounts of their misfortunes. In so doing, claimants offered their own view of the meaning of poverty beyond the technical requirements established by the War Department. Their accounts portray the effects of aging, infirmity, and disease on themselves and family members. They describe family struggles with misfortunes and explain their efforts to sustain households and kin networks.

More than a self-portrait, their claims reflect the larger cultural values assumed, if not imbued, in early-nineteenth-century American families. Even among the poorest, these aging veterans reflect the extraordinary value placed on self-sufficiency.[1] Veterans who received private charity or public relief appealed for the pension to restore their independence. Claimants who feared they were becoming dependent pleaded for the pension to ensure continued self-sufficiency. These claims implied a reluctance if not dread of relying on charity or poor relief for support.

The second value displayed in these claims, which was inseparable from self-sufficiency, was patriarchy. Veterans portrayed themselves as struggling to retain their status and authority as heads of households. They claimed that with the pension they could continue to be the principal source of support for their families, especially those that contained young or disabled children or older children who cared for their parent. With the pension providing a lifelong income, fathers could also control an orderly transition of their households as sons moved away or assumed title of the family farm. As seen in the case studies below that go beyond information found in the claims, some veterans used the pension to execute retirement contracts, which transferred their farms to sons while retaining a place for themselves on the homestead. Thus they ensured their self-sufficiency and independence as heads of households—albeit households reduced in size, often just to husband and wife. In these cases, pensioners and their children gained greater security and independence as well as a psychological benefit of unmeasured value. The pension removed many of the hazards that produced fear of households collapsing or conflict over the distribution of the father's property. For claimants who failed the means test, the pension was their safety net should they lose or divest their assets.

This chapter is based on the results of a random sample of 20,000 applicants. One white male in ten over the age of fifty-nine applied for the pension.[2] The proportion of blacks applying for the pension is difficult to determine, since race was not systematically recorded in pension applications. Only a handful of cases in my sample could be positively identified as black veterans. To some degree, the pension claims unveiled circumstances among survivors of the Revolutionary generation as a whole. The examination of the claims by the type of household also revealed more clearly than other analytical categories the interplay between age, wealth, and household composition.

PROFILE OF APPLICANTS

About half the applicants lived in New England and almost a third resided in the Middle Atlantic States. While the average age of the applicants was sixty-five years, as a group they represented a wide range of ages: one in seven was in his fifties, nearly two-thirds were in their sixties, and almost a quarter were over seventy years of age. More than 80 percent of the applicants reported they were in poor health (Table 2.1): Silas Russell reported that he was "very infirm," Daniel Rider swore that he was "in bad health," Henry Hallowell said he was "weak in body," Henry Buzzell claimed to be "feeble," Joseph Stevens stated that his health was "broken," and Reuben Clark complained of "afflictions.[3] Richard Hallstead said he had a "weak heart." Philo Philips, "a man of color," suffered from "rheumatism," the most commonly reported medical complaint. Israel Manning reported "afflictions of the kidneys," and Ichabod Beckwith said he had "palsy and fits." A few applicants were physically disabled. Samuel Mitchell testified that he was blind.[4] As Louise Gray notes in this volume, the elderly often cited such ailments as the key reason for needing charity or public support. Veterans' claims underscored how infirmities, especially rheumatism,

Table 2.1
Applicants' Health Categories

	Frequency	Percent	Valid Percent	Cumulative Percent
"Infirm"	544	62.0	62.0	62.0
Medical Claim	176	20.1	20.1	82.1
Healthy	4	.5	.5	82.6
Not Mentioned	153	17.4	17.4	100.0
Total	877	100.0	100.0	

Source: Resch, *Suffering Soldiers*, 220.

diminished their capacity to be self-supporting, and more important perhaps, to fulfill their roles as husbands and fathers.

Most claimants were poor, as officially measured by the war department's means test. Nearly one veteran in eight (13.4 percent) was penniless. About half the other claimants reported assets valued at less than $50. Only one applicant in five reported owning real estate. Taken as a whole, the average value of claimants' property was $129. Generally, claimants' inventories contained a few household items, some farm implements or artisan tools, and possibly one or two animals such as a cow or pig. Hardly any of the veterans reported an income. Using a crude measure derived from veterans' claims and aggregate wealth reported for New York residents, it appears that applicants were well below the average wealth. In 1819 the state of New York reported an average of $204 per person in real and personal property.[5] By comparison, in 1820, after dividing the amount of wealth per household by the number of people in the household, the per capita wealth of veterans in New York was $28, or about one-ninth the average wealth of residents in the state.[6] Regardless of state or region, applicants reported owning a meager portion of the nation's wealth. If these data are extrapolated for the population as a whole, claimants were at the bottom of the economic ladder. To emphasize their destitution, 22 percent of the claimants stated that they had once received, were receiving, or were about to receive private charity or public relief (Table 2.2).

Pension applications revealed a stratification of assets and deprivation that reflected the interplay of age and household structure (Table 2.3). On the bottom rung were solitary households where veterans claimed no other family members living with them. Veterans living with their wives were higher up that economic ladder. Veterans heading nuclear households were higher still, and those heading

Table 2.2
Source of Support for Applicants and Applicants Reporting They Would Seek Support

		Frequency	Percent	Valid Percent	Cumulative Percent
	Family, Friends, Town	152	17.3	17.3	17.3
	No Aid	676	77.1	77.1	94.4
	Would Seek	49	5.6	5.6	100.0
	Total	877	100.0	100.0	

Source: Resch, *Suffering Soldiers*, 203–204.

complex households were at the top. The analysis of household types suggested stages of growing dependency and fraying households and kinship networks.

SOLITARY HOUSEHOLDS

Veterans who reported no one else in their households were among the oldest and most desperate men, according to their claims. Comprising slightly more than 15 percent of the applicants, this group contained nearly half of all veterans above the age of seventy-four. On average, these veterans owned only $20 in assets, an average one-sixth the value of assets reported by applicants as a whole. Nearly half the solitary veterans, more than any other category of claimants, were penniless. One veteran out of twenty reported owning real estate, far fewer than claimants as a whole. Moreover, the relative absence of reported debt by this group (only 10 percent listed liabilities) suggests that these veterans had depleted their assets and were incapable of securing credit because they were incapable of paying their debts. It is not surprising that this group also had the highest rate of dependency. Nearly 40 percent of the solitary veterans reported having received charity from neighbors or poor relief from their communities. Their pleas for pensions eloquently revealed the dire effects of advanced age, declining health, grinding poverty, frayed kin networks, and diminished autonomy.

Poverty and illness had dissolved Elijah Caswell's household. In 1820 Caswell, sixty-eight years old, wrote in his pension application that he was unemployed, lived in Massachusetts, and possessed only $7 in assets. Caswell told the court that before receiving a pension in 1818, his invalid wife had been living in the local poorhouse. He reported, "when I got my pension, I took her out." He apparently placed her with another family, possibly to nurse her afflictions, because she did not reside with him when he reapplied for his pension.

Table 2.3
Household Types

Household Forms	Frequency	Percent	Valid Percent	Cumulative Percent
Solitary	132	15.1	15.1	15.1
Husband and Wife	233	26.6	26.6	41.6
Nuclear	400	45.6	45.6	87.2
Extended: Pension Applicant Head With Kin	18	2.1	2.1	89.3
Extended: Kin With Applicant	75	8.6	8.6	97.8
Multiple: Kin With Applicant	3	.3	.3	98.2
Multiple: Applicant With Kin	3	.3	.3	98.5
Applicant With Non-Related	13	1.5	1.5	100.0
Total	877	100.0	100.0	

Source: Resch, *Suffering Soldiers*, 203–204.

He swore that if he were not continued on the rolls, he could no longer aid her, and she would have to return to the poorhouse. Although they lived apart, Caswell pleaded for a pension to provide for his helpless wife.[7] Caswell received a pension.

Other solitary veterans who were dependent on the charity of friends pleaded for the pension so as to be restored to self-sufficiency. Henry Buzzell's plea left a record of rare detail, which illuminates conditions that were only implied in hundreds of terse supplications from other claimants. Buzzell's claim describes his failed struggle to remain an independent head of household. His application contained a desperate plea for the pension to prevent his fall into pauperism. In 1825 Buzzell, sixty-five, appearing before the court in Strafford County, New Hampshire, claimed to be a penniless, disabled farmer who was unable to support himself because of advancing age and deteriorating health. In addition, Buzzell told the court that his son Jacob had become poor and could no longer aid him. Buzzell told the court that in 1812 he had become "feeble" and had deeded his farm to son Jacob in return for Jacob's agreement to support his father for the remainder of his life.

Father and son had completed a retirement contract. A retirement contract was typically a deed of sale, generally between a father and a son, which required the son to support his parents in exchange for the father's property. These agreements were widely employed to provide security and care for parents and dependent kin. Although deeds were generally made when the parties were in good health, often the deeds were not executed until the owner became debilitated, or was near death, or after he had died. The unexecuted deed provided the father leverage to ensure compliance with its terms by retaining the power to name a new grantee. The unexecuted deed was also an insurance policy in case the grantee died before the owner. In such cases the father could transfer the property to another person in exchange for support and care.[8]

Buzzell swore that Jacob had lived up to their retirement contract until 1824, when an unexplained catastrophe impoverished Jacob. Buzzell testified, "Jacob has become poor and wholly unable to support me [or] to contribute to my relief and I am now entirely left destitute." He claimed, "I have no family [to aid me]." Buzzell had become wholly "dependent on charity" from friends. Infirmity and the failed retirement contract threatened to reduce Buzzell to pauperism. The old veteran hoped to regain his independence with the income from his pension. He probably hoped to aid son Jacob as well.[9] Buzzell's case is interesting particularly because no decision made by the War Department shaped the program more than the one to grant pensions to veterans who subsisted under a retirement contract. Even if their living conditions were sparse, as they probably were in many cases, such veterans were only technically poor as defined by the department's means test. Their assets, while no longer owned by the veterans, were still being used to support them. In honoring retirement contracts, the War Department used the pension as a family assistance program to shore up households as well as to aid individual veterans.

COUPLES' HOUSEHOLDS

A little more than a quarter of all applicants headed households that only contained a couple. As a group they were but a step above conditions reported by solitary veterans. Nearly 10 percent of these couples were penniless and another 52 percent had property worth less than $50. These veterans anguished over declining kin support, the grim prospect of becoming paupers, and the breakup of their households. Couples, however, were far more likely to be burdened by debts than were solitary veterans, which suggests their continued creditworthiness. One couple in five reported debts compared to one out of ten solitary veterans. If all their reported debts were deducted from their assets, the average value of their estates would decrease from $179 to $74.

Silas Russell's circumstances resembled those of other veterans and their wives who claimed to be nearing dependency. Russell, seventy-six years old, and his wife lived in Hillsborough County, New Hampshire. They had been cared for by their son. The veteran claimed to be "very infirm" and unable to work. He reported that his wife was "bed ridden." The old couple was penniless, and the court reported that their "son is now unable to render him a comfortable support."[10] Such claimants submitted heartrending appeals not only to support themselves, but also to provide for their spouses without the aid of charity or alms. These veterans were on the verge of pauperism as a result of misfortune, age, infirmity, and children's indigence. These appeals suggest that hundreds, perhaps thousands, of veterans and their wives were struggling to maintain households weakened by growing dependence, by deteriorating health, and by the weakening of kin networks that accompanied aging.

At the age of seventy-two, Bartholomew Stevens, from Somerset County, Maine, reported that he had been a pauper "before I received the bounty of Government." Stevens claimed that upon receiving the pension, he and his wife, also seventy-two, had moved in with their son, "a man of small property," who could not maintain them without income from the pension. Stevens avowed that if the pension were discontinued, he and his wife would have to leave their son's household and again become paupers. Despite their hardships, Stevens and his wife were probably more fortunate than many of their peers. With the income from the pension, one of their children had given them refuge and succor, and the veteran had restored his household with his wife with himself as its head.[11]

Many veterans, like Stevens, claimed that their assets were depleted, their health was failing, and that they were becoming increasingly burdensome to their children.[12] According to such testimony, the parent's dependence upon filial aid had only slowed their slide toward pauperism. As they became more dependent, veterans like Stevens tried not to saddle their children with any additional burden. The pension assured these veterans that they would remain or become self-sufficient. Moreover, in many cases the pension probably diminished anxieties, if not conflicts, by reducing the burdens of filial support.

NUCLEAR HOUSEHOLDS

The possibility of household dissolution and pauperism was especially troubling to claimants who headed nuclear families. They composed the largest block of applicants, 46 percent of the whole (Table 2.3). Nearly two-thirds of the veterans heading nuclear households were under age sixty-five, the average age of all claimants; only 5 percent of them were over age seventy-five. By contrast, a majority of solitary veterans were in their seventies, and 15 percent of the veterans heading couple households were over the age of seventy.

In general, veterans heading nuclear households reported seven times the wealth of solitary veterans, and they reported 50 percent more wealth than couples. Nearly 25 percent of these veterans owned real property.[13] On average these claimants reported estates valued at $141, which, in one out of four cases, included real estate. Despite possessing relatively more wealth than other groups of veterans, 40 percent of these claimants (twice the proportion reported by couples) were burdened with debts that nearly equaled their assets. This fact implies that these households were still actively intertwined with the commercial networks of their communities. Only a few of these veterans received charity from family and friends or, even more rarely, from public relief.

Nuclear households varied greatly in composition. Three quarters of them had children over the age of fifteen, mostly between the ages of sixteen and twenty-four. A quarter of the nuclear households had children under the age of fifteen. Another group of households had two sets of children, one composed of young children and the other composed of children nearing their majority. These household compositions occurred for various reasons. Some veterans had married late in life, or remarried younger women. Typically, however, this group of veterans was in their early sixties, and their wives were in their mid-fifties. Generally, they had two or three children in their households.

Some veterans reported in their claims that large households compounded their plight by depleting their health and meager assets. In a few instances, the presence of disabled children added to the veteran's distress. Many older claimants reported that young children were heavy burdens. Neal McGerry, an eighty-year-old veteran with a twenty-year-old wife and infant child, made this plea.[14] As the case studies below show, in the face of such woes, veterans pleaded to restore or sustain patriarchal households. In addition, their appeals portrayed their families as the principal source of comfort, welfare, self-respect, and social status. No doubt the approximately 47,000 kin who resided with claimants anxiously awaited the pension to ensure their own subsistence. Most veterans, so it seems, viewed the pension as a form of assistance for their whole family.

In 1820 Jonathan Stevens, who was fifty-eight years old, pleaded for the pension to maintain his fragile household. Stevens, his wife, fifty, and three children—daughters, whose ages were eighteen, twenty, and twenty-five—lived on his farm in Caledonia County, Vermont. He had purchased the farm with a down payment from his pension, which he had received in 1818. By 1820 his assets totaled $553. In accordance with War Department rules, the court deducted the $230 Stevens owed on his first mortgage, leaving him an estate valued at $323. This amount was midway between the means test's cutoff point of $200 in assets and the department's discretionary ceiling of $400 for exceptional cases. Stevens reported another $150 in personal debts, but these debts were not deducted from his estate. Stevens pleaded that he was at "half strength," that his oldest daughter was infirm, and that if the pension were not continued, he would lose his farm. Furthermore, he stated that he had purchased the farm "on the faith of my pension that I should thereby be able to pay for it." Stevens had used the pension to change his status from a landless farmer to farmowner and to strengthen his household, which included a debilitated child under his care. The department continued Stevens on the pension rolls, and presumably the household remained viable while the veteran lived.[15]

Similarly, George Ewing, sixty-seven years old, and his seventy-year-old wife expressed alarm that without the pension their children might depart their household, which would then surely collapse because the old veteran and his wife could not manage it without their help. Ewing reported that he suffered from a "painful illness," and that his wife was also unwell. Their two unmarried daughters, Abigail, thirty-nine, and Rachael [*sic*], thirty-five, who lived at home, cared for their parents. The relationship between daughters and parents appeared, however, to be fragile and strained. Ewing pleaded for the pension because he and his wife had "no person on whom I can claim for assistance save that of parental affections" which, he implied, were wearing thin. Love and filial duty were not sufficient, in Ewing's mind, to guarantee a viable household. He hoped to strengthen his household by using the pension to reduce his daughters' burden of parental support. In addition, Ewing implied that the pension would also be an insurance policy to maintain the veteran and his wife, should their daughters leave home or become infirm.[16] Similarly, Peter Crapo stated that he could not count on his son's aid in the future because "he is now of age" and would soon leave his parents' home to establish his own household. Crapo probably hoped that the pension would diminish the burden on their son and possibly encourage him to remain longer at home.[17]

Veterans such as Ewing and Crapo portrayed their households as on the verge of collapse because of poverty and because their children's aid was uncertain. Filial affection and duty had sustained some households, but veterans feared that these sentiments would not be strong enough to prevent children from striking out on their own. The pension claims show that normally veterans' children left home after reaching their twenties. Only one household in ten contained an adult child over age thirty. Among veterans whose households contained children over the age of fifteen, nearly twice as many reported daughters living with them as reported co-resident sons. Households like those headed by Crapo and Ewing were vulnerable to sudden collapse should the children depart.

Some veterans appealed for pensions to fulfill their patriarchal duties to dependents within their households. Solomon Cook claimed that poor health and advancing age made support of his young family increasingly difficult. The 66-year-old Cook had either married late in life or had remarried, and he was raising a young family. In 1820 he was living in Genesee County, New York, with his wife, thirty-three. The household contained seven children between the ages of one and thirteen. Cook reported that he had to support his oldest daughter even though she was employed outside his home. His estate consisted of some livestock and personal property, which totaled $41 in value. He swore that his debts exceeded the value of his assets, and he told the department that he was "dependent upon the Bounty of the Government for [the] support" of his family. Cook portrayed his household to be near collapse, especially under the strain of his failing health, indebtedness, and many young mouths to feed.[18]

A large portion (26 percent) of the veterans who headed nuclear households pleaded for pensions to support their infirm and disabled children. Applications from veterans John Wellman, Dan Weller, and Jeremiah Purdy described fragile family networks of mutual care that were on the verge of collapse. John Wellman, sixty-five, reported that he nursed his helpless son, twenty-three, and "feeble" wife. He also reported that his three sons, thirteen, seventeen, and nineteen years old, who resided at home, contributed to his support. Dan Weller, sixty-one, provided for his wife, fifty-eight, and cared for his idiot daughter, twenty-eight. They were assisted by their two young daughters, ten and thirteen. Jeremiah Purdy, sixty years old, headed a household composed of his wife, fifty-nine, his three daughters, eighteen, twenty-five, and twenty-six, and a son, fifteen. Purdy reported that his son was a cripple. Purdy's 25-year-old daughter suffered from consumption. The other children helped to sustain the household and to care for their ill sister and disabled brother. Without pensions the Wellman, Weller, and Purdy households were less likely to survive as refuges for disabled and helpless kin. Their claims suggest that the network of mutual family support that the society relied on to provide for the elderly, infirm, and disabled was on the brink of failure.[19]

Joel Atherton's claim more fully illustrates the conditions that led veterans like Wellman, Weller, and Purdy to make special appeals to preserve their households. In 1820 Atherton, fifty-six, lived on his farm in Portland, Maine, with his wife, fifty-four, and eight daughters who ranged in ages from eight to twenty-four. He reported that he could not work full time "on account of rheumatism," and he claimed that his two oldest daughters, Nancy, twenty-four, and Harriet, twenty-two, were "very feeble" and required parental care. Atherton stated that his other daughters, except the youngest, "are able in part to support themselves," and that his wife was in "comfortable health and able to do part of the housework." Atherton's estate consisted of forty acres of land, a barn and attached half-house, a cow, a yearling, five sheep, farm tools, and household items valued at $210. He also claimed $275 in debts, which he said could not be paid "without disposing of the little property I possess." Atherton faced the compound problems of contributing to the support of his young children and assisting his infirm older daughters at a time when rheumatism made him less able to work. In such cases, veterans cited their care for dependent members of their households as a special circumstance entitling them to a pension. In Atherton's case, despite an estate that exceeded the means test's first tier of $200, the department concurred and kept him on the rolls.[20]

Many veterans confronted bankruptcy along with ill health and frayed networks of kin support. They wrote that debt added the threat of financial collapse and pauperism. The fear of bankruptcy was particularly acute among claimants who headed nuclear households. These veterans revealed, possibly unintentionally, the effects of excessive debt on their households. Creditors' demands for payment could force parents to liquidate assets and cause them to become destitute and dependent. In Josiah Gary's case, his children, who felt exploited by their father, threatened to take him to court for debt if he didn't pay them for their years of labor on his farm. In 1820 Gary, sixty-four, who suffered from "palsy," lived in Windham County, Connecticut, with his wife, sixty, and two children. His assets amounted to $1,900, including farm land, barn, house, tools, livestock, and household goods. He owed various people $140 and indicated that he owed about $2,000 to his son, thirty, and daughter, thirty-three, for their "hard work for 10 years past" on the farm. He swore that both children wanted to be paid for their labor and that he was required either to give them the farm or sell it to raise cash to pay them. They had invested their labor to secure those assets; now they wanted to be paid off. In this case Gary's independence was threatened by his own children's demands to collect what was owed them. Gary claimed that if he received the pension he could pay his debt to his children by giving them his farm. While many claims stressed the bonds of affection binding households, Gary's case showed an intergenerational revolt. Debt and hard feelings triggered Gary's application for a pension. Gary's receipt of the pension ensured his independence as head of household apart from his estranged children.[21]

In other instances the threat of bankruptcy helped to retain older children in the household to assist their parents. Heavy debts endangered parental assets, threatened household viability, and endangered the legacies children had earned or expected to receive through inheritance. In these cases, indebtedness tied older children more closely to their parents' households. Thus self-interest reinforced cultural norms that prescribed that older children, especially females, remain at home to support their parents. Such was the case for William Blair of Peterborough, New Hampshire.

Blair was one of ten Continental Army veterans residing in Peterborough when the pension act passed. Eight of them received the pension in 1818. He was among the town's five pensioners who passed the means test in 1820. Before receiving the pension in 1818, Blair and his wife, along with their son, William Jr., and the son's wife, struggled to maintain the farm they shared. By 1818 the farm had been mortgaged to pay debts. The household's taxable assets were reduced to a single ox. In 1818, William Jr. paid $1.70 in taxes, which included his poll tax of $1.30. The veteran's poll tax was abated and the veteran paid no property tax because he had assigned his farm to creditors. The family's fortunes were near collapse. By 1820, having received his pension for two years, the veteran paid off his creditors and resumed full ownership of his farm. The household, composed of the veteran and his wife, and their son and his wife, recovered its former rank just below the midpoint of Peterborough's taxpayers.

In 1820, Blair accurately reported his circumstances when he told the court that he was seventy years old and lived with his wife, who was sixty-four, and owned no real estate. By then he had transferred title to the homestead to his sons while he and his wife continued to reside on the property. His assets were reduced to a cow worth $16 and a hog worth $8. Blair said that he was a farmer who owed "more than the above property" was worth. His son, William Jr., owned the farm, which he shared with his father, who had a life-lease to half of it. Blair passed the means test. The two households—father and son—remained independent and interdependent. They even prospered. In 1825 the veteran was taxed on his leased half-share of the farm, which consisted of one-half acre of mowing land, two horses, one cow, and twenty acres of wild land. With the aid of the pension between 1818 and 1825, by the time the elder Blair died, he had fulfilled his patriarchal obligation by providing for his wife and his parental duty by passing on his farm to his son. The pension had enabled the family to retain the homestead where William Jr. remained to raise his thirteen children and to care for his mother, who died in 1842 at age eighty-six. This case revealed the fragile nature of households and the value of the pension in providing security and stability.[22]

COMPLEX HOUSEHOLDS

Other veterans appealed for the pension to maintain households that had become refuges for grandchildren and ailing kin. Claimants heading complex households were among the least poor veterans who applied for the pension. They averaged $280 in assets, and a large proportion (40 percent) owned real estate. Most (85 percent) of these veterans headed households that contained their own older children and young grandchildren, generally under ten years of age. Less than one out of three of these households contained children under age fifteen; approximately 80 percent of these households reported children over age fifteen.

Only 1 percent of the claimants heading complex households reported nonkin living with them, and as a group, these were the wealthiest applicants. Their assets averaged $500 in value and more than half of them owned real estate. Typically, their households contained the veteran and his wife and one or two people living with them as hired help and caregivers. Rarely was one of their children living with them. For example, Joseph Hawes, sixty-five, and his wife, seventy-two, were poor, "weak," and in debt. They had hired their ten-year-old granddaughter "to live with us" and care for them.[23] On the other hand, some who were quite poor had taken in lodgers or children to earn money. In 1820 Abner Mitchell, seventy-two, and his wife, seventy, a black couple living in Lunenburgh, Massachusetts, were subsidized by the town to provide a room and board for two pauper children. The Mitchells reported $6 in assets.[24]

For Phineas Hamblett the pension was his safety net. In 1820 Hamblett, sixty-five, was living on his farm in Cheshire County, New Hampshire. His estate was assessed at $777 and he claimed debts totaling $253. The value of his property was well above the department's poverty line. Like so many other veterans, Hamblett's appeal focused on the household role as a refuge. He reported that he supported his 92-year-old mother-in-law, his 62-year-old deaf and blind wife, and their feeble 39-year-old daughter. Hamblett testified that although he was fairly well off and still in good health, he needed the pension's income because his ability to support the household and to care for his dependents was diminishing. Hamblett had probably hoped to persuade the department to make him an exception to the rule. The department rejected Hamblett's claim because he failed the means test. Despite being denied, he was welcomed to reapply for the pension if his assets fell below the department's means test.[25]

The pension saved William Diamond's household in Peterborough, New Hampshire. Diamond used the pension to sustain his household and to fulfill his patriarchal duties. Diamond was a war hero who had fought at Lexington, Trenton, and Princeton, and he had served various enlistments that totaled just more than two years. After the war, he moved to Peterborough, where he acquired a farm. He held a precarious place just above the bottom third of the town's taxpayers. In 1817, at age sixty-two, Diamond had divided his farm equally between his two unmarried sons, William Jr., thirty-three, and John, twenty-seven.[26] As part of the retirement contract, the sons agreed to support their father and mother in exchange for deeds to the properties. Titles to the farms, however, were not formally registered in William Jr. and John's names for another four and eleven years, respectively, possibly as a precaution to ensure compliance. Nevertheless, the town recognized the legality of these retirement contracts by taxing the father and sons on their respective portions of the divided estate.

In 1818 Diamond applied for the pension. He reported that he was "very destitute of property." Although this claim was exaggerated, Diamond was among the lowest third of the town's taxpayers, and his sons, as would be expected because of the equal division of his farm, occupied an even lower rank. The pension bolstered the family's fortunes. Soon after their father received his pension, Diamond's sons expanded their farms by buying land next to them. In 1820, when Diamond reapplied for the pension, he claimed that he owned no real estate, possessed $42 worth of livestock, and paid $6 annually for a life lease he held to thirty-two acres of land. Diamond reported that his household consisted of his wife, fifty-eight, and his daughter, Lydia, twenty-three, and Lydia's two children. Lydia had apparently been abandoned by her husband and had returned home sometime between 1818 and 1820. Diamond also told the court that "he was unable to work" and owed $50 in debts. He did not report that the town had taxed him on one acre of plowed land, one acre of mowing land, four acres of pasture, and a horse. Diamond acted as if the retirement contracts had been executed, and the town looked the other way when he omitted this taxable property from the inventory he submitted to the court. Though Diamond was not impoverished, townsmen may have considered the veteran deserving because they regarded him as a war hero for his role in the opening battle of the Revolution.

Continued on the rolls and guaranteed an income for life, Diamond executed the retirement contracts with his sons. On 16 March 1821, the veteran deeded part of his farm to his older son, William Jr., who soon established his own household. In 1824, at age thirty-nine, he married Lucinda Haggett, twenty-eight, of Peterborough. William Jr., his wife, and later their three daughters remained on his share of the homestead farm for most of their lives. The pension had helped Diamond's older son gain independence as the head of his own household. In October 1822, the veteran bequeathed the remaining share of his farm to his other son, John, who had married in 1821. The veteran retained a life lease to a small portion of John's farm. The old soldier, his wife, and

Table 2.4
Applicants' Occupation Categories

		Frequency	Percent	Valid Percent	Cumulative Percent
	Laborer	445	50.7	58.9	58.9
	Business or Profession	140	16.0	18.5	77.4
	Trade	171	19.5	22.6	100.0
	Total	756	86.2	100.0	
	None or missing	121	13.8		
	Total	877	100.0		

Source: Resch, *Suffering Soldiers*, 203–204.

possibly their daughter and grandchildren continued to share the farm with son John, his wife, and their young family. Father and son appeared to maintain their own households by dividing the farmhouse they shared into separate quarters. Both continued to be taxed separately for their shares of the farm. The veteran paid for his lease and likely contributed income from his pension to sustain this compound household.

Upon the veteran's death in 1828, Diamond's estate of $163 was reduced to $4 after his debts were paid. As he had claimed in 1820, the veteran owed as much as he owned. Nevertheless, he left John with clear title to the farm. John and his brother William Jr. remained below the midpoint of Peterborough's taxpayers for the rest of their lives. Neither brother exceeded the economic status of their father. John continued to support his mother until her death in 1855 at age ninety-three. The pension had helped to sustain the Diamonds' intergenerational household well into the nineteenth century.

CONCLUSION

Scrutinized under the means test, veterans conformed to the popular image of them as heroic, virtuous, and patriotic warriors.[27] Once they were Washington's young recruits, mostly teenagers and men in their early twenties, who had enlisted early in the war. By 1820 most claimants were laborers, artisans, or farmers in their mid-sixties (Table 2.4). Age and infirmity had reduced their ability to be self-supporting. Most no longer owned real property, and they were unable to work at full capacity. The means test revealed them as either destitute, poor, or propertyless. More than a fifth of the claimants relied either on charity or public relief, or were about to seek aid. Many were strapped with debts, which threatened to deplete their meager assets. Almost half were still responsible for young families, aged parents, or sick, insane, or invalid children who drained veterans' meager resources and health.

Solitary veterans were the most desperate lot. They were the oldest, most debilitated, and poorest of applicants. Those who had once been married witnessed the dissolution of their households because of poverty, illness, death of a spouse, and the departure or death of their children. Advanced age made their lives even more miserable. Almost half of them had become paupers or were on the verge of pauperism. For some, such as Henry Buzzell, dependency was imminent because a son's sudden poverty threatened an otherwise previously successful planned retirement. Solitary veterans pleaded to restore or to conserve their places as heads of households. In some cases these veterans anguished to fulfill their obligation to spouses and children who had been forced out of their households because of poverty. Even the most desperate veterans pleaded for autonomy through a pension rather than remain or become an object of private charity or a ward of the public.

Many, such as Peterborough's Blair and Diamond, had lived subsistence lives after the war. Both of these men had climbed to an economic level that hovered between the lower quarter and lower half of Peterborough's taxpayers. Blair and Diamond achieved a small, yet precarious, measure of independence as husbandmen and craftsmen. In 1815 Blair and Diamond, sixty-five and sixty respectively, entered the period of greatest risk to their households. Advancing age, increasing infirmity, and uncertain support from their children threatened to ruin their modest estates. Careful to fulfill their patriarchal roles, the two men provided for their retirement and their wives' care and helped their sons to establish their own households on the homestead. Nevertheless, at this critical juncture, their intergenerational networks were near collapse.

Based on inventories and pleas, thousands of veterans' households appeared to be in jeopardy of collapse like those headed by Blair and Diamond. Alarmed and fearful, veterans pleaded for pensions to stop their relentless slide toward dependence and loss of status, power, and self-respect as heads of households. Aging veterans reported that their households were collapsing due to infirmity, disability, age, diminished assets, and debts. Anxiety was especially great among veterans with young families and those whose households contained infirm wives, sick and disabled children, or grandchildren and elderly kin. Veterans dreaded the grinding forces that were crushing their households and undermining their status as patriarchal heads.

Viewed broadly, in many cases the receipt of veterans' pensions prompted the transfer of wealth from fathers to their children. More important, the pension liberated children from the traditional duty of supporting parents. It allowed children to take control of their own lives and it freed pensioners from dependence upon their children. Each generation gained greater independence, which *could* weaken family bonds. All the same, it seemed, in cases like Peterborough's pensioners, that the program nurtured stronger family relationships rather than weakening them. With receipt of the pension, the veteran's children were no longer burdened with the shame or guilt of abandoning him and their mother to the woes of poverty and charity. Pensioners like Blair and Diamond remained independent, sustaining their traditional patriarchal household, and strengthening intergenerational networks. Parents were delivered from the dread of dependency and the fear of pauperism. The pension appeared to temper the sense of obligation for children and the patriarchal demand for support—which could produce grudging compliance and resentment—with feelings of security and stronger bonds of affection. Thus the veterans' pension, awarded as both an honor for service and as assistance for elderly soldiers, reinforced personal and societal values of self-sufficiency, viable households, and patriarchy.

NOTES

1. For work on the history of aging and households, see the following: W. Andrew Achenbaum, *Old Age in the New Land* (Baltimore, MD: Johns Hopkins University Press, 1978); David Hackett Fischer, *Growing Old in America* (New York: Oxford University Press, 1978); Steven Ruggles, *Prolonged Connections: The Rise of the Extended Family in Nineteenth-Century England and America* (Madison: University of Wisconsin Press, 1987); and Daniel Scott Smith, "Behind and Beyond the Law of the Household," *William and Mary Quarterly* 3d. m. ser. 52, No. 1 (January 1995): 145–150.

2. That estimate is based on a Bureau of Census figure that in 1820 there were 211,000 white males above the age of fifty-nine. See J. Resch, *Suffering Soldiers: Revolutionary War Veterans, Moral Sentiment, and Political Culture in the Early Republic* (Amherst: University of Massachusetts Press, 1999), 204.

3. Silas Russell, Pension File S45128, Record Group 15, National Archives (hereafter abbreviated as RG, NA); Daniel Rider, Pension File W5705, RG15, NA; Henry Hallowell, Pension File S32800, RG15, NA; Henry Buzzell, Pension File S45529, RG15, NA; Joseph Stevens, Pension File S43175, RG15, NA; and, Reuben Clark, Pension File S12506, RG15, NA. Also see Christian Hubbert, Pension File S39754, RG15, NA. Hubbert said he was in "poor health."

4. Richard Hallstead, Pension File S44909, RG15, NA; Philo Phillips, Pension File S39013, RG15, NA; Israel Manning, Pension File S33043, RG15, NA; Ichabod Beckwith, Pension File S34023, RG15, NA.

5. *Niles Weekly Register*, 26 February 1820.

6. To arrive at this figure, I divided total court-assessed wealth for applicants from New York by the number of people reported in the households of applicants from New York.

7. Elijah Caswell, Pension File S34155, RG15, NA.

8. Resch, *Suffering Soldiers*, 160.

9. Henry Buzzell, Pension File S45529, RG15, NA.

10. Silas Russell, Pension File S45128, RG15, NA.

11. Bartholomew Stevens, Pension File W25074, RG15, NA.

12. Nathaniel Pardee, Pension File S43795, RG15, NA; Nathan Mann, Pension File

W9908, RG15, NA; Ephraim Stevens, Pension File S41198, RG15, NA; Jedidiath Russell, Pension File S45127, RG15, NA; George Buyers, Pension File S40768, RG15, NA; Daniel Condit, Pension File W449, RG15, NA; William Worster, Pension File S35148, RG15, NA; Thomas Gratton, Pension File S21773, RG15, NA.

13. By contrast, only 5 percent of solitary veterans and 20 percent of couple households reported owning real estate.

14. Neal McGerry, Pension File W8276, RG15, NA.

15. Jonathan Stevens, Pension File W2456, RG15, NA.

16. George Ewing, Pension File S35916, RG15, NA.

17. Peter Crapo, Pension File S43414, RG15, NA.

18. Solomon Cook, Pension File S43375, RG15, NA.

19. Dan Weller, Pension File W16466, RG 15, NA; John Wellman, Pension File S42317, RG15, NA; Jeremiah Purdy, Pension File W10937, RG15, NA.

20. Joel Atherton, Pension File W23472, RG15, NA.

21. Josiah Gary, Pension File S37003, RG15, NA. Also see Joseph Hinshaw, Pension File W24425, RG15, NA.

22. John Blair, Pension File S45296, RG15, NA; *Peterborough Tax List*, Peterborough Historical Society.

23. Joseph Hawes, Pension File S353596, RG15, NA.

24. Abner Mitchell, Pension File W15084, RG15, NA.

25. Phineas Hamblett, Pension File S44407, RG15, NA.

26. Jack Resch, "The Continentals of Peterborough, New Hampshire," *Prologue* 16 (Fall 1984): 180–183.

27. Resch, *Suffering Soldiers*, 65–92.

3

Social Lives of Elderly Women in Eighteenth-Century Toulouse

Sherri Klassen

> At the final performance, fifty people of all ages attended. Mme. de Cour-
> teille (the eldest of the family) stayed in her parlour playing trictrac with
> her old friends but now and then they would pop into the music room and
> watch what was then known as the *belle jeunesse.* . . . It seems that these
> gatherings, in which all generations came together, are a thing of the past.
> . . . I doubt if now could there anywhere be found such ease, harmony, good
> manners and lack of pretension as that which reigned in all the great houses
> of Paris.[1]

This passage was written by Mme. de la Tour du Pin. Written when she was
seventy-one years of age, the recollection describes elite Paris in 1789, more
than forty years earlier. Clearly seasoned with large measures of nostalgia, the
passage nonetheless corroborates many other sources that indicate that elderly
women in the eighteenth century did not withdraw from social life but instead
engaged in a wide variety of social activities within a broad network of friends
and family members. Both memoirs and notarial sources demonstrate a bustle
of activity and significant connections forged by older women both within their
age cohort and across generations.

Wills are particularly useful in demonstrating the breadth of social ties important to women in their old age. The wills written by women in Toulouse at
both the beginning and end of the eighteenth century show that elderly women
placed greater value than younger women on their extended family and friends.
Elderly women, like men and younger women, wrote wills for a variety of
reasons—to modify local custom, favor one heir over another, incorporate supplementary or sentimental bequests, or plan funeral and votive arrangements.

Inheritance law in the south of France allowed considerable power to the testator, and a great many women and men of all classes took advantage of their opportunity to direct their wealth from beyond the grave.[2] Wills demonstrate avenues of power for elderly women and point to the people over whom the elderly had influence.

Of the nearly 800 elderly women dying over the age of sixty in 1719–1720 and 1789–1790, I can make use of the wills of 107.[3] The vast majority of wills still extant were those that had been written in the last five years of life. In addition to this sample, I collected data on 400 wills taken at random from the same years of notarial documents.[4] This sample shows that almost as many women as men wrote wills in any given year, although their choices and circumstances seem to have differed. In 1719–1720, the general sample includes 101 wills written by women and 99 by men; in 1789–1790, 82 were written by women and 118 by men. The majority of those written by women were written when the woman was either single or widowed. Only 48 of the 183 testators in the general sample (26.2%) were married women. The general sample included women and men of all ages but was skewed slightly toward the elderly, since the majority of the testators wrote when they believed they were close to death.

Particularly in their ancillary legacies, women showed that they valued their friends and more distant kin, but these relationships with people outside the immediate family circle did not replace the conjugal family; they supplemented it. When an elderly woman's children outlived her, they were always mentioned in the will and received larger bequests than friends and extended family members.[5] Extended family and friends were, however, also significant. Relationships beyond the household and nuclear family included members of the natal family, in-laws, and friends, both age-mates and members of younger generations. Though some of those writing wills had no children of their own, quite a number of those with children also reached beyond the nuclear family and the household. Sixty-one percent of the women in both periods included supplementary legacies that extended beyond their own children and households or, in the case of those women without apparent living children, their next of kin. Figures 3.1 and 3.2 outline the percentage of women giving bequests only to their own children or next of kin, those who gave only to their children and household members, those whose giving may reflect that they had no living kin at all, and those whose extended giving clearly indicates a choice to reach beyond those most closely related to them. In the early period, most of these reflected relations to the testator's family of birth; by the end of the century, more were friends.

To some degree, the inheritance system in the south of France may have allowed women to feel freer with their estates than men. As the family patriarch, the aging man established his will in order to maintain the patriliny and the family property. In contrast with the case of female testators, as many as 59 percent of the heirs of male testators were within the nuclear family in 1719 and 1720, and this percentage increased to 68 percent over the course of the century. That men included more members of their conjugal family in their wills

Figure 3.1
The Breadth of Beneficiaries of Female Testators in 1719–1720

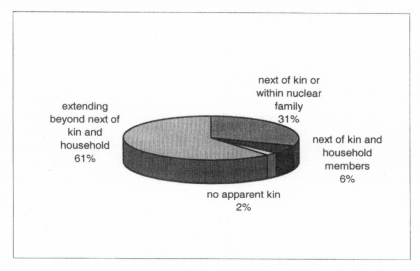

Source: Archives Departmentale Haute Garonne series 3E.

Figure 3.2
The Breadth of Beneficiaries of Female Testators in 1789–1790

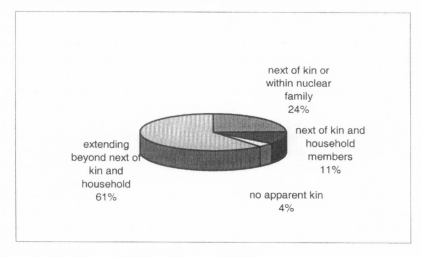

Source: Archives Departmentale Haute Garonne series 3E.

in the latter decades suggests a certain leveling of the family, showing that some men utilized their wills to offer tokens of affection to their otherwise disinherited offspring. The responsibility to maintain the family property, however, remained strong. Furthermore, because of the much higher incidence of remarriage among men than among women, elderly men were more likely to live enmeshed in a domestic environment into their old age. While the percentage of nuclear family heirs rose for men across the century, the percentage of beneficiaries from among extended families and friendships declined from 37 percent in 1719–1720 to 26 percent in 1789–1790. Women, whether they headed their own households or lived with others, had the freedom a patriarch lacked; they could use their wealth to smooth the imbalances caused by primogeniture and use their wills to acknowledge the valued relations that existed outside the household and conjugal unit.

Though the elderly women clearly valued members of their extended family, the most striking difference between their lists of heirs and those found in the random samples is the number of heirs not identified as blood relations or servants.[6] Many of these were identified explicitly as friends, some even as "dear friends." Others were named without a label of any sort. The form of the document offers some assistance in classifying these individuals, since the notaries fairly consistently drafted wills in such a way as to differentiate between relations, servants, and individuals unrelated by blood or marriage. In all cases, religious bequests began the will. As a rule, bequests to servants and members of the clergy followed. After these, bequests to the immediate family appeared, with family members who were clergy listed first or between the clerical and familial bequests. Bequests to extended family and godchildren followed, and friends appeared in the penultimate position, immediately before the announcement of the chief beneficiary or universal heir. Occasionally, the group of family bequests were listed after extended family and friends, but they remained distinctly divided into groups defined by the proximity of their relationship. More rarely, friends and extended family members were interspersed. In general, heirs were listed in order of the proximity of their kinship to the testator. Friends never appeared before siblings or spouses, but they were occasionally listed with cousins or with in-law relations. In this chapter, I have assumed that those individuals listed with friends or with extended family but not identified as extended family either explicitly or by name were also friends.

Figures 3.3 and 3.4 show the number of heirs mentioned according to their relationship to the testator. The data show a dramatic increase in the proportion of friends to receive bequests. The proportion of heirs from the nuclear family shrank in the general samples of female testators as well, but not as dramatically. The proportion of unrelated friends, on the other hand, rose only slightly in the general sample. The greater contrast is with the wills written by men. Only 9 percent (14) of the men in 1719–1720 left legacies to friends to whom they bore no relation. The proportion even shrank over the course of the century, moving down to 3 percent (16). Although the average number of bequests per will grew

Figure 3.3
Composition of Heirs, 1719–1720

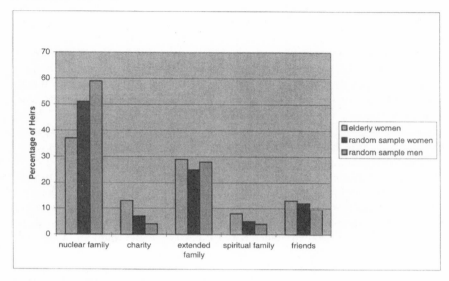

Figure 3.4
Composition of Heirs, 1789–1790

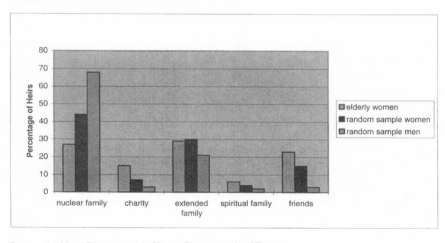

for every sample in my study, for men, this meant legacies left to more members of the nuclear family rather than to friends.

Most of the newfound friends for elderly women were other adult women. Fourteen legacies in 1719–1720 were left to female friends and 13 were to male friends. Only 5 of these female heirs and 7 of the males were minors. In 1789–1790, 75 legacies were left to members of the extended family and friends. In this case, 36 were legacies to unrelated friends. The difference is almost entirely in the body of legacies left to female friends; 22 legacies were left to female friends, of which only 5 were for girls who had not yet reached their majority. The 14 legacies left to male friends were also largely gifts to adults; only 1 mentioned that the heir was yet a minor. The important ties of friendship, therefore, seem to have been older and more predominantly female at the end than at the beginning of the century.

Not only did more elderly women mention friends in their wills at the end of the century, they also remembered friends of more varied social backgrounds. My samples of wills include women from various walks of life. In the beginning of the century, artisan women remembered friends who were also artisans; laborers and peddler women remembered others of that economic status; and nobility generally left legacies only to other nobles, reaching beyond their social class only to servants and for the purpose of charitable bequests.[7] By the end of the century, however, elderly women began spanning social barriers. Not only were landed nobles passing on their wealth to robe nobility, they also left legacies for friends of more diverse social background. Jeanne Marie Joseph Paignon was the unmarried daughter of a petty nobleman. She left a small cash bequest to the daughter of an innkeeper and another to the daughter of a sculptor. The bulk of her estate was also passed on to an unmarried female friend, though in this case only the friend's name and address are listed.[8] Anne de Labadens, also a noble, left a cash bequest for the daughter of one who made his living measuring grain and another for the daughter of her valet.[9] The bourgeoisie and master craftspeople were no more likely to restrict themselves to a single social group. Gabrielle Bitis, whose husband had been a bureaucrat, gave a covered silver dish to each of her two "good friends as a token of her friendship." The two friends were both grain merchants.[10] Servants also mixed with the artisan classes and with the elites. Jeanne Fourniér, a former servant, gave a piece of jewelry to Jeanne Marie Caillou, the daughter of a master shoemaker.[11] Jeanne Lafont, another servant, left a cash legacy to a woman of the administrative elite in "recognition of their friendship" and named a nobleman as her principal heir.[12]

Earlier in life, friendships may have grown out of professional acquaintances, but these seem to account for few of the friends mentioned in the wills written by elderly women. Out of 13 wills for which occupational data is available for both the testator and at least one of the unrelated heirs, only 1 included a bequest to a member of the same trade. This will was written in 1718 by Marguerite Bouxarine, widow of Guillaume Vieilhe, master shoe repairman. She made 8 bequests. Seven heirs were related either by blood or marriage, but 1 was mentioned only as the wife of another master shoe repairman.[13] Another woman, Jeanne Serene, though not identified with an occupation of her own, alluded to her trade in the will. Mme. Serene was the widow of a day laborer. In 1720 she wrote her will and explained that she had money owing to her from the widow of a shoemaker who sold saltpeter in a spot close to the church of the Inquisition. Mme. Serene had apparently provided the saltpeter and a case for the shoemaker's widow and was awaiting her portion of the profits. Clearly working as a petty merchant after her husband's death, Jeanne Serene named another woman, also a widow and also a merchant as her principal heir.[14]

Most of the friends mentioned shared the same general social status as the testator but not the same actual trade. Antoinette Brousse, the widow of a gardener, for example, named the wife of a tailor her principal heir, while the widow of a tailor offered small legacies for a printer and his sister.[15] Honorée Neutre was the widow of a builder in 1720 when, among 9 heirs, she included 2 granddaughters of a hatmaker.[16] Occupation may have introduced women to acquaintances, but the number of friendships without a trade alliance is more noteworthy.

For the vast majority of wills, unfortunately, data is incomplete for ascertaining the existence of a work relationship between the testators and their heirs. The work status of wives and widows is generally unspecified in wills; when the women worked at trades unrelated to their husbands', their bequests to friends in these trades would remain a mystery. When Antoinette Espitallier, widow of a porter, wrote her will in 1786, she named the daughter of a fisherman her principal heir. Both women, presumably, earned incomes as well, but the will offers no hints about whether the two women worked together or at entirely separate endeavors.[17] In addition to the 13 wills in which some indication of occupational status is given, another 17 wills mention friends but provide too little occupational data for any notion of the relationship.

For the majority of the testators who mention friends, friendship was but one of many relationships that the elderly women valued.[18] Jeanne Ourtigues, for example, left a small cash legacy for her niece even as she left the bulk of her estate to a male friend.[19] Marie Pigasse remembered her nephew as well as her universal heir, another unrelated male friend.[20] Catherine Monestier left cash for a niece and a nephew, gave an item of jewelry to one female friend, and named another her universal heir.[21] All these examples come from wills written in the 1710s. At the end of the century, estates were diffused at least as widely. Jeanne Lafont left cash legacies for 5 female friends before naming a male friend her universal heir.[22] Jeanne Fournier left legacies for 3 grand nephews and a grand niece, a godson and a female friend, as well as naming a male friend her principal heir.[23]

Though the ages of the heirs are never mentioned, some of the Toulousain women mentioned in the wills clearly represented longstanding friendships, women of the same generation as the testators. The two grain merchants mentioned by Gabrielle Bitis were likely contemporaries. When Jeanne Lambert wrote a bequest for Germaine Dalix, she described her as an "old and dear friend."[24] Dalix may have been younger than the 83-year-old Lambert, but the two women were likely of the same generation.

Memoirs also attest to the importance of age-mates to elderly women. In the passage cited at the opening, Mme. de la Tour du Pin praised the mix of generations but also described a situation in which age groups socialized for the most part in segregated groups. Elizabeth Vigée-Lebrun also recalled old women socializing together. While La Tour du Pin painted the socializing as pleasant, Vigée-Lebrun ridiculed the elderly women. She recalled laughing at the old aristocratic women who gathered together and sat in chairs along the side of a boulevard.[25] Mme. Roland passed a gentler judgment on the socializing of elderly women with friends. Though as a young girl the author found her grandmother's friend distasteful, she also noted that the grandmother appeared to have enjoyed her company and the occasion for gossip. Roland hastened to add, however, that her grandmother preferred her sister's company and, though these two teased each other in an air of familiarity, both led quiet, retired lives.[26]

Sisters appear frequently in the wills from Toulouse. Approximately 20 percent of the female testators in all my samples left legacies to at least one sibling, usually a sister. Male testators in 1719–1720 remembered their brothers more than their sisters. The number of bequests left by men for their siblings declined considerably over the course of the century, from 28 (28%) to 15 (12.7%). The same is not true for women. Older women left their sisters legacies that showed they were valued, though they were rarely the only heirs remaining. Marguerite Bouxarine had two living sisters when she wrote her will in 1719. Her sisters were not the only people in her life. She left bequests for 5 nieces and nephews, 1 goddaughter, and 1 adult female friend. Her sisters, however, received the largest bequests. One was given all the testator's clothing (except items specifically given to the other heirs) and the second sister was named universal heir.[27] Paule de Richard left the bulk of her estate to her sister-in-law and her brother's children with the provision that her sister have the use of the full estate during her life.[28] The two sisters Claire and Jeanne Généreux both wrote wills in 1715 and each named the other her universal heir.[29] These examples are drawn from various social groups. Marguerite Bouxarine was the widow of a master shoe repairman, Paule de Richard was a noblewoman, and the Généreux sisters were the daughters of a surgeon.

In addition to their friendships with women of the same generation, older women's social networks reached wide enough to capture women, men, and children of the next two generations, including nieces, nephews, godchildren, in-laws, and the children of friends. The presence of nieces, nephews, and grandnieces among the lists of heirs demonstrates a continuation of the connections to the natal family even beyond a close sibling relationship. Slightly more than one-third of the wills written by elderly women included legacies for nieces or grandnieces. In both periods, women mentioned nieces slightly more frequently than nephews, and men mentioned nephews slightly more often than nieces. While this pattern suggests a certain degree of gender segregation among the elderly, there were also enough heirs of opposite sexes to suggest that the social norms were by no means hard and fast cultural dictates.

Godparenting also seems to have been important for the older woman, especially when it fostered a relationship she already valued, such as the niece–aunt relationship. Of the nineteen nieces of elderly women to receive bequests from their aunts, seven (36.8%) were named as goddaughters as well as nieces. The proportion is much smaller in the women from the general samples (15.4%). Nephews/godsons do not appear at all as the heirs of elderly women, although they crop up occasionally in the general samples. A blood relationship was not, however, necessary for a strong spiritual relationship. The wills of elderly women suggest that a special bond existed between older women and their godchildren, only about one-third of whom were clearly related by blood. A successful spiritual relationship could exist within or outside the extended family.

Just as godparenthood created meaningful fictive lines of kinship, so too did marriage bring women into wider nets of social interaction.[30] Three women in the samples of elderly women left bequests for their daughters-in-law, and unlike the examples found in the general sample, the daughters-in-law in these examples do not appear to have been the testators' only friends or relations. After listing her provisions for funeral arrangements, Marie Lajoux declared that she had no living children. She left a small bequest for the daughter of a merchant and another small legacy for her granddaughter, Françoise Araignon. The universal heir was her daughter-in-law, Geraude Araignon, and mother of Françoise.[31] Certainly Marie Lajoux would have chosen differently had her son been living. Nonetheless, since she chose against the more customary practice of naming a grandchild universal heir, her will shows a sentimental attachment to her daughter-in-law. Anne de la Reiche de la Permartin wrote her will when several of her children were still living. Also a widow, she had been married to a councilor at the parlement of Toulouse. She came from the opposite end of the social spectrum from Marie Lajoux. Following custom, she named her eldest son as her chief beneficiary. In addition, she left smaller bequests to her two other sons and her two daughters. Her two grandchildren—one boy and one girl—received small legacies as well. Apart from small cash provisions left for servants, the only bequest to someone not related by blood was one left to her daughter-in-law. This heir received a ring valued at 1,000 livres.[32] Marie Lajoux and Anne de la Reiche de la Permartin both wrote their wills at the beginning of the eighteenth century. Antoinette Guille wrote hers in the 1780s. She was the widow of a day laborer with two children still living when she wrote her will. The first legacy listed was to Jeanne Galau, wife of her younger son Benoît. She allowed her daughter-in-law to choose among her *chemises*, hairpieces, handkerchiefs, and "generally anything she wishes for her own personal use" up to a value of 60 livres. She mentioned a larger bequest for her goddaughter, gave her eldest son and his children their legal entitlement, and then named Benoît (or his children) universal heir.[33] Jeanne Galau, then, received her own legacy in addition to benefiting from her husband being named universal heir. Although the commercial value was slight, the bequest demonstrates the significance that the relationship between mother and daughter-in-law could accrue.

In addition to her son's marriage, a woman's own brought a variety of relationships into her life. Paule de Richard, writing her will in 1717, left a sum to both her husband's nephew and his niece. After making a number of legacies to her own family members, she named her husband's sister her universal heir.[34] Paule de Capmartin, in 1790, left a cash bequest for her sister-in-law and a small legacy to be shared between her two brothers-in-law.[35] Dame Petronille D'Assezat left her husband's niece a silver breakfast set valued at 1,200 livres when she wrote her will in 1787. This was one of many legacies and was written "as a token of her affection."[36]

The relationships appearing in the wills were closer and more affective than simple acquaintanceship. The vast majority of the bequests left to friends and extended family members reflect relationships based on affection rather than family strategy. In many cases, the testators clearly stated their affinity. The purpose for these bequests was often clearly stated: They were signs of remembrance. When Gabrielle Bitis gave her two "good friends" a covered silver dish each, it was as "a token of friendship."[37] Jeanne Lafont showed her friendship toward four sisters, each receiving 100 livres "as a mark of recognition for her affection."[38] Petronille D'Assezat wrote that her legacy to M. Chalvet (possibly a nephew of her husband's) of a silver water pitcher as well as a small cash legacy was "a token of her friendship."[39]

Most of the bequests left to friends were, in fact, tokens in size as well as in intention. Of the 28 friends mentioned in the 1719–1720 wills, 22 were the recipients of small, token bequests. Thirty-six of the 51 friends in 1789–1790 received secondary bequests. The size and value of a token bequest varied from very small to quite considerable and reflected the relationship and the value of the entire estate. A token bequest was simply that—it was large enough to evoke memory without depriving the family of the lion's share. The smallest legacy to a friend was for 20 livres. This one was from Marianne Cambola, the widow of a royal official, Jean-Baptiste Serignol. She named her son her universal heir and supplemented her daughter's legal inheritance by 100 livres.[40] The woman's estate, then, was large enough that she could feel comfortable adding a small supplement to her daughter's bequest. Her friend's legacy was very much smaller than that given to family. When Catherine Guillermin gave a gold watch valued at 200 livres to a male friend of hers, she would not have considered this a major portion of her estate. She was the widow of a nobleman and had been able to supplement her younger son's inheritance by more than 6,000 livres.[41] Small bequests like these could serve to remind the heirs of their friendship but did not supersede family ties.

Though cash bequests were a very common form of token, legacies in precious and nonprecious goods became more common for elderly women in the later eighteenth century. Jewelry and items made of silver or gold were growing favorites, and a few women left bequests of furniture, clothing, or linens. Fran-çoise Couderc left jewelry to both a male and a female friend. They may have been brother and sister; the will gave a M. Bessayre a ring and Mlle. Bessayre a ring and a bracelet.[42] Amande Escoffre left a number of cash bequests to family members but left all her jewelry, as well as some furniture and linens, to an unrelated female friend and bequeathed her *chemises* to a male friend.[43] Marie Jean St. Germaine gave a gold watch valued at 200 livres to a female friend.[44] Practical items, such as housewares, cooking utensils, furniture, or clothing, were rarely found in bequests to friends. The only four women to give items of furniture in 1789–1790 all gave wardrobes, a piece of furniture that was both valuable and versatile. Unlike a kitchen table, a wardrobe may well have been a decorative piece of furniture as well. Linens and clothing were very rare as gifts for friends, although they appear frequently in bequests to family members. Testators seem to have chosen the items in their legacies for both their monetary and their sentimental value. Although the number of material bequests was growing in legacies to both men and women, women were always more likely than men to receive goods instead of cash. In 1719–1720, male friends received only cash bequests and in 1789–1790 only 6 of the 19 men to receive bequests were given legacies composed of goods. Friendships with women, then, were far more likely to be cemented with the help of material culture.

When women gave items of clothing, they demonstrated a familiarity with the heir through their awareness of the fashion and tastes of the recipient. Mme. Petronille D'Assezat was most particular in the clothing that she included in her will. She left the bulk of her estate to her only son but gave a large bequest to her daughter as well. In addition to a cash legacy, the daughter was given a choice between all her mother's silk dresses and a Persian "four seasons" dress. She also gave the daughter her coiffes made of English lace and three pairs of lace sleeves or cuffs (*manchettes*) and a golden snuffbox.[45] The daughter seems to have opted for the Persian dress, since this was missing from the estate inventory, while a long list of silk dresses remained. Clothing frequently went to daughters but also sometimes passed to nieces and grandnieces and, occasionally, friends.

Many of these bequests stated that the clothing was intended for the use of the recipient, and legacies such as Mme. D'Assezat's show an awareness of the tastes of the younger heirs and the particular items of clothing that would be of value to them personally. The elderly assumed that the clothing in their possession could and would be worn and appreciated by women considerably younger than themselves. The fashion choices of the elderly differed little from those of the next generation, thus allowing the elderly to use their clothing as tokens of affection and living remembrances of the ties of family and friendship even beyond the grave.[46]

With the exception of clothing and linens, all the items bequeathed were durable as well as valuable; they were items that could serve as a token of remembrance for many years to come. Simple gifts of jewelry, precious housewares, linens, or clothing demanded nothing of the heirs except that they cherish the memory of their friend. The vast majority of the legacies were given with no conditions whatsoever.

A few of the bequests that crossed generations, on the other hand, contained evidence of patronage, coercion, or manipulation. These did not represent friendship among equals. These testators sought to perpetuate their memory not only with tokens but also by assisting their heirs and influencing their life choices. Most typically, legacies to young nieces and grandnieces were intended to be portions of their dowries, while legacies to young men were intended to help them begin a trade. Paule de Richard left money to both nieces and nephews for their marriage. One niece was to have 500 livres a year from a 4,800-livre investment until her marriage, and one nephew received the interest from a 1,000-livre investment until his marriage.[47] Honorée Neutre wrote a provision in her will for a wedding gift of 200 livres for her niece Toinette. If the girl did not marry, the money was to remain in the estate.[48] Jeanne Guimbaud left items for her grandniece's trousseau—linens and a small chest—as well as a 60-livre wedding gift.[49] Marguerite Bouxarine's nephews were to receive their legacies of 30 livres each when they took up a trade or when they were twenty-two years of age.[50] Linked bequests show concern for the heirs' future and were meant to help the recipients along the paths destined for them. Failure to follow this path carried financial penalties.

Occasionally, especially in bequests written to godchildren, women sought spiritual rewards in return for their largesse. When Paule de Richard wrote her will in 1717, she asked that her goddaughter not only pray for her but also orchestrate the minutely detailed funeral ritual she had stipulated earlier in the will and arrange for all the appropriate masses to be said in her honor.[51] Mme. de Richard, in return, left her goddaughter furniture, paintings, and an annual pension. While none of these were explicitly religious items, the paintings were quite likely depictions of religious themes. Estate inventories recorded that this was invariably the case for paintings found in the houses of deceased elderly women. Such paintings were not a common bequest; they appear only twice in the wills of elderly women and, in both cases, the pieces of art were passed on to goddaughters.[52]

One woman went beyond giving symbols of her spiritual attachment and gave a legacy meant to fulfill part of her role as educator of her godchild. Marianne Raymond wrote her will in 1719 and died the same year. She left only two bequests, one naming her husband her universal heir and the other detailing the legacy that was to be left to her niece and goddaughter. This girl, Marie Anne de Larroche, was to receive 3,000 livres when she married or when she reached the age of twenty-five. Until that time, the interest from this sum was to be used to pay for a convent education. Furthermore, Mme. Raymond wrote that M.

Larroche, the testator's brother-in-law and the heir's father, was not to have control of the funds at all. Should he not wish to send Marie Anne to a convent school, the money was not to be kept by Marie Anne or her father but was to pass instead to the testator's brother.[53] Although she could not definitively steer her goddaughter's education from beyond the grave, Mme. Raymond could use the leverage of the inheritance to influence her brother-in-law's decision.

Provisions like these disappeared by the end of the century. Only one will of the 1780s sample requested prayers in return for the gift. The same will gave a set of three legacies that were linked to a life stage; Amande Escoffre left 600 livres to her three grandnieces to help in the preparation of their first communions.[54] This is an interesting bequest, linked not only to a moment in the children's life course but also to a religious ritual, and presumably not too far in the future. When spiritual relationships remained, the testators of the late eighteenth century generally waived their heirs' obligations. Especially in legacies to goddaughters, testators continued to bequeath objects of religious significance, though they ceased to request prayers. Such objects included art, devotional literature, and jeweled crosses.[55] These gifts as likely signified a fitting remembrance of shared devotions in life as legacies intended to assure spiritual rewards. With or without a spiritual component, the familiarity expressed in the wills suggests a close social relation. The women knew their heirs well enough to choose items of personal significance. The testators clearly longed to remain in the memories of their living friends and family and gave goods that could then extend elements of their friendship beyond their own deaths.

The social interaction that fostered these relationships occurred, at least in part, within the woman's home. The contents of an elderly woman's estate demonstrate the extent of her involvement in social entertaining at home. Estates were inventoried for a variety of reasons in eighteenth-century Toulouse. Heirs frequently requested an inventory when bequests required a division of goods or a delay before the inheritance could be delivered. Inventories were conducted before items were sold, but they often occurred only after specific legacies had been fulfilled. The accuracy of the inventory depends on the diligence of the notary and the heirs requesting the document. Since the purpose of the inventory was often to evaluate the monetary worth of the estate, items of little value were sometimes mentioned only in passing. The notaries and the heirs nonetheless attested with their signatures that the document contained an accurate accounting of all the items found in the household of the deceased.

I have estate inventory information for 14 women who died over the age of sixty in eighteenth-century Toulouse.[56] Four of the women died in the 1710s or 1720s and 10 of them died in the 1770s or 1780s. Of these women, 4 were nobles, 3 were of merchant or professional families, 4 were of the artisanal milieu, and 3 were either laborers or indigent. All but 3 of the women were widows at the time they died. The women lived in apartments ranging in size from one to nine rooms. Several of the women had a distinct kitchen and all left evidence that they cooked within their homes. Table 3.1 outlines the items

Table 3.1
Items Indicating Social Activity and Entertaining in the Estate Inventories of Elderly Women, 1700–1720 and 1770–1790

	Deceased	Social status	folding beds	chairs	tables	folding tables	coffee pots	plates	games
1700-20	Bar	Nobility	1	76	7		3	56	2
	Castets	Worker		4	1			3	
	Gilis	Artisan		76	10	7		138	
	Lambert	Worker							
1770-90	Barra	Doctor	1	16	4	1	7	138	
	Bonnes	Artisan	1	43	5	1		84	
	Cambon	Merchant		18	5	1	1	33+	
	Cazaux	Merchant							
	D'Assezat	Nobility	2	19	4		7	24	
	Forgues	Artisan		13	2	1		12	
	Gérie	Nobility		23	6	2	5+	191	1
	Labadens	Nobility	1	61	8	2		59	
	Legueur	Destitute		10	1	1		24	
	Puntis	Artisan	1	17	1			24	

Source: ADHG series 3E as follows: Bar 3E11880; Castets 3E1890; Gilis 3E11916; Lambert 3E11925; Barra 3E13910; Bonnes 3E11880; Cambon 3E11885; Cazaux 3E11886; D'Assezat 3E6502; Forgues 3E11911; Gérie 3E1290; Labadens 3E11925; Legueur 3E11926; Puntis 3E11926.

found in the inventories indicating social activity and entertaining. The chart contains only those items that were housed in locations offering easy access for frequent or occasional use. Valuables, for instance, were often tucked away in a chest or closet away from the front of the apartment, sometimes among financial papers or linens. These items included jewelry and objects of silver or gold. Precious plates, cutlery, or goblets were stored away; regular housewares, on the other hand, appeared in the front rooms and in accessible cabinets.

The presence of folding furniture suggests the need for versatility of space to accommodate varying numbers of residents or guests. Several of the women in this sample were prepared for the possibility of an overnight guest or for the need of an additional bed for a servant. Beds appeared in many of the rooms and were clearly folded and stored until need arose for their use. Folding tables also suggest a fluctuating level of need. These tables never served as the woman's primary or sole table. Instead, a single noblewoman like Anne de Labadens housed ten tables within her nine-room apartment, of which two were folding tables. On a smaller scale, Marguerite Barra, the widow of a doctor, kept five tables in her two rooms, and one of these was collapsible. Even Madeleine Legueur felt the need for two tables in the room that she shared with three other women. The women must have been very short of space, and it is hardly surprising that one of these tables could be folded and stored. Folding furniture allowed the women to convert their dwellings from a space appropriate for themselves alone into one more appropriate for short- or longer-term visitors.

The large number of chairs prevalent in each of the women's apartments attests to a pattern of social activity involving groups of visitors all sitting and engaging in conversation. The chairs kept the women's apartments in a state of readiness for receiving guests and hosting large gatherings. They varied in quality but were generally usable. Many were described as "stacking" chairs, which is rather fortunate considering the amount of space 76 chairs must have taken in the apartment of an artisan like Françoise Gilis.

Eating and drinking appears also to have played a role in entertaining. Though it plays no major role in the memoirs of the period, several of the estate inventories show the presence of at least one coffeepot in the household and a large number of plates. Goblets and bottles of wine could also be found in a few of the households. Wine and coffee may have served personal consumption habits, but more than one coffeepot per household suggests entertaining and shared beverages. In addition to their coffeepots, Jeanne Marie Françoise Gérie and Magdelaine Barra also held onto a dozen or more coffee cups. The large quantity of plates includes pewter, porcelain, and pottery plates but does not include silver plates and does not include platters, bowls, tureens, or other, more specialized items of tableware. Only the three women—Jeanne de Lambert, Margueritte Castets, and Marie Cazaux—who lived as pensioners in furnished rooms did not have in their possession enough plates to serve well beyond their own personal needs.

When conversation grew tedious, the elderly resorted to games of chance. Two of the inventories in my sample contained evidence of gaming. Thérèse Génie owned a board or table game known as the jeu de poteau and Margueritte de la Bar owned two card tables. Such diversions are social in character. The memoir literature abounds with descriptions and indictments of elderly women who passed their days playing games and gambling. Apart from poteau, elderly women were apparently fond of trictrac (backgammon) and Loto, both of which involved gambling.[57] Reading provided another diversion for these elderly women. Six of the women died with books in their households.[58] Reading may have occurred in private or have formed a part of the social intercourse with visitors reading aloud to each other. Such endeavors in leisurely entertaining and amusements provided the setting for the development of close friendships beyond the level created from work and neighborhood acquaintances.

The estate inventories provide a window into the households of women who died while they were still the heads of households or, at least, who maintained some independent living space. The numerous women who, instead, lived with their relations may have experienced a more withdrawn lifestyle, focusing their emotional attachment, as the moralists wished, solely on their own children and grandchildren.

For the most part, however, the indications provided in wills and estate inventories suggest that women were socially active in their later years, developing strong, affectionate relationships with both their extended families and a number of friends. Although Mme. de la Tour du Pin observed this scenario wistfully, as an occurrence of the past, many of the characteristics she described indicate the beginnings of a modern pattern of social aging. The growing importance of affective friendships for women as they aged and their this-worldly focus point more to modern than early modern trends. Further research into the social dimensions of aging in the nineteenth and twentieth centuries may well uncover an acceleration of these trends, incorporating more and more the use of leisure goods to expand social networks and provide a framework for social activity.

NOTES

1. Henriette-Lucille, Marquise de La Tour du Pin Gouvernet, *Journal d'une femme de cinquante ans* (Paris: Librairie Chapelot, 1914), 159.

2. An overview of inheritance laws and customs in both the south and north of France can be found in David Troyansky, *Old Age in the Old Regime* (Ithaca, NY: Cornell University Press, 1989), 127–130. On inheritance strategies of families at the end of the eighteenth century in the south of France, see Margaret Darrow, *Revolution in the House: Family, Class and Inheritance in Southern France, 1775–1825* (Princeton, NJ: Princeton University Press, 1989); and Anne Zink, *L'Héritier de la maison: géographie coutumiere du sud-ouest de la France sous l'Ancien Regime* (Paris: Éditions de l'École des Hautes Études en Sciences Sociales, 1993).

3. The wills were found in Archives Départmentale, Haute-Garonne (ADHG), series 3E. These 107 wills were written by women whose age at death and other information could be clearly identified within the relevant archival sources.

4. This sample includes up to 10 wills from each of the notaries in Toulouse for the years 1719 and 1789. When a register contained more than 10 wills, I selected 10 written at different points of the year. I did not select based on gender.

5. The inheritance system in the south of France can account for the women showing a lack of preference for their eldest sons, since Toulousain men practiced primogeniture and favored this child over all others. The women would not, however, have assumed that their husbands' estates had or would provide for their other offspring and family members.

6. Servants were also very important in these wills. See a longer discussion of their role in my dissertation: Sherri Klassen, "Aging Gracefully in the Eighteenth Century: A Study of Elderly Women in Old Regime Toulouse," Ph.D. diss., Syracuse University, 1996. On servants in eighteenth-century France, see Cissie Fairchilds, *Domestic Enemies: Servants and Masters in Old Regime France* (Baltimore, MD: Johns Hopkins University Press, 1978); and Sara Maza, *Servants and Masters in Eighteenth-Century France: The Uses of Loyalty* (Princeton, NJ: Princeton University Press, 1983).

7. For example, Marguerite Bouxarine, the widow of a master cobbler, left a copper pitcher and two pressing irons to the wife of another master cobbler (ADHG 3E 5952); Jeanne Serene, also a widow, made her living selling saltpeter outside the Church of the Inquisition. In her will, she passed all her meager belongings to Gaillarde Hugon, another widow and another peddler woman (ADHG 3E 5954); Marie Lajoux was the widow of a day laborer. She gave some linens and a small cash bequest to Bertrande Dazieu, the daughter of a shopkeeper (ADHG 3E 6000).

8. ADHG 3E 10915.

9. ADHG 3E 1183.

10. ADHG 3E 6488.

11. ADHG 3E 1095.

12. ADHG 3E 2123.

13. ADHG 5952.

14. ADHG 5954.

15. ADHG10762; ADHG 1063.

16. ADHG 3E 3980.

17. ADHG 10686.

18. Five of the 10 wills remembering friends in 1719–1720 and 15 of the 21 in 1789–1790 named a friend the principal heir. In 1 case in 1719–1720 and 7 cases in 1789–1790, the friend was the sole heir listed. In these cases, the estate was simply too small to divide or the friend was the sole person of major interest to the testator. These few women may well have fit the stereotype of an old age passed in poverty and loneliness.

19. ADHG 3E 1103.

20. ADHG 3E 7410.

21. ADHG 3E 7321.

22. ADHG 3E 2123.

23. ADHG 3E 1095.

24. ADHG 3E 6447.

25. Elizabeth Vigée-Lebrun, *Souvenirs* (Paris: Éditions des Femmes, 1984), 43. Originally published in 1835.

26. *The Memoirs of Madame Roland, a Heroine of the French Revolution*, trans. and ed. Evelyn Shuckburgh (London: Moyer Bell, 1989), 157–161.

27. ADHG 3E 5952.

28. ADHG 3E 10927.

29. Claire Généreux 3E 6447; Jeanne de Généreux 3E 6445.

30. In the south of France, the eldest son and his wife customarily resided with the son's parents. A number of scholars have explored the ensuing relationships in peasant households. Anthropologists and historians of the family such as Martine Segalen, Jean-Louis Flandrin, and Peter Laslett view this family system as exploitative of the young daughters-in-law. It is supposed that a young woman entering the household of her mother-in-law would feel powerless and cowed by the older woman's authority. When she herself becomes the family matriarch, she turns her years of resentment against her own daughter-in-law, thus perpetuating the cycle. See Martine Segalen, *Mari et femme dans la société paysanne* (Paris: Éditions des Musées Nationaux, 1980); Peter Laslett, ed., *Household and Family in Past Time* (Cambridge, Eng.: Cambridge University Press, 1972); Jean-Louis Flandrin, *Familles, parenté, maison, sexualité dans l'ancienne société* (Paris: Hachette, 1976). There is, however, little evidence of serious conflict between mother-in-law and daughter-in-law. Although court records shed considerable light on conflict between husband and wife, female in-laws are infrequent antagonists. Conflict is examined by Roderick Philipps, "Women, Neighbourhood and Family in the Late Eighteenth Century," *French Historical Studies* 18, no. 1 (1993): 1–12; and Alan Williams, "Patterns of Conflict in Eighteenth-Century Parisian Families," *Journal of Family History* 18 (1993): 39–52. Wills suggest that in-law relationships were not dysfunctional as a rule and were sometimes even close.

31. ADHG 3E 6000.

32. ADHG 3E 3980.

33. ADHG 3E 10760.

34. ADHG 3E 10927.

35. ADHG 3E 1070.

36. ADHG 3E 6488.

37. ADHG 3E 6488.

38. ADHG 3E 2123.

39. ADHG 3E 1063; ADHG 3E 6488.

40. ADHG 3E 4014.

41. ADHG 3E 1095.

42. ADHG 3E 10996.

43. ADHG 3E 1063.

44. ADHG 3E 10761.

45. ADHG 3E 6488.

46. Though older women did tend to own more clothing in dark colors than younger women, estate inventories show that the variety and styles owned by elderly women also appear in those of the younger women. Social status and wealth played a more significant role than age in determining dress in eighteenth-century France. See Daniel Roche, *La Culture des apparences* (Paris: Fayard, 1989), which explores this theme in depth.

47. ADHG 3E 10927.

48. ADHG 3E 3980.

49. ADHG 3E 4625.

50. ADHG 3E 5952.

51. ADHG 3E 10927.

52. Antoinette Guille, ADHG 3E 10760, and Paule de Richard, ADHG 3E 10927.

53. ADHG 3E 6449.

54. ADHG 3E 1063.

55. Samuel K. Cohn Jr. argued that in Siena a similar decline in coercive spiritual bequests resulted from legislation in the eighteenth century. No such legislation can explain the pattern in Toulouse (Samuel K. Cohn Jr., *Death and Property in Siena, 1205–1800: Strategies for the Afterlife* [Baltimore, MD: Johns Hopkins University Press, 1988]).

56. These inventories are housed in ADHG series 3E as follows: Bar 3E11880; Barra 3E13910; Bonnes 3E11880; Cambon 3E11885; Castets 3E1890; Cazaux 3E11886; D'Assezat 3E6502; Forgues 3E11911; Gérie 3E1290; Gilis 3E11916; Labadens 3E11925; Lambert 3E11925; Legueur 3E11926; Puntis 3E11926.

57. See, for example, Mme. de la Tour du Pin, cited in the opening, Vigée-Lebrun, *Souvenirs*, 43. I have been unable to find a description of the "jeu de poteau."

58. These women were M. Bonnes 3E13910; J. Cambon 3E1185; P. D'Assezat 3E6502. Most of the books were devotional literature, with a certain number unspecified. The titles and authors were only occasionally provided.

4

Women and Aging in Transatlantic Perspective

Anne Kugler

Women's experience of old age in pre-industrial societies included important continuities with their younger years in their reliance on networks of family and kin and their placement within interlinking hierarchies of rank and gender. The process of growing older also varied considerably with women's financial standing, state of health, marital status, and age. A number of studies have established these fundamental parameters for the study of female old age in a number of countries, but a crying need for comparative work remains. One might ask as well whether the experiences of later years for women were fundamentally affected by geography—for instance, by whether they lived in Britain or in North America. Were social standing, wealth, and years equally important in affecting old age on both sides of the Atlantic, or did the environment of the New World offer new possibilities or problems for women as they aged? If, as David Fischer suggests, traditional patriarchal ideology, including respect for elders, gained particular weight when North America was being colonized, did older white women benefit?[1] Or did they gain from a flatter social hierarchy and an ideological premium on the concepts of liberty and equality in a frontier world populated by proportionately many more freeholding farmers than in north-western Europe? On the other hand, might the development of the ideals of liberty and equality during the formation of the new republic actually disadvantage older women if they involved rejecting hierarchies in which women might hold elevated places, such as aristocracy and age?[2]

Developing a transatlantic picture of aging for women where women are able to speak for themselves through their own personal writings is an especially difficult endeavor, even in the world of gender history. Alongside the standard problem of actually finding material written by women—restricted further to those women who were sufficiently rich, leisured, and inclined to write—the existence of such evidence for women who have survived to old age is a rarity on either side of the Atlantic.[3] The following set of three paired comparisons of six financially secure older women from the "long" eighteenth century furnishes the opportunity for sustained exploration of the lives and words of women who, when compared in their strong similarities and suggestive contrasts, illuminate especially vividly both the fundamental connections between the old world and the new and the variety of possibilities inherent in each environment.[4] These six women's experiences from roughly the age of fifty through their seventies and eighties indicate two significant continuities in the aging experience—the centrality of religion and of networks of family and friends—that underscore the fundamental survival of English patterns of spiritual and social life in the new world.[5] Accordingly, they further Terri Premo's assertion that the patriarchal family remained at the core of women's experience as they aged, and that despite the limitations of this familial identification for women, it did provide important connections, support, and fulfillment as they left the years of childbearing and child rearing for which they were supposedly primarily designed.[6] Furthermore, this domestic context might offer ways in which women in the vigor of their older years—fifties and early sixties—could use that family identification and especially motherhood not only for support at home, but as a means of extending influence and power outside the immediate realm of the family to create a fulfilling and even authoritative position for themselves in the wider society.

The divergences between these pairs of women, however, also bring into relief variations in the aging experience depending on both environment and individual temperament. While the more stratified, bureaucratic England might construct limitations on older women's mobility and authority because of the expectations of a traditional hierarchical society, for a few women with money, high social status, and good connections, England's cosmopolitan environment might offer more access to political power and social interaction than eighteenth-century North America.

RELIGION AND OLD AGE

The first comparison demonstrates most vividly the continuity in religious outlook on both sides of the Atlantic in the closeness of the experience of two deeply devout women, despite the secularizing, rationalizing eighteenth-century context. The life of Mary Hopkinson (1718–1804), Anglican gentlewoman born in England and settled in Philadelphia with her American lawyer husband, closely parallels that of Sarah Savage (1664–1752), farm wife and member of a noted family of Dissenting ministers near Bristol. Both women compiled reflections and extracts from readings, intending them to be instructive legacies for their descendants; both presumed to remonstrate with men over the issue of clerical qualification; and both perpetuated by word and example the model of upright, prayerful Christian life. These two women most clearly exemplify the importance of religion in the aging experience of women in the eighteenth century,[7] particularly as it enabled pious older women to speak, advise, and reprove.

Sarah Savage

Sarah Savage was the daughter and sister respectively of Dissenting preachers Philip and Matthew Henry. She was well trained, therefore, in the practice of Presbyterianism and had even been taught basic Hebrew by her father. Her daily routine included devotional exercises and hearing and outlining sermons—in other words, an active, knowledgeable pursuit of her faith. She married a farmer, John Savage, and produced four surviving children. Shortly before her fiftieth birthday she explicitly commented on her aging in terms that reinforce the theme of bodily decay, yet are couched in an entirely religious and providential understanding:

I have entered my declining years. Finding those that look out of the windows beginning to darken, I am obliged to use glasses. I find my strength fails. Yet, as to these infirmities, several things comfort me—They are only natural and common, not hastened by my own sin, and folly—I, otherwise, enjoy a very great measure of health, and can be in any post of usefulness, not having been confined to my bed or chamber for almost three years. But, the greatest support of all is—the good hope of everlasting rest—that, when my earthly tabernacle shall be dissolved, I shall have a heavenly mansion provided for me, where I shall see God, and my glorious Redeemer.[8]

Despite her explicit discussion, upon entering her fifties, of experiencing two symptoms of decline—decreased physical strength and weakened eyesight—Sarah Savage did not think of herself yet as entering a period when the infirmities of old age would actively impede her daily routine of household work, daily devotions, visits from family and friends, and delight in and care of grandchildren.[9] When she was fifty-seven, for instance, she contrasted her own need to prepare for decay in the future with the present condition of a woman in worse shape (and presumably older) than herself: "I was much affected to hear a poor old woman of our society complain of decays. . . . Lord, pity, and help under such decays, and let me be more busy now, and endeavor to lay up something in store against such an evil day."[10]

It was also while in her fifties that Sarah Savage, from her position as mother of a grown and prosperous family and her long experience in religion, wrote a reproving letter to the curate of her parish in 1717, protesting his sermon against Dissenters on the previous Sunday: "The distinct charge we had yesterday from you of schism pride arrogance etc I cannot account light, especially from one, who should stand in the place of God to guide, and instruct in the way to heaven I therefore think it invidious to judge mens hearts which none but God can do." Having claimed the right of conscience while warning against clerical pride, she reminded this priest of her family's deference toward the established church and criticized both the style and substance of his preaching:

> I was much affected many years ago with a sermon I wrote from you [i.e., took notes on] . . . I wish you would preach and pray as you did then. . . . I think there is no family but ours in the parish, that are accounted dissenters, yet you know we are true friends to you and the Church as any one in the parish. . . . I have heard many complain that you speak so low, that they can scarce hear, but I observed yesterday you could raise your voice, but if I had foreseen our treatment, I believe my seat would have been empty.[11]

In this combination of deference and pointed reproof, Sarah Savage was fortified by her diligent attendance at Church of England services—a symbol of obedience to the state despite maintaining her own religious principles. She could also draw on her long experience in and knowledge of sermon delivery, because of which she possessed the ability to judge the appropriateness of his choice of topics and the correct way to carry out his calling. This attitude to the clergy resurfaced in her sixties, when having read an old sermon of her father's she commented, "Methinks, as I grow old, I have more delight and sweetness in my old sermon notes. . . . I heartily bless God for the gifts and abilities of our younger ministers. But I am comforted to think that I have not now my foundation to lay. I had then the best helps, so that my roots were watered with wine."[12] In this context, Sarah Savage depicted her old age as a period of spiritual fruition and suggested in consequence that she was trained and spiritually qualified in a way that the ministry could not replicate.

Although Sarah Savage found her sixties to be blessed with the fruits of long religious experience, this period also included one of the most devastating experiences of old age, the loss of her husband in 1729. Sarah's understanding of this event drew on a providential framework as she struggled to find comfort amidst her grief, but it is also notable that she recounted this blow as relatively merciful because of her age and its attendant circumstances: "Lord, help me to behave myself well under this sharp dispensation. I own the mercy of God to me in outward things. I am not forsaken of my friends, but the contrary. . . . I am not left in debt, and with children little. Surely all these mercies should make me thankful." Being widowed in her mid-sixties, then, was qualitatively different, in positive ways, from what it would have been in earlier years. Not only was she not facing the daunting prospect of raising children on her own, she could understand her husband's death as part of the Christian experience of moving through stages in life, through death, and on to eternal life in due season as part of God's plan: "God's sovereignty should silence me, and his wisdom satisfy. It is well with my husband. It is well. All is well that God doth. My time after him is not likely to be long."[13] Sarah could render her loss intelligible and bearable partly through her own advancing years and prospect of soon joining her husband.

A few months later, perhaps as a way of creating a new focus for her life, Sarah wrote explicitly of the function of her diary as a learning device and exemplar for her descendants. Drawing on her advanced years as a qualification for wisdom, she claimed the ability of the aged to distance themselves from worldly things, to recognize their insubstantiality, and moreover, to have the authority to teach this wisdom to descendants even once she was physically gone:

I have had such plentiful experience of the goodness of God to me through all the way in which he hath led me in this wilderness, that I cannot but think it a duty to leave an acknowledgment of it under my own hand, for the quickening and encouragement of my dear children and grandchildren who have this evil world to pass: "A dangerous and tiresome place."[14]

Sarah Savage expanded her children's spiritual inheritance—casting her life in terms of the providences afforded her by God, but also recognizing her own increasing frailties—when in her seventieth year she wrote a spiritual autobiography. She prefaced her brief account "Finding decays, especially in my memory, I think it not improper to leave this testimony under my hand of that kind Providence which has followed me all my days" and ended with "The health I have in my old age is, surely, a great mercy. . . . I have the use of reason, and peace in my own conscience, those unspeakable blessings."[15] Even at this later stage of her old age, when failing memory was one of her motivations for recording her life, it is notable that Sarah Savage claims lucidity and tranquility as special blessings—the very things she would need to face the prospect of imminent death and judgment.

Two years later, Sarah moved in with one of her married daughters. In doing so, she completed the transition from helpmate, child raiser, and household manager to elderly contemplative. Relieved of the responsibility of managing a household, she expressed concern at the loss of traditional feminine "usefulness," asking, "And now I am here, Lord, what wilt thou have me to do? I am encouraged to find some good, praying people, with whom I hope to spend a happy eternity."[16] Even after two years of living in this environment, she still made references to this lack of a clear domestic role, exclaiming, "O that I may be some way useful even in old age!" but also suggesting a way to constructively redefine her "usefulness": "I can delight in a pen and a book, and opportunity to devote myself to God."[17]

Sarah Savage reiterated this conception of herself in old age as "useful" to her relatives not now in terms of domestic labor but in terms of religious edification, when she looked back at previous volumes and reaffirmed her continued writing: "hoping it may be useful to some of mine, when I am in the dust, for their quickening, and encouragement in the narrow way." Moreover, she went on to quote her brother's annotations on Deuteronomy 3:22 to demonstrate that this kind of guidance for her descendants was a particular duty of the old:

"Those that are aged, and experienced in the service of God, should do all they can to strengthen the hands of those who are young."[18]

When Sarah Savage died in 1752, her niece depicted the event as the natural completion of a life of piety, verifying Sarah's own self-depiction: "My dear aunt Savage died . . . and in a good old age (almost eighty-eight) was gathered to her people. . . . She had lived a holy, cheerful life; made religion her business. . . . She was useful, beloved, meek, humble, charitable. She is gone to receive her reward—joined by the society she loved. May I ever remember such examples as these."[19]

Mary Hopkinson

Across the ocean and in an Anglican rather than Dissenting framework, Mary Hopkinson nonetheless experienced a very similar kind of old age. Born in England as a member of the lesser gentry, Mary grew up in Antigua and married Thomas Hopkinson, a Philadelphia lawyer. Unlike Sarah Savage, she was widowed in 1751, when only thirty-three, and left with seven children to care for. Despite her "small estate," she managed to have her older son Francis trained in the law, and her two oldest daughters married well.[20]

Like Sarah Savage, on the strength of her experience and piety Mary Hopkinson felt that she knew what qualified a man to be a good member of the clergy. When she was nearly fifty she used her spiritual knowledge and her authority as a mother to warn her son of his deficiencies in the moral qualities necessary for entering the priesthood:

if you enter into the ministry with a high sense of the importance of the sacred office you take upon you, and constantly pray to God . . . that your corrupt affections may be mortified, and that he would teach you obedience, humility, patience, meekness . . . and bring them into practice, before you presume to preach them to others, then although your talents may not be shining, yet you may be enabled to do much good to the souls of others.[21]

When Mary Hopkinson was in her sixties and seventies, she wrote and extracted from books passages useful for holy living and preparation for her own death. In addition, like Sarah Savage, she hoped to leave edifying work for her descendants in aid of their pursuit of salvation. She dedicated her commonplace book to her eldest daughter, Elizabeth Duche: "You have often desired my dear child, you might have this book, when I had done with it, and all sublanary [sic] things. I with the greater pleasure comply with your request, as I know you have a true relish for the contents."[22] The contents were comments on and extracts from readings on religious doctrine and practice—Mary Hopkinson's personal assessment of the basic armor needed to fortify a good Christian.

Again like Sarah Savage, in late old age Mary Hopkinson turned to functioning as a living exemplar once she had moved in with a granddaughter and was no longer managing a household herself. Here too, the "usefulness" of old women was at issue. In eulogizing her grandmother, Mary's granddaughter praised not only her service as a moral model, but her continued productive capacity: "She was all goodness; ten thousand sermons upon charity and self-love could not have the effect as one such example. . . . she walked frequently in the nursery . . . to talk to the children, who were very fond of her" and sewed, up to the last day of her life, when she "made up four caps."[23]

In transatlantic perspective, Mary Hopkinson and Sarah Savage demonstrate the greatest line of continuity, in time and space, between the old world and the new. For aging women, religion, of whatever denomination, provided a world-view that gave meaning and significance, both to the good moments and the tragedies, and especially to the approach of death and the right use of length-ening years in preparing for salvation. Both these women had a theological outlook that strongly focused on Providence, on a benevolent and merciful God even when he inflicted trials, and on the strong hope of salvation through his Grace, even if Sarah Savage was a predestinarian and Mary Hopkinson assuredly was not. Both these women spent their last years cohabiting with their descen-dants, serving as living testimony to the practice of piety and its rewards in old age and as a teaching example to the next generations. In female descendants' reports of their deaths, these women received recognition for having fulfilled that role well on earth, and thus might expect happiness in heaven, which was, after all, the whole point of human life.

RANK, POLITICS, AND OLD AGE

The second pair of women in this chapter elucidates the furthest extent of political power available to older women in either setting and demonstrates that they could use their familial and religious positions—as mothers of influential adult sons and as mature, pious churchwomen—to exercise a number of forms of authority. Lady Rachel Russell (1637–1723) of London and Woburn Abbey, herself of ancient noble lineage and widow of famous Whig political martyr Lord William Russell, parlayed motherhood and aristocratic privilege into an active and powerful political and economic career. Abigail Adams (1744–1818) of Massachusetts, from an influential old Puritan family and wife of farmer, lawyer, and one-term second president John Adams, had a voice in church affairs and patronage because of her husband's temporary holding of the highest office in the new republic and as a mother in the fortunes of her son and future president John Quincy Adams. In comparing these two women's activities, how-ever, it is notable that Rachel Russell, living in the presumably more constricted, confining traditional society of England, was the more unapologetic and exten-sive wielder of political power, precisely because of the advantages she gained from her rank and from the English patronage system. The experiences of these two women suggest that older noblewomen in England might use these positions with more confidence and to more effect than might the wives of officeholders in the United States because the advantages of aristocratic birth could offset the disadvantages of gender in ways that were not replicated in the new American republic.

Lady Rachel Russell

Rachel Russell was the daughter of Thomas Wriothesley, the fourth earl of Southampton, and Rachel Massue de Ruvigny de la Maison Fort, a Huguenot noblewoman. By the time she married her second husband, William, Lord Russell, Rachel was an extremely wealthy heiress who retained legal control over her own estates.[24] In 1683, when Rachel was forty-six, Lord Russell was executed for involvement in the Rye House Plot. After a lengthy period of intense grief, Lady Rachel returned to the world in her early fifties. She supervised her children's education, arranged their marriages, and managed her own and her family's vast estates.

After the Glorious Revolution, her symbolic position as the saintly widow of a Whig martyr and her wealth, rank, and contacts offered Rachel exceptional political influence. She had already initiated a secret correspondence with Mary II before the Revolution; once her in-laws, the earls of Bedford and Devonshire, became privy councilors, Rachel could also use those channels to obtain favors for kin and friends.

Lady Russell also cultivated relationships with many of the notable clerics of the day, including John Tillotson, who owed his position as dean of St. Paul's partly to her influence, and who sought her advice on whether he should accept the appointment when King William asked him to be archbishop of Canterbury: "And now, Madam, what shall I do? my thoughts were never at such a plunge. I know not how to bring my mind to it. . . . I hope I shall have your prayers, and would be glad of your advice." Rachel responded: "I see no place to escape at; you must take up the cross, and bear it. . . . 'tis God calls you to it." To which Tillotson replied:

I am obliged to your Ladyship beyond all expression, for taking my case so seriously into your consideration, and giving me your mature thoughts upon it. . . . I weighed all you wrote . . . having not only an assurance of your true friendship and good will for me, but a very great regard and deference for your judgment and opinion. . . . I had almost forgot to mention Mr. Vaughan's business; as soon as he brought your Ladyship's letter hither to me, I wrote immediately to Whitehall and got the business stopped.[25]

This exchange portrays Rachel as instructor and Tillotson as deferential student, leaping to fix a problem for Rachel's kinsman (Mr. Vaughan), despite the fact that he was about to become the highest-ranking bishop in the Church of England. Once archbishop, Tillotson continued to solicit her opinion, especially about clerical appointments connected to her family's property holdings in London, and she used him as an intermediary in requests to Queen Mary.[26]

Lady Russell was able to act even more authoritatively when she personally owned the right of presentation to a benefice. In checking the references of a Mr. Swayne, she both acknowledged and claimed the responsibility of prudently wielding such power in telling Sir Robert Worsley:

I am persuaded that in a just regard to the weight of the matter, and to me who ask it from you, if you know any visible reason that he is not a proper person for such a preferment, that you will caution me in it; for I profess to you, Sir, I think the care of so many souls is a weighty charge; and I have been willing to take time to consider whose hands I put these into.[27]

The height of Rachel Russell's expression of authority comes at age sixty-four, in a letter of thanks to King William for the success of her petition to elevate the earl of Rutland to a dukedom, where she spoke as answering for the whole extended clan, saying, "As you will lay an eternal obligation on that family, be pleased to allow me to answer for all those I am related to; they will look on themselves equally honour'd with Lord Rutland, by your favour to his family, and I am sure will express their acknowledgments to your Majesty in the most dutifull manner."[28]

In 1711 her son, her second daughter, and her kinsman the duke of Rutland all died. In the face of this triple bereavement, her political activity lessened, even as her correspondence to grandchildren continued and her life of religious introspection increased. Her own good health continued to 1717, by which time failing sight and tremors curtailed her writing. Nonetheless, in 1720 she launched a legal claim on estates in France left by the death of a cousin and petitioned George I for help in this effort. She was still pursuing this suit at her death in 1723 at the age of eighty-six.

Rachel Russell is the extreme example of a woman situated by her rank, wealth, connections, and the manner and fact of her widowhood to play an active role in the political nation, especially the Church. If she did not act officially, then certainly neither did she act clandestinely, but rather operated through the normal channels of kinship connections and client–patron relations that staffed the state and influenced its policies. Lady Russell's fifties and sixties were the height of her exercise of a number of forms of power, an exercise that only diminished significantly with loss of health and loved ones in her early seventies. Because of her birth, Rachel Russell could enter this world with self-confidence and the expectation of deference to her rank, a self-confidence that peaked in her later years when she spoke as family representative, dispensed political advice, and placed job candidates.

Abigail Adams

The power and self-confidence of Rachel Russell's rank and wealth, exercised in the political arena by a vigorous matriarch in her mature fifties and sixties, contrast in some notable respects with the example of Abigail Adams, who, like Rachel Russell, involved herself in the political and ecclesiastical life of the nation, finding places for her kin, advising on politics, and consulting over filling clergy positions. Abigail Adams, however, could not hope to match the age, dignity, and wealth of Rachel Russell's pedigree. She worked to further her family interests in the less hierarchical, less bureaucratic new republic, without a national established church or the corresponding right of a privileged class to staff numerous positions within that church. Nor was her husband's position permanent, either socially or politically. Consequently, Abigail Adams's experience of the vigorous phase of old age ran along the same lines as Rachel Russell's in some respects, but demonstrates the narrower reach and lesser power of a mature woman placed at the top of American society.

During the Revolution Abigail Adams had seen her role as stand-in for her husband during his absence as a temporary aberration—a patriotic sacrifice of her wifely claims in favor of her husband's public service career and the needs of the emerging nation.[29] In similar vein did she view her elevation to the position of First Lady and the corresponding need to leave her own home for Philadelphia and take on extensive hostessing and ceremonial duties. In this new situation, and now being fifty-two years old, the First Lady also explicitly attributed her reluctance to assume the burden of the position to her advanced age: "At my time of Life, the desire or wish to shine in publick life is wholly extinguished, the retirement to (peacefield, the name which Mr. A. has given his farm) is much more eligible to me."[30] This assertion of preference for a retired life, while appropriate to someone of her age, stands in notable contrast to Lady Russell's heightened social visibility during her fifties.

This public role brought with it not only ceremonial duties, but new forms of family obligation, as well as new ways to fulfill those obligations. Mrs. Adams helped defend her husband against press attacks by using her connections to plant rebuttals in the newspapers, and she helped advance her nephews' careers by finding them positions in her husband's administration—one as the president's secretary, the other a clerk for the Supreme Court.[31] Rather than confidently asserting noble privilege, however, as Lady Russell had done in the context of English aristocratic society, Abigail Adams depicted her activity in terms that supported the ideology of the new American republic. Writing to her sister of her patronage efforts, Mrs. Adams insisted on the candidate's own merit and devalued the claims of traditional nepotism:

Judge Cushing mentioned to Judge Chase that Mr. Cranch was a nephew of mine, to which he replied, that Mrs. Adams wish should be his Law. This tho' very polite in the Judge, I am far from wishing should influence him or the other Gentlemen. If I did not think Mr. Cranch a person well qualified for the office, I would not recommend him if he was my own son.

In this report, as well as reprioritizing the claims of merit and blood, Abigail simultaneously indicated the weight of her influence and disclaimed any authority on that front. While judges afforded her respect because of her position, Mrs. Adams herself, in putting her request in terms of a meritocratic new ideal, undercut the opportunity for older women to exercise authority on behalf of their male kin's careers.

America was also a problematic environment for Abigail Adams's interest in the appointment of a new minister in her home congregation in Quincy. The new nation not only was without the established church or property rights to benefices that so aided Rachel Russell, the very process of choosing clergy in Massachusetts by discussion in a public meeting made women's participation more difficult than in England, where the whole question could be decided by private correspondence or personal visits among the political and social elite. Here, too, as in the case of political appointments, much as she did expect to possess some influence in the selection of a candidate, Abigail Adams disclaimed a voice in the process, expressing outrage that a male acquaintance would make her preferences known during a public discussion: "I could not believe that any Gentleman would have had so little delicacy or so small a sense of propriety as to have written a mere vague opinion, and that of a Lady too, to be read in a publick assembly as an authority. . . . little did I think of having my Name quoted on any occasion in Town meeting."[32]

Mrs. Adams's last recorded political actions were as a 66-year-old mother who intervened in her son's career, not so much to help him advance professionally as to insist that he respond to the claims of the family as well as the claims of the nation. John Quincy Adams was ambassador to Russia when Abigail Adams wrote to President James Madison requesting her son's recall because his wife was ill. When shortly afterward Madison offered John Quincy Adams a place on the Supreme Court,[33] Abigail Adams urged that he accept the position in terms that acknowledged the imperatives of Divine Will and of service to the state but also ascribed considerable weight to the imperatives of family duty, particularly toward aging parents. Here too, unlike the confident assumption of compliance in Rachel Russell's correspondence, there is a hint of the diffidence of Abigail Adams's previous letters:

I will not impose my judgement as a Law upon you, but I will say I consider it a call of providence to you. . . . I believe you can be more extensively useful to your country in this than in any other employment, certainly you can be of more benefit to your Children by being able to superintend their Education, and should the lives of your parents be prolonged a few more years, your presence will prolong and heighten the few remaining pleasures and comforts which remain to advanced age.[34]

After Mrs. Adams's death in 1818, John Adams explicitly compared Rachel Russell and his wife in terms that ignored both their social disparity and their political activity while emphasizing the very quality that their kin attributed to Sarah Savage and Mary Hopkinson—religious virtue:

This Lady was more beautiful than Lady Russell, had a brighter genius, more information, a more refined taste, and at least her equal in virtues of the heart; equal fortitude and firmness of character, equal resignation to the will of heaven, equal in all the virtues and graces of the Christian life.[35]

INTROVERTED AND EXTROVERTED OLD AGE

The last pair of women illuminates extreme contrasts in health and sociability. At one end of the scale, Hester Lynch Thrale Piozzi (1741–1821) of London, Bath, and Wales exemplified robust intellectual and physical health and extroverted delight in witty society. Her love for an Italian musician meant that she experienced her later years alienated from her kin and focused instead on social circles, travel, and writing for publication. With a persona centered on sociability, Hester Piozzi both reaped the benefits of creating networks, and suffered some drawbacks in living such a determinedly social existence, which may correspond to a certain level of disjunction in her early and later experience of aging.[36] At the other end of the scale is Elizabeth Drinker (1735–1807) of Philadelphia, mother of a large and prosperous Quaker family. She led an intensely private, kin-centered, house-based, understated life, drawing strength from children, grandchildren, and medicinal concerns. Consequently, her fifties were different only in degree from her early seventies.

Hester Lynch Thrale Piozzi

Two entries ten days apart in Hester Lynch Thrale Piozzi's *Thraliana* already indicate some of the hallmarks of this woman's decades from her fifties to her eighties. On 9 April 1791, marking the onset of menopause and assessing her condition at fifty, she wrote: "I believe my *oldest friend* is at last going to leave me, and that will probably make a change in my health, if not induce the loss of it for ever. . . . I am now exactly fifty years old I think, and am possessed of great corporeal strength blessed be God, with ability to endure fatigue if necessary." On 19 April she lamented, "How shockingly this volume of Thraliana is written compared with foregoing ones!! I am frightened to see how my hand writing is degenerated, and eyesight goes away so horribly fast, that it injures my powers of composition." Hester Piozzi was explicit and dramatic, her health robust, but undercurrents of insecurity and alarm lurked just below the surface. She sought the recognition of the social world for her wit and conversation, interacting not so much with her family as with circles of friends and acquaintances. Daughter of a moderately prosperous family in Wales, she married Henry Thrale in 1763, produced four surviving daughters, and enlivened London society as part of Dr. Samuel Johnson's circle. After being widowed in 1781, she gained considerable notoriety for publishing her recollections of Dr. Johnson and for marrying Gabriele Piozzi, an Italian musician. Hester Piozzi then embarked with her new husband on a tour of his native land, a voyage that outraged her children and provoked social ostracism.

In her new life as Mrs. Piozzi, she began at the age of fifty-five to write a history of the world. This ambitious and indeed presumptuous project for a woman was in some respects legitimated by her advancing years, a time when sober scholarly subjects should have been especially interesting, and when her own experience and accumulated wisdom might be sufficient to the task. Despite the validation provided by her age, the scale of the project prompted fears of social ridicule on precisely that front. She expected to take five years, and worried, "If death catches me (as 'tis most likely) before the period arrives. . . . The people will say that at my age such a project was no other than ridiculous and that to entertain hope of ever finishing so large and comprehensive a work, was insolent anticipation; but if by God's mercy the volumes should be completed— they *may* be really useful to some, and entertaining to others, and may bring me in a Thousand Pounds."[37]

Despite the loss of friends and break with her daughters, Hester Thrale Piozzi's second marriage was happy, her health reasonably good, and for the decade of her fifties, engrossed as she was in her husband, her writing, and rebuilding a social circle, she was hopeful and productive.

In her early sixties, however, the onset of her husband's ultimately fatal bouts of gout curtailed their travel, their social engagements, and her opportunities for sustained writing, as she nursed Mr. Piozzi during his lengthening periods of acute illness. Moreover, her history (called *Retrospective*) when completed was neither a critical nor a commercial success, and her contemporaries were dying in ever more alarming numbers, which she saw as a manifestation of her own increasing vulnerability to death. Noting the demise of Mr. Murphy, one of the last of Dr. Johnson's circle, Mrs. Piozzi depicted herself as gradually losing the mortality buffer provided by the existence of other survivors from those days, saying, "Lord Westcote lives to stand a while longer like a long shadow in the setting sun, covering and shading my small person from death the destroyer."[38] In preparation for this increasingly imminent event, the Piozzis even built a burial vault for themselves.[39]

Notwithstanding her mounting concern with her own mortality, in 1805 Hester Piozzi took up a new and difficult foreign language: "I'll study Hebrew to divert ennui and pass the summer months away—Shameful! If not criminal resolution! to endeavour to rid myself of *time* who is so near ridding the world of me."[40]

Gabriele Piozzi died in 1809, and Mrs. Piozzi was again a widow, but now facing her seventies on her own. She began this stage of her life by embarking on a new lengthy work, *Lyford Redivivus, or a Grandames Garrulity*, an etymology that unfortunately lived up to its title. It was drawn from her language studies but went very wide of the mark in straining for improbable and inaccurate derivations of English words from Hebrew. Its ill-advised publication drew contemptuous reviews. Her last years, from 1811 to 1821, were mostly spent in a self-inflicted state of perilous finances, straining for continued public and familial appreciation. Interpretations of this period of her life differ: she either enjoyed her new acquaintances at Bath and retained a reputation for impressive powers of conversation, or she spent a miserable decade, not writing anything worthwhile, increasingly isolated, disappointed in both her children and the uncertainty of social applause.[41] It is certainly true that in her writings from this period, there is a strain of desperation and bitterness. Shortly after she had given all her real estate to her adopted heir (who continued to press her for money), she was forced to find cheap lodgings in Bath. She portrayed her reduced circumstances with scathing self-pity: "My Aunt—with the Boarding house: A New Farce acted without much applause even from her nephew by poor wretched HLP—I think I shall really be driven quite down."[42]

Even after the extraordinarily public celebration of her eightieth birthday, a seemingly triumphant validation of the continuing vitality and social success of the very old, she wrote that her "comfort is that she is likely soon to escape the truly uneasy situation of out living friends and enemies—and standing alone upon the stage of life till hiss'd off for being able to furnish no further amusement."[43]

Despite this pessimistic assessment of her position in late old age, it is notable that when Hester Piozzi died, she too was eulogized, as Mary Hopkinson and Sarah Savage were, in precisely the terms in which she had depicted herself— only in this case, those terms were primarily intellectual and social, rather than religious. Her friend Mrs. Pennington (notably not any of her daughters) wrote an obituary (again, notably not a private letter) that characterized Mrs. Piozzi's significance as "descended on both the paternal and maternal sides from the ancient and respectable families of the Salisburys and Cottons . . . but still more distinguished as the intimate friend of . . . a coterie never surpassed in talent and acquirement, in this or any country. The vivacity of this lamented lady's mind was a never failing source of pleasure to all who had the good fortune to enjoy her society, while the brilliancy of her wit, tempered by invariable good humour and general benevolence, delighted all who approached her, and offended none."[44]

Elizabeth Drinker

On 1 January 1802, at the age of sixty-seven, Elizabeth Drinker wrote in her diary: "When in tolerable health I can be as happy, and more so, at home than anywhere else . . . as my sister seems to choose looking after the family, I have the more leisure to amuse my self in reading and doing such work as I like best. My health is such, that I cannot go much abroad, but can stay pleasantly at home when my mind is at ease, and I never go out from my family to look for comfort."[45] This reflection on the occasion of the New Year encapsulates much of Elizabeth's experience of middle and old age, in a life that was centered entirely on family and home, dictated by invalidism, and permeated with concern for her own and her loved ones' health. Elizabeth Drinker was born to a merchant family in 1735 in the same Philadelphia house in which her mother had been born. After her marriage in 1761 to trader and prominent Quaker Henry Drinker and one move in 1771 to a new house, she lived there for the rest of her life, hardly leaving the premises save for visits to her children nearby.[46]

Elizabeth Drinker kept a journal of the weather, the precise health status of her children, grandchildren, and husband, illnesses experienced and remedies tried, and her family and friends' visits, interspersed with occasional comments on fires and epidemics in Philadelphia, news, and her reading and sewing. Her old age was a nearly seamless continuum of chronic illness, absorbing motherhood and grandmotherhood (especially in visits to and from, and nursing of her two sons and three daughters and their families), and quiet, domestic, sometimes solitary pursuits of reading, writing, and sewing. As Elizabeth Drinker herself noted, "There is such a sameness in my way of living every day, that I have little to say."[47]

Although Elizabeth subscribed to Quaker principles of pacifism, abolition of the slave trade, and sobriety and modesty in dress and decorum, her intense interiority extended to the issue of attendance at weekly Meeting, to which she went rarely by her fifties, and not at all in her sixties and seventies, despite her husband's active participation in the governance and spiritual life of the sect.[48] Nor is her diary punctuated with explicit religious sentiment, or self-reflection, unlike those of the women examined above. Ordinarily reserved and understated, the only expressions of emotion pertain to her children's welfare. "No wife or mother, is more attached to her near relative[s]"[49] was her accurate self-characterization.

This woman's old age was experienced in an environment circumscribed by illness and narrow emotional family focus. In this small, domestic world, Elizabeth Drinker also seems contented and fulfilled, always excepting her perpetual indispositions. While she felt age approaching, and regretted the idea of separation from her children in death ("How near are my children to my heart. I must soon leave them, may the Lord preserve them!"),[50] nonetheless "May we be thankful for the favours received" was her prayer at the end of 1806 and indeed of many years.[51] The only real break in this scene was when her eldest daughter died of cancer in 1807. Elizabeth Drinker lamented her loss with uncharacteristic emotion and reiterated her grief in subsequent diary entries. Perhaps most tellingly, she herself died two months later at the age of seventy-two.

Elizabeth Drinker chose to rely exclusively on family rather than cultivating an external circle of friends as part of her support network. Had she wished, she certainly had the opportunity to make connections with the outside world, living as she did in the thriving port city of Philadelphia. Nonetheless, even if she had been so inclined, Elizabeth Drinker could not have replicated the scale of Hester Piozzi's social life of summers at fashionable watering holes and country estates in England and abroad and winters in London with the literary elite of the nation. Opportunities for interaction and movement were greater and more varied in the huge, commercial, cultural, and political hub of London than they were in the cities of the United States, so that while Elizabeth Drinker's environment did not impede her sociability, Hester Piozzi's was a positive encouragement to hers.

CONCLUSION

Sarah Savage, Mary Hopkinson, Rachel Russell, Abigail Adams, Hester Piozzi, and Elizabeth Drinker all share some major characteristics in their old age, so that in many respects, the Atlantic divide was not a divide at all. They expressly noted their increasing physical debility, starting in their fifties but most especially in their sixties and seventies; citing declines of eyesight, hearing, handwriting, energy, strength, and memory. They commented on the imminence of death, expecting it at any time from their fifties on, and considering life's continuance a surprising gift from God. They lamented the loss of friends and family, recognizing it as one of the particular trials of old age. With the exception of Hester Piozzi, they enjoyed their children (notably their daughters) and especially grandchildren, with whom contact was frequent, and in two of the cases, ended up residing with a daughter or granddaughter. They all read extensively (both in devotional works and in most cases in other forms of literature), keeping up an active intellectual life throughout their old age. In fact, intellectual pursuits were particularly suited to their old age, free as they were from childbearing and other concerns of younger years, and perhaps looking for a new focus in life appropriate to their age. They claimed for themselves experience, wisdom, and a degree of detachment very much along the lines of moralists' depictions of a rational, tranquil, contemplative old age. Their fifties, while separate from earlier decades by the fact of menopause and grown children, were because of continued vigor and sociability, as well as fewer losses to and a greater remove from death, nonetheless in most cases significantly different from their later sixties and seventies. In all cases, religious belief permeated their outlook, practice, and expression, and for Mary Hopkinson and Sarah Savage it became nearly all-absorbing. Moreover, this wholehearted spirituality translated on a number of occasions into judgments on, and influences over, the clergy, thus providing a sphere of authority over men and a male institution that was legitimated by piety as well as by social status and age.

Nonetheless, differences in environment and temperament contrast most notably in two areas: the extent to which an older woman through her family, rank, and existing channels of patronage could exercise political influence; and the directions in which women might look for support and fulfilling lives as they aged, either within a small family circle and home or in a much wider, cosmopolitan array of friends and acquaintances. Paradoxically, the traditional, highly socially stratified and bureaucratized world of England in the eighteenth century might, therefore, have offered to a very small number of women at the top ranks of society or in literary circles the most extensive opportunities for the exercise of political and economic authority, and for the cultivation of alternative ties and intellectual stimulation to that of the family. A specific set of unusual freedoms and authorities for a few aging women, then, might be found not in the beckoning unpopulated frontiers of the new world, but in the old.

NOTES

1. Inaugurated by David Fischer, *Growing Old in America*, 2d ed. (New York: Oxford University Press, 1978), in the American case and Keith Thomas, "Age and Authority in Early Modern England," *Proceedings of the British Academy* 62 (1976): 205–248, in the English, the most lasting argument has been over the degree to which the elderly were afforded greater respect in their later years because of the ideal of age hierarchy combined with their demographic scarcity, or instead disparaged for declining abilities and usefulness. For further developments on the English side, see Peter Stearns, ed., *Old Age in Pre-Industrial Society* (New York: Holmes and Meier, 1982); Margaret Pelling and Richard Smith, eds., *Life, Death and the Elderly: Historical Perspectives* (New York: Routledge, 1991); Paul Johnson and Pat Thane, eds., *Old Age from Antiquity to Post-Modernity* (New York: Routledge, 1998). On the American side, see W. Andrew Achenbaum, *Old Age in the New Land: The American Experience Since 1790* (Baltimore, MD: Johns Hopkins University Press, 1978); John Demos, "Old Age in Early New England," in *Past, Present and Personal: The Family and the Life Course in American History* (Oxford, Eng.: Oxford University Press, 1986); Thomas Cole, *Journey of Life: A Cultural History of Aging in America* (Cambridge, Eng.: Cambridge University Press, 1992).

2. For discussion of the implications of republicanism for women, see Mary Beth Norton, *Liberty's Daughters: The Revolutionary Experience of American Women 1750–1800* (Boston: Little, Brown, 1980), esp. 298–299. On the question of rejection of old world aristocracy and its connection to a new individualistic male identity, see Michael Kimmel, *Manhood in America: A Cultural History* (New York: Free Press, 1996).

3. The most comprehensive survey of older women in America is Terri Premo, *Winter Friends: Women Growing Old in the New Republic 1785–1835* (Urbana: University of Illinois Press, 1990). For England, see Lynn Botelho and Pat Thane, eds., *Women and Ageing in British Society Since 1500* (London: Longman, 2000).

4. For an eloquent defense of this kind of small-scale comparative method, see Natalie Davis's Preface to *Women on the Margins: Three Seventeenth-Century Lives* (Cambridge, MA: Harvard University Press, 1995), 2–4, where she explains to her subjects, "I put you together to learn from your similarities and differences. . . . I wanted to show where you were alike and where you were not, in how you talked about yourselves and what you did. . . . I wanted to have a Jew, a Catholic, a Protestant so I could see what difference religion made in women's lives, what doors it opened for you and what doors it closed, what words and actions it allowed you to choose. . . . I asked what advantages you had by being on the margins."

5. Mary Beth Norton even argues for an intensification of English patriarchal structures in the first century of colonial settlement in New England in *Founding Mothers and Fathers* (New York: Knopf, 1996), 12–13. See also Sherri Klassen's chapter in this volume for women's reliance on networks of friends as well as family in early modern France.

6. Premo, *Winter Friends*, 11, 21–99. See also C. Dallett Hemphill's argument for the primacy of family and gender hierarchy over age hierarchy: "Age Relations and the Social Order in Early New England: Evidence for Manners," *Journal of Social History* 28, no. 2 (Winter 1994): 271–290.

7. See Premo, *Winter Friends*, 131–177, for the importance of religion in American women's worldview.

8. J. Williams, *Memoirs of the Life and Character of Mrs. Sarah Savage* (Philadelphia: Presbyterian Board of Publication, 1818), 138 (June 1714).

9. *Memoirs*, 227 (10 May 1724), 99 (15 February 1721).

10. *Memoirs*, 221 (27 February 1722).

11. Diary of Sarah Savage, British Library AddMS 45538.

12. *Memoirs*, 60 (29 October 1727).

13. *Memoirs*, 107–109 (27 September–1 October 1729).

14. *Memoirs*, 139 (15 February 1730).

15. *Memoirs*, 143–144 (1734).

16. *Memoirs*, 156 (7 September 1736).

17. *Memoirs*, 157 (14, 20 March 1738).

18. *Memoirs*, 235–236.

19. *Memoirs*, 167.

20. Biographical details from Maryland Historical Society Redwood Family Papers Family Tree for the Hopkinsons; and letter of Benjamin Franklin to Mr. James Burrows, an account of Mary Hopkinson and her family. Redwood MS 1530.1 Box 3, 10 May 1765.

21. Maryland Historical Society, Redwood MS 1530 Box 4, July 1766.

22. Mary Johnson Hopkinson's Commonplace Book (1780–1798), first page, Maryland Historical Society, Redwood MS 1530 Box 6.

23. Maryland Historical Society Redwood MS 1530 Box 4, Letter Emily Hopkinson to Anne Hopkinson Coale, 14 November 1804.

24. Lois Schwoerer, *Lady Rachel Russell: One of the Best of Women* (Baltimore, MD: Johns Hopkins University Press, 1988), 1, 31.

25. *Letters of Lady Rachel Russell from the Manuscript in the Library at Woburn Abbey* (London: Dilly, 1773), 159–163.

26. Regarding requests to Queen Mary, see *Letters of Rachel, Lady Russell* (Philadelphia: Parry and McMillan, 1854), 285 (1691). Regarding clerical positions, see, for example, Schwoerer, *Lady Rachel Russell*, 194.

27. *Letters*, 202–203 (1696).

28. *Letters*, 203–204. See also Schwoerer, *Lady Rachel Russell*, 215.

29. Edith Gelles, *Portia: The World of Abigail Adams* (Bloomington: University of Indiana Press, 1992), 3, 15, 30–42.

30. Edith Gelles, *First Thoughts: Life and Letters of Abigail Adams* (New York: Twayne, 1995), 128.

31. Gelles, *First Thoughts*, 146–147.

32. *New Letters of Abigail Adams* (Boston: Houghton Mifflin, 1947), 96 (6 June 1797).

33. Adams Papers, Reel 411, 30 June 1811; cited in Gelles, *Portia*, 205.

34. Adams Papers, Reel 411, 4 March 1811; cited in Gelles, *Portia*, 205.

35. Gelles, *First Thoughts*, 172.

36. See Katharine Kittredge's chapter in this volume for more on Hester Thrale Piozzi.

37. *Thraliana: The Diary of Hester Lynch Thrale [Later Mrs Piozzi] 1776–1809*, vol. 2, ed. Katharine Balderston (Oxford, Eng.: Clarendon Press, 1951), 952 (20 January 1796).

38. *Thraliana*, 1067 (21 June 1805).

39. *Thraliana*, 1044 (September 1803).

40. *Thraliana*, 1064 (20 May 1805).

41. For the positive version, see James Clifford, *Hester Lynch Piozzi (Mrs. Thrale)*, 2d ed. (New York: Columbia University Press, 1987), 429–455; for the negative, see William McCarthy, *Hester Thrale Piozzi: Portrait of a Literary Woman* (Chapel Hill: University of North Carolina Press, 1985), 254, 259–264.

42. Pocket Diary, 15 August 1814; cited in McCarthy, *Hester Thrale Piozzi*, 259.

43. Pocket Diary, 4 March 1821; cited in McCarthy, *Hester Thrale Piozzi*, 264.

44. *The Intimate Letters of Hester Piozzi and Penelope Pennington*, ed. Oswald Knapp (London: John Lane, 1914), 372.

45. *Diary of Elizabeth Drinker,* vol. 2, ed. Elaine Crane (Boston: Northeastern University Press, 1991), 1483. Abbreviated hereafter as *Drinker Diary*.

46. *Drinker Diary*, x–xii.

47. *Drinker Diary*, vol. 3, 1697 (21 October 1803).

48. *Drinker Diary*, vol. 2, 1020 (10 April 1798).

49. *Drinker Diary*, vol. 2, 1595 (2 December 1802).

50. *Drinker Diary*, vol. 3, 1857 (22 August 1806).

51. *Drinker Diary*, vol. 3, 1994 (31 December 1806).

PART II

Interacting with Institutions to Thrive or Survive in Old Age

5

Old People and the Flow of Resources Between Generations in Papal Rome, Sixteenth to Nineteenth Centuries

Angela Groppi

In recent years many studies have contributed evidence that there is no linear progression toward a welfare state. There are instead cyclic oscillations in which the state, families, and charitable institutions redistribute the tasks of caring for the weakest and neediest in a manner that, despite being unequal, is often complementary. Requesting and providing assistance occur within contexts that are determined by the amount of assistance from the individual states, the laws, the personalities, and the needs of those who request relief, as well as those who provide it. These contexts are the result of different public and private interests meeting and colliding in an attempt to define their own spheres of aid and responsibility.[1]

My research on intergenerational relations and familial and social solidarity in papal Rome between 1500 and 1800 is set within this perspective. It aims to recreate the levels of familial and social responsibility toward the old and new generations and to understand individual and collective acts of assistance. These are part of the dialectic between charity and social welfare, between voluntarism and systems of obligation, and between informality and formality.

In order to evaluate the quality and the level of relief offered to the elderly by their own children, relatives, or in-laws, most studies have used a series of indicators linked to "voluntary" options. These include cohabitation, the geographic distance between the respective residences, and contractual maintenance agreements in exchange for real and personal property, as well as gift-giving.[2] My study prefers another indicator, the right of maintenance, which demonstrates how intergenerational solidarity is sometimes the far-from-voluntary consequence of an objective obligation that is imposed by the laws regulating the circulation and transfer of material resources among members of the same family.

At the same time, I attempt to clarify a recurring question in the historical debate on the respective responsibility of family and community in furnishing assistance to the elderly.[3] To do this I have interlaced the analysis of the legal liability of family to maintain destitute relatives with an assessment of the role of charity and relief institutions charged in the past with providing for the elderly. The association of these two fields of analysis is also demanded by the fact that the obligation of families for their dependent members is derived from a particular legal relationship in which the dynamic of rights and responsibilities is not a concern only of the private sphere. This dynamic also concerns the public sphere and interest, because the burden of the indigent and chronically ill who are not supported by their families represents a collective liability not only in terms of the costs of assistance but also as a potential social danger.

THE FRAMEWORK OF PAPAL RELIEF

There is no need to stress here the central role that the problem of pauperism assumed in Rome, as it did in the rest of Europe, between the sixteenth and eighteenth centuries. The general outlines of both charitable and repressive efforts are already well known, as is the fact that this is the period that saw the transformation of the poor into a sociological category and the triumph of a new "technical" dimension to the dispensation of charity that gave rise to numerous treatises and several relevant relief activities.[4]

Among the charitable institutions of papal Rome there was the *Ospizio Apostolico dei Poveri Invalidi* (Apostolic Hospice of the Poor Invalids), the largest hospice of the city, which is further distinguished by the recurring historiographic attention paid to it.[5] Pope Innocent XII founded the hospice between 1692 and 1693, availing himself of the cooperation of a group of Oratorians and Jesuits. What is often underscored in the history of this institution is how the Apostolic Hospice ceased to be a place where beggars were confined, becoming instead a shelter for impoverished orphans and the elderly of both sexes, only a few years after the issuing of its founding papal bull. It will also be remembered that many cardinals and the pope himself were perplexed by the capture and incarceration of beggars that the first statutes of the hospice had provided for; so much so that the actual practice of confinement was much less prevalent than had been announced by many published proclamations. A few months after its establishment, it was already deemed opportune to open the doors to those poor who desired their freedom (22 April 1693), and the imprisonment of beggars was definitively abandoned in 1696.[6] This transformation is normally read as the failure of the papal undertaking, related also to the general "public opinion" that viewed the confinement of beggars as an inopportune or even iniquitous gesture. In reality, abandoning the forced confinement of beggars was not a "reconversion" but simply a withdrawing from one of the two fronts on which Pope Innocent XII had decided to act. Not only was the capture and punishment of beggars part of the founding principals of the Apostolic Hospice, but so too was the relief of both young and old invalids, *corpore vel aetate*.

In papal Rome experimentation with charity spanned the sixteenth through the seventeenth centuries. Renouncing the imprisonment of beggars in 1696 appears to have been a choice in favor of a more benevolent assistance and a policy that did not regard the problem of pauperism solely as one of public order. Instead it helped those who risked sliding into indigence and destitution, and thus it interrupted the emblematic detention of the dangerous poor. Here was a fundamental change in the pattern of the papal government of the city and the state. Relief no longer affected only the most marginal and limited sections of the society, but had an impact on the very basis of its organization and became an instrument of social stability in the hands of the political powers; a social stability particularly difficult in Rome, a city teeming with pilgrims, seasonal workers, and vagrants, where the fragility of the economy made most work even more precarious than elsewhere in Europe.[7]

The papal legacy of the late seventeenth century was therefore not a generic and punitive charity toward the indigent and beggars, but rather a heritage of assistance that was broadening into a form of social security. This increasingly involved well-defined, selected segments of the population who found themselves in monetary and moral straits. These included the ill, elderly, young boys and girls, orphans and foundlings, and honest women, as well as penitent sinners, widows, and women separated from or abandoned by their husbands. A vast number of institutions such as hospitals, shelters, confraternities, and dowry funds provided them with assistance. These institutions were often quite small and they were incorporated into a network fusing charitable acts with social policy.[8]

In this framework the Apostolic Hospice can be a useful starting point for analyzing and grasping the dimensions of the pontifical relief that provided for not only the subsistence but also the well-being of the population. This relief came from the simultaneous, although differentially weighted, interactions involving families, social and religious communities, institutions, and the state.

HELP FOR THE AGED

The Apostolic Hospice undertook and reorganized a series of relief options that had previously been in operation at the *Ospedale dei poveri mendicanti di San Sisto* (Poor Beggar's Hospital of Saint Sixtus) founded by Pope Sixtus V in 1587. The history of the similarities and differences of these two institutions, and that of their destinies, which began to converge in 1692 when the old Hospital of Saint Sixtus was incorporated into the newer hospice, still remains to be written. Here I shall confine myself to explaining a few of the elements that are useful in identifying the nature of the provision of assistance for the elderly of both sexes that took root and shape in Rome between the end of the sixteenth and the beginning of the nineteenth centuries.

Also at the Hospital of Saint Sixtus, the predilection for confining and repressing the beggars who were swarming in the streets and churches of the city soon ended. The goal of collecting "all beggars who are now in the city, which have neither family nor lodging in Rome," according to the invitation of the *Bando per li poveri mendicanti di Roma* (Announcement to the Poor Beggars of Rome), which the delegates of the hospital issued on 6 December 1590, was curtailed within a few years and transformed into a limited and less repressive offer of assistance.[9] The "new" offer expected the presentation of a request from the needy and the selection by the administrators of the institute based on those characteristics that identify and define the image of the deserving poor who were to be taken in.[10]

In 1596 the Hospital of Saint Sixtus decided that there "will be maintained only the destitute poor who have no other help, and who are unable to earn a living by begging or by any other means." Others, who despite being elderly, blind, crippled, or unable to work were able to beg, were given a sign to attach to their left shoulders that authorized them to ask for alms in the city. At the same time a questionnaire came into use to determine the chief traits that contributed to the creation of a profile of the deserving poor. This set of questions, with but minor variations, was still considered valid by the Apostolic Hospice during the eighteenth century. On the basis of this body of information, the deserving poor were identified as believers; as natives or residents of the city for a certain number of years; as carrying on a trade even if he or she was no longer able to practice it; or as belonging to a weakened, but not necessarily absent, family unit; as being a "weak" property holder, that is, not possessing sufficient property to guarantee subsistence, but not necessarily without real or personal property.[11]

Parallel to voluntary confinement, which characterizes a large part of Roman relief activities, an operation of identification and classification of the city's population was put into effect. During this process the population was placed within precise systems of rights and duties that defined the history of assistance and social protection for a lengthy period thereafter. Over the centuries, these systems were refined and modified in a complex allotment of responsibilities that at times found families, institutions, and the state working on opposing, but frequently complementary, sides. From this interplay came the reciprocal influences and manipulations between individuals and institutions over the circulation of resources that deserve being reconstructed in a larger perspective than the overly unidimensional one of social control.[12]

Once "vagrants and strolling beggars" were left to their destiny,[13] the elderly became a privileged population in hospices, such as that of Saint Sixtus, in which the real poor were defined as those "who had not *so much* [my emphasis] as to be able to live, nor the possibility of procuring such by their own labor, or are either elderly and decrepit or blind, or crippled either by age or infirmity."[14] Later the aged were also numerous in the Apostolic Hospice, where two communities of elderly men and elderly women were found alongside those of the boys and girls.

OLD AGE AND THE DUTY OF WORKING

When does old age begin? What is the age that authorizes the elderly to state that they are in need of assistance? There were no clear answers at any time to these questions in seventeenth-century papal Rome. It is only when the Apostolic Hospice was founded in 1692 that the Oratorian Francesco Marchesi set the threshold at seventy years of age in the first statutes. It must be added, however, that the manuscript reveals a moment of hesitation, for a cancellation shows that sixty was first written.[15] This threshold remained in force for a good part of the eighteenth century, until it was lowered to the age of sixty in 1779.[16]

Nevertheless, age in and of itself, even when it was determined more rigorously, was never a sufficient reason to authorize admission. Old age alone exempted neither women nor men from the task of supporting themselves. This was configured as an inescapable duty in a society where the problem of senile dependence had no mandatory chronological age. Disability due to age had to be demonstrated, despite the fact that it was provided for.[17]

The Hospital of Saint Sixtus issued some *Notificazioni* (Orders) between 1655 and 1676 establishing that the "poor applicants" who submitted requests to be admitted also had to present documentation specifying not only their age but also indicating from what "infirmity of the limbs" they suffered.[18] Consequently, many people quickly declared various types of infirmity due to illness or injury. Infirmity began to be either certified by physicians or attested to with *fedi* (testimonials) issued by the parish priest, or both, at the beginning of the eighteenth century. Parish priests also often certified the state of poverty of those who applied to be admitted, since the first statutes of Saint Sixtus stipulated that neither the "hale and hearty" nor those "able to live by the sweat of their brows" were to be admitted.[19] In any case, once they were admitted, neither advanced age nor the loss of self-sufficiency exonerated them from the obligation of either performing chores in the institution or even working outside its walls.

Many shoemakers, tailors, dressmakers, cooks, carpenters, masons, barbers, washerwomen, spinners, and weavers were admitted to Saint Sixtus to perform these specific, essential tasks for the community, as later happened in the Apostolic Hospice. The decree of 24 September 1691 stated that no inmates were to be admitted whom a physician had not first certified, and whosoever was unable to help in the hospital was not to be admitted.[20]

A number of inmates also worked for craftsmen or entrepreneurs outside the institute. In such cases the institute confiscated their wages, or at least part of them, to defray the cost of their maintenance. A decree of 18 July 1625 proclaimed that "all the poor of this institution who are able to perform any work at all, including spinning, must give half their earnings to our hospital or otherwise quickly depart."[21] The portion expected by the institute was later reduced to one-third, a practice that was also adopted by the Apostolic Hospice. During the eighteenth century the latter institution authorized some men to work outside its walls, leaving daily and returning at night to sleep. Several blind men were in this group, and they had their "labor market," being "requested by some artisans either to work or to turn grindstones."

Work was an indispensable obligation for all the inmates and thus a basic element in the institutional organization. Each person taken into the hospice was expected to work, including the *poveri benestanti* ("poor well-off"), as they are called in the regulatory plan, *Governo generale dell'Ospitio de' Poveri questuanti ristretti nel Palazzo Lateranense*, probably compiled by the Oratorian Francesco Marchesi toward the end of 1692.[22]

The first duty of every individual was to support himself or herself by his or her own labor. Only decrepitude or chronic illness authorized the elderly to apply for admission and cease working. Otherwise work spanned the entire existence of men and women, as much inside as outside the institution. A quintessential example is the case of Giulia Cantagalli, a woman who asked to be admitted to the Hospital of Saint Sixtus on 10 August 1691 as "desirous of spending her final years in this place." She declares she is one hundred ten years old and has always worked. "I have managed to earn something by spinning, because even though I am so old I still spin and do some other things to support myself even though I am unmarried."[23] The expectation was that older individuals would continue to work until they were absolutely unable to do so. This is also corroborated by the admission requests presented to the Apostolic Hospice by ninety-five women and seventy-one men in the following century, between 1724 and 1727. They hastened to assert that their pressing needs, an aggregate of illness, infirmity, and decrepitude, made it impossible to obtain food and clothing by their own efforts as they had always done.[24]

FAMILIAL DUTIES

Although illness, old age, and the inability or reduced ability to work were all necessary reasons to be entitled to institutional assistance, they were not sufficient grounds in and of themselves. Admission to a relief institution depended on proving that the applicant was without any possible support from relatives. An order issued by the Apostolic Hospice in 1701 specified that those admitted not only had to be invalids "due to age or infirmity," but also "must be paupers, possessing nothing neither able to earn their living by their own efforts nor having relatives who are obliged or able to maintain them."[25] Institutional relief efforts in papal Rome, at least those that were planned and systematic, were mobilized only in cases where those family members having the primary responsibility for aiding their kin were either absent or powerless to support their destitute relatives.

The assignment of kin responsibility for relatives was extant from the earliest years of the Hospital of Saint Sixtus. One of the questions directed to suppliants before admittance, was, "If he has a wife, children, and how many, and where, and what sort of other relatives, and where."[26] It is during the seventeenth century, however, that the responsibility of family for their dependent members came to be redefined in an increasingly rigid and precise manner.

References to the family group's substance, composition, and residence were always included in the examination of those applying for admission to the Hospital of Saint Sixtus from the mid-seventeenth century, while in the earlier reports this information was often omitted.[27] Also during the same period, restrictions on the admission of poor spouses were introduced, whereas previously both individuals and couples were regularly accepted at Saint Sixtus. A decree of 16 January 1644 ordained that all women "who have husbands outside" were to be discharged, while a second dated 6 March 1649 decided to "take note of all who have wives to send them away."[28] There was a growing conviction that whoever had a living spouse could have or should have relied on spousal assistance, which, as Susannah R. Ottaway has recently noted, is generally ignored in the relevant historical literature.[29] This was a trend that became increasingly formalized over time, until spouses were officially limited to domiciliary relief when the Apostolic Hospice was founded. Regarding those who were married, a decree of 7 January 1693 further specified that "said charity is to be given only to those without anyone to maintain them, and rejecting those who do not deserve it since they have children or relatives who can maintain them."[30]

The duty for family members to support each other became more precise during the eighteenth century. The burden of care for the elderly population appears to have fallen principally on spouses and children, especially male offspring. According to the regulations of the Apostolic Hospice, the elderly who were admitted "must not be married, since it is not possible to help everyone, those who have no help from anyone must be favored." The candidates specifically could not have male children "because His Holiness does not intend for this charity to relieve children of their burden of maintaining their Parents which falls on them, regardless of the poverty of the Children, and the impossibility to do so, except in some special cases."[31]

It was not by chance that the elderly who hoped to be admitted to the Apostolic Hospice immediately specified in their petitions either that they were without children or how those relatives who might have helped them would have been plunged into dire poverty by doing so.[32] Angelo Micucci, for example, who was eighty-four years old and had been a combmaker for sixty years, needed assistance because he was no longer able to practice his craft, "but above all because the son who supported him has passed on to a better world." Margarita Narcisi, an old spinster, worked as long as she was able. Now, at the age of seventy, "she lives with her widowed sister and her sister's two daughters who have not enough to live on."[33]

Contrary to what was to happen in the rest of the Italian peninsula, first the

Hospital of Saint Sixtus, and later the Apostolic Hospice, verified the absence of relatives with extreme diligence.[34] The poor were asked not only to relate their cases in their petitions, but to furnish their personal information and addresses as well. In this way the "visitors," introduced in 1655, were able to trace the applicant, question neighbors and the parish priest, and assess the truth of what had been declared.[35] Strict controls were put in place, especially from the mid-seventeenth century, to assure that admission was an option only when no family member was able to assist the destitute relative. Institutional documents describe how numerous admission requests were rejected after children, husbands, and wives were located.[36]

It is worthwhile keeping in mind that a departure from the rules was anything but unusual in the Roman society of the time, where the system of protections and recommendations was a functional system of governing.[37] Behind the wide variety of both male and female servants who were found among the inmates, we can also find some nobles and prelates who intervened on behalf of the elderly members of their *familia* (servants of household), and whose recommendations made it possible to overlook an age not really advanced or a kinship group not so very scarce. In addition, the recurring admission of elderly soldiers from the *Castel Sant'Angelo* fortress, the symbol of the sovereign pontiff's power in the city, discloses a special relief program reserved for the servants of the state, which the pontiff himself promoted. Neither was it rare for elderly married couples to gain entrance to the men's and women's communities at the same time, or at times that were falsified, despite the requirement of widowhood. This transpired when reciprocal authorization was granted before the notary of the institution and often involved bestowing some real or personal property on the institution.

This was not an unusual proceeding.[38] Donations of sums of money, homes, vineyards, lands, and so on by those admitted dot the entire history of Saint Sixtus and later of the Apostolic Hospice.[39] The possession of property was useful to men and women not only to negotiate irregular admissions, but also to assure them better treatment during their stay. In 1726 Domenico Taveggi asked "to end the last days of his life in the holy place of San Michele a Ripa" and stated that he was ready to deposit one hundred scudi to be admitted quickly and to enjoy a few more personal comforts than the other inmates. These comforts concerned ways of eating, sleeping, and dressing that he himself said in his petition were habitually granted to those who "pay more than the others upon admission." The administrators in their turn negotiated for the good of the Hospice, and on 13 August 1726 decided that Taveggi was able to enter and enjoy the requested privileges, paying, however, one hundred and fifty scudi instead of the thirty scudi that eighteenth-century regulation required at the moment of admission.[40] The amount of thirty scudi corresponded to the cost of a year's maintenance and was paid either by a benefactor, the pauper being admitted, or a family member who wished to shift the onus of maintaining a relative onto the shoulders of a charitable institution.

THE RIGHTS AND DUTIES OF MAINTENANCE

In papal Rome, taking on the responsibility of feeding and lodging an individual by a charitable institution was never without a price, given the very rigid legislation that carefully determined familial obligations to maintain the needy. The obligation of maintaining destitute relatives, which is a determining factor in intergenerational relationships, took root in the remote past. It is the Justinian Code that was the basis for determining "blood ties," even though the expression *jus sanguinis* also encompassed *jus coniugii* and *jus affinitatis*, the reciprocal obligation to maintain paternal and maternal ascendants, descendants, and, although in less certain terms, brothers, sisters, husbands, and wives. This precept became established and refined by glossators and postglossators who clearly defined familial obligations, the nature of obligations, and the terms of fulfilling them: "alimentorum nomine generaliter veniunt omnia, quae sunt necessaria ad honestam, et congruam vitae humanae sustentationem" ("with the term maintenance we mean all those things that are necessaries for an honest and proper lifestyle").[41] Not simply food but clothing, lodging, and medical expenses were part of one's maintenance, since they were indispensable elements of existence, as were the expenses involved in raising and educating the younger generation. The claim for maintenance was based on a proven state of indigence and the inability to provide for one's own support, and on the existence of a relative whose financial condition allowed him or her to take on the burden of doing so. To the judge fell the task of assigning the amount of assistance on the basis of the economic and social circumstances of the person who was bound to do so, as well as the needs, circumstances, and age of whoever had this right.

Without substantial modifications, this right is part of the *jus commune* of a number of Italian states with inflections and emphases that vary in the regions of Longobard or Roman law and various local acts. This is particularly emphasized by the canon law maxim that states that denying maintenance to whom it is due is equivalent to killing that person.[42] It is found in the Pisanelli Code of 1865, the first Italian civil code written after the Unification, and in all codes predating the Unification. In Rome, where the pontifical government held power until 1870, the right of maintenance was regulated until the end of the eighteenth century by the statutes of the city, which were reformed by Pope Gregory XIII in 1580 and by a later series of papal regulations organizing civil legislation.[43]

The principle that the family provide the major portion of the maintenance of those in difficulty was valid in many societies, including the English one, where an early widespread network of public assistance was set in place with the Poor Laws. Nevertheless, a legal definition is one thing and the practical application of the law is another. Many studies of English society stress not only the scarcity of maintenance lawsuits that were not on behalf of husbands, wives, or illegitimate children, but also the limited cultural obligations on children to maintain their own elderly parents: the obligations of married sons and daughters were first to their spouses and their children.[44]

The situation was noticeably different in papal Rome, where the legal liability to maintain elderly parents and relatives was avoided only in extreme cases. This obligation became increasingly rigid during the eighteenth century when a bull of Pope Clement XIV granted the *Tribunale del Cardinal Vicario* (Cardinal Vicar's Court) exclusive jurisdiction in maintenance suits so as to speed judicial decisions.[45] The jurisdiction of the Cardinal Vicar's Court in these cases was periodically reconfirmed and continued until 1870, except from 1798 to 1799, during the Roman Republic, and from 1809 to 1814, during the period of Napoleonic domination, when the activity of the court was suspended.

The needy who were not voluntarily assisted by their own family members had the right to bring legal action against them by filing a case with the court. The claimants had to furnish certificates from the parish priest or two witnesses proving their "extreme poverty" and the ensuing need for assistance. They also had to document that the family members who were obliged to maintain them were able to do so. At this point, the court summoned the defendants and sought to persuade them to tender a monthly sum based on their ability to pay. When arbitration failed, the court issued a decree stating the amount that had to be deposited once or twice monthly with the notary of the court.

The examination of a thousand economic decrees dating from 1769 to 1817 in which the Cardinal Vicar's Court ruled on accusations against relatives who balked at maintenance payments makes it possible to reconstruct the legal and procedural dynamics of familial responsibilities in papal Rome.[46] On the whole, Roman society appears to be rather rigorous in its imposition of the hierarchy of reciprocal responsibilities among relatives by marriage and blood, with its obligations and debts to be honored. The framework of the responsibilities of maintenance was wider than in other European contexts, comprising parents, children, husbands, fathers-in-law, grandfathers, brothers, uncles, nephews, and occasionally some women (wives, daughters, mothers-in-law, aunts).[47]

In Rome particularly we find a very uncompromising system of obligations and control in place against children who resisted helping their parents. Among the 1,010 decrees, where it is possible to determine the relationship of the plaintiff to the defendant, most cases concern children who were obliged by the Cardinal Vicar's Court to maintain their own parents. These make up 32.3 percent of the total, compared to 21.6 percent of husbands who had to maintain their own wives and children and 15.5 percent of grandfathers and paternal uncles who had to maintain their grandchildren, nieces, and nephews. Among the parents who claimed and obtained the right of maintenance were 245 mothers, 69 fathers, and 12 parental couples. The children ordered to provide maintenance were predominantly sons, except for one case of a daughter who was made responsible for her father's maintenance and two cases that required a widow to assume her husband's duties toward his mother. Family responsibilities were supported and controlled by public intervention in the papal capital, and children carried the bulk of this support.

Using both persuasion and compulsion, Roman families were forced to accept those tasks of care and assistance that the law defined as natural, but which so many tried to shirk. The poor who were not "naturally" maintained by their own relatives had a powerful ally in the Cardinal Vicar's Court, which made every effort to convince or compel whoever had the duty to deposit the maintenance pension. This summary proceeding was not prejudiced by any judicial court proceedings, although longer and more complicated, that could be pending in parallel. The obligation that the Cardinal Vicar's Court imposed was an answer to an urgent need; the pontiff, in the name of the right to life, was the guarantor that this relief was not to be delayed. This was a right that was not to be subject to the lengthy proceedings of many lawsuits, since, as the words of Pope Clement's bull proclaimed, "venter non patitur dilationem" ("the stomach can't suffer delay").

Thanks to an expeditious procedure dispensing with needless details or formalities, the Cardinal Vicar's Court made its rulings swiftly. Usually no more than one or two months passed between the filing of the complaint and the decree enjoining the initial maintenance payment. The time was quite brief, considering that it included investigating the details of the case, depositing testimony, and gathering information from the parish priests. The court was not only rapid but also assiduous in ensuring that the parties complied with its decrees and was diligent in keeping track of changes in the financial status and circumstances of both of them. The regularity of the payments was tightly controlled. The maintenance payments were deposited with the notary of the Cardinal Vicar's Court, who entered the sums in the registers set aside for the declarations of deposits and collections, which either the two parties or their representatives signed before two witnesses.[48] After the complaints of claimants, there frequently were new injunctions, at times accompanied by seizures of belongings or wages, to pressure those relatives who had stopped making payments—after only a few months in some cases.

The court was very careful to evaluate even the smallest fluctuations that altered the circumstances of the original situation. Over the years new decrees reflected changing circumstances, since, as one petition noted, "every complaint must be not only supported by the law, but also and principally based on means."[49] The sums to be paid were now and again suspended, reduced, or voided after an interminable correspondence that the obligors produced to demonstrate impoverishment due to illness, loss of employment, or financial ruin. Those entitled to maintenance, meanwhile, wasted no time in pointing out the improved financial conditions of their relatives, hoping to obtain an increase in their maintenance allotments, always carefully balanced between needs and resources. Antonio Fineschi, for example, who was past seventy, sent a petition in 1835 to obtain an increase in the monthly amount provided by his son. To this end, he included not only a medical certificate that proved his inability to work, due to "nervous confusion," but also an affidavit signed by four witnesses who stated that his son was the proprietor of a barber shop and had been living quite comfortably for some time. Since the son had no children to support, he was easily able to pass additional money to his father.[50] This was an important piece of information, for there were many sons who refused to help their own parents by advancing the argument that their first duty was to their children. In pontifical Rome, however, this was not always an effective excuse. On 3 July 1844, the parish priest of Santa Maria del Popolo declared that there was no doubt that Luigi and Girolamo, the two sons of the widowed Anna Maria Benedetti, were obligated to maintain her despite being "burdened by their families and earning little during these summer months, [but] if they had one more child they would have to support it."[51]

The Cardinal Vicar's Court meticulously investigated everyone's condition of life in its attempt to arbitrate conflicting interests, sanctioning financial responsibilities in accordance with varying assets. These responsibilities were assigned along the lines regulating the transmission of property. If mothers more often turned to their adult sons, wives to husbands, unmarried sisters to their brothers, young widows with younger children to brothers-in-law, fathers-in-law, or at times to their own fathers, it was because the line of succession excluded women from inheriting either from their ascendants or descendants, just as males in the agnatic line had the advantage over collateral males. Instead of inheritance, however, women were entitled to dowries and maintenance.[52]

In the attempt to regulate the rights of subsistence, the court intervened in interfamilial dynamics and tried to foster an agreement among the parties that was not exclusively concerned with economic needs. The dictates of the court often betrayed a knowledgeable awareness of the risks created by cohabitation based more on economic than affective reasons. To avoid these situations, the Roman authorities were willing to be very discreet and flexible. A decree of 21 June 1808 against three brothers, Clemente, Marcello, and Giovanni Battista Fabiani, for the maintenance of their mother and sister initially determined that the mother and sister "may themselves choose to be maintained in the home of one or another." This request was annulled a few days later at someone's request, one does not know whose, and the second decree stipulated that "they shall pay as much to the sister as to the mother, five scudi a month."[53]

This flexibility in the enforcement of the decrees and in the enjoining of reciprocal duties represents the other side of the coin of a society particularly exacting and rigid in measuring and regulating familial responsibilities. Taking into account the particular exigencies of individuals and family groups was one way to secure the cooperation of the families involved in poor relief. Charitable assistance was a duty that the pontiff was not able to avoid honoring without diminishing one of the basic symbols of his sovereignty; Roman Catholic charity was an indispensable element in assuring Rome's role as a model and leader of civilization.[54]

There was, however, a price to pay for this stringent assignment of familial responsibilities that, in regard to the assistance provided to the older generations, was perhaps more rigid in papal Rome than elsewhere. The increased legal liability of the Roman family to maintain their dependent members ended by bringing about an even heavier debt of gratitude toward its own subjects that the state incurred. The *Moto-proprio* of 1 May 1828, with which Pope Leo XII regulated the pensions of pontifical civil servants, entitled not only widows and children to pension checks, but also those parents "lacking other means of subsistence and unable to earn their own living, that were maintained by their sons, while they were alive, thanks to the salary that they drew from the state." These parents were entitled to a portion of the pension, along with the widow, minor children, and unmarried or widowed daughters.[55] This is the sole known example from the modern Italian pension scheme of a reversionary pension that was to be shared by the parents of the deceased while the widow and children were living.[56]

In the course of time, the state demonstrated that it was more or less willing to assume the duty of the head of the family to maintain the members of its family according to a sliding scale. This allows one to grasp the character of the responsibility allotted to the family, the breadth of public protection, and the degree of the state's involvement in the well-being of the "citizens." In this way the reversionary annuity became a sort of prize, particularly in its original outlines, that the state awarded to whoever had been the breadwinner of his household. He had worked without having placed on the community the burden of maintaining his family members who were not self-sufficient due to age, illness, or gender. A perspective thus emerges wherein the implementation and evolution of the pension system may offer a useful indicator for understanding the variable relationship between the family's and the state's responsibility toward the old and young generations.

CONCLUSIONS

The example of Rome highlights how the obligation to support the elderly was the outcome of a long, entangled battle between families and collectivity. The amount of responsibility apportioned to each of these two poles was the result of incessant negotiation between micro and macro systems of solidarity. The right of maintenance played a strategic role in such a dynamic. This view transforms the family into an institution of support and obligations and furnishes an exceptional field of observation for inquiring into the construction of kinship systems in Western society. The legal imposition of the obligation of familial assistance begins a competition between families and those institutions in charge of providing relief to the needy.

Familial responsibility, ostensibly traced back to natural law and *jus sanguinis* as a moral duty, takes shape at the height of a power struggle between individuals and institutions. The latter, owing to the community's interest in providing for the indigent, try to limit the individual's right to relief to the family, but such familial solidarity evidently is not the natural outcome of blood and marriage bonds. The family did not automatically represent a financial solution to its members: Relatives and relatives-in-law strenuously defended their own objectives of survival or well-being by their shrewd use of charitable institutions, through which they strove to share the burden of the old and the new generations. The result was a game of mutual manipulation by individuals and institutions over the collective circulation of resources mobilized to help the needy. The end result of this game was a social system wherein welfare responsibilities and welfare provisions belonged to both the family and the collectivity.

NOTES

1. Cf. M. A. Crowther, "Family Responsibility and State Responsibility in Britain Before the Welfare State," *Historical Journal* 25, no. 1 (1982): 131–145; Peter Laslett, "Family, Kinship and Collectivity As Systems of Support in Pre-industrial Europe: A Consideration of the 'Nuclear-Hardship' Hypothesis," *Continuity and Change* 3, no. 2 (1988): 153–175; Richard Wall, "Les Relations entre générations en Europe autrefois," *Annales de démographie historique* (1991): 133–154; Martin Daunton, ed., *Charity, Self-Interest and Welfare in the English Past* (London: University College London Press, 1996); Peregrine Horden and Richard Smith, eds., *The Locus of Care: Families, Communities, Institutions, and the Provision of Welfare Since Antiquity* (London: Routledge, 1998).

2. Hans C. Johansen, "Growing Old in an Urban Environment," *Continuity and Change* 2, no. 2 (1987): 297–305; Sonya O. Rose, "The Varying Household Arrangements of the Elderly in Three English Villages: Nottinghamshire, 1851–1881," *Continuity and Change* 3, no. 1 (1988): 101–122; Peter Laslett, *A Fresh Map of Life: The Emergence of the Third Age* (London: Weidenfeld and Nicolson, 1989); Gísli Ágúst Gunnlaugsson and Loftur Guttormsson, "Transition into Old Age: Poverty and Retirement Possibilities in Late Eighteenth- and Nineteenth-Century Iceland," in *Poor Women and Children in the European Past*, ed. John Henderson and Richard Wall (New York: Routledge, 1994), 251–268; André Burguière, "Les Rapports entre générations: Un problème pour l'historien," *Communications* 59 (1994): 15–27; Jacques T. Godbout, *Le Langage du don* (Montreal: Fides, 1996).

3. See David Thomson, "The Welfare of the Elderly in the Past: A Family or Community Responsibility?" in *Life, Death, and the Elderly: Historical Perspectives*, ed. Margaret Pelling and Richard M. Smith (London: Routledge, 1991), 194–221; Pat Thane, "Old People and Their Families in the English Past," in *Charity, Self-Interest and Welfare in the English Past*, ed. Martin Daunton (London: University College London Press, 1996), 113–138.

4. Jean-Pierre Gutton, *La Société et les pauvres en Europe, XVIᵉ–XVIIIᵉ siècles* (Paris: Presses Universitaires de France, 1974); Luigi Fiorani, "Religione e povertà: Il dibattito sul pauperismo in Roma tra Cinque e Seicento," *Ricerche per la storia religiosa di Roma* 3 (1979): 43–131; Bronislaw Geremek, *La pietà e la forca: Storia della miseria e della carità in Europa* (Rome: Laterza, 1986); Michele Fatica, *Il problema della mendicità nell'Europa moderna (secoli XVI–XVIII)* (Naples: Liguori, 1992); Brian Pullan, "Support and Redeem: Charity and Poor Relief in Italian Cities from the Fourteenth to the Seventeenth Century," *Continuity and Change* 3, no. 2 (1988): 177–208; Brian Pullan, "New Approches to Poverty and New Forms of Institutional Charity in Late Medieval and Renaissance Italy," in *Povertà e innovazioni istituzionali in Italia dal Medioevo ad oggi*, ed. Vera Zamagni (Bologna: Mulino, 2000), 17–43.

5. Michele Fatica, "La reclusione dei mendicanti a Roma durante il pontificato di Innocenzo XII (1692–1700)," in Fatica, *Il problema della mendicità nell'Europa moderna*, 161–215; Pia Toscano, *Roma produttiva tra Settecento e Ottocento: Il San Michele a Ripa Grande* (Rome: Viella, 1996).

6. Archivio di Stato di Roma (ASR from here on), Ospizio Apostolico di S. Michele (OASM from here on), b. 233, *Decreti di congregazioni generali per l'Ospizio Apostolico dal 1692 al 1699*, and b. 234, *Decreti di congregazioni particolari per l'Ospizio Apostolico dal 1692 al 1699*.

7. Angela Groppi, "Roman Alms and Poor Relief in the Seventeenth Century," in *Rome—Amsterdam: Two Growing Cities in Seventeenth-Century Europe*, ed. Peter van Kessel and Elisja Schulte (Amsterdam: Amsterdam University Press, 1997), 180–191.

8. Angela Groppi, *I conservatori della virtù: Donne recluse nella Roma dei Papi* (Rome: Laterza, 1994).

9. ASR, OASM, b. 166, c. 7.

10. On the dividing line between the deserving and undeserving poor, see Sandra Cavallo, *Charity and Power in Early Modern Italy: Benefactors and Their Motives in Turin, 1541–1789* (Cambridge, Eng.: Cambridge University Press, 1995); see also Jeremy Boulton, "Going on the Parish: The Parish Pension and Its Meanings in the London Suburbs, 1640–1724," in *Chronicling Poverty: The Voices and Strategies of the English Poor, 1640–1840*, ed. Tim Hitchcock, Peter King, and Pamela Sharpe (Basingstoke, Eng.: Macmillan, 1997), 26–33.

11. ASR, OASM, b. 192, *Interrogationi da farsi alli poveri, li quali dovranno esser accettati nel Hospitale di Ponte Sisto, ò indrizzati ad altri Hospitali, overo meritaranno la licenza di mendicar per Roma* (Rome: Appresso li Stampatori Camerali, 1596).

12. See Lynn Botelho, "Aged and Impotent: Parish Relief of the Aged Poor in Early Modern Suffolk," in *Charity, Self-Interest and Welfare in the English Past*, ed. Martin Daunton (London: University College London Press, 1996), 91–111.

13. This option is expressly stated in the *Statuti dell'ospedale di S. Sisto*, n.d. [1678?], chapter 3 (ASR, OASM, b. 36), which specifies that paupers must be admitted "only if they choose, so that they be not malcontents who disturb the tranquility of the community."

14. ASR, OASM, b. 36, *Statuti dell'ospedale di S. Sisto*, n.d. [1678?], chapter 22.

15. Rome, Biblioteca Vallicelliana, ms. P 199, cc. 591–596, *Regole dell'Ospizio Apostolico stabilito per il soccorso de' Poveri Invalidi dalla Santità di N. Sig. Innocenzo XII*.

16. *Istruzzione per i Poveri Uomini, e Donne, Ragazzi, e Ragazze, che desiderano essere ammessi nell'Ospizio Apostolico de' Poveri Invalidi*, 1 agosto 1725; Giuseppe Vai, *Relazione del Pio Istituto di S. Michele a Ripa Grande eretto dalla Santa Memoria di PP. Innocenzo XII* (Rome: Stamperia di S. Michele a Ripa, 1779).

17. The ability of the elderly to help themselves has recently attracted the attention of Susannah R. Ottaway: "Providing for the Elderly in Eighteenth-Century England," *Continuity and Change* 13, no. 3 (1998): 391–418; see also Margaret Pelling and Richard Smith, Introduction to *Life, Death, and the Elderly: Historical Perspectives*, ed. Margaret Pelling and Richard M. Smith (London: Routledge, 1991); Thomas Sokoll, "The Household Position of Elderly Widows in Poverty: Evidence from Two English Communities in the Late Eighteenth and Early Nineteenth Centuries," in *Poor Women and Children in the European Past*, ed. John Henderson and Richard Wall (New York: Routledge, 1994), 207–224.

18. ASR, OASM, b. 166, cc. 12 and 15; see also the case of the rural hospitals in Hesse analyzed in this book by Louise Gray.

19. ASR, OASM, b. 36, *Statuti dell'ospedale di S. Sisto*, n.d. [1678?], chapter 22.

20. ASR, OASM, b. 232, *Decreti di Congregazione per l'ospedale di S. Sisto dal 1687 al 1693.*

21. ASR, OASM, b. 226, *Decreti di Congregazione per l'ospedale di S. Sisto dal 1619 al 1657.*

22. Rome, Biblioteca Vallicelliana, ms. P 199, cc. 581r–591v. The "poor well-off" were those who paid more or less substantial sums when they were admitted in return for such privileges as private rooms, or the right to eat in their own rooms and not in the communal dining room.

23. ASR, OASM, b. 203, *Esami de' poveri dell'ospedale di S. Sisto dal 1691 al 1694.*

24. ASR, OASM, bb. 193 and 194.

25. ASR, OASM, b. 264.

26. ASR, OASM, b. 192, *Interrogationi Da farsi alli poveri, li quali dovranno esser accettati nel Hospitale di Ponte Sisto.*

27. ASR, OASM, b. 200, *Esami de' poveri dell'ospedale di S. Sisto dal 1647 al 1663.*

28. ASR, OASM, b. 226, *Decreti di Congregazione per l'ospedale di S. Sisto dal 1619 al 1657.*

29. Ottaway, "Providing for the Elderly."

30. ASR, OASM, b. 233, *Decreti di congregazioni generali per l'Ospizio Apostolico dal 1692 al 1699.*

31. ASR, OASM, b. 32, *Ristretto della Fondazione, e Regolamento de' Poveri Invalidi dell'Ospizio di S. Michele, e Conservatorio di S. Giovanni in Laterano nello stato, in cui presentemente si trova* (Rome: Stamperia di S. Michele a Ripa, 1726).

32. On the presence or possibility of kin support, see Tim Wales, "Poverty, Poor Relief and the Life-Cycle: Some Evidence from Seventeenth-Century Norfolk," in *Land, Kinship and Life-Cycle*, ed. Richard M. Smith (Cambridge, Eng.: Cambridge University Press, 1985), 351–404.

33. ASR, OASM, bb. 193 and 194.

34. Cf. Sandra Cavallo, "Patterns of Poor Relief and Patterns of Poverty in Eighteenth-Century Italy: The Evidence of the Turin Ospedale di Carità," *Continuity and Change* 5, no. 1 (1990), 65–98; Cavallo, *Charity and Power.*

35. ASR, OASM, b. 226, *Decreti di Congregazione per l'ospedale di S. Sisto dal 1619 al 1657.*

36. ASR, OASM, 2d part, b. 19, *Visite de' poveri, 1715–1724.*

37. Groppi, *I conservatori della virtù.*

38. See also Sandra Cavallo, "Family Obligations and Inequalities in Access to Care in Northern Italy, Seventeenth to Eighteenth Centuries," in *The Locus of Care: Families, Communities, Institutions, and the Provision of Welfare Since Antiquity*, ed. Peregrine Horden and Richard Smith (London: Routledge, 1998), 90–110.

39. ASR, OASM, b. 43, *Memorie di Istromenti diversi dal 1587 al 1714.*

40. ASR, OASM, b. 198, *Memoriali e fedi diverse dal 1664 al 1728.*

41. Lucius Ferraris, *Bibliotheca canonica juridica moralis theologica . . .* (Rome, 1784–1790; first edition 1747) ad vocem *Alimenta.* The classic texts on Alimenta were the treatises by Bartolo da Sassoferrato, *Tractatus alimentorum* (Paris, 1517); Giovanni Battista Pontano, *De alimentis cuiusque generis liber* (Rome, 1579); Giovanni Pietro Sordi, *Tractatus de alimentis* (Venice, 1604).

42. Antonio Marongiu, "Alimenti. Diritto intermedio," in *Enciclopedia del diritto* (Milano: Giuffrè, 1958), 21–24.

43. Angela Groppi, "Il diritto del sangue: Le responsabilità familiari nei confronti delle vecchie e delle nuove generazioni, Roma secc. XVIII–XIX," *Quaderni storici* 92 (1996): 305–333; Mirella Mombelli Castracane, *La codificazione civile nello Stato pontificio* (Naples: Edizioni Scientifiche Italiane, 1987).

44. Jill Quadagno, *Aging in Early Industrial Society: Work, Family and Social Policy in Nineteenth-Century England* (New York: Academic Press, 1982); Lynn Hollen Lees, "The Survival of the Unfit: Welfare Policies and Family Maintenance in Nineteenth-Century London," in *The Uses of Charity: The Poor on Relief in the Nineteenth-Century Metropolis,* ed. Peter Mandler (Philadelphia: University of Pennsylvania Press, 1990), 68–91; Crowther, "Family Responsibility"; Thomson, "Welfare of the Elderly"; Thane, "Old People."

45. *Chirografo della Santità di Nostro Signore PP. Clemente XIV felicemente Regnante concesso al Tribunale del Vicariato di Roma* (Rome: Stamperia della Revenda Camera Apostolica, 1772).

46. The classification has taken into account two blocks of decrees issued between 1769 and 1783 and between 1806 and 1817: ASR, Tribunale del Cardinal Vicario (TCV from here on), b. 342, *Deposito d'alimenti, 1769–1775*; ivi, b. 340, *Registro delle suppliche per le cause d'alimenti, 1775–1783*; ivi, b. 343, *Registro delle cause di alimenti dall'anno 1806 a tutto l'anno 1834.*

47. Crowther, "Family Responsibility"; Thomson, "Welfare of the Elderly."

48. ASR, TCV, bb. 345–363, *Registri dei depositi e delle consegne agli assegnatari degli alimenti dal 1775 al 1870.*

49. Archivio Storico del Vicariato di Roma (ASVR from here on), Atti della Segreteria del Vicariato (ASV from here on), pl. 131, Nicola Armanni's petition of 5 November 1842.

50. ASVR, TCV, Appeals for maintenance, payments, etc. 1830–1835, not cataloged.

51. ASVR, ASV, pl. 138, fasc. B.

52. Maria Teresa Guerra Medici, "L'esclusione delle donne dalla successione legittima e la constitutio super statutariis successionibus di Innocenzo XI," *Rivista di storia del diritto italiano* 56 (1983): 261–294; Christiane Klapisch-Zuber, *La Mmaison et le nom: stratégies et rituels dans l'Italie de la Renaissance* (Paris: Éditions de l'École des Hautes Études en Sciences Sociales, 1990); Thomas Kuehn, *Law, Family and Women: Toward a Legal Anthropology of Renaissance Italy* (Chicago: University of Chicago Press, 1991); Giulia Calvi, *Il contratto morale: Madri e figli nella Toscana moderna* (Rome: Laterza, 1994); Renata Ago, "Ruoli familiari e statuto giuridico," *Quaderni Storici* 88 (1995): 79–101; Angela Groppi, ed., *Il lavoro delle donne* (Rome: Laterza, 1996).

53. ASR, TCV, b. 343, *Registro delle cause di alimenti dall'anno 1806 a tutto l'anno 1834.*

54. Groppi, "Roman Alms and Poor Relief in the Seventeenth Century"; Maura Piccialuti, *La carità come metodo di governo: Istituzioni caritative a Roma dal pontificato di Innocenzo XII a quello di Benedetto XIV* (Turin: Giappichelli, 1994).

55. *Moto-proprio della Santità di Nostro Signore Papa Leone XII sulle giubilazioni . . .* (Rome: Stamperia della Reverenda Camera Apostolica, 1828).

56. In the Provinces of the Kingdom of Sardinia, the 27 June 1850 act on military pensions provided that the pensions could revert to the parents of the deceased only if

he had left neither a widow nor children. Emilio De Bernardi and Domenico Felice Gioliti, eds., *Raccolta delle leggi, decreti, rescritti, regolamenti circolari ed istruzioni dei cessati governi delle provincie italiane sulle pensioni di servizio civile e militare . . .* (Florence: 1869–1876).

6

The Experience of Old Age in the Narratives of the Rural Poor in Early Modern Germany

Louise Gray

The debate surrounding the position of the elderly in pre-industrial society is one that has been accorded a great deal of interest in recent years and has been studied from a variety of vantage points, including demography, medicine, literature, and social history. To date, however, the main focus has rested upon the period immediately surrounding the onset of industrialization. A central feature of this work has entailed a comparative assessment of the social position of the old both within a household and in a communal setting. Debates over the existence of the "golden age of ageing" have held an important position, as have studies questioning the existence of "a simple causal relationship between the status of the aged and societal development" and the "scarcity value" of the aged themselves.[1] Prime areas of concern have been the effect of industrialization upon the social and economic position of the elderly, and the place of the elderly within a familial and social framework. Upon the premise that its treatment of the elderly is an acid test of the society in question, much time has been expended in seeking out largely statistical evidence to assess this criterion.

One criticism leveled against previous historical investigations of old age has been that "old age . . . has attracted attention rather than the elderly themselves."[2] This is particularly true of European studies of the period from the sixteenth to the mid-eighteenth century, especially among the few German works devoted to this topic.[3] Specific research into the experience of the aged is rare—at best, the elderly are mentioned in passing, usually under the rubric of widowhood, or as one category of hospital inmate.[4] It is notoriously difficult for the historian to unearth a sense of the daily lives of individuals in early modern society. This is especially true when one is concerned with the plight of the poor—those faceless masses whose voices, as is often lamented, remain hidden in the available documentation.

Some important discrepancies have arisen within studies of early modern old age to date that are directly related to the sources that historians have used. The dearth of surviving records with comprehensive information on the social and physical welfare of early modern paupers means that the period is frequently underrepresented in social histories of old age.[5] The elderly are, however, overrepresented in early modern documents relating to poor relief, giving us the impression that old age should be uniquely equated with poverty. As one historian has commented, "as people aged they dipped further and further into poverty, even if they had not previously been poor."[6] While not denying the impoverishment and deprivation that befell many of the elderly in the early modern period, we must bear in mind that these records seem to privilege the elderly. We must thus beware of making sweeping generalizations about this social group that the records themselves may not bear out. In addition, we must remember that the presence of the elderly within other historical records might be hidden from our view. This is primarily due to an absence of information within the sources relating to a person's age—a case that is especially true for females.[7] Caution must be taken when utilizing documentation relating to the elderly poor if we are to avoid grouping the elderly together as if their shared seniority implied shared experiences, regardless of their social or economic position.[8]

The tendency has been to regard old age as a social problem to the extent that the actual experience of this phase of life among the elderly poor is all too frequently missing from the equation.[9] In real and practical terms, what did it mean to be poor and old in the sixteenth and seventeenth century? How did old age affect a person's ability to labor, and what effect did this have, especially among a class that was dependent for its survival upon its ability to work? How did one arrive at the point of applying for entry into a hospital? Through an analysis of petitions written by, and on behalf of, the elderly poor in Hesse, Germany, this chapter will endeavor to shed light upon the expectations and reality of old age among the rural populace, from both an individual and a communal vantage point. The setting for this study is thus both localized and specific, dealing with one particular group of the elderly poor (the petitioners) in this particular region of Germany. Experiences of old age will be discussed through a consideration of changes in the social and economic role and importance of the aging individual. Rather than merely categorizing these petitioners as aged and poor, I will investigate some aspects of the meaning of this status for these individuals. Through this approach, I will reveal the ways in which the elderly continued to see their social standing as being interconnected with their prior occupational history. Moreover, I will illustrate the continued employment of these individuals, and the mechanisms through which they adapted their lifestyles to cope with the infirmities of old age. The important role of both begging and immobility within the life-cycle histories of the elderly in Hesse will also be revealed. From the vantage point of the Hessian pauper petitions, this chapter will investigate how the individual supplicants experienced old age.

PAUPER PETITIONS AND THE HESSIAN TERRITORIAL HOSPITALS

The institutions at the center of this chapter are territorial or state hospitals (*Landesspitäler*), established in rural Hesse by the Protestant ruler Landgrave Philipp the Magnanimous. Founded in the Reformation period, they had previously belonged to the monastic orders and had been brought under state control through secularization. The hospitals were allowed to retain a proportion of their monastic wealth and were to be run from the proceeds of this revenue—thus they were, theoretically at least, self-financing.[10] The concept behind their foundation was that they would offer free shelter and care to the sick poor from the surrounding countryside. In contrast to other contemporary medical institutions, which predominantly offered short-term care to "curable" cases, the *Landesspitäler* offered long-term care to the "incurable" poor. The Hessian hospitals' clientele differed greatly from that of other *Incurabili* hospitals. In the latter, the incurables were usually young and were often suffering from some form of contagious disease, such as dermatological and venereal diseases.[11] The *Landesspitäler* catered to a wider variety of ages, and the inmates were predominantly suffering from conditions that, while chronic, were not immediately life-threatening.

The perceived link between old age and poverty is well documented in historical studies.[12] This connection is echoed in the provisions of the Hessian welfare policies that were established during the Reformation. Communities established poor relief in the form of community chests, through which each parish was supposed to provide alms for their poor.[13] One of the aims was "the improved care of persons suffering from infirmity and the ailments associated with old age."[14] Institutionally, old age was defined as over sixty years of age; in one Hessian hospital's rules, "it would be then that one would be so broken down that he could not earn his bread."[15] The emphasis on decrepitude was further enhanced in the *Landesspitäler* ordinance of 1534, written by the superintendent of the hospital. It stated that "persons under the age of sixty were only allowed to be taken in, when their impotence was such, that they were fit for nothing else."[16] In a sense, therefore, for their applications to be considered, the incapacitation of the younger applicants had, in theory at least, to mirror that of their elder counterparts. In sixteenth-century Hesse it seems that sixty years was seen as a benchmark.[17]

The Hessian authorities not only viewed old age as a distinct phase of life but, irrespective of gender, also perceived those persons over sixty years old as being more likely, physically at least, to be incapable of supporting themselves. The benchmark further suggests that the "over-sixties" were a large and needy enough group to receive this recognition, and the establishment of the *Landes-*

spitäler also suggests that society as a whole was failing to care for this sector of the population.[18] The existence of these institutions adds further weight to Keith Thomas's conjecture that "the golden age" of aging and communal and familial provision for the elderly are, in reality, largely mythical—at least in the case of the poorer members of society.[19] For applicants to these Hessian hospitals, the locus of care within the family and community had broken down to such an extent that the elderly were now required to turn to the state.[20]

This chapter looks at a perhaps uniquely rich source on the elderly poor: the pauper petitions received by two of the state hospitals, Haina and Merxhausen. Haina, established in 1533, specifically served male patients, and Merxhausen served women. The surviving petitions allow us to glean insights into the experience of old age in a manner akin to that evinced in studies of the English pauper letters of the late eighteenth and nineteenth centuries. While mentally ill patients were also admitted into these hospitals, this chapter will focus on persons suffering from predominantly physical ailments.[21] In contrast to bureaucratic and administrative sources that document the poor as a silent group, the pauper petitions provide us with detailed information on the elderly's experience of old age through their own voices. Written by or on behalf of the elderly petitioners, this correspondence provides "a rare direct personal record of what the poorest people of society felt and thought, including such intimate matters as the suffering from illness and the experience of old age."[22]

To gain entry into a *Landesspitäl*, an applicant had to petition the landgrave or the hospital superintendent (*Obervorsteher*). To qualify as deserving of assistance, petitioners had to be poor, incurably ill, and resident in the Hessian countryside. In addition, applicants were to have led a pious and honest life and to be wholly without means of support.[23] Officials at the time were as aware as historians are of the problems of ascertaining the authenticity of the contents of these documents.[24] To this end, petitions needed to be corroborated by local officials and a local pastor. Not infrequently, reports were also offered by the applicant's family or neighbors, and upon occasion by a surgeon or doctor—in sum, "the epistolary advocates of the poor."[25]

Critics of this form of documentation are quick to dismiss many potentially important findings as being purposely emotive, and written with a fixed agenda in mind.[26] While the issue of rhetoric must be considered to prevent sweeping generalizations from being made, the rhetoric itself reveals much about the presumptions and expectations of the period. Features common to a variety of petitions that have been dismissed as formulaic strategies could also be read as demarcating issues that were deemed to be important at the time of the petitions' composition. If, for instance, enough people were stressing the extensive period in their life during which they had worked, it would seem reasonable to assume that a willingness to work was deemed an important component of the makeup of the "worthy poor."[27] Perhaps more important, it illustrates that the individuals in question would equate their social standing and identity—and hence their worthiness of assistance—with their employment history. This issue has become increasingly important in recent historical studies that have brought into question the notion of the submissive pauper.[28]

The question of rhetoric can also be addressed from another perspective. It is notoriously difficult for a historian to be able to reach inside the mentality of a previous age and to distinguish hyperbole from truth. All the same, the necessity of obtaining confirmation of a person's status from so many different sources made lying nearly impossible in these petitions. In areas of overlap, in which the reports concur with each other, we are most likely to find the truth—or at least a version of the truth that all parties agreed upon.[29] Through an astute and careful reading of such sources, the historian is able to gain a unique insight into the world of the elderly rural poor and to compare these findings to current historiography.

AGING AS AN ILLNESS? THE DEBILITATING EFFECTS OF OLD AGE

Pauper petitions served to justify and explain a person's need for assistance. In addition, they offer historians important insights into the life histories of the poor, including their perception of life-cycle events. We are given indications of how the applicants experienced the onset of old age. In her petition of 1619, for example, Curdt Schrieber's widow referred to being "besieged by old age."[30] Similarly, in 1616, the widow Kuna Scheffer from Löhlbach explained that she was suffering from "the difficult burden and frailty of old age." As a result, she was afflicted with problems of comprehension. She described herself as an imbecile. Furthermore, her hands shook, and all her limbs felt tired and heavy. She was consequently no longer able to earn her keep and was also unable to "collect alms from the doors of other people." A similar predicament confronted Gertraudt Ewel, from the village of Buphain.[31] Her application of 1616, when she was almost eighty years old, revealed that her husband had died approximately nine years earlier, and since that time she had lost her physical strength through old age and had suffered all manner of illnesses and infirmities. As is so common in these petitions, she was consequently unable either to earn her own keep or to collect alms from other people.[32]

Such infirmities were not the sole preserve of female applicants. Similar physical problems cross the gender divide. This is evidenced, for example, in the 1716 documentation relating to Jacob Schöneweiß, a "poor, old, and now almost blind man." Jacob recounted: "[I have spent] almost all my life, from my youth onwards, as a cowherd." Through this occupation he had been able to support himself. He was unable to do this any longer as a result of "both old age and disability and failing sight." Unless he was guided, he was unable to find his way. As a result, he had been forced to give up his job as a cowherd. His poor wife was "also old and of advanced years [and] without accommodation, shelter, or food," and he was reduced to searching for his sustenance "at the doors of other people." His failing eyesight meant that he was unable to continue begging, for he could not mobilize himself without someone to assist him. Jacob was at a loss as to how to improve his situation. Entry into Haina was his last hope.[33]

"Old age" assumes its own force. In common with the printed literature of the period, one gains the impression from the petitions that certain ailments and illnesses were viewed as accompanying this phase of life and were therefore explained from that vantage point. Blindness, frailty, and immobility were frequently seen as being irrevocably linked to the experience of old age. In a sense, it is almost as if old age itself was being portrayed as the overriding illness. It may be suggested that, as modern anthropological studies have shown, there is an "altered presentation of illness in many old people," in which certain symptoms more common to the elderly are connected to their age, and to a large extent, even expected.[34] Whereas numerous petitions from younger applicants state that God had burdened them with their afflictions, this stance is rare in the petitions regarding the elderly. It could be argued that such an expectation of illness continues today—if not from the vantage point of the medical profession, then at least from the subjective viewpoint of the elderly. As the anthropologist Dorothy Jerrome has shown in her modern study of old age, the elderly seem to expect to suffer from a certain number of physical difficulties as part and parcel of their seniority.[35] The evidence of the Hessian petitions suggests that these self-perceptions also existed in the early modern period.

The language of the petitions suggests that the notion of the graduated experiences of old age was a common theme in the popular mind, and that the differentiation between various stages of life was incorporated into the linguistic usage of the populace. (Whether and how this "knowledge" was connected to learned works from this period is a question that constraints of space will not permit to be included in this chapter.) It may be that such divisions were based upon observation and experience—in many respects, the obvious. While the precise age divisions of such "stages" related largely to the individual, it appears that the petitioners distinguished between someone being "old" (*alt*) and of "advanced old age" (*hohen alter*). The latter term seemed to denote those who had been both forced to give up any forms of employment and were unable to collect alms. It was usually during this latter phase that hospitalization was sought.[36] The word "decrepit" (*abgelebt*) sometimes seems to have been a formulaic augmentation of "advanced old age."

In the minds of the elderly Hessian poor at least, old age was connected with declining health, against which humanity was powerless.[37] Notably, it seems that this phase of life was most frequently associated with physical conditions that involved some form of weakening—most commonly, a lack of physical strength involving loss of mobility and stamina. The petitions depict old age as a time of (seemingly rapid) decline and loss of physical attributes, whether of sight, hearing (occasionally, reason), or, as will be illustrated, with fundamental mobility. A common literary trope regarding old age can be seen in the 1515 Shrovetide play (*Fastnachspiel*) in Gengenbach, Germany. Here, the elderly person is portrayed as being discontented, deaf, and blind. He explains that his "legs creak" and he requires two crutches to facilitate his mobility. To him, old age is an "evil guest."[38] In the Hessian petitions, however, one has the sense that it is only within the later phase of old age—the phase that provokes the application for admission—that such discontentment sets in. As illustrated below, many of the petitions also reveal the continuing social and economic role of the elderly; they were frequently able to labor and support themselves for a considerable time before applying for admission. The experience of old age was in many respects, therefore, much more multifaceted than popular or learned culture would suggest. It is to questions of the ability of the elderly to earn their keep that this chapter will now turn.

SURVIVAL STRATEGIES AMONG THE ELDERLY

In his seminal essay on aging in seventeenth-century England, Keith Thomas asserted, "for those whose earning capacity depended on their physical strength, old age had little to commend it."[39] Because of the criteria for admission to a *Landesspital*, the association between physical incapacity—connected, as has been shown, to old age—and enforced retirement as evinced in the petitions is perhaps unsurprising.[40] For the laboring poor, with no possessions of their own to fall back on, being unable to work could irrevocably weaken one's social position.[41] The applicants frequently described their social situation in terms of their past and present employment opportunities. Wherever possible, the elderly used their employment by the state in an effort to secure themselves a position in the territorial hospitals.[42] This is particularly true of cases where the applicant—or, in the case of female applicants in particular, a member of their immediate family—had previously served as a pastor, in military service, or in one of the hospitals in question. Such a device was a further attempt by claimants to add weight to their cases, from a position where their only form of power or only bargaining tool stemmed from the wretchedness of their existence.

(In the case of hospital employees, from the 1650s onward, the state was responsible for providing for the widows and children of a deceased employee. This usually took the form of providing food or money. Whether one was more likely to gain a place as a hospital inmate if an individual or their relatives worked in the hospital is a matter that requires further research. It is not unthinkable, however, that having lived within the hospital community for many years, a former employee would have had an advantage over other applicants, for they would probably have had more of a chance to develop the social bonds that might prove fruitful to them in the future—particularly among the hospital administrators.)

In her work on England, Margaret Pelling has suggested that the elderly were expected to fend for themselves, undertaking even the most menial jobs. Studies of pauper censuses in England reveal a system wherein the elderly were expected to perform various tasks, including laundering and nursing, in return for poor relief.[43] Perhaps to an even greater extent, Angela Groppi's chapter in this volume reveals the expectation on the part of authorities that old age by itself should not rule out a capacity to work.[44]

The elderly adapted their lifestyle and occupations to fit their physical capabilities, which altered as the years passed. They managed their old age and the various ailments that they suffered by changing their occupations and lifestyles as far as possible to match their abilities. In 1672, for instance, Andreas Senff, a former employee of Haina, petitioned Regent Landgravin Hedwig Sophie for entry into the hospital. Senff recounted his lengthy service at Haina. First, he had worked for twelve years as a wool weaver. Subsequently he had been a clothworker, serving the poor. For the past thirteen years, he had worked in the kitchens at Haina and had also been involved in many other general tasks of service. In his advanced old age, however, and after much hard work, he was suffering from "poverty, hunger, and misery." He appealed to the Landgravin to prevent him from being expelled from the hospital now that he was unable to perform his work. Instead, because of his many years of hard work and his advancing years, he wished to be admitted to Haina, and to spend the short time that was left of his life there. The Landgravin agreed to this request—in principle, at least.[45] This document can be seen as charting, in brief, the life-course of this individual. While we have no details on the reasons for the changes in career, it may be that the move from employment as a clothworker to a kitchen hand was connected to his advancing age. At any rate, it is certain that he regarded his age as the ultimate cause of his inability to work.

In his study of the self-help mechanisms in early modern Bordeaux, Martin Dinges has asserted that begging was not included among the support strategies of individuals within a parish.[46] The opposite is true in rural Hesse. Although nominally forbidden in the territory, begging is a recurrent and fundamental theme within the life-cycle strategies of the petitioners. The frankness and frequency with which this topic is addressed in these documents suggests that the practice of seeking alms was an accepted, or at least tolerated, aspect of life in the communities of the applicants, if not also further afield. Such an apparent discrepancy might be explained by recourse to notions of the "deserving poor" and communal care networks. Unlike the work-shy vagrant—a familiar figure in the ordinances of the time—the applicants were the "worthy poor" whose ability to work and support themselves had been negated by their age and their physical and mental incapacities, rather than by insubordination and laziness. The aged resorted to petitions usually only when they were not only physically (or mentally) incapable of working, but also unable even to go out and collect alms.[47] Crucially, references to alms collecting and begging usually appear in a manner that suggests that the elderly regarded this practice as a form of work—perhaps the final phase of their employment life cycles.[48] The elderly seem to have been able to cope sufficiently with many illnesses and weaknesses. It was only when mobility became "too arduous" or impossible for them, and they were therefore unable even to go out and seek alms for themselves, that they became wholly incapable of sustaining themselves. It was at this point in a person's life cycle that admission would likely be sought.

The 1630 petition of Hans Liese illustrates the ways in which the aging process affected one's lifestyle. Liese recounted that he was a carpenter by trade and that, for many years, he had worked on construction projects for the Landgrave's father and his grandfather. He had served both as a pious subject, acting loyally and obediently. At the time of his application, Liese was an eighty-year-old man who had lost both his hearing and his sight. He was also unable to stand, and, according to the local pastor, his reason and his sense had also been wrested from him. Because of his physical infirmity, he was unable to earn a living and was forced to rely upon the charity of pious Christians. Although some form of charity might have been available to him, he was physically unable to reach it and could therefore not benefit from it. He requested that, due to his old age and impotence, he be granted admission to Haina for the short time that remained of his life.[49]

It was not only men who charted their career paths within the petitions. In 1713 the widow Susannen Leÿsen, describing herself as sixty-five years old, requested entrance into Merxhausen "due to her age and frail condition." We learn that, as a result of a fall many years before, she had damaged her back so badly that "the bone stuck out a long way." Ten years earlier she had given up her house to her daughter and son-in-law and had stayed with them up until now. She had managed, many years previously, to provide herself with a meager diet by acting as a form of messenger. She had often been sent on journeys between ten and thirty miles away. In spite of the fact that she was "really small and not unlike a dwarf," she was still considered capable of undertaking such employment, although the underlying implication may have been that her size and physical condition made the job increasingly difficult. Susannen—and seemingly her daughter and son-in-law—had many debts, and she was without even the smallest amount of money. In her advanced old age she was unable to undertake her delivery work any longer and was therefore also unable to feed herself.[50] It would appear that, although she resided with her family, she was responsible for providing herself with her own food and provisions.

In Hesse, the early modern experience of old age appears to have progressed through these three basic stages: namely, enforced "retirement" from paid labor, through physical incapacity, a subsequent inability even to continue to collect alms (most commonly from mobility deficiency), and at last, application to a territorial hospital. Having survived on communal charity for as long as possible, the invalid turned to the state to provide its own form of care—namely, the territorial hospital. The authorities were content to let the family and community be the first point of call for aid to an individual. It was only when all such resources had been exhausted that the state was called upon to step in and offer institutionalized care.[51]

THE SUBJECTIVE EXPERIENCE OF OLD AGE

We cannot simply explain the process by which illness was encompassed under the rubric of old age in terms of the low life expectancy among these supplicants—that is, that their nearness to death overrode the question of their incurable state. Whereas many elderly requested entry into the hospital for "the short period of time" that was left of their lives, this formula was common to many of the petitions and was not restricted to those of an advanced age. In the years for which comprehensive lists of patients in Haina survive (from 1717), it is evident that many of these elderly patients went on to reside in the hospital for many years. Johannes Stroh from Geismar, for example, entered the hospital in 1712, at the age of sixty-eight, and remained there until his death in 1719. Ditmaar Eÿerdantz entered the hospital as an "old and impotent man" in 1709 and stayed there until 1726, when he died. Barthel Schäcke from Vöhl spent from 1717 until 1723 in Haina.[52]

Nor can the references to the limited life expectations of the petitioners simply be dismissed as a rhetorical device to arouse sympathy and assistance. It is common for historians to assume that those applying for entry into institutions were all too eager to go to such places. Nevertheless, one gains a sense from these sources that, in some cases at least (and especially where they concerned the elderly, and where the invalid was responsible for facilitating his or her own petition), the opposite may in fact have been true. Entry into the hospitals seems to have been very much the last resort for those considered in this chapter. In the majority of cases, it would appear that only when they were wholly unable to support themselves—as aforementioned, usually because they were physically incapable of moving very far—were these applications made. It could thus be argued that the stigma that was attached to entering such hospitals ensured that only the neediest poor applied for entry. An unwillingness to enter these institutions might not simply be due to the institutions themselves but might also relate to the subjective experience of the petitioner. The elderly Hessian petitioners accepted their increasing infirmities as a part of the aging process but did not deem this in itself to be sufficient cause for them to be incapable of caring for themselves.[53] As modern anthropological studies have shown, it would appear that a personal expectation of some form of physical hardship in one's advancing years means that the elderly's subjective view of their health may differ from the perceptions of others. According to Jerrome, for example, "feeling well and enjoying good health does not depend on the absence of physical illness in old people."[54]

CONCLUSION

An in-depth study of the pauper petitions from the Hessian territorial hospitals allows one to gain a glimpse into the experience of old age in the rural society of early modern Germany. Obviously, by the nature of their objectives, these sources focus upon a specific and localized sector of the elderly—namely the sick, elderly poor who applied for admission into the Hessian *Landesspitäler* of Haina and Merxhausen. This is, however, a social group whose voices often go unheard in the surviving documentation of the sixteenth and seventeenth centuries, and, for that reason, the exercise can still provide valuable insights.

Evidence from the petitions suggest that the elderly among the early modern rural poor, surviving on an "economy of makeshifts,"[55] viewed illness in a highly subjective way. Many of the applicants had been suffering from a variety of physical ailments for quite some time before their petitioning for a place in a hospital. Illness and the necessity of assistance and care were, in many ways, defined in terms of mobility and activity. Frequently, it was only when one was wholly unable to labor (in the widest sense of the term), and was rendered immobile, that one applied to the hospital.

Within a format reminiscent of the stages of life, the petitioners defined and described their advancing years and their worsening condition. Their final descent into advanced age and incapacity was swift. At its simplest, the onset of old age meant that one was forced to cease working or to undertake a job that was less physically demanding. For many petitioners, advanced old age meant that one was unable to do anything other than beg. Ultimately, decrepitude meant that even begging was impossible. A close study of the petitions thus reveals extra facets to the life cycle of the elderly that have previously been neglected by historians—namely the use of begging as a tool of self-help, the issue of immobility especially, and the finding that in spite of old age many people would deem themselves capable of providing for themselves until they were literally unable to go out in search of sustenance. The onset of immobility thus signified an important watershed into the final stage of the life cycle.

Similarly, the importance of begging as a strategy for survival by the elderly, and the authorities' apparent tolerance for these activities by the aged, is linked to the notion of reciprocal care in this period. The petitions reveal that the applicants were frequently extremely conscious of their place within the community, often stressing previous forms of employment. In a sense, they felt worthy of charity through their age and their previous services to the community. The possible loss of communal identity and subsequent stigmatization that one might have faced upon entering an institution may explain a perceived resistance to the hospitals. Alternatively, this reticence may be explained by looking at the notions of subjective views of health as mentioned here.

For the elderly of Hesse, the hospital was their last resort—in many senses, not just for the individual, but also for a community that frequently could not afford to continue to subsidize chronic invalidism through the provision of alms.[56] The local community, however, not only seems to have been willing to give alms but also apparently played a central role in the network of care. There was a progression from communal charity to institutional charity. These are seen as separate and subsequent phenomena, and not as alternative sources of assistance. This might be explained by the fact that once one entered a *Landesspital*, one could stay there for the rest of his or her life, or it might be a sign of staggered power and authority. In the first instance one was responsible for oneself and one's family. When this failed, one would turn to the authority of the community, and then subsequently to state support in the form of institutions.

By placing the elderly at the center of a study concerning old age, one is able to gain a deeper understanding of the reality of old age in this period. By studying the experiences of the elderly, one gains insight not only into the life-course of an individual, but also into the broader changes within society. Far from the marginalized and ridiculed figures portrayed in literature, the elderly in the petitions reveal that, despite their poverty and their infirmity, many of these people still regarded themselves as fulfilling a social function (usually expressed either through their own employment record or that of their spouse or offspring). To a large extent, they believed themselves capable of making their own decisions about how their life-course was to progress. Admittedly, their social situation may have rendered many such decisions little more than choices against which there was little alternative. Nevertheless, the experiences of the elderly as evinced in these documents reveal a continuing attempt on the part of the aged to adapt their lifestyles so that they could cope with their infirmities. Although their ultimate inability to be self-sufficient is evidenced in the very act of petitioning, their efforts to adapt offer us an alternative perspective of old age in early modern rural Hesse than is perhaps gleaned from statistical studies of poor relief and household structure.

NOTES

I wish to thank Lynn Botelho, Sandra Cavallo, Vivian Nutton, Susannah Ottaway, and the late Roy Porter for their comments on this chapter. I also want to extend my thanks to the archivists at the Hessische Staatsarchiv Marburg for their assistance, and especially to Christina Vanja at the Archiv des Landeswohlfahrtsverbandes Hessen (henceforth referred to as LWV) for the generous help that she has extended toward me. This chapter stems from my Ph.D. research, which was made possible by the funding of the Wellcome Trust. I wish to express my gratitude to the Trust for their support.

1. Keith Thomas, "Age and Authority in Early Modern England," *Proceedings of the British Academy* 62 (1976): 205–248.

2. Margaret Pelling and Richard M. Smith, Introduction to *Life, Death and the Elderly*, 2d ed., ed. Margaret Pelling and Richard M. Smith (London: Routledge, 1994), 1. See also David Troyansky, *Old Age in the Old Regime: Image and Experience in Eighteenth-Century France* (Ithaca, NY: Cornell University Press, 1989), 4.

3. For example, Robert Jütte, "Aging and Body Image in the Sixteenth Century: Hermann Weinsberg's (1518–1597) Perception of the Aging Body," *European History Quarterly* 18 (1987): 259–290; Manfred Welte, "Das Alter im Mittelalter und in der Frühen Neuzeit," *Schweizerische Zeitschrift für Geschichte* 37 (1987): 1–32; Peter Borscheid, "Der alte Mensch in der Vergangenheit," in *Zukunft des Alterns und gesellschaftliche Entwicklung*, ed. Paul B. Bates and Jürgen Mittelstrass (Berlin: de Gruyter, 1992), 35–61; Peter Borscheid, *Geschichte des Alters: Vom Spätmittelalter zum 18. Jahr-*

hundert (Münster: Deutscher Taschenbuch Verlag, 1987). For a critique of Borscheid's work, see David Troyansky, "Balancing Social and Cultural Approaches to the History of Old Age and Ageing in Europe: A Review and Example from Post-Revolutionary France," in *Old Age from Antiquity to Post-Modernity*, ed. Paul Johnson and Pat Thane (London: Routledge, 1998), 96–109. The relative lack of work in Germany on this subject is further suggested in the bibliography entries on the elderly in Paul Münch, *Lebensformen in der Frühen Neuzeit* (Berlin: Neuausgabe, 1998), 510. See also Dietrich von Engelhardt, "Altern zwischen Natur und Kultur: Kulturgeschichte des Alters," in *Alter und Gesellschaft,* ed. Peter Borscheid (Stuttgart: Hirzel, 1995), 13–24.

4. It can be argued that much of the information on the "experience" of old age in the early modern period has come from studies wherein such an analysis was not their primary objective. Regarding hospitals, see, for example, Anne-Marie Kinzelbach, *Gesundbleiben, Krankwerden, Armsein in der frühneuzeitlichen Gesellschaft: Gesunde und Kranke in den Reichsstädten Überlingen und Ulm, 1500–1700* (Stuttgart: Franz Steiner, 1995), 100, 325, 327–328, 341. Compare to Annette Boldt-Stülzebach, "Das Leben im Hospital—Die Altersversorgung in der Stadt Braunschweig im Mittelalter und in der Frühen Neuzeit," in *Geschichte des Alters in ihren Zeugnissen von der Antike bis zur Gegenwart,* ed. Gerd Biegel (Braunschweig: Braunschweigisches Landesmuseum, 1993), 47–54. On widowhood, see, among others, Heide Wunder, *"Er ist der Sonn, sie ist der Mond": Frauen in der Frühen Neuzeit* (Munich: Beck, 1992), especially ch. 7; Dagmar Freist, "Religious Difference and the Experience of Widowhood in Seventeenth- and Eighteenth-Century Germany," in *Widowhood in Medieval and Early Modern Europe,* ed. Sandra Cavallo and Lyndan Warner (London: Longman, 1999), 164–178. It must be remembered that widowhood was not implicitly connected to old age.

5. On German sources, see, for example, Robert Jütte, "Poverty and Poor Relief," in *Germany: A New Social and Economic History,* vol. 2, *1630–1800,* ed. Sheilagh Ogilvie (London: St. Martin's Press, 1996), 385–389.

6. Robert Jütte, *Poverty and Deviance in Early Modern Europe* (Cambridge, Eng.: Cambridge University Press, 1994), 36.

7. See the comments of Margaret Pelling, "'Who Needs to Marry?' Ageing and Inequality Among Women and Men in Early Modern Norwich," in *Women and Ageing in British Society Since 1500,* ed. Lynn Botelho and Pat Thane (London: Longman, 2001), 31–41.

8. See also Lynn Botelho and Pat Thane, Introduction to *Women and Ageing in British Society Since 1500,* ed. Lynn Botelho and Pat Thane (London: Longman, 2001), 2.

9. See, among others, George Minois, *History of Old Age—From Antiquity to the Renaissance* (Cambridge, Eng.: Polity Press, 1989).

10. Heinrich Boucsein et al., eds., *800 Jahre Haina. Kloster. Hospital. Forst: Eine Ausstellung des Landeswohlfahrtsverbandes Hessen in Zusammenarbeit mit der Ev. Kirchengemeinde Haina* (Kassel, Ger.: Landeswohlfahrtsverbandes Hessen, Referat Öffentlichkeitsarbeit, 1986), 70. Regarding the monastic wealth of Haina, see especially J. Letzner, *Kurtze Beschreibung des Klosters Haina in Hessen,* in Kuchenbecker, *Anaecta Hassiaca,* Collection 4 (1730), 305–368, ch. 3; also Otto Liemke, "Das Kloster Haina im Mittelalter: Ein Beitrag zur Baugeschichte der Cistercienser Deutschlands," unpublished Ph.D. diss., Königliches Technisches Hochschule zu Berlin, 1911.

11. Sandra Cavallo, *Charity and Power in Early Modern Italy: Benefactors and Their Motives in Turin, 1541–1789* (Cambridge, Eng.: Cambridge University Press, 1995), esp.

123–125; Cavallo, "Family Obligations and Inequalities in Access to Care," in *The Locus of Care: Family, Community, Institutions and the Provision of Welfare Since Antiquity*, ed. P. Horden and R. M. Smith (London: Routledge, 1998), 90–110.

12. See, among others, Thomas Sokoll, "Old Age in Poverty: The Records of Essex Pauper Letters, 1780–1834," in *Chronicling Poverty: The Voices and Strategies of the English Poor, 1640–1840*, ed. Tim Hitchcock, Peter King, and Pamela Sharpe (Basingstoke, Eng.: Macmillan, 1997), 127–154; Jütte, *Poverty*, 36–40; Claire S. Schen, "Strategies of Poor Aged Women and Widows in Sixteenth-Century London," in *Women and Ageing in British Society Since 1500*, ed. Lynn Botelho and Pat Thane (London: Longman, 2001), 13–30.

13. See especially Walter Heinemeyer, "Armen- und Krankenfürsorge in der hessischen Reformation," in *450 Jahre Psychiatrie in Hessen*, ed. Walter Heinemeyer and Tilman Pünder, Veröffentlichungen der Historischen Kommission für Hessen No. 47 (Marburg, Ger.: Elwert, 1983), 1–20. Perhaps the best general history of these hospitals to date is to be found in this volume.

14. Heinrich Schenk, *Geschichte des Hospitals Haina und Merxhausen nebst einem Lebensbild des Begründers* (Frankenberg, Ger.: 1904), 4.

15. Cited in William John Wright, *Capitalism, the State and the Lutheran Reformation in Sixteenth-Century Hesse* (Athens, Ohio: 1988), 191.

16. German transcription cited in Karl Demandt, "Die Hohen Hospitäler Hessens: Anfänge und Aufbau der Landesfürsorge für die Geistesgestörten und Körperbehinderten Hessens (1528–1591)," in *450 Jahre Psychiatrie in Hessen*.

17. Regarding institutional benchmarks of old age, see Shulamith Shahar, *Growing Old in the Middle Ages: "Winter Clothes Us in Shadow and Pain,"* trans. Yael Lotan (London: Routledge, 1997), 12–19, ch. 10; and Lynn Botelho, "Old Age and Menopause in Rural Women of Early Modern Suffolk," in *Women and Ageing in British Society Since 1500*, ed. Lynn Botelho and Pat Thane (London: Longman, 2001), 43–66.

18. Some urban institutions in France, the Low Countries, and northern Italy also appear to have "consistently identified the elderly as a category of inmate that was disproportionately large in relation to its share of the local population." See Pelling and Smith, Introduction, n. 78. Compare, among others, to Jütte, "Poverty and Poor Relief," 383–385.

19. Thomas, "Age and Authority," 205–248.

20. On the issue of care networks, see Horden and Smith, *Locus of Care*, esp. Martin Dinges, "Self-Help and Reciprocity in Parish Assistance: Bordeaux in the 16th and 17th Centuries," 111–124; Cavallo, "Family"; Jütte, *Poverty*, 83–99.

21. See, especially, Sokoll, "Old Age," 127–154; K.D.M. Snell, *Annals of the Labouring Poor: Social Change and Agrarian England 1660–1900* (Cambridge, Eng.: Cambridge University Press, 1985); J. S. Taylor, *Poverty, Migration and Settlement in the Industrial Revolution: Sojourners' Narratives* (Palo Alto, CA: The Society for the Promotion of Science and Scholarship, 1989).

22. Sokoll, "Old Age," 127. These sources also offer the historian a viewpoint against which to compare opinion found in contemporary popular and learned culture. Such a focus is unfortunately outside the scope of this chapter.

23. It is evident, however, that in cases of mental illness patients were also taken from the towns if they were deemed to be a danger to the community and if the locale had insufficient resources to care for the invalid. In these instances, admission was granted

only upon payment to the hospital, and in some cases, upon exchange of patients, wherein an urban person suffering from a mental illness would be sent to one of the territorial hospitals on the condition that his or her town hospital accepted a poor person in his or her place. Exceptions also seem to be made in the case of children. See, among others, Christina Vanja, "Die Versorgung von Kindern und Jugendlichen in den hessischen Hohen Hospitälern der Frühen Neuzeit." *Vortrag Internationales Festkolloquium "Waisenhäuser vor und nach August Hermann Franckes Gründung 1698*; Halle a. d. S., 21–23 September 1998 [unpublished paper]. I wish to thank Frau Dr. Vanja for allowing me access to this work.

24. On this point, see also Troyansky, "Balancing."

25. Sokoll, "Old Age," p. 135.

26. Akihito Suzuki, "The Household and the Care of Lunatics in Eighteenth-Century London," in *The Locus of Care: Family, Community, Institutions and the Provision of Welfare Since Antiquity*, ed. P. Horden and R. M. Smith (London: Routledge, 1998), 153–175.

27. Eligibility for assistance rested upon an individual being considered "worthy" of assistance. These institutions were not designed to cater to the "unworthy poor"—such as beggars or vagrants—against whom a variety of ordinances were promulgated throughout this period.

28. See, for example, Geoff Hudson, "Ex-Servicemen, War Widows and the English County Pension Scheme, 1593–1679," unpublished Ph.D. diss., Oxford University, 1995.

29. On pauper letters as documents, see especially Sokoll, "Old Age," 127–154; Pamela Sharpe, "Survival Strategies and Stories: Poor Widows and Widowers in Early Industrial England," in *Widowhood in Medieval and Early Modern Europe*, ed. Sandra Cavallo and Lyndan Warner (London: Longman, 1999), 220–239. Compare, for example, to Natalie Zemon Davis, *Fiction in the Archives: Pardon Tales and their Tellers in Sixteenth-Century France* (Cambridge, Eng.: Polity, 1987).

30. LWV, *Bestand* 17, Reskripte.

31. Both these cases can be found in LWV, *Bestand* 17, Reskripte.

32. Ibid.

33. LWV, *Bestand* 13, Reskripte, 1716.

34. John Brocklehurst, "Aging and Health," in *The Social Challenge of Ageing*, ed. David Hobman (London: Croom Helm, 1978), 159.

35. Dorothy Jerrome, *Good Company: An Anthropological Study of Old People in Groups* (Edinburgh, Scot.: Edinburgh University Press, 1992), 93–94. See also Brocklehurst, "Aging," 163. On the "curability" of old age, see, among others, Hans-Joachim von Kondratowitz, "The Medicalisation of Old Age: Continuity and Change in Germany from the late Eighteenth- to the Early Twentieth-Century," in *Life, Death and the Elderly*, 2d ed., ed. Margaret Pelling and Richard M. Smith (London: Routledge, 1994), 134–164; Roy Porter, "Senile Dementia," in *A History of Clinical Psychiatry: The Origin and History of Psychiatric Disorders*, ed. German Berrios and Roy Porter (London: Athlone, 1995), 52–62; G. Fennell, Chris Phillipson, and Helen Evers, *Sociology of Old Age* (Milton Keynes, Eng.: Open University Press, 1988), 39–41; Pat Thane, "Geriatrics," in *Companion Encyclopaedia of the History of Medicine,* 2d ed., vol. 2, ed. W. F. Bynum and Roy Porter (London: Routledge, 1997), 1092–1115. Compare to Colin Jones and Laurence Brockliss, *The Medical World of Early Modern France* (Oxford, Eng.: Clarendon Press, 1997), 62; Kinzelbach, *Gesundbleiben*, 298.

36. Compare, for instance, to Joel T. Rosenthal, *Old Age in Medieval England* (Philadelphia: University of Pennsylvania Press, 1996), 101–103. See also Shahar, *Growing Old*, esp. 98–170; Nicholas Orme, "Sufferings of the Clergy. Illness and Old Age in Exeter Diocese, 1300–1540," in *Life, Death and the Elderly*, 2d ed., ed. Margaret Pelling and Richard M. Smith (London: Routledge, 1994), 62–73.

37. Rosenthal (*Old Age*, 106–107) describes it as an "inescapable process."

38. Borscheid, *Geschichte*, 13.

39. Thomas, "Age and Authority," cited in Pelling and Smith, Introduction, 4.

40. The issue of retirement in the early modern period is a contentious one that space restrictions prevent this chapter from addressing. (See among others, Rosenthal, *Old Age*.) For the purposes of this chapter, I take retirement as meaning the enforced ending of one type of employment through ill health.

41. Compare to Margaret Pelling, "Old Age, Poverty and Disability in Early Modern Norwich: Work, Remarriage and Other Expedients," in *The Common Lot: Sickness, Medical Occupations and the Urban Poor in Early Modern England*, ed. Margaret Pelling (London: Longman, 1998), 134–154.

42. This process is similar to the findings of work by both Rosenthal and Shahar in their studies of the medieval petitions for retirement from a variety of state and church employment.

43. Pelling, "Old Age," pp. 134–154; Andrew Wear, "Caring for the Sick Poor in St Bartholomew's Exchange: 1580–1676," *Medical History*, Supplement No. 11 (1991): 41–60. Compare to, among others, Richard Connors, "Poor Women, the Parish and the Politics of Poverty," in *Gender in Eighteenth-Century England: Roles, Representations and Responsibilities*, ed. Hannah Barker and Elaine Chalus (London: Longman, 1997), 126–147; Merry Wiesner, *Gender, Church and State in Early Modern Germany* (London: Longman, 1998), 146, 149, 157; Wiesner, *Working Women in Renaissance Germany* (New Brunswick, NJ: Rutgers University Press, 1986), especially 92–93.

44. This can be compared, for example, to the discoveries that have been made by Imhof and Schumacher in their study on causes of death in Giessen and its surrounding areas in the eighteenth and nineteenth centuries. Arthur E. Imhof and Helmut Schumacher, "Todesursachen," in *Historische Demographie als Sozialgeschichte: Giessen und Umgebung vom 17. zum 19. Jahrhundert*, part 1, ed. Arthur E. Imhof (Darmstadt, Ger.: Hessische Historische Kommission für Hessen, 1975), 559–625, esp. pp. 615–616, figs. 16 and 17. The belief in a continual capacity to work is also evident in the territorial hospital policy that all capable persons should perform some light work. See Louise Gray, "The Self-Perception of Chronic Physical Incapacity Among the Labouring Poor: Pauper Narratives and Territorial Hospitals in Early Modern Rural Germany," unpublished Ph.D. diss., University of London, 2001, ch. 6.

45. LWV, *Bestand* 13, Reskripte.

46. Dinges, *Locus*, 113. Regarding begging in rural areas, see also the comments of Robert Jütte in "Poverty and Poor Relief," 393–395, 398 (also n. 21 on the common chest in general). Compare to Kinzelbach, *Gesundbleiben*, esp. 124.

47. The mentally ill were also accepted as inmates in the *Landesspitäler*. This chapter, however, focuses upon the physically incapacitated petitioners.

48. Regarding issues of life-cycle strategies, see, among others, Tim Wales, "Poverty, Poor Relief and the Life-Cycle: Some Evidence from Seventeenth-Century Norfolk," in *Land, Kinship and Life-Cycle*, ed. Richard M. Smith (Cambridge, Eng.: Cambridge University Press, 1984), 351–404.

49. LWV, *Bestand* 13, Reskripte.

50. LWV, *Bestand* 17, Reskripte.

51. See also Wright, *Capitalism*, 189.

52. LWV, *Bestand* 13, Kuchenjahresrechnungen. Such findings can be compared to the modern notion, as asserted by Marian Robinowitz, that "in hospitals [today] a young patient might be described as a long-term patient, while an old one is said to be taking up a bed." Cited in Shahar, *Growing*, 6. Compare also to Vivian Nutton, "Medieval Western Europe, 1000–1500," in *The Western Medical Tradition 800 B.C. to A.D. 1800*, ed. Lawrence Conrad et al. (Cambridge, Eng.: Cambridge University Press, 1996), 152.

53. This is particularly clear in cases where the caregiver is also aged, but the caregiver applies for his or her charge to be admitted into the hospital. For more information, see Gray, "Self-Perception," ch. 4. On familial care networks, see ibid., ch. 5.

54. Jerrome, *Good Company*, 94.

55. Olwen Hufton, *The Poor of Eighteenth-Century France, 1750–1789* (Oxford, Eng.: Clarendon Press, 1974), 69.

56. Examples of this occur especially in times of famine and war.

7

"Labor and Sorrow": The Living Conditions of the Elderly Residents of Bocking, Essex, 1793–1807

Jane Pearson

> We saw two large townships called Braintree and Bocking,
> Where the tale of distress was of late years most shocking.[1]

It seems unlikely that the elderly population of any eighteenth-century English village or town was ever a group in the sense that its members possessed a common identity. Although theoretically united through longevity, bodily weakness, bereavement, and approaching death, the prevailing social hierarchies preserved the economic inequalities of life into old age. The records that historians use to identify and to analyze aspects of the life of old people in the past often do not possess the completeness necessary to study the old as a group. Old people are more often studied *within* a group such as the bereaved or the poor, not all of whose members are old. This chapter uses a combination of sources from the English parish of Bocking, Essex, to consider the living conditions of the elderly, particularly in relation to socioeconomic groups and gender. It covers the years 1793–1807, a period when Bocking became the place in Essex that endured the highest poor rate. In both 1793 and 1807, Bocking vestry organized a census of the village.[2] For the purposes of this chapter, the information on the censuses is supplemented by an annotated map of Bocking dated 1803, a fine collection of probate wills, apprenticeship lists, Anglican and Nonconformist parish registers, both of which specify age at death, and some Poor Law records. Using these records collectively allows the old people of Bocking to be viewed as a group for a short but significant period. The period was significant because it saw the collapse of Bocking's industrial base—its long-established woolen cloth trade. As a result, most of the households in which the elderly lived also experienced sudden change. This chapter examines these changes as they affected old men and old women of different socioeconomic status.

In the late eighteenth century, Bocking was an industrial village on the northeastern side of Braintree in Essex.[3] The 1801 national census gave the population of Bocking as 2,680, which was much larger than the average Essex village of that time.[4] In mid-August 1793 Bocking's vestry decided to carry out a survey of inhabitants. Information was collected street by street, household by household. The "names, qualities and professions" of the heads of all households were noted, together with their gender and some indication of their age.[5] The reason for making the survey was not specified, but its interest in dependent age groups suggests a vestry initiative to explain, forecast, and, perhaps, control the vestry's spending.[6] Thirteen and a half years later, in December 1807, the vestry clerk, Betts Andrews, undertook a repeat house-to-house census, using the same categories, if not the same route, as the 1793 census taker. These two household lists identify the existence, if not always the name, of the inhabitants who were thought (or who claimed) to be over the age of seventy.

The vestry censuses are not problem-free as sources. In both there are clerical errors to be corrected.[7] Second, the only individuals who are named are the household heads, which means only about 21 percent of the population can be identified by name. In a few cases the addition of the word *junior* assists identification. Fortunately, Bocking's parish registers include not only the age at death but also information on the relationship of the dead to the living—"child of" or "wife of"—which assists the process of identification (provided it is assumed that men lived with their wives and children). Information on social status and domicile can be found in wills, the ratepayer and rate disbursement lists (records regarding the collection and distribution of the poor relief "tax"), and the listing of owners and occupiers of land and houses that supplements the 1803 map of Bocking.[8] These records allow the accuracy and completeness of the census record to be checked. They also enable some enlargement of the "moment in time," which is all that a census can capture. A third potential problem is the ability of people in the past to know their ages and to give them correctly when asked.[9] The Bocking censuses identify inhabitants over the age of seventy, but when such people came to be buried, the register tells a familiar story. According to the burial register, there should have been twice the number of over-seventies than were actually recorded for the census in August 1793. The burial register confirms the identity of old people who remained in Bocking until they died; it gives the names of old people who died as inmates of the workhouse or as lodgers (who are counted but not named on the census), and it gives the names of any who were accidentally omitted from the census or who moved into Bocking after the 1793 census was made.[10] Finally, I have accepted Bocking's vestry decision that seventy was the critical age for dependency to be counted, even though the over-sixties are perhaps a more usual cohort to represent the old in the eighteenth century.

The 1793 census specifies a total population of 2,936.[11] The 1807 census specifies a total population of 2,376.[12] Thus, in the space of thirteen and a half years, the population of Bocking declined by 560, or 19 percent. The loss, almost equally divided between males and females, was greater in the period after the 1801 government census.[13] Of course, the loss was not only of individuals. There was also a loss of households and families. In 1793, 632 household heads are listed, and in 1807, 546—a loss of 14 percent.[14] In effect, 86 households (the equivalent of a small village) had disappeared and had not been replaced. No empty houses are recorded in 1793, but seven are recorded in 1807.[15] The average size of household in 1793 was 4.5, and in 1807, 4.2. Clearly, Bocking became a roomier town in the thirteen years under review.

In the eighteenth century, Bocking was primarily a baize-weaving town, its textile industry organized by succeeding generations of two regional clothiers— Savill and Nottidge—both of whom owned premises in Bocking. There were also a declining number of smaller clothiers in the parish. In 1793, 43 percent of the town's households were primarily engaged in some aspect of the wool trade.[16] This compared with about 26 percent of households engaged in farming and building trades (including all "laborer"-headed households). By 1807 this picture had changed markedly. A mere 18 percent of households were now defined by a wool trade occupation, while those dependent on farming, a building trade, or laboring had increased to 33 percent. It is clear on the evidence of the census that some of those who were unable to leave changed both their residence and their occupation within Bocking.[17] Most of the weaver households had no property-ownership stake in the town. Some of them departed, leaving behind a parish in which 24 percent of its household heads could not name their occupation. This compares with 7 percent in this condition in 1793. In over little more than a decade, Bocking had ceased to be a baize-weaving town and had become, however temporarily, a town with a serious unemployment problem.

How might this significant economic and demographic change have affected the way the elderly lived in Bocking? Since, as I shall show, about half the over-seventies were living in extended households in 1793, this depression-induced exodus carried grave implications for them. Whether or not they were head of the household, whether or not they were (or intended to be) in receipt of poor relief, the likelihood is that none of the elderly, whether richer or poorer, could avoid or, in some cases anticipate, the challenges brought about by economic collapse. The ratepayers among them would be forced either to pay more or to accept that they could no longer afford the status of paying rates. The ability of the over-seventies to live independently might even be under threat, especially if they lived with an increasingly impoverished or desperate-to-move kinsman or adult child. In addition, if the elderly poor moved from the place in which they had spent their vigorous years, could they be sure their pensions would still reach them? If they moved, they would lose their access to the charitable monies with which rich clothiers had generously endowed Bocking over the previous two centuries.[18] For the very poor old people, accustomed to augment their shilling-a-week pension with a little light odd job or nursing work,

Table 7.1
The Households of the Old As Identified in the Censuses of 1793 and 1807

Domicile	1793		1793		1807		1807	
	Old men	%	Old women	%	Old men	%	Old women	%
Workhouse	11	25	12	34	8	27	10	26
Alone	2	5	1	3	3	10	9	24
Household of 2	7	16	7	20	8	27	12	32
Household of 3+	24	55	15	43	11	37	7	18
Total	44	101	35	100	30	101	38	100

Source: Essex Record Office: The Bocking Censuses, D/P 268/18/1–2.

the stronger and more able-bodied unemployed, now present in greater numbers, might reduce their opportunities to earn.

THE HOUSEHOLDS OF OLD MEN AND WOMEN

The 1793 census shows there were 79 people over the age of seventy living in Bocking. By 1807, their numbers had fallen, by 14 percent, to 68. Both censuses give only the name of the household head. While this name might refer to any one of the adult members (of the appropriate gender) of the household, making it difficult to identify the elderly resident, in fact, as already indicated, there are in the sources additional clues that can be used to decide, in many cases, whether the elderly resident is the named household head. By these means it is possible to compile a list of the names of most of the elderly residents (living out of the workhouse) of Bocking at both census dates. None of the old men identified in 1793 survives as a *name* on the 1807 census, although at least one was alive, being later entered in the burial register. Only 3 of the old women named on the 1793 census are to be found on the 1807 census. Given their advanced age, this is not surprising. However, when we take the names of men and women over seventy on the 1807 census and search for them in the census of thirteen years earlier, there is considerably more continuity. Over two-thirds of the old men and three-quarters of the old women living in Bocking in 1807 had been working in Bocking in 1793.[19] In other words, the majority of the elderly living in Bocking in 1807 had also been living there in 1793. During a period of swift economic depression, when 19 percent of the whole population and 14 percent of the households had departed, the elderly as a group stayed put. As we shall see, their living conditions changed dramatically.

Table 7.1 sets out the size of the households in which Bocking's old people lived at both census dates and includes aged workhouse inmates. It clearly shows that, at the first census date, old people were most likely to live in households with three or more members.[20] For the 24 old men in this situation, the average size of their household was 5.7 people. For the 15 old women, it was 5.8 people. However, these larger households differed in their composition. The old women's households contained more women and fewer children than did the comparable old men's households.[21] The greater numbers of children present in the old men's households probably reflects the greater opportunities for child labor in these households. However, where the old man was the only man in the household—and usually the household head—he lived with two or three adult women. It seems likely, judging from his status designation, that in most of these cases, the old man's household contained adult female servants. It is probable that around a quarter of these larger households were not poor and that the old man in question was enjoying retirement or semiretirement without any necessity to make alternative living arrangements. Any problems associated with old age would have been assisted by the presence of servants or family members under the same roof. By contrast, around 40 percent of these old women's households enjoyed the potential comfort of a coresident adult woman.

Another difference between the households was the gender of the household head. In almost every case, the larger households in which old men lived were headed by a man. This was not the case for the old women, one-quarter of whom lived in a female-headed household.[22] Only one-quarter of the old women were the heads of their households, whereas the majority of the old men seem to have been, at least nominally, the head whether or not they were involved in the day-to-day work.[23] Of the 4 old women who achieved headship of a large household, 3 were widows carrying on their deceased husband's enterprise, and the fourth was a widow taking in lodgers. The 1793 census thus reveals that, on the eve of economic disaster for the town, the majority of the over-seventies were living in large households of 3 to 13 people. A substantial minority of these households were in circumstances comfortable enough to be ratable. Twenty-nine percent of the old men's households paid rates, compared to 40 percent of the old women's households. For those who were not so fortunate, the old men remained in the working household, typically run by a man and with several members under fifteen years of age. The majority of the old women lived in households that were similar in function but attenuated by a general absence of young children and, in a quarter of cases, by the death of the (male) household head.

The economic downturn changed this picture dramatically. By 1807, the percentage of old people living in the town's larger households halved and, for old women, this was no longer the most likely type of household for their dwelling.[24] The average size of the larger households in which old men lived had scarcely changed—at 5.3 it was almost identical with the 1793 figure. As before, all these households were headed by a man, but the old men were now much less likely than before to share the household with another adult man.[25] In other words, whether he liked it or not, the old man was the head of the household.

In addition, only 18 percent of their households were now made up of children under fifteen years old. In these figures we see the demise of Bocking's trading households, which had been dominated by men and filled with children. The average size of the households inhabited by old women in Bocking had declined significantly by 1807 to 4.5. The percentage of children in their households had almost halved, and they were now even less likely to be headed by a woman.[26]

One of the more significant changes in the living arrangements of old people in Bocking lies in their diminishing access to the larger households. In 1793, before the downturn in trade, elderly men and women were most likely to be found living in households whose occupants were engaged in trade or who were wealthy enough to employ several servants. By 1807, old people were much less likely to live in the larger, busier households. It was not that Bocking's households had declined much in size. Rather, the composition of these larger households had altered so that, by 1807, they contained around 10 percent more women and 10 percent fewer children.[27]

In 1793 the next most likely domicile for the over-seventies in Bocking was the workhouse. At neither census did the workhouse accommodate a majority of the old people. In Bocking in 1793, 29 percent of the over-seventies lived in the workhouse, making up 37 percent of the workhouse inmates. Thirteen years later, in 1807, the figures were 26 percent of their number living in the work-house, making up 41 percent of the workhouse numbers.[28] So although the actual number of the old living in the workhouse had declined a little, the proportion of the elderly to which the workhouse catered had remained virtually unchanged. A little under a third of the elderly in Bocking composed a little over a third of the workhouse inmates. Since the total number of poor had increased, this suggests that the workhouse may have chosen to support the elderly rather than other needy groups in the town.[29]

In Bocking in 1793, 14 old men and women (18 percent) lived in a household of just two people. Three of these households were certainly old married couples. The additional evidence of the burial records suggests that the majority of the others were sharing with spouse or kin and that most of the old men remained head of the household. Two of the old men were in lodgings. In 1807, 20 old men and women (29 percent) lived in households of two. At this date, old women were more likely to live in a household of two than they were to live in the workhouse. The same was not true for the old men. In 1807 there were 8 old married couples and the remaining 3 old men lived with a younger woman, presumably wife, daughter, or maidservant, since, in every case, the old man was the head of the household. Of the 5 old women who were not living with their old husband, 2 lived with a younger man and 3 with a woman, and in 4 of these cases a woman was head of the household. In sum, around a quarter of the over-seventies in Bocking, around the turn of the eighteenth century, lived in households of just 2 members and, in more than half the cases, the other coresident was their spouse. In most cases the old man retained his headship of the household and in all cases he shared with a woman. A minority of old women (around 30 percent) shared with a woman, presumably a reflection of their greater longevity and, possibly, of their own choice or of an overseer's decision.

Finally, as Table 7.1 shows, in 1793, 2 old men and 1 old woman lived alone in this overcrowded industrial village. Since none of them was named on the August poor rate disbursement listing and none of them left a will, they were probably maintaining their independence through prior savings or investment. Widow Medcalf, for instance, was a ratepayer, the widow of a butcher.[30] Thirteen years later, in 1807, solitary living had become more common, with 3 old men and 9 old women living alone. Only 1 of the 3 old men, and 3 of the 9 old women, had been a household head in Bocking thirteen years previously.[31] Several, in their middle age, had been associated with a trade and thus with economic independence.[32] In addition, it seems that most of these individuals had lived in Bocking throughout their middle age and had family living in the town. These solitary individuals made up 18 percent of the old people in the census—an increase of 14 percent since 1793. The whole population of Bocking had decreased in these years by 20 percent, to the extent that the later census reveals several empty houses. This means that it is possible that the solitary elderly were so by choice, and that this choice had not been available to them thirteen years earlier when empty houses were not to be found. Some of the wills written around the last decade of the eighteenth century certainly give the impression that properties were uncomfortably packed with tenants. Samuel Clay Sr., bay weaver, for instance, whose will is dated 1787, left a dwelling house and weaving shop, part brewhouse, and orchard in his own occupation. He also left "three rooms or dwellings in Bocking" in the occupation of Widow Sly, Widow Taylor, and Mary Peers; "three rooms in Bocking and part of the brew house" in the occupation of Widow Clarke, Widow Denton, and James Peers; and "three messuages in Bocking and half of the orchard" in the occupation of John Tiffen and John Collis.[33] Thus, four messuages, including working premises, an orchard, and a brewhouse, seem to have housed a total of nine households.

During this short period, the old people of Bocking had, generally speaking, begun to live in smaller households. As we have seen, the average size of Bocking households had remained virtually the same so this finding bespeaks a significant alteration for the old. Eighteen percent fewer old men were, in 1807, living in an extended household, but 11 percent more were living with only one other person. The proportion living alone had doubled to 10 percent. For old women, the percentage living in the workhouse had slightly diminished, but 24 percent of them were now living alone, 21 percent more than at the previous census. Sixty-three percent lived in a household of 2 or more in 1793. This percentage had declined to 50 percent by 1807. In other words, old men were still most likely to be living in extended households, but old women were now more likely to live in households of 2. They were now, in contrast to old men, almost as likely to be solitary as to be workhouse inmates. The evidence suggests, however, that some of these solitary women were not paupers or ex-workhouse women. Four of them were ratepayers on small properties. Clearly these are small numbers, but they are also identifiable individuals responding to changing economic circumstances. It would be possible to argue that, for these old women, the migration of families out of the parish had improved their ability to live independently. It may also be the case that they had been left to fend for themselves without the benefit of family support.

So, when the old men and old women identified on the censuses are compared, some suggestive differences in their households are apparent. First, more old women than old men lived in the workhouse. By 1807, however, although old women were still there in greater numbers, the proportions had evened out. Twenty-six percent of both old men and old women were now inmates. Second, fewer old women than old men lived in the large extended households. The likelihood is that old men retained headship of their enterprises even if the enterprise was actually run by a son whose family and workers or servants were also household members.[34] Old women seem to have been *more* likely to cede the household to a son and *less* likely to remain living in the household subsequently. Perhaps their "choices" were more constrained by the expectations of others than a widowed old man's would have been. Third, the gender composition of the households in which old men and old women lived was different. In 1793 the households in which old men lived were male-dominated, containing in total 82 men and boys and 68 women and girls. Women dominated the households in which old women lived. They contained 67 women and girls but only 35 men and boys. This is an unexpected finding, since both censuses show that nearly twice as many households in Bocking housed more women than men.[35]

These findings strengthen the argument that men retained economic power into their old age while their (old) widows did not, but it still does not explain why old women lived predominantly with women. Some other explanation is necessary that might involve community pressure of some kind, perhaps directed by the lower social status accorded to widows in comparison to widowers, cultural imperatives concerning seemliness and reputation, an economy that favored women's employment—such as spinning—or even the ability of old women to make a personal choice.[36] I have already suggested that old women, whose access to the larger households was more limited than old men's, were more affected by a housing shortage and an overcrowded parish. By 1807, the gender difference was less marked. Although old men continued to live in larger households than old women, those households were no longer male-dominated. The households in which old men now lived had, in total, 31 male and 32 female members. The households in which old women lived had 20 male and 43 female members. In other words, one effect of Bocking's economic collapse was felt in the households of old men. Either they could no longer rely on a son's support once their trade had failed or they could not take the risk of accompanying their sons when they chose to take their trading skills elsewhere. Evidently, they were unable to substitute the missing household members with male servants, journeymen, or laborers.

Fourth, and in connection with the last point, at both dates old men were more likely than old women to live in households containing children.[37] Fifteen of the 24 old men in the households with more than 2 inmates were in this position (62 percent) as against 6 of the 15 old women (40 percent). Finally, by 1807, old women were nearly three times as likely to live alone as were old men. Living alone has usually been seen as a function of economic weakness, but not all these women were paupers. This probably explains why more of them did not lodge together. These women were able to choose to live alone once there was sufficient spare accommodation to allow it. At the same time, their solitary condition might be a direct result of the migration of younger kin.[38]

The records show that the majority of Bocking's old people stayed in the town and experienced the economic downturn, the decreasing population, and the escalating poor rate. Their increasing economic weakness, whether expressed in the difficulty of finding sound tenants for their properties, the lack of work, or the departure of trusted kin and neighbors, is expressed in the changes in their household structures. The indications are that old men could maintain their hold on power conferred by property or a trade until death, their households attracting grown men and young families. Once they could no longer claim this economic power, their households degenerated to the style of the rest of the village, dominated by women. An old man with property or a trade had a power over his son and his daughter-in-law that an old woman apparently did not have. The situation may have been qualitatively different for old women as well. They seem to have gained living space and even the dignity of a home of their own once the economy of Bocking faltered. Women's skills, perhaps, were less likely than men's skills to diminish significantly in middle age. In addition, while their spinning skills might be less marketable as a result of the economic downturn, their nursing, childcare, cleaning, kitchen, and mending skills would always be in demand.

THE SIGNIFICANCE OF SOCIOECONOMIC STATUS TO THE OLD MEN AND WOMEN

To what extent were the old people of Bocking able to make choices about where and how they lived? Clearly, their socioeconomic status is deeply implicated in this question. In order to consider this question more closely, I shall compare the elderly residents who paid rates with those who did not. Although Bocking was described as a village, it was different in important respects from villages whose economy was purely based on agriculture. This is most noticeable when lists of ratepayers are considered. In a nonindustrial rural Essex village, such as Great Tey, ratepaying households represented about half of all households in 1729, and about one-third by the early nineteenth century.[39] In Bocking, such a calculation is more problematic. The list of Bocking parish ratepayers for September 1803, for instance, has a total of 512 names for a parish that, according to the censuses, had around 590 households.[40] This suggests that 87 percent of Bocking's households were paying rates. No less than 174 entries were for properties rated on a £1 rental value. We have already noted that Bocking's rates were second to none in Essex in this period. They were collected from an extraordinarily high number of households, in 32 percent of cases at the rate of £1 a year and in 26 percent of cases at £2 a year. It seems, then, that Bocking expected a much larger proportion of its inhabitants than was normal to contribute to the poor rate, even at the little sum of five shillings a time. The old were not exempt. For the cohort of 118 old people derived from the 1793 census and the burial records, the 1803 rate list suggests that at least 44 of them (37 percent) were paying rates—32 on properties with a rental value of £1 and £2, and 4 on properties with a rental value over £11.[41] This finding reflects the fact that, at that date, around half Bocking's old people counted in the census typically lived in larger trading households and were able to maintain their status and influence in the village by virtue of their close association with such enterprises.

The argument that the social status of old men with property or a trade must have been considerable can be further developed by considering the amount of their continued contribution to the parish poor rates. Eight of the 44 old men identified in the 1793 census were ratepayers and three of them owned land in the parish. According to the quarterly parish rate made in the same week as the census (6 August 1793), these men paid a total of £22.5.0.[42] Four more men, who were over seventy according to their subsequent burial record, paid £6.10.0.[43] Thus these 12 wealthier old men together produced enough in rates to pay for one year's maintenance of no fewer than 43 elderly widows, who typically received one shilling a week from the rates. All these contributing old men stayed in Bocking and were buried there.[44] They were among the fortunate householders who could manage to weather the economic depression. The 8 old women who paid rates also remained in Bocking until they died. Their households usually contained one other woman, and none housed a child.

Even though the ratepaying burden was widely spread, most of the old people were not ratepayers, and this places them firmly among the town's poorest inhabitants. To the 22 old men in this category identified in the census, I have added 13 whom the burial records claim would have been over seventy when the census was taken. Of these 35 old men, none of whom owned ratable property in Bocking, 26 (74 percent) stayed to be buried there. The comparable figure for old women was 16 (56 percent). The other difference that connected poverty and migration was the composition of the household. For the old men and the old women alike, the average size of the household was greater by two persons for those who left town. The crucial two were children under fifteen years of age. In addition, the old women's households that departed were, on average, smaller by one man than the departing old men's households. Thus, on both counts, poverty and migration were probably rather more strongly related for old women than old men.

So, in this period of swift economic decline, the fortunes of the elderly residents were closely associated either with the possession of ratable property or with the fact that they shared their accommodation with children. Property holding allowed them to stay, cushioned from destitution and household disintegration, but only a minority was in this position. Clearly women who paid rates were normally either the widow or the unmarried daughter of a (deceased) ratepayer. Except among the wealthier families, such widows and unmarried daughters were not normally left a ratable legacy. A household's children were, presumably, both a potent economic asset and, on their own account too, a good reason to seek better conditions elsewhere.[45] It seems that the old people attached to such a household also departed. This, no doubt, explains some of the out-of-town relief arrangements and the begging letters that the vestry was obliged to organize and to make provision for. It is perhaps surprising to find that none of the ratepaying old women lived with children, not even with a young maid of all work. Nineteenth-century censuses often reveal grandchildren coresident with their grandparents and old women taking in child lodgers. Bocking's ratepaying widows and spinsters seem not to have opted for a child companion. Alternatively, this may be one example of the vestry clerk not enquiring too deeply into the composition of a household that he did not expect would harbor claimants; or it may be an accident of small numbers.

CONCLUSION

In the 1790s, at St. Mary's parish church in Bocking, a funeral took place on average once or twice a week. During the service the congregation would have heard the following discouraging words: "The days of our age are threescore years and ten; and though men be so strong, that they come to fourscore years; yet is their strength then but labor and sorrow."[46]

In the early 1790s, less than 2 percent of the burials were for the over-seventy age group. Almost one-third of the old people were buried from the workhouse, and half lived (and died) in households of three or more. So, whatever else might be said of the living conditions of the very old in Bocking, they did not labor and sorrow in isolation. Between 1793 and 1807, however, the 19 percent reduction in the population of Bocking does seem to have changed the living conditions of the old people in a number of significant ways. As we have seen, although most of the elderly stayed in Bocking, they were less likely to be members of the town's larger households. They were more likely to live alone or as a couple. In addition, whatever their socioeconomic status, they became less likely to share their roofs with children. Households containing children were most likely to leave and to take all the children, but not necessarily the old man or woman, with them. The decision to take or to leave the old person (or the choice of the old person to stay or go) was closely associated with the household's socioeconomic status.

Depopulation and economic depression did not increase the old people's labor and sorrow equally. As the population of Bocking parish began to decrease in the early 1790s, the amounts collected for the relief of poverty increased. For the calendar year of 1792 the amount collected was £1,995. Within two years the collection was over £3,000; in 1801 and 1803 it was over £8,000. This amount would have provided 307 families with ten shillings per week for the whole year and seems an extraordinarily large sum even given the fact that 24 percent of the 546 household heads on the 1807 census had no occupation.[47] The explanation is that the town supported a large number of paupers who lived out of the parish.[48] The number of ratepayers increased by 284 percent between 1793 and 1803, and a large number of cottagers were asked to pay five or ten shillings a year and to become ratepayers for the first time in their lives. Some of these cottagers were old people who had already ceded property to the next generation of their family. This must have increased the usual anxieties of aging for them, making their declining years poorer than they had expected. Nevertheless, the elderly ratepayers remained in the parish throughout the depression, increasingly living in smaller households.

The evidence suggests that the situation in Bocking affected old men differently from old women. However, the playing field was unlikely to have been level to begin with. Wright's study of eighteenth-century Ludlow claims that widows rarely managed to both stay in the town and recover the level of prosperity they had enjoyed as wives of town traders.[49] Bocking's population had about 10 percent more women than men at both census dates—1793 and 1807. Most households contained more women than men, but only 8 percent of households were all female. In other words, although Bocking clearly offered opportunities for women's work such as spinning or domestic service on farms and in the victualing trade, there is no evidence of a subculture of all-female households such as Pamela Sharpe found in Colyton.[50] Bocking was not unusual, in that more women than men reached the age of seventy and more old women than old men were impoverished. Most of the old women evidently did not possess rights in the household equivalent to the old men, and they also had fewer opportunities to leave. Their chances of living in larger households dwindled considerably. Since it was the larger, poorer households that were considerably more likely to pack up and leave, the old women were more likely to miss this opportunity and be left behind. As economic hardship clutched the parish, their cohort living in the workhouse equaled in number those who lived alone, collecting a small weekly pension and laying it out solely on their own needs.

By contrast, the old men enjoyed the economic advantage of their sex. Bocking's evidence shows that it was old men, not old women, who lived in male-dominated households containing young children and that this seems to have been the sort of household that had the energy necessary to leave the hopeless economic depression and seek better opportunities elsewhere. The old men did not always accompany the migrant household. Some died before the act, others stayed behind, living alone or in the workhouse. In some cases, no doubt, it was the death of the old man that released his son's family to try its fortune elsewhere, just as, in agricultural parishes of eighteenth-century Essex, the death of a smallholder or farmer father quite often preceded by only a few months the wedding of his inheriting son.[51] Since relief could be sent to a pauper who had migrated, a decision *not* to migrate may indicate the old man's reluctance to leave home—his final important economic decision. Alternatively, it might indicate his son's *first* important economic decision—to leave the old man behind. In good times, an old man could expect to retain his position in the household he started up even through the experiences of bereavement, retirement, and failing strength. Bocking's records show that this expectation held for the wealthier, ratepaying households but ceased to hold for those families who were either too poor to pay rates or who had young children under their roofs. These were the very households that were most likely to migrate in search of work. This suggests that the poorer old men must have been particularly hard hit by the economic downturn. Unlike their wealthier old neighbors in Bocking, it seems likely that they felt compelled to migrate along with their grandchildren. Those who decided to leave were not ratepayers, and the likelihood is that the more substantial men had more to lose by leaving. Certainly they did not leave and were able to live out their remaining years in the place where they had earned their living and raised their families.

One of the most unexpected findings, on comparing the two Bocking censuses, is the increase in solitary living for the elderly. The word *solitary* is a socioeconomic category and carries a weight of meaning to do with emotional isolation and social neglect. We do not expect to find the elderly living alone in eighteenth-century records.[52] Sokoll's study of Ardleigh in 1796 and Braintree in 1821 confirms that elderly paupers did not live alone. They lived as kin or lodgers in someone else's household or they moved in together. As we have seen, this pattern changed in depressed, late-eighteenth-century Bocking. The elderly women increasingly *did* live alone while the elderly men found themselves in smaller households than previously. The wealthy elderly bought themselves assistance and company. The elderly poor, when single or widowed, were likely to be herded into lodgings or the workhouse. Among the poor, only old *married* couples could expect the decency of retaining their home. It is more than likely, however, that a bereaved old man or woman desired to retain this decency. Certainly, among the rural middle sort, male testators were in the habit of giving their widow specified rent-free houseroom and yard space for her remaining years.[53] We can infer from this that the property-holding elderly would have chosen to remain in their property on bereavement whether or not that involved solitary living, which was one of the reasons for the woman's dowry provision. As for the poor, it is impossible to be sure when solitary living was synonymous with independence or with loneliness, with respect or with neglect. The answers to such questions remain unclear, largely because of the implications of age, social status, and poverty.

Clearly, the link between age and pauperization, with all that pauperization entails for lack of choice, is closely related to gender and marital status. The evidence from Bocking suggests that widowed old men fared better than widowed old women. First, they were more likely than old widows to retain the bereaved household and to enjoy its superior economic strength and the associated opportunity to depart once economic depression set in. Secondly, poverty was likely to strike women at an earlier age than men. Sokoll has argued that the poor *man's* life cycle began to decline toward pauperization after the age of sixty, and the poor widowed *woman's* after the age of forty.[54] Bocking's evidence shows that old men who retained their status as household heads, even of the larger, failing enterprises, did not become pauperized. Possession of a property with as little as £1 in rental value put many, including some of the over-seventies, onto the ratepayer list during the worst years of the depression.

This chapter has concentrated on a short period in one community to examine how the living conditions of a group of elderly people changed as a result of a swift and devastating economic downturn. An exceptional time and some exceptional sources allow a glimpse of individual and household responses to economic stress and an opportunity to gauge the ability of old people to participate in decision making that directly affected their lives and their way of living. If exceptions prove the rule then the experience of Bocking's old people at the end of the eighteenth century should encourage historians of aging, at the very least, to be sensitive to the significance of local economic circumstances and issues of gender and class to the way of life of old people in the past. Thinking about old people as a group—a group that includes rich and poor, male and female, married, single, and bereaved, the economically active and the retired—implies renewed attention to their position in the community and to their enduring *contribution* to the community. It allows us to consider, if not satisfactorily to answer, questions to do with old people's retained or relinquished ability to choose such significant issues as where and with whom they might live. Ultimately, such an approach discourages "ageist" conclusions and encourages a more realistic appreciation of the potential for dignity and strength contained in the small proportion of a community who achieved riper years.

NOTES

1. Ann Hoffmann, *Bocking Deanery: The Story of an Essex Peculiar* (Chichester, Eng.: Phillimore, 1976). On 91, she quotes this piece of doggerel, attributing it to "the author of *Journal of a Very Young Lady's Tour from Canonbury to Aldeborough*, published (in rhyme) in 1804."

2. Essex Record Office (hereafter ERO) D/P 268/18/1–2.

3. T. Sokoll, "Household and Family among the Poor: The Case of Two Essex Communities in the Late Eighteenth and Early Nineteenth Centuries," unpublished Ph.D.

diss., Cambridge University, 1988. Philip Morant writes, "This fine and large parish is not a town, but one of the most considerable villages in this county, and part of it extends into what appears the heart of the town of Braintree" (*The History and Antiquities of the County of Essex*, vol. 2 [Chelmsford, Eng.: E.P. Publishing and Essex County Library, 1978], 383—originally published in 1763–1768).

4. A.F.J. Brown, *Prosperity and Poverty; Rural Essex, 1700–1815* (Chelmsford, Eng.: Essex Record Office, 1996), 1.

5. Three age groups were specified within the census, children up to fifteen years of age, people over seventy, and those in between.

6. Bocking parish registers had been noting the word *poor* beside some names from 1783. These were presumably those in receipt of relief (ERO D/P 268/1/3).

7. In several places the gender totals do not correspond to the age group totals, a girl having been wrongly entered as a boy, for instance. In such cases the correction was made according to the totals, which were not altered.

8. ERO D/DO P2.

9. E. A. Wrigley and R. S. Schofield, *Population History of England,1541–1871* (London: Arnold, 1981), 109–111, 202–203. Margaret Pelling argues that "a lack of absolute precision" in recording ages should not deflect historians from accepting "as a broad principle the reliability of contemporary perceptions of age, state of health and family structure" ("Old Age, Poverty, and Disability in Early Modern Norwich: Work, Remarriage and Other Expedients," in *Life, Death and the Elderly: Historical Perspectives*, ed. Margaret Pelling and Richard M. Smith [London: Routledge, 1991], 78, 80).

10. As I shall indicate, for some purposes I have included both the census and the register cohorts.

11. This was made up of 1,340 males and 1,596 females. Forty-four men and 35 women were over seventy; 530 males and 564 females were under the age of sixteen. There were 766 men and 997 women between the ages of sixteen and seventy.

12. This was made up of 1,066 males and 1,310 females. Thirty men and 38 women were over seventy; 517 males and 499 females were under the age of sixteen. There were 519 men and 773 women between the ages of sixteen and sixty-nine.

13. 276 men and 286 women were lost; 258 left before 1801 and 304 after 1801. The loss for the years 1793–1801 was 9 percent, and for the years 1801–1807 was 10 percent.

14. Both figures exclude the inhabitants of the workhouse.

15. However, the rate list for August 1793 shows four empty houses and one mill and one wool hall empty.

16. There were 6 wool manufacturers, 51 wool combers, 5 card makers, 171 weavers, and 40 spinners listed as household heads.

17. For instance, the 1793 census identifies 75 weavers living in Bocking Church Street. By 1807, 48 of them had disappeared as household heads, 9 remained in Church Street but with another occupation, 4 remained but were unemployed, and 3 had moved elsewhere in Bocking. Parish records show that, by 1799, 13 of them had been interred in the Anglican churchyard in Bocking.

18. Morant (*History and Antiquities*, 388–389) lists two almshouses to accommodate fifteen, a charity school, and nine separate bequests (in addition to the setting up of the workhouse), which provided money, food, and clothing to the poor and to specified groups such as "poor honest traders" and "poor not receiving collection."

19. Of the 7 who were not found, the family name and trade were found for 4 of

them, suggesting that the old man in the 1793 list was counted by the census taker but was not then the household head.

20. This was the case for 49 percent of them. Nine lived in households of three people, 5 in households of seven, 3 in households of eight, and 1 each in a household of nine, ten, twelve, and thirteen.

21. The percentages of men, women, and children in the old men's households were 39, 32, and 29 respectively. The percentages for the old women's households were 33, 49, and 18. There were 40 children in the old men's households and 16 in the old women's households.

22. The status of the female household heads was given as weaver, farmer, widow, and the respectable trader's title of "Mrs."

23. Eight belonged to the wool trade; several had gentry status. Wills give additional supporting evidence. Laslett's opinion is that an extended household was more likely to be headed by the older man (Peter Laslett, *Family Life and Illicit Love in Earlier Generations: Essays in Historical Sociology* [Cambridge, Eng.: Cambridge University Press, 1977], 200). See also S. J. Wright, "The Elderly and Bereaved in Eighteenth-Century Ludlow," in *Life, Death and the Elderly: Historical Perspectives*, ed. Margaret Pelling and Richard M. Smith (London: Routledge, 1991), 124.

24. Seven lived in households of three, 6 lived in households of four, 2 lived in households of five, 1 lived in a household of six, and 2 lived in a household of nine.

25. Seventy-five percent in 1793 had declined to 45 percent in 1807.

26. Twenty-seven percent in 1793 had declined to 14 percent in 1807.

27. Susannah Ottaway, "The Old Woman's Home in Eighteenth-Century England," in *Women and Ageing in Britain Since 1500*, ed. Lynn Botelho and Pat Thane (London: Longman, 2001), 111–138; Richard Wall, "The Residence Pattern of Elderly English Women in Comparative Perspective," in *Women and Ageing in Britain Since 1500*, ed. Lynn Botelho and Pat Thane (London: Longman, 2001), 139–165.

28. These are, nevertheless, high figures according to some sources. For example, Thomson suggests, for the mid-nineteenth century, a figure of 10 percent. David Thomson, "The Welfare of the Elderly in the Past: A Family or Community Responsibility?" in *Life, Death and the Elderly: Historical Perspectives*, ed. Margaret Pelling and Richard M. Smith (London: Routledge, 1991), 207–208.

29. Laslett's view is that "old men . . . showed a greater tendency to live as lodgers or in institutions if they lacked spouses." Laslett, *Family Life and Illicit Love*, 200. To the male parish overseers and the workhouse master, an old woman may have been a more attractive inmate than an old man, better able to contribute to community life and work. See Susannah Ottaway, "The Decline of Life: Aspects of Ageing in Eighteenth-Century England," unpublished Ph.D. diss., Brown University, 1998. In Chapter 6 she suggests that the overseers may have seen old people as taking up a disproportionate amount of their time rather than their budget and they were thus inclined to send them to the workhouse in the interests of efficiency.

30. William Medcalf, butcher, who wrote a will, was probably her son (ERO 352BR30).

31. Their occupations in 1793 were (male) weaver and (female) victualer, weaver, and spinner.

32. Two of the widows had been married to, respectively, a miller and a carpenter.

33. ERO 94AR1.This is one of several wills also depicting tenements crowded with lodger-tenants. Mary Peers and widow Clarke were both in receipt of poor relief.

34. It is also possible that a daughter-in-law could be more easily persuaded to share with her husband's father than with his mother.

35. 44 percent of households were female-dominated and 24 percent male-dominated in 1793. In 1807, 42 percent were female-dominated and 24 percent male-dominated. Twenty-seven percent had equal numbers of men and women at each date. Four percent of households were of solitaries in 1793 and 8 percent in 1807. The population of Bocking, at both census dates, had around 250 more female than male inhabitants.

36. Olwen Hufton, "Women Without Men: Widows and Spinsters in Britain and France in the Eighteenth Century," *Journal of Family History* 9 (1984): 355–374.

37. If old women were valued as child minders, allowing younger women more time to earn, they can rarely have been minding coresident children.

38. It might also be seen as a problem of the source—was the census counting lodgers as solitary householders?

39. Jane Pearson, "The Rural Middle Sort in an Eighteenth-Century Essex Village: Great Tey, 1660–1830," unpublished Ph.D. diss., University of Essex, 1997, 114.

40. Thirty-one of the names are listed more than once for separate properties (ERO D/P 268/11/3).

41. This does not include the widows of ratepaying men who were buried between 1793 and 1803.

42. The total rate collected in August 1793 was £538.2.6, produced by 190 ratepayers, 20 of whom were excused. There were typically four such collections per annum at this period (ERO D/P 268/11/3).

43. One of the four, John King Sr., weaver, was excused from his payment.

44. Farmer Crackenthorpe was buried in the Nonconformist burial ground, the others in the churchyard of St. Mary's, Bocking parish church.

45. See Wrigley and Schofield, *Population History of England*, 444, on the subject of dependency ratios. Wrigley and Schofield make the point that old people and children retained value as people who produced at least something while consuming less than full-bodied workers.

46. The Order for the Burial of the Dead in the Church of England, *Book of Common Prayer*, contained a reading of Psalm 90.

47. Sokoll writes that between one-fifth and one-quarter of Braintree's poor received £3–£4 per annum—that is, a maximum of one shilling and sixpence ha'penny per week (Sokoll, "Household and Family," ch. 8).

48. Sokoll makes the same point for the adjacent parish of Braintree that "no less than a fifth of the paupers chargeable to Braintree lived elsewhere" (Thomas Sokoll, "Old Age and Poverty: The Record of Essex Pauper Letters, 1780–1834," in *Chronicling Poverty: The Voices and Strategies of the English Poor, 1640–1840,* ed. Tim Hitchcock, Peter King, and Pamela Sharpe [London: Macmillan, 1997], 140).

49. Wright, "Eighteenth-Century Ludlow."

50. Pamela Sharpe, "Literally Spinsters: A New Interpretation of Local Economy and Demography in Colyton in the Seventeenth and Eighteenth Centuries," *Economic History Review* 44, no. 1 (1991): 46–65.

51. Pearson, "Rural Middle Sort."

52. Wright, "Eighteenth-Century Ludlow"; Sokoll, *Household and Family.*

53. Pearson, "Rural Middle Sort," 163.

54. Sokoll, "Household and Family." Sokoll defines the pauper household as one where a member claims regular poor relief. See also C. Phythian-Adams, *Desolation of*

a City: Coventry and the Urban Crisis of the Late Middle Ages (Cambridge, Eng.: Cambridge University Press, 1979). On p. 91 Phythian-Adams writes of widowhood as being "a social version of old age." See also Susannah R. Ottaway, "Providing for the Elderly in Eighteenth-Century England," *Continuity and Change,* 13, no. 3 (1998): 391–418.

PART III

Image and Reality: Social Experience Versus Cultural Representations of Old Age

8

Old Age in Early Modern Castilian Villages

David Vassberg

EARLY MODERN CASTILIAN VILLAGE SOCIETY

In the 1500s Spain became the greatest power on earth, with a vast overseas empire and a military that remained the dominant force in Europe for more than a century. The largest, wealthiest, and most populous part of Spain during this Golden Age was Castile (Figure 8.1), and the overwhelming majority of Castilians were peasant farmers who lived in villages.[1] Therefore, it is vital for scholars to understand the nature of Castilian village society during this period. Here we are employing *village* in a broad sense, for any organized rural community of modest size, whether a *lugar* under the administrative control of a larger municipality or a *villa* possessing jurisdictional autonomy.

This chapter explores the topic of old age in early modern Castilian villages. One might think that the topic would have been the subject of a substantial body of scholarly work. Unfortunately, that is not the case: The elderly of early modern Castilian society have been almost totally neglected, except for Luis S. Granjel's recent book *Los ancianos en la España de los Austria* (1996). Unfortunately, Granjel's book is of limited value for our purposes. Based almost entirely upon printed (and overwhelmingly literary) sources, it deals primarily with the urban elite of Habsburg Spain (i.e., the privileged 10 percent of the population). The *rural* elderly (i.e., old people from the 90 percent majority) are rarely present in his book, and they seldom receive more than passing mention in other scholarly publications.

Our study of the elderly is handicapped by the fact that we know relatively little about Castile's households during this period. Historical studies of Castilian

Figure 8.1
Iberian Kingdoms in the 1500s and 1600s

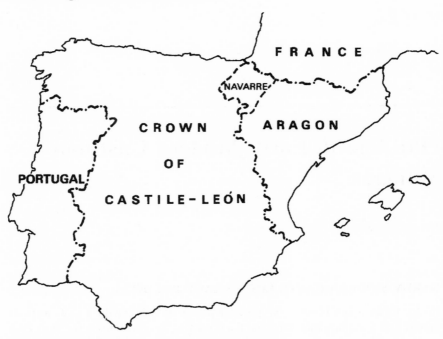

Source: Adapted from Vassberg, *Village and Outside World*, 4.

households almost invariably begin with the easily accessible mid-eighteenth-century cadastral survey, leaving the sixteenth and seventeenth centuries largely untouched. Social historian Sheldon J. Watts lamented that we did not even know with certainty whether the dominant rural family in early modern Spain was of the nuclear type. Historical demographer Francisco Chacón Jiménez noted more recently that there remained considerable uncertainty on this point, and on countless other important issues as well.[2] This remains largely true, despite the publication of a number of helpful studies in the interim. Thus our study of the elderly in early modern Castile lacks the advantage of a substantial body of supportive secondary works dealing with the topic.

   An underlying reason for this is the difficulty of obtaining detailed household information for rural Castile in this period. The overwhelming majority of villagers were illiterates who left no written accounts for posterity. Fortunately, however, Castile's villagers made their way into a variety of documents such as local governmental accounts, censuses, parish and notarial registers, and transcriptions of lawsuits. These documents provide glimpses into village society. By supplementing the surviving documentary records with folkloric and literary sources, along with a smattering of information from scholarly works, we can learn much about the rural elderly. All these sources indicate that the elderly in sixteenth- and seventeenth-century Castile did not form a uniform subgroup. On the contrary, the elderly were an exceedingly heterogeneous component of the society of the day. Their diversity is reflected in contemporary literary and popular depictions of "old folks." The diversity of the village elderly is clearly recorded as well in various governmental records. As a first step toward examining the condition of the early modern Castilian elderly, let us address the issue of who were the "old" during this period.

HOW OLD WAS "OLD?" AND HOW MANY OLD PEOPLE WERE THERE?

The world's great writers have often proven to be perceptive observers of their times. This is certainly true of Golden Age Spanish authors, who are frequently used as a source of historical information that is difficult or impossible to obtain from the extant documentary records.[3] Cervantes's famous knight-errant Don Quixote de la Mancha may be considered a literary stereotype demonstrating some of the characteristics of old age. The literary Quixote was only about fifty,[4] hardly enough to be considered "elderly" today, but definitely on the threshold of old age during the period of our chapter. The picaresque novelist Alonso de Castillo Solórzano called a fifty-year-old hermit an "elderly fellow" and a "venerable old man." Vicente Martínez Espinel, a friend of Cervantes and himself a poet and novelist, made reference to "an old fellow, as much as fifty." The famous Golden Age writer Quevedo was convinced that *he* had reached old age when he turned fifty-two.[5] In sum, when we read of "old" people in sixteenth- and seventeenth-century Spanish literature, we must remember that they were not necessarily of a really advanced age.

The *Relaciones* (responses to questionnaires sent by Castile's royal government to the towns and villages of the realm in the 1570s) comprise an exceptionally rich primary source of information about rural society. Fortunately, five volumes of *Relaciones* have been published, for towns and villages in the provinces of Madrid, Toledo, and Ciudad Real.[6] The *Relaciones* questionnaires do not directly address the question of old age. But question 17 inquires whether the site of the village is "healthy or unhealthy," and in their responses, a small number of villages provided clues to what they considered "old."[7] The village of Campillo approached the topic by reporting that "many people reach the advanced age of seventy and above." San Martín de Valdepusa raised the definition of advanced age considerably higher, saying: "This area is more healthy than infirm, because . . . there are always elderly men and women who reach eighty and ninety years." Ballesteros affirmed that it was "a healthy place, and has seen people live to a hundred."[8]

It is clear that Castilians of the day had various definitions of "old." Some believed that old age could begin as early as fifty. On the other hand, the residents of villages where longevity was commonplace seemed to reserve *old* for

Figure 8.2
Modern Provincial Divisions, for Locating Villages Mentioned in Text

AB-Albacete; AL-Almería; AV-Avila; BA-Badajoz; BU-Burgos; CA-Cádiz; CC-Cáceres; CN-Coruña; CO-Córdoba; CR-Ciudad Real; CU-Cuenca; GR-Granada; GU-Guadalajara; HU-Huelva; J-Jaén; LE-León; LO-Logroño; LU-Lugo; M-Madrid; MA-Málaga; MU-Murcia; OR-Orense; OV-Oviedo; P-Palencia; PO-Pontevedra; SA-Salamanca; SG-Segovia; SE-Seville; SO-Soria; SR-Santander; TO-Toledo; VA-Valladolid; ZA-Zamora.

Source: Map adapted from Vassberg, *Village and Outside World*, 8.

a far more advanced age. The difficulty of defining *old* complicates the task of counting how many "old people" there were.

Village censuses provide one of the most useful sources for information on the elderly, and for studying other aspects of early modern society. These censuses provide verbal snapshots of households, sometimes including information about the elderly and their position in society. My chapter utilizes computerized data from unpublished manuscript fiscal censuses of fifteen villages representing eight Castilian provinces during the period 1553–1664.[9] (See Figure 8.2.) Unfortunately, few of these censuses include precise data about people's ages, and when age information *is* reported, it is usually only for children. Fortunately, most of my censuses provide enough information (sometimes explicit, and sometimes apparent from the family organization) to permit establishing *approximate*

Table 8.1
Approximate Age Categories in Fifteen Castilian Villages

Category	Frequency	Percent	Valid Percent	Cumulative Percent
De pecho (< 1 yr, approx)	17	.7	1	1
Pequeño (1-4 yrs, approx)	74	2.9	4.2	5.2
Niño (5-9 yrs, approx)	142	5.6	8	13.2
Muchacho (10-19 yrs, approx)	373	14.7	21	34.2
Por casar (over 20 yrs, approx)	108	4.2	6	40.2
Adult (25+ yrs, approx)	992	39.0	55.7	95.9
Viejo ("old" or grandparent)	73	2.9	4.1	100
TOTAL (cases with age information)	1,779	70	100.0	
Hijo (child, with no age suggested)	502	19.7		
Missing (no age information)	262	10.3		
TOTAL (includes cases w/missing info.)	2,543	100.0		

These categories are often arbitrary, but they follow whenever possible the terms used in the census, i.e.: *de pecho* (nursing); *pequeño* (small child); *niño* (child); *muchacho* (older child); *por casar* (marriagable); and *hijo* (son). Following the Spanish custom, the table employs masculine forms, but all categories included both males and females.

Source: The Archivo General de Simancas, Expedientes de Hacienda, Legajos 45, 61, 65, 66, 81, 155, 274, 281, 316, 321, 356, 363, and 371.

age categories.[10] I have employed seven such age categories to construct Table 8.1.

The proportion of *viejos* (only 4.1 percent) in Table 8.1 seems to be unrealistically low. Other scholars have calculated that around 10 percent of Spain's pre-industrial rural population were sixty years old or above, and this percentage seems to have been also true of pre-Revolutionary France.[11] There are several explanations for the apparent underreporting in our sample. In the first place, the last two categories in Table 8.1 (adult and *viejo*) are troublesome. Adults were normally villagers with local citizenship, reserved for those over the age of twenty-five unless married before that age and accorded early adult status.[12] However, "citizens" (i.e., adults) could be elderly people not identified as such in the census. My use of the category *viejo* poses problems not only because of its inherent vagueness, but also because I decided to include grandparents in the category unless other facts made it clear that they were not "old." Notice that I have placed the category *hijo* along with the missing cases. That is because *hijo* is not a reliable age indicator: although the term literally means "child," suggesting youth, it can also mean "son" or "daughter" of *any* age, including advanced adulthood. With those caveats in mind, when we examine Table 8.1 we must take into account that while only 4.1 percent of valid reported cases[13] were *viejos*, this proportion might be substantially greater if we were able to add to it those "adults" and "*hijos*" that should rightly belong there. We can easily imagine that the figure really should be around 10 percent.

An important factor determining the proportion of elderly was *where* they lived. In pre-industrial times (far more than today), the physical location of a village had a significant impact on the residents' general health and longevity.[14] Question 17 of the *Relaciones* inquires whether the site of the village is "healthy or unhealthy." The overwhelming majority of villages responded with terse answers such as "healthy," or "rather unhealthy." Fortunately for historians, however, some of the villagers availed themselves of the opportunity to wax eloquent over the merits, or the disadvantages, of the place where they lived. These more articulate responses sometimes include information about how the physical environment of the village affected longevity. The citizens of La Despernada demonstrated an awareness of the importance of location when they reported, "[Our village] is a warm and salubrious and sheltered place, which produces good and healthy people." A high and well-drained location was no guarantee of a healthy population. Paracuellos reported, "There are few elderly people, because the village is out in the open and on an elevation, and the church lies at some distance from the village. And the doctors say that the church is the principal cause of the unhealthiness of the village, because it is so exposed to the winds, and this is very harmful to the people."[15]

An unhealthy site was likely to produce an above-average mortality rate. The weakest members of society—infant children and the elderly—were the most vulnerable. Consequently, we should not be surprised that villages reporting unhealthy locations typically also reported that the local residents did not live long. Chillón was somewhat cautious about the insalubriousness of its location, but it remarked that "there are few old people in the village, and for that reason we don't consider it to be overly healthful." The village of Alameda gave a similar report, observing that "This village is in a very level and pleasant place but is somewhat unhealthy because of its many springs and streams, and we deduce that for that reason there are few old people here."[16]

Molinillo reported that it was in a "cold and unhealthy location." This negative judgment was partially contradicted by the fact that the Molinillo natives who prepared the report were all old men: seventy, seventy-two, and sixty-seven years of age. Calling itself definitely unhealthy was Luciana, located at the confluence of the Bullaque and Guadiana rivers. According to the *Relaciones*, Luciana suffered cold winters, with much ice and fog, and uncomfortably hot summers because the surrounding mountains kept moderating winds from reaching the village. In conclusion, the villagers declared, "It is an unhealthier place than any in the entire district. Not many children survive here, and few people of this village—whether men or women—reach advanced age, and they are sickly."[17]

Fortunately, there were also villages in healthful locations where many people reached a ripe old age. One of these was Villanueva de los Infantes, which reported, "The area where this village is located . . . is considered to be a healthy place, and one can see that clearly because there are elderly people and few infirm." Similarly, Corral de Almodóvar declared that it was "healthy, considering the elderly people who have lived there."[18] The champion village for health and longevity according to the *Relaciones* was Nombela, positioned on the slopes of a small mountain range called the Berrocal de Nombela. The residents recounted several examples of remarkable longevity:

This is a healthful location, because it has no [endemic] contagious diseases, and few ordinary illnesses. The residents by today's standards live long and healthy lives, and they get along very well despite their age, especially those over seventy years old. There are old folks who walk eight or nine leagues[19] behind a pair of animals. And if they live in the village they don't leave it. They can walk straight and perfectly well without a cane if they wish. And they have excellent memories undiminished by their age, and this can be seen every day. At present [in the village] there are elderly people of eighty and ninety whose faculties and memory are so good that they serve throughout the area as reliable eyewitnesses of past events and lineages. And there have been old people of a hundred ten and a hundred twelve so agile and with such good memories that they seemed no older than fifty. And [this village] is so healthful for the elderly that one oldster of over ninety was on his way to mass and fell into an open grave that had been dug for a burial, and he broke a leg. But he healed so completely that afterward for many years he was as good as ever, and this same man later married a maiden of over sixty, and lived as a married man another five or six years. It is reported that there was another old fellow who reached a hundred twelve, and was so healthy and agile and mentally alert that we used to go to him as an archive of information about the past. And it transpired that one Sunday while he was apparently healthy except for his age, when the mass was over he stood up in the middle of the village church and removed his hat, and in the presence of the entire village he said "Gentlemen, for the love of God forgive me if I have in any way offended you, because God forgives me and forgives you all." Then he went home, and a few days later he died as a good Christian. And he had a brother who reached one hundred ten. We recount this to demonstrate how healthy our old people are.[20]

As we have seen, the definition of *old* was flexible, and the number of elderly people varied with environmental and other conditions. Although the proportion of elderly folks in early modern Castilian villages was relatively small, Golden Age Castilian villagers were keenly aware of the old and very old in their midst. We shall now turn our attention to how the elderly were perceived by their contemporaries.

ATTITUDES TOWARD OLD AGE

Period folkloric proverbs and stories give us some idea of contemporary attitudes toward old people. Sixteenth-century proverbs portrayed the elderly in diverse, and frequently contradictory, ways. Some depict them as shrewd and often underhanded individuals willing to exploit any opportunity for personal advantage. A collection published by the Marqués de Santillana in 1508 includes the proverb "The old man in his village, and the young man in the outside world, can lie as much as they please," meaning that the elderly can safely misrepresent past events that no one else has witnessed.[21] A variation of this theme is the proverb: "That's why the Devil knows so much, because he is old." The crafty oldster also appears in several Golden Age Spanish folkloric tales.[22] On the other hand, we find proverbs extolling the elderly for their wisdom gained from years of experience. For example, "If you want good advice, go to an old man" and "The oldster who cannot predict is not worth a sardine," meaning that old people's practical experience enables them to give seemingly prescient advice.[23] Their wise counsel was not always followed, because in Alonso de Barros's *Proverbios morales* (first published 1598), we find the sardonic comment: "These crazy young people never profit from advice [presumably offered by their elders]."[24]

The proverbial elderly in Spanish folklore are also admired for their patience. For example, "Bit by bit, the old woman spins the bundle [of fiber to be transformed into yarn or thread]." And they are extolled for their energy and their ability to get things done, as in the proverbs "The old man plants a vine, and he harvests the grapes" and "When an old woman dances, she raises a lot of dust" and also for their frugality, as in the proverb "The old woman used the weeds [presumably for cooking], and she left neither green nor dry ones."[25]

On the other hand, the elderly are frequently the butt of ridicule in Spanish folklore. A rather mild example is "An old man and an oven are both heated through the mouth: the first with wine; and the second with firewood," referring to the tendency of many old men toward immoderate drinking. Folkloric derision of the elderly more often than anything else is associated with romantic attachments or marriages that are considered inappropriate for persons of advanced age. The proverb "Elderly lover, winter with blossoms," calls attention to the absurdity of an aged Romeo; while "An old man who marries a young girl will live with a cheating wife, or will die tolerating her unfaithfulness." Along the same vein: "No one is more willing to pardon an insult than a lovesick old man."[26] Neither did folklore limit its derision of elderly lovesickness to males of the species. In the Golden Age traditional tale "La vieja enamorada," a lovesick old woman convinces a young man to marry her, but she foolishly agrees to his stipulation that she spend their wedding night out of doors. Chilled from the cold and damp weather, she sickens and dies within a few days.[27] On the other hand, the proverb "An old hen makes good soup," in addition to its literal meaning, carries a *double entendre* appreciative of the amorous potential of women of a certain maturity.[28]

Above all, Spanish folklore depicts the elderly as handicapped creatures to be pitied for the frailty and infirmities associated with advanced years. The pain of old age is noted in two proverbs gathered by Gonzalo Correas (b. 1571): "Where there is jealousy, there is love; and where there are elderly, there is pain" and "Around Saints Justo and Pastor [i.e., in autumn] the walnuts ripen, the girls fall in love, and the old women suffer from aches and pains."[29] And Alonso de Barros's sixteenth-century *Moral Proverbs* repeat the theme of the suffering elderly: "There is no one with a long life who has not had long suffering"; "Never did I see a man happy after he had grown old"; and "Nor [did I see] suffering that the old did not have, and more so if they were poor."[30] If not for their suffering, the elderly are pitied in folklore for their physical debility. The Correas proverb "A punishment by an old woman never makes an impression" expresses this, as does the traditional saying "The old man because of flagging strength, and the youth from lack of experience, [both] spoil things."[31]

Spanish literature is another source for attitudes about old age. Literary giants such as Cervantes offered discerning and often caustic comments about the society of their day. Mateo Alemán's *Guzmán de Alfarache* (1599–1602) recounted a classical story about the ages of man. The Roman god Jupiter decreed that a man would spend the first thirty years of his life enjoying himself. Then between ages thirty and fifty he was sentenced to live like a donkey, working hard at his profession to provide for his household. Between fifty and seventy he would live like a dog, barking and growling under inferior conditions and with scant gratification. And between seventy and ninety he would live like a monkey, aping the defects of his species. This story was also used by the famous playwright Lope de Vega and by the Jesuit philosopher and writer Baltasar Gracián, who added that during the final (monkey) stage of life, one would become senile and play with children. Along similar lines, elsewhere Gracián wrote that man would be a peacock at twenty; a lion at thirty; a camel at forty; a snake at fifty; a dog at sixty; a monkey at seventy; and nothing at eighty.[32]

Golden Age literature, like the folklore of the period, expresses ambivalent attitudes toward old age, ranging from profound respect to the most heartless derision. Good examples of the former may be found in *La Celestina* (1499) by Fernando de Rojas: "Prudence can only be found in the elderly" and "Good advice comes from the elderly." From the mouth of Don Quixote: "We must respect the elderly, even if they are not of the knightly class." And from Cristóbal Suárez de Figueroa's *El pasajero, advertencias utilíssimas a la vida humana* (1617), an eloquent tribute to the virtues of the elderly: "Age confers wisdom, prudence, good judgment, and everything else essential for making correct decisions."[33]

All that being said, Golden Age Spanish literature portrays the elderly in a negative light more often than in a positive one. Examples are not difficult to find. Fernando de Rojas in *La Celestina* ticked off a lengthy inventory of the unpleasant effects of old age: "Who can count, señora, the damages [caused by old age], with its inconveniences, its tiresomeness, its anxieties, its ailments, its chills, its fevers, its discontent, its peevishness, its grief, that wrinkling of the face, that change of hair from its original and fresh color, that loss of hearing, that weak-sightedness, with your eyes in the shadows, that sinking of the mouth, that falling out of teeth, that lack of strength, that halting walk, that tedious eating?" These were physical problems associated with age. There were also behavioral changes in many elderly folks. The Franciscan friar Antonio de Guevara's *Libro primero de las Epístolas familiares* (1542) forcefully denounced the sinful lifestyle of many that he saw: "It is of little advantage to have gray hair, and a wrinkled face, if on the other hand you are youthful in vices, and childish in thinking; and from this it follows that the sinful and dissolute oldsters are weary of life and terrified of death. The wicked old people with immoral lives are not sad and disconsolate for any other reason than the fact that they know that they only have a few years left in which to enjoy their depravity." Another negative characteristic frequently attributed to the elderly was miserliness, in Golden Age literature often considered to be typical of advanced age.[34]

It is not surprising that in a patriarchal society such as Golden Age Spain, old women fared considerably worse than old men in literary representations. By the standards of the day, a woman's worth was related to her reproductive capacity; consequently, her value diminished earlier than that of a man of similar socioeconomic circumstances. "Sterility is the trousseau of old women," declared the protagonist of *La pícara Justina* (1604), a sentiment repeated with mordant unkindness in the burlesque dialogues of Golden Age theatrical and novelesque portrayals of elderly women. In Lope de Vega's *La Dorotea* (1632), a female character remarks ruefully: "Women do not last as long as men" and "Men of all ages have choices, and can follow professions and hold offices; by then [when elderly] they are wealthier, and are more highly esteemed. But we women serve only as building material for their children, and if not for that, what function do we acquire in society?"[35]

In those rare cases when elderly women are portrayed in a positive light, they are likely to be accorded masculine (i.e., good rather than bad) qualities. Gonzalo de Céspedes y Meneses, for example, in *Historias peregrinas y ejemplares* (1623), praised an old woman with the phrase "a lady of much quality and even *manly* prudence."[36] The sentiment and language probably reflect the typical male viewpoint in Golden Age Castile.

THE EXPERIENCE OF OLD AGE IN CASTILIAN VILLAGES

Thus far we have dealt primarily with *perceptions* of aging and old age. We must now explore the reality of Castilian village society as depicted in contemporary censuses (bearing in mind that these, too, were colored: by the perceptions of the enumerators as well as the biases of their informants). Both the recorded perceptions and the available data indicate that the elderly in some respects occupied a privileged position in village society, but in many respects they found themselves at a disadvantage vis-à-vis their younger neighbors.

My fifteen-village database includes a category for primary and secondary occupations. Unfortunately, my censuses categorize less than half of the *viejos* in this way.[37] In both primary and secondary levels, however, the overwhelming majority[38] of the listed elderly are "dependents" not associated with an occupation at all. This indicates that people identified as *viejos* in the censuses were normally past working age. As we would expect from a rural population, most *viejos* who *were* attributed with an occupation were *labradores* (peasant farmers). It is hard to know exactly what the designation means, because some people might have been identified as *labradores* merely because that was a prestige category in the rural world. A so-called *labrador* could be only marginally active, hiring others to perform all fieldwork, and perform agro-pastoral activities only on a subsistence basis. If the occupational status on this point is somewhat equivocal, the database clearly shows a gender difference: *All* females in the *viejo* group are dependents.[39] From this we may surmise that elderly females were far more likely than males to attach themselves to the family of a son, daughter, or other family member. Those who did so were almost always widowed.

Widowhood and Remarriage

Documentary sources indicate that widowhood was a condition frequently associated with old age. In fact, 61.6 percent of the *viejos* in my fifteen-village database were widowed or previously widowed persons.[40] Widowhood, of course, was by no means limited to the elderly,[41] for it affected a large proportion of the inhabitants of early modern Castilian villages. Widowhood was far more likely to affect females than males: in fact, four-fifths of all widowed persons were women, a gender proportion also true of widowed *viejos*.[42] It is hardly surprising, then, that the phrase "old widow" appears frequently in early modern documents.

An obvious remedy for the difficulties accompanying the loss of a spouse was to find a suitable replacement. Some widowed persons undoubtedly found it impossible to remarry because of unattractive physical, familial, or personality characteristics. For others, remarriage was simply not an agreeable option. Some women—particularly substantial property owners—preferred to maintain their independence rather than to fall again under the domination of a husband. Many widows were probably pressured by family not to wed again. The Church was ambivalent on the question of remarriage: on the one hand, preaching the virtue of saintly abstinence while, on the other hand, recognizing the emotional, physical, and economic benefits of second matrimonial unions.[43] My fifteen-village database suggests that only about 6.1 percent[44] of ever-married persons had remarried. This figure surely is far too low, probably because of incomplete reporting by census takers. Other scholars who have analyzed seventeenth-century Castilian marriage records have found that between one-fifth and one-quarter of all weddings involved at least one previously married partner.[45]

We have evidence that nearly half the widowed persons of either gender entered into second nuptials. According to Gómez-Cabrero and Fernández de la Iglesia, the likelihood of remarriage in seventeenth- and early-eighteenth-century Mocejón (Toledo) depended upon the age of the surviving spouse at the moment of widowhood. Gender was also a factor: while the combined totals for all ages show little gender difference, *young* widowed *females* were more likely to re-marry than males of the same age; and *older* widowed *males* were more likely to remarry than females of the same age. It is regrettable that the Mocejón analysis placed everyone over the age of fifty in a single category; but even so, the tendencies seem to be quite clear. Evidence from Mocejón during this period (which we suspect is close to the Golden Age Castilian norm) also shows that older men who lost a spouse were much quicker to remarry (an average of 20.3 months compared to 49.4 months) than were women of the same age.[46]

Elderly Villagers in Complex Households

My census data indicate that at any given moment three-quarters (74.7%) of Golden Age rural Castilian households were of the simple (or nuclear) type. Another 14 percent were solitary households, meaning that approximately 9 out of 10 households were in these two categories. The bulk of the remaining 11.3 percent were extended, multiple, and pluri-conjugal household types.[47] It is well to remember that Castilian families, like those in the rest of Europe, did not remain frozen in one type of household structure. They were highly dynamic, evolving over time with the maturing of children, the aging of their parents, and other changing conditions. The Castilian (and general *European*) ideal was for a married couple to live by themselves in their own household, a sentiment expressed in the Castilian proverb "A married man wants his own home." Pressing economic or family needs frequently required this ideal to be set aside, at least temporarily. For example, a newly married couple often lived for a while with a parent until they could afford to set up a separate household. This was the situation of Pedro Cano and his wife, who in 1629 were living in the household of Alonso Paján, her widowed father.[48] In the normal order of things, the young couple would establish their own separate household as soon as they were able. That presumably would leave old Alonso Paján alone. A census of Villardefrades (Valladolid) describes the normal household evolution over time, reporting that in 1589 the widower Christóval Carnicero lived alone "because all his children are married and living in their own homes in this vil-lage."[49]

Although the widowed elderly might pass through a period of independent (i.e., solitary household) living, eventually (especially if they were female) they tended to move in with family members. Before that happened, there might be a transitional period during which the children living in the same village would provide assistance. In Castellanos (Burgos), for example, the widow Ana de Barcena ("poor, and harvesting neither grain nor wine") lived by herself in 1584. According to a census of that year, "her children give her food."[50] Although all *male* widowed persons in my database headed their *own* households, I have other documentary evidence of widowers also moving in with relatives as a survival strategy, particularly when they were economically distressed. For example, a certain Juan de Lara lived with a son in the village of Villoria, in Burgos province. A 1575 census indicated that Lara was "poor and widowed, and has even lost his citizenship."[51] Elderly people who had never married would not be able to move in with a son or daughter and might have to look for assistance from a convent, monastery, or hospice. Marcos Martínez, for example, a sixty-year-old living in Tamarón (Burgos) in 1668, was described as "poor and with no family"—language expressing sympathy for a situation that was perceived as highly undesirable, in a society where one's children were expected to furnish the kind of assistance that in today's developed world is provided by social security systems.[52] Nevertheless, persons like the said Marcos Martínez might be able to find other kin to give them a place to live.[53]

The elderly were not only guests, but also hosts in the formation of complex households. In Espartinas (Seville), for example, a 1631 census shows the widower Francisco Limón "the elder" as the head of a household that included his thirty-year-old daughter Jacinta and the old man's granddaughter Leonor, "who served him." In this case, there is no mention of a husband for Jacinta, and so we may speculate that she was either widowed or an unwed mother.[54] We should add that the idea of a grandchild (or other relative) as a servant was by no means rare in the rural world, and the service aspect of the relationship was often explicit in censuses. The widow Leonor Fernández, for instance, in 1582 had a maidservant named Catalina Martínez living with her. The widow's own granddaughter, Catalina was from a neighboring village three kilometers down the road.[55]

Adoption, Guardianship, and the Elderly

One reason for the formation of complex households was that family loyalty encouraged people to take responsibility for raising the orphaned children of close relatives. This was especially true of grandparents, who could protect their own bloodlines by taking their orphaned grandchildren into their homes.[56] For example, in 1578 Hernando de Ayala had an orphaned granddaughter in his household.[57] Madalena González, a widow living in Espinosa de la Ribera (León) in 1582, had the company of her grandson Juan, child of the widow's deceased son.[58] In 1628 the widow Juana Rendera was keeping her eight-year-old orphaned grandchild Diego.[59] In 1627 the widower Cristóbal Esteban had three orphaned grandchildren living with him.[60] The last was a fairly prosperous household, but kin loyalty compelled many families to become foster parents of orphaned relatives even when they presumably could ill afford the expense.

Many solitary individuals and childless couples, out of a desire for companion-
ship as well as love of family, became foster parents of their orphaned nieces,
nephews, and grandchildren. For example, the widow Mari Vicenta seems to
have lived alone before opening her home to an orphaned niece and nephew.[61]

Besides adoption by a host family, another method for providing for orphans
and half-orphans was to place them under the supervision of a guardian. Guardianship in Castilian law was designed to protect the person and property of
individuals who by reason of age or other conditions were not fully competent
to act on their own behalf, and who had no father to do it for them. In accordance
with this precept, the guardian had to be someone who *did* possess the requisite
physical, mental, and legal abilities to exercise the *patria potestas* (parental
authority).[62]

The famous late-thirteenth-century Castilian *Siete partidas* (or *Partidas*) specified that the preferred guardian should be the person designated in the parent's
will.[63] This was normally the surviving parent, or if both parents were dead,
another close relative, usually an uncle. In 1564, for example, Domingo Martínez was the guardian of a niece whose father had died.[64] Although guardians
could be of either sex, males were far more likely than females to be entrusted
with the care of an orphan or half-orphan. In fact, 89 percent of the guardians
listed in my fifteen-village database were men. Only 6 percent were officially
classified as *viejos*, but as we have indicated earlier, the *viejos* appear to have
been grossly undercounted, and it is quite possible that the elderly represented
far more than 6 percent of guardians.

Because feeding and clothing a child could be troublesome and expensive,
guardians, even when close relatives, did not necessarily welcome their orphaned
kin into their households. Instead, many guardians sent their charges out to work
as life-cycle servants in another household or even in a different village. In that
way the guardians could obtain financial advantage from what otherwise might
have been an unwelcome expense. For example, Agustín Díaz, who was the
guardian of twelve-year-old Francisca Pedrera, sent her away from his village
to work in the city of Ávila.[65]

Poverty, Old-Age Care, Inheritance, and Dowries

Not all old people were poor, by any means, but the elderly rich were com-
paratively rare in Golden Age Castilian village society. In the history of aging,
there is a close association of old age with poverty. The *Siete partidas* considered the elderly to be poor by virtue of their age and accompanying physical
debility.[66] Unfortunately, at this point my database does not include enough
economic information about *viejos* to permit statistical analysis. There is ample
documentary evidence, however, indicating that old people in early modern Castilian villages tended to be poor. A census of Herreruela (Cáceres) from 1586
contains many examples: Catalina Alonso, "old, widowed, and very poor";
María Salgada, "old, widowed, and very poor"; Gil Domínguez, "old and poor";

and María Domínguez, "old, widowed, and very poor." In fact, *everybody* in this village labeled old was classified as either poor or very poor.[67]

Because old age was so often synonymous with poverty, early modern villagers were justifiably concerned about what would happen to them in their declining years. As we have seen, the elderly were often (not to say usually) taken in by their children or other relatives. Providing assistance to aged parents or other kinfolk was perceived to be a familial responsibility not requiring a quid pro quo. To be sure, insofar as they were physically able, the old folks in the household (along with children and everybody else) shared in both domestic chores and the tasks of field, flocks, and other familial economic enterprises. This participation in household activities was not considered to be payment for services rendered. The long-term care of one's parents (and to a lesser degree to other relatives) was thought of as the honorable thing to do, even if it entailed personal sacrifice. The topic was (and remains even in today's world) a complex one with myriad overtones. It was tacitly understood that since the parents had supported their children when they were weak and vulnerable during early life, the children would reciprocate by supporting their parents when they were similarly weak and vulnerable in old age.[68]

Villagers approaching old age did not have to rely solely upon the sense of familial responsibility to ensure that they would be cared for in their declining years. They could also use property transfers (inheritance, gifts, and dowries) to bind their children (or other kin) more securely to their obligation to provide shelter and sustenance. The question of inheritance is crucially important to understanding the rural world, because rural people needed property (land, livestock, and tools) for the agro-pastoral activities to support themselves and their families. The topic is exceedingly complex and is worthy of book-length treatment on its own. Here we can merely touch the surface of a highly important topic that has yet to receive the scholarly attention that it deserves.[69]

Inheritance in Castile was solidly based upon Roman law. The late-medieval *Partidas* faithfully followed the Justinian Code, a Roman heritage reiterated in the *Laws of Toro* (1505), which remained the basic law governing Castilian inheritance until the nineteenth century. But despite the longevity and hypothetical uniformity of the Roman heritage, there were significant regional and class differences in the transmission of property from generation to generation. In theory, the Romano-Castilian system provided for an equitable division of an estate between heirs. But actually, the law allowed considerable latitude in apportioning shares. Four-fifths of the estate formed what was called the *legítima*, of which two-thirds (i.e., 66⅔% of the 80%) had to be divided equally among all legal heirs (legitimate children if living, otherwise grandchildren or parents). The remaining one-third (i.e., 33⅓% of the 80%), called a *mejora*, could be added to the share of a child, or could be combined with the one-fifth of the estate that could be freely bequeathed, to form a *mayorazgo*, or entailed estate.[70]

Egalitarian (or, at least quasi-egalitarian) inheritance practices encouraged sons to leave the paternal household when they married, thus creating new nuclear families. Within this context, some parents sought to enhance their chances for good treatment in retirement by promising an extra-generous share of their property to the child that they considered the most obedient, respectful, and generous. Allyson Poska has found that parents in early modern Galicia (the northwestern part of the Crown of Castile-León) drew up written contracts providing generous gifts, dowries, and inheritances for favored children *explicitly in exchange for long-term care*.[71] It seems likely that a broader study of notarial records would find quite similar practices in other parts of Castile. We know that it was a widespread Castilian custom for elderly parents to give the usufruct of their lands to whichever child took them in. Rewards for long-term care could also be settled through wills executed near the end of life, giving that child who had provided the most assistance a larger portion than that given to his or her siblings.[72]

CONCLUSION

It is always misleading to make broad statements, because generalizations tend to mask even the most kaleidoscopic diversity. The elderly in early modern Castilian villages were certainly a heterogeneous group. Our evidence shows that they were present in all socioeconomic categories and in all household types. We have considerable evidence nevertheless of a close association between old age and poverty, even according to the definitions used in preindustrial times, when nearly all rural people had a living standard that we would regard as abject poverty. The precariousness of normal rural life, greatly exacerbated by the debility of old age, caused many elderly people to seek guarantees of good care in their declining years by selectively distributing their property among their children through gifts, dowries, and extra inheritance shares. To be sure, offering rewards for good care did not always bring the expected results. All the same, the practice provides an interesting nuance about the relations between the old and the young, and between parents and their children.

Contemporary attitudes toward the rural Castilian elderly were as diverse as the elderly themselves, often expressing opposite or even contradictory characteristics: healthy and infirm; wise and foolish; miserly and generous; and wealthy and impoverished. Our folkloric, literary, and documentary evidence, however, indicates that the elderly tended to rank among the most economically disadvantaged in Golden Age Castilian villages.

NOTES

1. David E. Vassberg, *Land and Society in Golden Age Castile* (Cambridge, Eng.: Cambridge University Press, 1984), 1–3; and Vassberg, *The Village and the Outside World in Golden Age Castile: Mobility and Migration in Everyday Rural Life* (Cambridge, Eng.: Cambridge University Press, 1996), 25–66.

2. Sheldon J. Watts, *A Social History of Western Europe, 1450–1720: Tensions and Solidarities Among Rural People* (London: Hutchinson University Library, 1984), 37; and Francisco Chacón Jiménez, "Nuevas tendencias de la demografía histórica en España: Las investigaciones sobre historia de la familia," *Boletín de la Asociación de Demografía Histórica* 9, no. 2 (1991): 79–98.

3. Many Hispanists have recognized this. Perhaps the best example is Noël Salomon, *Recherches sur le thème paysan dans la "comedia" au temps de Lope de Vega* (Bordeaux, Fr.: Feret et Fils, 1965), subsequently published as *Lo villano en el teatro del Siglo de Oro*, trans. Beatriz Chenot (Madrid: Editorial Castalia, 1985). Another is Ricardo del Arco y Garay, *La sociedad española en las obras de Lope de Vega* (Madrid: Real Academia Española, 1941); and del Arco, "La ínfima levadura social en las obras de Cervantes," in *Estudios de historia social de España*, vol. 2, ed. Carmelo Viñas y Mey (Madrid: Consejo Superior de Investigaciones Científicas, 1952), 209–290. To give a personal example, I cited literary examples dozens of times in my recent *Village and Outside World*.

4. Miguel de Cervantes Saavedra, *El ingenioso hidalgo Don Quixote de la Mancha* (Madrid: Editorial Castalia, 1978) (Part 1 first published in 1605, and Part 2 in 1615), Part 1: 1.

5. Cited in Luis S. Granjel, *Los ancianos en la España de los Austria* (Salamanca, Sp.: Universidad Pontificia, 1996), 22, 23.

6. *Relaciones histórico-geográfico-estadísticas de los pueblos de España hecho por iniciativa de Felipe II: Provincia de Madrid; Reino de Toledo; Ciudad Real*, ed. Carmelo Viñas y Mey and Ramón Paz (Madrid: Consejo Superior de Investigaciones Científicas, 1949–1971).

7. See copies of the questionnaires in the published volumes for Madrid, Toledo (primera parte), and Ciudad Real.

8. For Campillo, see *Relaciones: Toledo*, primera parte, 206; for San Martín, *Relaciones: Toledo*, segunda parte, 1: 380; and for Ballesteros, *Relaciones: Ciudad Real*, 120.

9. The villages (selected because of the quality of household data) are Adobezo (Soria); Alberguería de la Sierra (Salamanca); Caballar (Segovia); Castellanos (Burgos); Castrillo de Rucios (Burgos); Cerveriza (Soria); Ciruelos (Segovia); Compludo (León); Frandovínez (Burgos); Gallinero (Soria); Marzales (Valladolid); Miranda de Duero (Soria); Peñaflor de Hornija (Valladolid); Priaranza del Bierzo (León); and Santovenia de Campos (Palencia?). I have not located the last village on a modern map (it may have disappeared). The province is an educated guess, based upon the "Campos" in the name and the neighboring villages mentioned in the census. There are 2,543 individuals in my fifteen-village database. The censuses are found in the Archivo General de Simancas, Expedientes de Hacienda, Legajos 45, 61, 65, 66, 81, 155, 274, 281, 316, 321, 356, 363, and 371 [hereafter, AGS, EH].

10. Nearly 90 percent of individuals in the database (2,281 out of 2,543) have either a precise or an approximate age reported. Precise ages (which we must view with great distrust because they were frequently rounded off) were given for only 408 individuals (i.e., 16%) of the 2,543 in my database.

11. For Spain, see Pedro Carasa Soto,"Vieillesse et pauvreté en Castille, 1750–1900," paper presented at the Tenth International Congress of Economic History, Louvain, Belgium, 1990; María Antonia Fernández Ochoa, *Luarca y la Tierra de Valdés, 1650–1830: población, sociedad y economía* (Luarca-Valdés, Sp.: Ayuntamiento de Valdés, 1995), 79; and Benjamín García Sanz, *Los campesinos en la sociedad rural tradicional: marco*

institucional, producción, presión fiscal y población (Tierra de Curiel y Tierra de Peñafiel, siglos XVI–XVIII) (Valladolid, Sp.: Diputación Provincial, 1989), 371–374. For France, see Antoinette Fauve-Chamoux, "Aging in a Never-Empty Nest: The Elasticity of the Stem Family," in *Aging and Generational Relations over the Life Course: A Historical and Cross-Cultural Perspective*, ed. Tamara K. Hareven (Berlin: Walter de Gruyter, 1996), 77–78.

12. Vassberg, *Village*, 14–18.

13. Incidentally, male and female *viejos* were about equal in number (respectively 36 and 37).

14. On this point, see Luis de Hoyos Sáinz and Nieves de Hoyos Sancho, *Manual de folklore: La vida popular tradicional en España* (Madrid: Colegio Universitario, Ediciones Istmo, 1985), 424–431; and Mary J. Dobson, *Contours of Death and Disease in Early Modern England* (Cambridge, Eng.: Cambridge University Press, 1997).

15. *Relaciones: Madrid*, 237, 420.

16. *Relaciones: Ciudad Real*, 202; and *Madrid*, 15.

17. *Relaciones: Ciudad Real*, 337, 278–279.

18. *Relaciones: Ciudad Real*, 587, 210.

19. One league measures about 3½ miles.

20. *Relaciones: Toledo*, segunda parte, 2: 149–150.

21. *Refranero clásico*, 27.

22. *Cuentos folklóricos*, 95, 127.

23. *Refranero español*, 434, 472.

24. *Refranero español*, 31.

25. *Refranero clásico*, 31, 60; *Refranero español*, 472.

26. *Refranero español*, 37, 472, 473.

27. *Cuentos folklóricos*, 262.

28. *Refranero español*, 472.

29. *Refranero clásico*, 123, 166. The cited saints were preadolescent brothers martyred in fourth-century Spain.

30. *Refranero español*, 28, 48, 55.

31. See respectively, *Refranero clásico*, 101, and *Refranero español*, 472.

32. The references are to Lope's *El cuerdo en su casa* and to Gracián's *Agudeza y arte del ingenio*, and to *Oraculo manual y arte de prudencia*, all cited in *Cuentos folklóricos*, 91–93.

33. Examples cited in Granjel, *Ancianos*, 29, 30.

34. Granjel, *Ancianos*, 33–35.

35. Granjel, *Ancianos*, 133–135.

36. Granjel, *Ancianos*, 137 (emphasis added).

37. Primary occupations are given for 45.2 percent and secondary occupations for 39.7 percent

38. As a primary occupation, 73 percent were dependants, and as a secondary occupation the figure was 86 percent "Dependents."

39. Castilian law regarded women in general, and particularly *old* women, to be weak creatures in need of assistance, according to María del Pilar Rábade Obradó, "La mujer trabajadora en los ordenamientos de Cortes, 1258–1505," in *El trabajo de las mujeres en la Edad Media hispana*, ed. Angela Muñoz Fernández and Cristina Segura Graíño (Madrid: Asociación Cultural Al-Mudayna, 1988), 124, 139.

40. This includes not only 28 widowed persons, but also 16 previously widowed (but

remarried at the time of the census), and 1 person presumed widowed. There were 73 *viejos* in the sample.

41. Only 17 percent of ever-widowed persons in my database were *viejos*, but we must remember that the elderly were surely far more numerous than the 4.1 percent labeled *viejos*. If we extrapolate consistent with the plausible estimate of 10 percent elderly, we get 42.5 percent of widowed persons presumed to be elderly.

42. Twenty-two of 28 widowed *viejos* in the database (78.6%) were women. By way of comparison, in late-eighteenth-century Valdés (in Spain's Cantabrian region) roughly 70 percent of widowed persons were females. See Fernández Ochoa, *Luarca*, 79, 83.

43. Mariló Vigil, *La vida de las mujeres en los siglos XVI y XVII* (Madrid: Siglo Veintiuno, 1986), 195–200; and Heath Dillard, *Daughters of the Reconquest: Women in Castilian Town Society, 1100–1300* (Cambridge, Eng.: Cambridge University Press, 1984), 61, 64–65.

44. Figure obtained by adding the percentages of 2nd, 3d, and 4th marriages to the twice- and thrice-widowed.

45. Ángel Gómez-Cabrero and María Soledad Fernández de la Iglesia, "Familia y fecundidad en Mocejón (1660–1719). Una reconstrucción de familias," *Boletín de la Asociación de Demografía Histórica* 9, no. 1 (1991): 73–75; Bartolomé García Jiménez, *Demografía rural andaluza: Rute en el Antiguo Régimen* (Córdoba, Sp.: Diputación Provincial, 1987), 71–72; Alfonso Rodríguez Grajera, *La Alta Extremadura en el siglo XVII: Evolución demográfica y estructura agraria* (Cáceres, Sp.: Universidad de Extremadura, 1990), 47–48; Ramón Lanza García, *La población y el crecimiento económico de Cantabria en el Antiguo Régimen* (Madrid: Universidad Autónoma de Madrid, and Servicio de Publicaciones de la Universidad de Cantabria, 1991), 327–333; Laureano M. Rubio Pérez, *La Bañeza y su Tierra, 1650–1850: Un modelo de sociedad rural leonesa: Los hombres, los recursos y los comportamientos sociales* (León, Sp.: Universidad de León, 1987), 120; and García Sanz, *Campesinos*, 331.

46. Gómez-Cabrero and Fernández de la Iglesia, "Familia y fecundidad," 74–75.

47. From my fifteen-village database. To be precise: 2.3% extended; 0.5% multiple; 5% pluri-conjugal; 0.9% *both* pluri-conjugal *and* extended; and 2.6% nonfamily. Pluri-conjugal households contained resident children from previous marriages.

48. This was in Bormujos (Seville), according to a census in AGS, EH, 237. The proverb cited above can be found in *Refranero español*, 131.

49. The census of Villardefrades is in AGS, EH, 433.

50. The Castellanos census is in AGS, EH, 61–23.

51. The census for Villoria is in AGS, EH, 368–7.

52. The census of Tamarón is in AGS, EH, 442–2. The tradition of familial assistance is described by María Ángeles Hernández Bermejo, *La familia extremeña en los tiempos modernos* (Badajoz, Sp.: Diputación Provincial, 1990), 274–276; and by Ruth Behar, *The Presence of the Past in a Spanish Village: Santa María del Monte* (Princeton, NJ: Princeton University Press, 1986), 94–103.

53. A niece or nephew, for example, might open their home. A concrete example of this was Juan Rodríguez, who had an aunt living with him. See a 1586 census of Fuentepinilla (Soria), in AGS, EH, 42.

54. The Espartinas census is bound in parchment near the end of AGS, EH, 272.

55. The widow lived in Espinosa de la Ribera (León), and the neighboring village was Mataluenga. See a census in AGS, EH, 273. On the topic of kin-servants, see also Vassberg, *Village and Outside World*, 88–89.

56. Hernández Bermejo, *Familia extremeña*, 274–276; and Beatrice Gottlieb, *The Family in theWestern World from the Black Death to the Industrial Age* (Oxford, Eng.: Oxford University Press, 1993), 8, 194–195.

57. This was in Puerto de Santoña (Santander), and the grandfather had a housekeeper to look after the child. See a census in AGS, EH, 368.

58. In this case, the deceased son had been a priest, which possibly explains why the child was with his grandmother rather than his mother. See a census of Espinosa in AGS, EH, 273.

59. This was in Villoruela (Salamanca), according to a census in AGS, EH, 437.

60. Esteban lived in Marzales (Valladolid). One of the grandchildren had lost both parents, while the other two had lost their mother and were seemingly abandoned by their father. In any case, the grandfather's household was a prosperous one, because it included two servants and a son who was in the clergy (but *not* the local parish priest). See a census in AGS, EH, 316.

61. This was in Villar de la Vieja (Salamanca) in 1570, according to a census in AGS, EH, 434–441.

62. The juridical aspects of Castilian guardianship are summarized by M. Sierra Pomares, "Tutela" and "Tutor," vol. 30 of *Enciclopédia jurídica española* (Barcelona, Sp.: Francisco Seix, 1911), 470–481, 489–492; and by Luis Moutón y Ocampo, "Curatela," vol. 6 of *Nueva enciclopédia jurídica*, dir. Carlos-E. Mascareñas (Barcelona, Sp.: Francisco Seix, 1975), 167–169. The *Partidas* code was followed "to the letter" in fifteenth-century Paredes de Nava (Palencia), according to Juan Carlos Martín Cea, *El mundo rural castellano a fines de la Edad Media: El ejemplo de Paredes de Nava en el siglo XV* (Valladolid, Sp.: Junta de Castilla y León, 1991), 340.

63. Sierra Pomares, "Tutela," 473; and Martín Cea, *Mundo rural*, 340–341.

64. This was in Gallinero (Soria), and the niece (from his wife's family) was living with them. See a census in AGS, EH, 281. Almost all censuses that list such information include guardians who are uncles.

65. At the time of the census, incidentally, the young girl had already spent eight months working in Ávila. See a 1654 census of Santa Cruz de Pinares (Ávila) in AGS, EH, 382. Life-cycle service in rural Castile is analyzed in David E. Vassberg, "Life-Cycle Service As a Form of Age-Specific Migration in the 16th and 17th Centuries: Rural Castile As a Case Study," in *Les Migrations internes et à moyenne distance en Europe, 1500–1900*, vol. 1, ed. Antonio Eiras Roel and Ofelia Rey Castelao (Santiago de Compostela, Sp.: Xunta de Galicia, 1994), 385–402.

66. Carmen López Alonso, *La pobreza en la España medieval: Estudio histórico-social* (Madrid: Centro de Publicaciones, Ministerio de Trabajo y Seguridad Social, 1986), 43–44.

67. The Herreruela census is in AGS, EH, 34. On old age and poverty, see also Pedro Carasa Soto, "Vieillesse" and "Las clases populares urbanas y el mundo de la pobreza en Castilla" in *Proceedings of the Congreso Internacional de Historia: El Tratado de Tordesillas y su época* (Tordesillas, Sp.: V Centenario del Tratado de Tordesillas, 1995).

68. Ramón Lanza García, *Población y familia campesina en el Antiguo Régimen: Liébana, siglos XVI–XIX* (Santander, Sp.: Universidad de Cantabria, Ediciones de Librería Estudio, 1988), 124–182; Hernández Bermejo, *Familia extremeña*, 270–276; and Behar, *Presence of the Past*, 97–103.

69. We draw the reader's attention to Máximo García Fernández, *Herencia y patrimonio familiar en la Castilla del Antiguo Régimen (1650–1834): Efectos socioeconóm-*

icos de la muerte y la partición de bienes (Valladolid, Sp.: Universidad de Valladolid, 1995). This work is an excellent study of inheritance and family holdings in Castile. Regrettably, it is limited to the period 1650–1834. Golden Age Castile (encompassing the previous century and a half) has yet to be studied in its own right. Fortunately, much of what García Fernández has to say appears to be also true of Castile's Golden Age.

70. Francisco Chacón Jiménez, "Continuidad de costumbres y transmisión de la propiedad en el sistema familiar castellano, siglos XVI–XVIII," in *Historia social de la familia en España: Aproximación a los problemas de familia, tierra y sociedad en Castilla (ss. XV–XIX)*, ed. Francisco Chacón Jiménez (Alicante, Sp.: Diputación de Alicante/ Instituto de Cultura "Juan Gil-Albert," 1990), 47–59; García Fernández, *Herencia y patrimonio familiar*, 24–30, 143–238; and Margarita María Birriel Salcedo, "Mujeres y familia: Fuentes y metodología," in *Conceptos y metodología en los estudios sobre la mujer*, ed. Bárbara Ozieblo (Málaga, Sp.: Universidad de Málaga, 1992), 58–61.

71. Allyson M. Poska, "The Economics of Aging: Dowry Contracts, Property Exchange, and Parental Care in Early Modern Galicia," paper presented at the Thirtieth Annual Conference of the Society for Spanish and Portuguese Historical Studies, San Diego, California, 1999.

72. Hernández Bermejo, *Familia extremeña*, 270–271; Lanza García, *Población y familia*, 151–158, 163–165; and Behar, *Presence of the Past*, 97–103.

9

Stereotypes and Statistics: Old Women and Accusations of Witchcraft in Early Modern Europe

Alison Rowlands

"The age of witch hunts thought first in terms of old women, just as we do," wrote Erik Midelfort in 1972 in his seminal work on witch hunting in south-western Germany.[1] Keith Thomas and Alan Macfarlane had already reached similar conclusions in their equally important works on England and Essex respectively, with Thomas noting in 1970 that "witches were primarily women, and probably old ones, many of them widowed," and Macfarlane suggesting a year later that "suspected witches were characteristically middle-aged or old."[2] Since then many other historians of early modern witchcraft have reached—or based their work upon—the same conclusion: that old women were tremendously vulnerable to accusations of witchcraft.[3] Lyndal Roper most recently reiterated this idea in a wonderfully thought-provoking article in which she argued that child-witches became the focus of fears about evil in eighteenth-century Germany in what constituted a shift away from an "old symbolic structure of witchcraft" within which old women had been the main locus of contemporary anxiety about witches.[4] Referring to this old symbolic structure, Roper contended that

The witch-hunt as it operated in the sixteenth and seventeenth centuries had offered a clear way of dealing with evil, by locating the source of evil in an old woman. Old women were disproportionately represented amongst the victims of the witch craze; and the old woman was the abiding stereotypical witch.[5]

The idea that old women—who may often also have been poor or widowed—were exceptionally vulnerable to accusations of witchcraft during the early modern period has also been emphasized in Brian Levack's excellent overview text-book of the early modern witch hunts;[6] it also emerges in more general works on gender and widowhood in early modern Europe.[7] It has thus attained the status of what might be described as an accepted orthodoxy among a wide academic audience, ranging from the undergraduate to the professor and beyond the narrow field of witchcraft specialists.

Starting from the premise that it is good historical practice periodically to revisit and question such orthodoxies, and in the light of recent research done by witchcraft scholars who have postulated new explanatory frameworks for witchcraft accusations, this chapter will reexamine the stereotype of the witch as old woman in the sixteenth and seventeenth centuries.[8] In those centuries legal prosecutions for the crime of witchcraft in Europe reached their all-time high and generated the most evidence about witchcraft beliefs among both the elites and the lower orders. Did contemporaries imagine that old women were more at risk of being thought of as witches by their neighbors than other age-gender groups? If they did, does the statistical evidence on age culled from the records of witch trials suggest that this belief translated into a much greater vulnerability of old women to formal accusations of witchcraft? In exploring answers to these questions, I will argue that the witch-as-old-woman stereotype is supported by literary and anecdotal evidence, but that statistical evidence on the ages of accused witches shows that a far broader range of people of all ages and both genders were formally accused of witchcraft before Europe's courts by their neighbors. There was thus a significant disjuncture between the image and the reality of the identity of early modern Europe's accused witches, which has been rendered largely indistinct through the tremendous power that the witch-as-old-woman stereotype has exerted on witchcraft scholarship. In this chapter I will critically examine the existing historiography and draw on my own research into witch trials in the Lutheran German imperial city of Roth-enburg ob der Tauber in order to demonstrate and problematize this disjuncture and suggest a new set of questions we might most fruitfully ask about the connections between age and the vulnerability to accusation of early modern Europe's alleged witches.

Rothenburg ob der Tauber and its rural hinterland experienced a restrained pattern of witch trials between the mid-sixteenth and early eighteenth centuries as a result of a lack of enthusiasm for the formal prosecution of alleged witches on the part of both the lower orders of the area and the city's secular and ecclesiastical elites.[9] Some twenty-eight cases involving allegations of maleficent or diabolic witchcraft were tried in the city during this period, involving a total of sixty-five individuals who were tried as witches or questioned formally on suspicion of witchcraft: only three of them—all women—were ultimately exe-cuted.[10] There were no chain-reaction witch panics in Rothenburg, during which suspects were tortured into confessing that they were witches and naming their accomplices, and which resulted in large-scale executions; such witch panics were anyway the exception rather than the rule throughout early modern Europe.[11] Rothenburg, then, offers the chance to examine the alleged witch under relatively normal circumstances: where there was a trickle rather than a flood of formal trials and where executions were kept to a bare minimum. Rothenburg also offers exceptionally rich sources for those allegations of witchcraft that were formally tried: several seventeenth-century cases, for example, run to hundreds of pages. Such detailed sources best enable the historian to trace the life histories—and thus the possible ages—of alleged witches, and to establish the complex and often lengthy processes of interpersonal conflict that lay behind the making of witchcraft accusations against particular individuals.[12]

THE WITCH-AS-OLD-WOMAN STEREOTYPE

Anecdotal and demonological evidence suggests that early modern people from across the social spectrum did indeed seem to think that old women were particularly vulnerable to being imagined as witches. In commenting on the outbreak of witch trials in the Electorate of Trier in 1590, for example, Cologne city councilor Hermann Weinsberg noted that "in this manner [i.e., by means of witch trials] one can most rapidly get rid of old women and hateful people."[13] Tyrolean physician Hippolytus Guarinoni also devoted particular attention to the reasons old women became witches in his *Von Grewel der Verwüstung menschlichen Geschlechts* of 1610, explaining that

they are so unfairly despised and rejected by everyone, enjoy no-one's protection, much less their affection and loyalty. . . . so that it is no wonder that, on account of poverty and need, misery and faint-heartedness, they often . . . give themselves to the devil and practise witchcraft.[14]

The belief that old women were at greater risk of being associated with witchcraft also seems to have been held lower down the social hierarchy. For example, in his excellent account of witchcraft persecutions in early modern Bavaria, Wolfgang Behringer noted that "in many cases the aged suspects themselves are recorded as complaining that every old woman was now under suspicion."[15] In support of this point he cited the example of Anna Widmann, a seventy-year-old woman from Hemau, who said at her trial in 1618 "that the children call all old people witches."[16]

The idea that older women were more likely than other people to be witches was an even more marked feature of early modern demonological writing, although it was emphasized most strongly in the works of skeptics who argued against the necessity of witch trials.[17] The most famous skeptic to write in this vein was Johann Weyer, court physician to Duke William II of Berg, Jülich, and Cleves, in his 1563 demonology, *De praestigiis daemonum*, in which he made the witch-as-old-woman stereotype central to his argument against the reality of witchcraft and against the need to prosecute and execute witches.[18] Weyer explained that the devil exploited the inconstancy of women in general and of old women in particular in order to delude them into believing that they had flown to witches' dances, had had sex with demons, and had worked maleficium, when none of these events had actually happened. According to Weyer, witches were women who

being by reason of their sex inconstant and uncertain in faith, and by their age not sufficiently settled in their minds, are much more subject to the devil's deceits, who, insinuating himself into their imagination, whether waking or sleeping, introduces all sorts of shapes, cleverly stirring up the humours and the spirits in this trickery.[19]

They therefore constituted no real threat to either the well-being of their neighbors or to the security of Christendom and did not need to be formally tried for their imaginary crimes.

Weyer's idea of the witch as a harmless, melancholic old woman, whose gender and age rendered her mind particularly susceptible to the devil's influence, was taken up by later skeptical writers. In 1591, for example, German demonologist Johann Georg Godelmann argued that the devil had particular power over "worn-out, stupid, ignorant old women, who were badly instructed in the Christian faith and reeling in their understanding."[20] This idea was also central to skeptical writing in England, with Reginald Scot noting in 1584 that

One such sort of such as are said to bee witches, are women which be commonly old, lame, bleare-eied, pale, fowle, and full of wrinkles; poore, sullen, superstitious, and papists; or such as knowe no religion: in whose drousie minds the divell hath gotten a fine seat: so as, what mischeefe, mischance, calamitie, or slaughter is brought to passe, they are easilie persuaded the same is done by themselves; imprinting in their minds an earnest and constant imagination thereof. They are leane and deformed, shewing melancholie in their faces, to the horror of all that see them.[21]

Like Scot, English skeptic John Gaule utilized a very similar image of the alleged witch in 1646 in *Select Cases of Conscience Touching Witches and Witchcraft* in order to criticize the credulity of people who were too eager to suspect "every old woman with a wrinkled face, a furr'd brow, a hairy lip, a gobber tooth, a squint eye, a squeaking voyce, or a scolding tongue" of witchcraft.[22]

The skeptics' argument that alleged witches were nothing more than deluded old women who needed better religious instruction and medical help rather than to face the full rigors of the law was, of course, intended to underline the absurdity and cruelty of witch trials to their contemporaries and also to ridicule what they saw as the popular credulity and superstition which underpinned the whole system of belief in witchcraft.[23] However, this argument may have had other, less positive effects. The descriptions given by the skeptics of old women almost invariably descended to the level of uncomplimentary caricature, stressing as they consistently did their physical ugliness, mental weakness, lack of piety, susceptibility to temptation, and tendency toward irascibility. This caricaturization may well—albeit unwittingly—have added support to (as well as reflected) a more general strain of early modern misogyny that was directed particularly against old women and which can also be found in contemporary ridicule and hostility directed against widows and allegedly sexually predatory older women.[24] Moreover, because it suited their overarching argument against witch trials to emphasize the witch-as-old-woman stereotype, skeptical writing probably did much to strengthen this stereotype and consequently paid relatively little attention to those accused witches who did not fit so neatly with its age and gender profile.

The point about this demonological stereotype was that it was just that: a stereotype. We need to be cautious about assuming that it translated in a straightforward manner into actual accusations of witchcraft against aged women, given that relatively little is yet known about the influence of particular demonologies either on the development of popular beliefs or on actual trial procedure in individual cases. As Ian Bostridge points out,

We should not confuse the business of the prosecution of witches . . . with either the "discourse of witchcraft" (narrowly and unproblematically defined as a body of texts) or the belief in witchcraft (often parlously psychologistic, individualistic and awkwardly placed for historical analysis). There is no universally valid connection between these three, although they can overlap.[25]

Malcolm Gaskill has also made the point that we should not assume unproblematic connections between prosecution, discourse, and belief in relation to witchcraft. Gaskill tested the conclusions of Thomas and Macfarlane "that witches in England were usually female, economocially marginal, elderly and rarely had living husbands" against ecclesiastical and secular court records from early modern Kent.[26] Gaskill concluded that, while English trial pamphlets, like demonological writings, tended to stress the witch-as-old-woman stereotype in imagery as well as text, formal accusations of witchcraft in Kent were made against a wider and more varied range of suspects and on the basis of an almost infinite range of social conflicts. His conclusions concur with much of the recent work done on witchcraft accusations in early modern Germany, from which it has long been clear that "every form of conflict lends itself in principle to a transference onto the level of witchcraft,"[27] and that the range of witchcraft suspects was correspondingly potentially equally broad.

These findings should thus make us cautious in accepting too uncritically textual descriptions or pictorial portrayals of witches as old women, without testing as stringently as possible the degree to which this stereotype was, in fact, reflected in the reality of actual accusations of witchcraft. As Gaskill notes, quoting Bob Scribner,

witch-stereotypes "came to have a cultural life of their own among both the learned and the unlearned [who] could both believe in the broad stereotype of witchcraft, while being wholly sceptical of its particular application to their own circumstances."[28]

We can perhaps discern a tension between the power of the witch-as-old-woman stereotype and an awareness that a far wider range of people might plausibly be accused of witchcraft even in the few examples of contemporary belief about witchcraft that I offered earlier. For instance, Hermann Weinsberg mentioned old women and "hateful people" as those most likely to become caught up in witch trials: the latter category could cover anyone believed to be malevolent by their neighbors,[29] while Anna Widmann suggested that old people in general rather than old women in particular were at greatest risk of being called witches by children.[30] Moreover, after explaining why old women might give themselves to the devil, the physician Guarinoni went on to say that it was hardly surprising that they did so, given that "strong men, rich people, youngsters, and those of high social status often did the same and worse with far less justification."[31] His entire passage can thus be read as implying that anyone, regardless of age or gender, could be accused of witchcraft during the early modern period, a point that the following discussion of the statistics that we have on accused witches categorized according to these two variables will demonstrate was, in fact, the case.

AGE STATISTICS OF ACCUSED WITCHES: PROBLEMS AND INTERPRETATIONS

Age statistics of accused witches taken from the records of witch trials obviously offer the historian the best way to test whether the witch-as-old-woman stereotype was reflected in the reality of formal accusations. In all too many cases, however, the trial records simply do not give us this information. Macfarlane noted this problem in 1970, commenting that, while contemporary demonologists like Reginal Scot and William Perkins "suggested that witches were, almost without exception, 'old,' " in most instances the indictments for specific cases did not record the ages of suspects. Despite the fact that Macfarlane's conclusions about accused witches' ages in early modern Essex have often been reproduced and referred to by other historians,[32] he was able to establish the ages of only fifteen alleged witches who were tried in 1645: two were aged forty to forty-nine; three, fifty to fifty-nine; seven, sixty to sixty-nine; and three, eighty to eighty-nine.[33] This, with other impressionistic evidence from pamphlets, led Macfarlane to suggest that "in Essex, the likeliest age for a witch was between fifty and seventy."[34] Erik Midelfort, another historian whose pioneering work on witch trials in southwestern Germany has done much to suggest that old women were especially vulnerable to accusations of witchcraft,[35] has on closer inspection a similar paucity of statistical information on accused witches' ages. Midelfort provided tables of the ages of child witches from seventeenth-century Calw and of the percentages of adults and children executed for witchcraft in seventeenth-century Würzburg,[36] and also referred in passing to the ages of certain self-confessed and accused witches, which ranged from five to eighty years.[37] However, his book offered no overall statistics on the

Table 9.1
Percentages of Witches Aged Over Fifty Tried in Various Parts of Early Modern Europe and New England

Author	Place	Number under 50	Number Over 50	Percent Over 50
Villette	Dept. Nord, France	23	24	51%
Demos	Salem, Mass.	69	49	42%
Monter	Basel	1	9	90%
	Freiburg	2	7	78%
	Geneva	24	71	75%
	Valangin	2	7	78%
	Val de Travers	6	12	66%
	TOTAL	35	106	75%
Macfarlane	Essex	2	13	87%
Bever	Württemberg	13	16	55%
Muchembled	Cambresis	6	7	54%

Source: Edward Bever, "Old Age and Witchcraft in Early Modern Europe," in *Old Age in Pre-Industrial Society*, ed. Peter N. Stearns (New York: Holmes and Meier, 1982), 150–190.

percentage of old women accused of witchcraft in southwestern Germany between 1562 and 1684, doubtless because the sources did not consistently provide adequate information on this issue and because he was dealing with such a large number of trials.[38]

Appended to an essay written in 1982, Edward Bever's table (Table 9.1) remains the most extensive collection of statistics on the ages of accused witches available.[39] It is worth closer critical attention for this reason and also because it forms the basis of Brian Levack's table of ages of accused witches in his textbook, *The Witch-Hunt in Early Modern Europe*, which is much used in undergraduate courses on the history of witchcraft.[40] In it, Bever compares the numbers of accused witches under and over fifty years old in various areas for which statistics were then known.

According to Bever's analysis, people over the age of fifty were significantly overrepresented among the accused witches in relation to the proportion of the overall population that they constituted. He therefore concluded that witchcraft accusation was linked in important ways to old age in sixteenth- and seventeenth-century Europe and New England and particularly to the onset of menopause in women and to the gender- and class-specific problems that the aging process posed for women of the lower orders during this period.[41]

Bever's table provides a valuable starting point for thinking about possible connections between age and vulnerability to witchcraft accusations, but we need to treat it with a certain degree of caution rather than just accept it at face value. To begin with, it is based mainly on known ages of suspected witches, so we are left with a considerable dark figure for the alleged witches of each area about whose ages we know nothing. For Essex, for example, Bever has cited only the 15 women of known age taken by Macfarlane from the 1645 assizes. They formed part of a larger group of 37 tried at this time; the ages of the other 22 suspects are unknown.[42] Should we assume that these 22 were of roughly the same age-distribution as the known 15, or should the percentage of those over fifty be calculated on the basis of 15 out of a total of 37 suspects, which gives the lower figure of 41 percent? Moreover, the 37 suspects tried in 1645 constituted only a fraction of the 314 people known to have been prosecuted under the witchcraft statutes between 1560 and 1680 at the Essex Assize and Quarter Sessions courts. These 314 in turn constituted two-thirds of those known to have been accused of witchcraft in early modern Essex, but this still leaves us with a significant number who were prosecuted at borough and ecclesiastical courts in the county.[43] The 15 alleged witches of known age from 1645, therefore, were merely the tip of an iceberg of accused individuals. Below the waterline we know relatively little about the ages of suspected Essex witches, and we should be wary of assuming that they reflected proportionally the age-range of the fifteen middle-aged and elderly suspects from 1645, particularly as Bever himself suggested that it may have been more likely that older rather than younger suspects would have had their ages recorded by clerks, because they were more noteworthy.[44] It is thus unclear from Bever's table whether there really was significant regional variation in the proportion of accused witches fifty years old and above, or whether the variation in these figures simply reflects the different percentages of known ages of alleged witches for the various areas listed.

Another problem with Bever's table is that, while he is keen to use it to support his argument that vulnerability to accusations of witchcraft was linked to the onset of menopause in women, he does not break his age-statistics down according to gender. Neither does Levack in his reproduction of Bever's figures, although he does provide a separate table a few pages earlier showing that women dominated the total numbers of witches prosecuted in some of the same areas, making up 81 percent of those accused in the Department of the Nord, 78 percent of those accused in New England, 76 percent of those accused in Geneva, 93 percent of those accused in Essex, and 82 percent of those accused in southwestern Germany.[45] The exact relationships between age and gender are not tabulated, however, and Levack's discussion of the connections between old age and witchcraft is couched entirely in terms of "the most common stereotype of the witch, that of an old woman," thereby leaving the reader with the impression that all old witches were female.[46]

In some instances, of course, accusations of witchcraft *were* gender-specific: all 37 of Macfarlane's witches from the Essex Assizes of 1645 were women.[47] However, in other cases a closer look at the individual authors' own figures

Table 9.2
Ages and Genders of 165 People Accused As Witches During the Salem Witchcraft Outbreak for Whom Minimal Information Is Available (1692)

Age	Male	Female	Total
Under 20	6	18	24
21-30	3	7	10
31-40	3	8	11
41-50	6	18	24
51-60	5	23	28
61-70	4	8	12
Over 70	3	6	9
Total	30	88	118

Source: John Demos, "Underlying Themes in the Witchcraft of Seventeenth-Century New England," *American Historical Review* 75 (1970): 1311–1326.

shows that some of the old witches were old men. For example, John Demos's analysis of the ages and genders of accused Salem witches reads as in Table 9.2.[48]

Demos's more detailed analysis showed that, while 75.5 percent of the accused witches above fifty years old were women, 24.5 percent of them were men. This is a not inconsiderable proportion and suggests that, just as men made up an average of around 20–25 percent of the total number of witches accused of witchcraft in many parts of Europe,[49] they probably constituted the same overall proportion of old witches. Moreover, while Demos concluded that the Salem witches "were predominantly married or widowed women, between the ages of forty-one and sixty," his analysis showed that a not inconsiderable proportion of all the women accused of witchcraft were forty years old and below (37.5 percent).[50] By dividing the Salem suspects according to the ten-year band into which their ages fell, then, as well as by their gender, Demos showed that the range of ages of accused witches was much wider than the witch-as-old-woman stereotype would have us believe. Bever chose to organize the statistical material in his overview table (Table 9.1) around the age of fifty because he wanted to emphasize the apparent importance of menopause in explaining women's greater vulnerability to accusations of witchcraft, although he in fact suggested in his essay that menopause during this period began at the age of forty.[51] However, when Bever also categorized ages in the different regions in ten-year bands in subsequent tables in the appendix to his essay, the tables showed the much wider range of ages from which suspected witches might plausibly be drawn.[52]

I have attempted to tabulate my Rothenburg material using the same gender and age-range categories as Demos did for Salem.[53] In Rothenburg no exact age was recorded for an adult witch until 1629, although this became fairly standard

Table 9.3
Ages of Alleged Witches in Rothenburg ob der Tauber Which Can Be Established
with Relative Certainty (1549–1709)

Age-Range	Male	Female
Under 20	5 (youngest = 6 years old)	7 (youngest = 8 years old)
21-30	3	5
31-40	2	3
41-50	4	4
51-60	3	8
61-70	1	1
Over 70	1 (oldest = c. 88 years old)	1 (oldest = 88 years old)
Total	19 (from total of 19 alleged male witches)	29 (from total of 46 alleged female witches)

Source: Alison Rowlands, Narratives of Witchcraft in Early Modern Germany: Fabrication, Feud and Fantasy (Manchester: Manchester University Press, forthcoming), Appendix I.

practice thereafter.[54] Before then, however, it is often possible to establish roughly the probable ages of alleged adult witches from their own testimony (about their ages at marriage, the ages of their husbands, the numbers of children they had had, and so on); the testimony of neighbors about them; and the presence of married offspring in trials as either co-accused witches or accusers.[55] The ages of self-confessed child witches were recorded from the first time they appeared in Rothenburg's records (1587) because the issues of the validity of their testimony and of their legal treatment were so closely linked to their ages.[56] I have included self-confessed witches—most of whom were children or teenagers—in my analysis, because the fact that they were arrested or formally questioned on suspicion of witchcraft showed that contemporaries took the possibility that youngsters could be witches perfectly seriously. I do not think that their cases were qualitatively different from those in which adults accused their adult neighbors of witchcraft, as certain other historians of witchcraft seem to believe.[57] I have also included in my tables those people who were called before Rothenburg's councilors for formal questioning on suspicion of witchcraft without subsequently being arrested and prosecuted for witchcraft: The fact that they were suspected and questioned shows that contemporaries believed that they might be witches, while the fact that they did not become the focus of full-scale trials themselves reflected the reluctance of Rothenburg's elites to allow witch trials to get out of hand.[58]

Of the remaining 17 alleged female witches in Rothenburg, another 3 were probably in their late twenties or early thirties, and another 7 in their forties or fifties, resulting in the totals for the broader age ranges displayed in Table 9.3.

The ages of the remaining 7 female witches could have been anywhere from the late twenties to their early sixties, which would probably also add numerical weight to the broad age-range of around thirty to sixty. (See Table 9.4.) Finally,

Table 9.4
Broad Age-Ranges of Alleged Female Witches in Rothenburg ob der Tauber
(1549–1709)

Age-Range	Number of Female Witches
Under 20	7
21-40	11
41-60	19
61-80	1
Over 80	1
Total	39

Source: Alison Rowlands, *Narratives of Witchcraft in Early Modern Germany: Fabrication, Feud and Fantasy* (Manchester: Manchester University Press, forthcoming), Appendix I.

if we look at the female witches for whom age is known with greatest certainty (Table 9.5) and who were accused by other people rather than confessing to witchcraft themselves, we might tentatively conclude that, within the forty-to-sixty age grouping, women fifty years old and above ran a slightly higher risk of becoming the subject of a legal investigation into an allegation of witchcraft.

On the whole, however, I would caution against the interpretation of this statistical data as providing unequivocal support to the idea that old women were—as the witch-as-old-woman stereotype seems to suggest—tremendously vulnerable to accusations of witchcraft. To begin with, although most alleged witches in Rothenburg were female (46 out of 65, or 70.8 percent), more than a quarter were male (19 out of 65, or 29.2 percent).[59] Moreover, despite a bunching of suspects in the forty-to-sixty age range, accused and self-confessed witches came from a wide age-range, from six-year-old self-confessed witch Hans Gackstatt, who claimed he had gone night-flying with his mother in 1587, to 88-year-old Anna Maas, accused in 1673 of having seduced her maidservant into witchcraft.[60] This range of suspects occurred despite the fact that Rothenburg never experienced large-scale episodes of severe witch trials; it was only during such episodes, according to some historians, that one would expect the witch-as-old-woman stereotype to break down and a far more varied range of suspects to be accused.[61] My sense is that early modern people were quite capable of imagining women and men of all ages plausibly as witches at all times, and not simply during episodes of severe persecution when the supply of supposedly "stereotypical" old women allegedly "ran out." To fail to take this heterogeneity of suspected witches into account testifies to the immense influence that the stereotype of the witch-as-old-woman has exerted over the historiography of witchcraft. It also does those alleged witches who were neither female nor particularly old a major disservice, as it seems to suggest that we are judging their experiences in the jails and interrogation chambers of early modern Europe as somehow less valid, less worthy of study, and less comprehensible than those of older women.

Table 9.5
Ages of Women Accused of Witchcraft in Rothenburg ob der Tauber Which Can
Be Established with Greatest Certainty (1549–1709)

Name	Marital Status	Year of Trial Involvement	Age
Barbara Bratsch	Single, maidservant	1652	23
Margaretha Rost	Married	1641	27
Anna Brodt	Married	1587	Late 20s/early 30s
Eva	Married	1627	30/early 30s
Elisabetha Kraft	Married	1602	34-37
Anna Maria Knöspel	Married	1689	50
Anna Schuhmacher	Widow for 20 years	1709	53
Catharina Leimbach	Married	1652	53 or 54
Appolonia Glaitter	Married	1671	56
Margaretha Horn	Married	1652	60
Anna Dieterich	Widow for 2 years	1629	61
Anna Maas	Married	1673	88

Source: Alison Rowlands, *Narratives of Witchcraft in Early Modern Germany: Fabrication, Feud and Fantasy* (Manchester: Manchester University Press, forthcoming), Appendix I.

Second, I think that historians of witchcraft need to think far more carefully about what any bunching of accused witches within the age-range of forty to sixty years might actually mean for the connection between the age and the vulnerability of any particular individual to accusations of witchcraft. This is because the age at which any individual was formally accused of witchcraft in the early modern period was often just the final stage in what had already been a long and complex story of interpersonal tensions between themselves and their neighbors, in the course of which both sides had for years preferred to look to nonlegal methods for mediation of their conflicts.[62] Evidence from many parts of Europe shows that individuals who were ultimately accused of witchcraft had often been reputed as witches among their neighbors for anything from fifteen to forty years by the time they were tried; many would have escaped formal accusation altogether simply by dying before their neighbors ventured to take this risky step against them.[63] A significant proportion of Rothenburg's female witches had lived in their communities as reputed witches for many years before being formally accused of witchcraft. Twenty of the 38 girls and women who were accused of witchcraft there, rather than confessing to witchcraft of their own volition, had preexisting reputations as witches (52.6 percent); when the duration of their reputation was specified by witnesses, it ranged from six to many years, the average being around eighteen years.[64] Instead of focusing too exclusively on the connections between old age and vulnerability to accusations of witchcraft, then, we need to ask a new set of questions about age and aging in relation to alleged witches. At what age might they first have gained reputations as witches and why? How did their reputations develop, and did this development coincide in any significant ways with particular events in their lives and those of their neighbors? Finally, at what age were they most likely to be formally accused of witchcraft by their neighbors and why?[65]

These questions are best answered with the help of detailed trial records by means of which we can try to reconstruct the life stories of alleged witches and their accusers and to elucidate the complex processes of social and psychological interaction between accuser and accused witch over potentially lengthy periods of time. I have attempted such a detailed reconstruction elsewhere.[66] Here I can only offer a few hints about the ages at which reputations for witchcraft were first developed and about the ages at which accusations were finally made against reputed witches. To begin with, we need to be aware of the fact that it was possible for an individual to first gain a reputation as a witch at a surprisingly young age. Witchcraft in early modern Europe was believed to be an art that was passed on by the proficient to those younger than themselves, particularly within families and households. Many women would therefore have first gained a reputation as a witch by simply being born into a family where a parent was already a reputed witch. Marrying into a family of reputed witches or going into service with a mistress who was a reputed witch could also be enough to gain a woman a reputation as a witch by association; again, this would have occurred at a fairly young age, in the teens in the case of going into domestic service and in the twenties in the case of first marriage. Other women could gain reputations as witches as a result of what might be described as almost entirely random factors: because they had the bad luck to be blamed by a neighbor for a misfortune, for example, or—as was more usually the case in Rothenburg and its hinterland villages—because they were too successful at something that was highly valued within their communities (such as dairying) and were deemed to have achieved their success by supernatural means.[67] The first gaining of a reputation for witchcraft, then, may well have been a feature of childhood, adolescence, or early adulthood for many individuals. Whether they ever went on to be formally accused of witchcraft would depend on a variety of factors: their social, marital, and economic status, their relationships with their neighbors, how they coped with their status as a reputed witch, their luck, and their longevity.

Much more attention has been devoted by historians to the question of why women in their forties and above ran a higher risk than other age and gender groups of being accused of witchcraft. Macfarlane suggested that it was more likely for older women to be poor, reliant on their neighbors for material support, and therefore more likely than other age-gender groups to find themselves in the conflict-ridden relationships with their neighbors from which witchcraft accusations might emerge.[68] Midelfort suggested that older women were more likely to be widows and thus vulnerable to witchcraft accusations because they lacked the protection that husbands could provide in communal conflicts.[69] Bever and Lyndal Roper have suggested that older women's vulnerability to accusations of witchcraft was connected in some important way to menopause. Bever postulated that the effects of menopause itself caused certain women to behave in aggressive ways, which had greater potential for conflict with their neighbors,[70] while Roper argued that early modern society was socially and culturally conditioned to view the no-longer fertile bodies of postmenopausal women with particularly strong feelings of horror and revulsion and thus to imagine such women most readily as the maleficent witches who harmed and killed instead of nurturing life.[71] I have critically evaluated these various explanations elsewhere and found none of them entirely convincing.[72] My sense is that the reasons for any individual's vulnerability to an accusation of witchcraft are to be found in the complex dynamics of individual cases, rather than in grand explanatory models such as those listed above. One general clue to the greater vulnerability of women aged forty to sixty to accusations of witchcraft may be found, however, in contemporary ways of thinking about power and its exercise and can be illustrated by way of conclusion with the following example of a witchcraft accusation from Wettringen, one of Rothenburg's hinterland villages, in 1652.[73]

In 1652 Catharina Leimbach, the 53- or 54-year-old wife of the village blacksmith, was accused of witchcraft by her neighbors, the Schürz family. Eight-year-old Barbara Schürz claimed that she had been seduced into witchcraft by Catharina and taken by her to witches' dances, but it was Barbara's stepmother, 38-year-old Eva Schürz, who was the main source of the suspicions raised against the older woman. In addition to believing that Catharina had such power over Barbara that she could spirit the child away from under her parents' noses, Eva believed that Catharina was secretly entering the Schürz household at night in order to steal the milk from Eva's cows so that she could make more butter and cheese than Eva, and that she posed a threat to the well-being of the child with which Eva was pregnant when she made these accusations in 1652.

Various points of significance can be drawn from this case. The first is that, while Catharina was in her fifties when accused, she had had a reputation for being able to work witchcraft (particularly in relation to the magical stealing of milk) for at least eighteen years within Wettringen. It seems to have been Eva's anxieties about her impending childbirth, rather than anything that Catharina had specifically said or done, that finally prompted Eva's formal accusation in 1652. Second, Eva's anxieties about Catharina seem to have revolved around a perception of her power and expertise: her power over Eva's stepdaughter and livestock and her perceived greater success in the important skill of dairying. John Demos and Robin Briggs have both suggested that midlife—the ages of forty to sixty—was imagined by contemporaries as the time during which the possession and exercise of power were deemed to peak. It was therefore perhaps not surprising that anxieties around the theme of witchcraft—which was a type of power, if a maleficent and negative one—would have been more likely to increase in relation to reputed witches at this time of their lives.[74] Finally, however, the Wettringen case reminds us once again that the issue of the relationships between age and witchcraft are far more complex than the witch-as-old-woman stereotype would have us believe. Catharina Leimbach was in her fifties when accused of witchcraft in 1652, but she was married and prosperous in comparison to her neighbors, not poor and socially isolated. Moreover, she was accused of witchcraft along with her 63-year-old husband and their 23-year-old maidservant, while self-confessed witch Barbara Schürz, at eight years of age, became a focal point of the council's investigation into the case.[75] The reality of the identity of possible witches in early modern Rothenburg, then, was by no means simply a reflection of the image suggested by the witch-as-old-woman stereotype, and it is only at this level of the individual case-study that we will best be able to tease out and explain the disjuncture between the two.

NOTES

This chapter is a much-shortened version of the paper that I presented at the *Old Age in Pre-Industrial Society* Conference held at the Gerontology Institute, Ithaca College, 9–11 September 1999. I would like to thank conference organizers Lynn Botelho, Katharine Kittredge, and Susannah Ottaway for inviting me to attend, the UK's Arts and Humanities Research Board for financing my travel there, and several Essex University colleagues (Joan Davies, Julie Gammon, Jeremy Krikler, Steve Smith, and John Walter), Susannah Ottaway, Lynn Botelho, and Herbert Eiden for their comments on drafts of this chapter.

1. H. C. Erik Midelfort, *Witch Hunting in Southwestern Germany 1562–1684: The Social and Intellectual Foundations* (Stanford, CA: Stanford University Press, 1972), 187. Midelfort also noted (187–188) that this stereotype of witches as "old, secluded, peculiar women" broke down when trials were most severe in the seventeenth century.

2. Keith Thomas, *Religion and the Decline of Magic*, rev. ed. (London: Penguin Books, 1973), 671; Alan Macfarlane, *Witchcraft in Tudor and Stuart England: A Regional and Comparative Study*, rev. ed. (London: Routledge, 1999), 162.

3. See, for example, Deborah Willis, *Malevolent Nurture: Witch-Hunting and Maternal Power in Early Modern England* (Ithaca, NY: Cornell University Press, 1995), 18–19; Gerhard Schormann, *Hexenprozesse in Deutschland*, 2d ed. (Göttingen: Vandenhoeck und Ruprecht, 1986), 118–119; E. William Monter, *Witchcraft in France and Switzerland: The Borderlands During the Reformation* (Ithaca, NY: Cornell University Press, 1976), 115–124; Wolfgang Behringer, *Witchcraft Persecutions in Bavaria: Popular Magic, Religious Zealotry and Reason of State in Early Modern Europe* (Cambridge, Eng.: Cambridge University Press, 1997), 161–162, and *Hexen: Glaube, Verfolgung, Vermarktung,* 2d ed. (Munich: C. H. Beck, 2000), 17. Behringer has, however, argued elsewhere that the gender, age, and social status of accused witches could vary regionally and chronologically and agrees with Midelfort that the witch-as-old-woman stereotype broke down in severe trials; see Wolfgang Behringer, "'Erhob sich das ganze Land zu ihrer Ausrottung': Hexenprozesse und Hexenverfolgungen in Europa,"

in *Hexenwelten: Magie und Imagination vom 16.–20. Jahrhundert*, ed. Richard van Dül-men (Frankfurt am Main: Fischer Taschenbuch, 1993), 131–169.

4. Lyndal Roper, " 'Evil Imaginings and Fantasies': Child-Witches and the End of the Witch Craze," *Past and Present* 167 (2000): 107–139.

5. Ibid., 123.

6. Brian P. Levack, *The Witch-Hunt in Early Modern Europe*, rev. ed. (London: Longman, 1995), 141–145.

7. See, for example, Merry E. Wiesner, *Women and Gender in Early Modern Europe* (Cambridge, Eng.: Cambridge University Press, 1993), 218–238; Pamela Sharpe, "Sur-vival Strategies and Stories: Poor Widows and Widowers in Early Industrial England," in *Widowhood in Medieval and Early Modern Europe*, ed. Sandra Cavallo and Lyndan Warner (Harlow, Eng.: Longman, 1999), 220–239; Elizabeth Foyster, " Marrying the Experienced Widow in Early Modern England: The Male Perspective," in *Widowhood in Medieval and Early Modern Europe*, ed. Sandra Cavallo and Lyndan Warner (Harlow, Eng.: Longman, 1999), 108–124.

8. See particularly the recent work by Robin Briggs, *Witches and Neighbours: The Social and Cultural Context of European Witchcraft* (London: Harper Collins, 1996); Malcolm Gaskill, "Witchcraft in Early Modern Kent: Stereotypes and the Background to Accusations," in *Witchcraft in Early Modern Europe: Studies in Culture and Belief*, ed. Jonathan Barry, et al. (Cambridge, Eng.: Cambridge University Press, 1996), 257–287, and "The Devil in the Shape of a Man: Witchcraft, Conflict and Belief in Jacobean England," *Historical Research* 71 (1998): 142–171; Rainer Walz, *Hexenglaube und mag-ische Kommunikation im Dorf der Frühen Neuzeit: Die Verfolgungen in der Grafschaft Lippe* (Paderborn, Ger.: Ferdinand Schöningh, 1993); Johannes Dillinger, *"Böse Leute": Hexenverfolgungen in Schwäbisch-Österreich und Kurtrier im Vergleich* (Trier, Ger.: Spee, 1999); Walter Rummel, *Bauern, Herren und Hexen: Studien zur Sozialgeschichte sponheimischer und kurtrierischer Hexenprozesse 1574–1664* (Göttingen, Ger.: Vanden-hoeck und Ruprecht, 1991); Alison Rowlands, *Narratives of Witchcraft in Early Modern Germany: Fabrication, Feud and Fantasy* (Manchester, Eng.: Manchester University Press, forthcoming).

9. For further discussion of these themes, see Rowlands, *Narratives of Witchcraft*, chapters 1 and 2.

10. The three executed were Magdalena Dürr (in 1629, after also being found guilty of infanticide), Anna Margaretha Rohn (in 1673, who claimed that she had been pos-sessed since 1664), and Barbara Ehness (in 1692, after also confessing to attempted murder by means of poison). See Rowlands, *Narratives of Witchcraft*, Appendix I, for a full list of Rothenburg's witchcraft cases.

11. See Briggs, *Witches and Neighbours*, 1–13, 397–411.

12. See, for example, my article analyzing the case of Appolonia Glaitter, who was tried in 1671 at the age of 56, who was reputed to have been a witch from the age of twenty-two, and whose trial generated around 300 pages of legal documentation: Alison Rowlands, "Witchcraft and Old Women in Early Modern Germany," forthcoming in *Past and Present*.

13. Cited by Schormann in *Hexenprozesse in Deutschland*, 118: "Man kann der alter weiber und verhaster leut nit balder quidt werden, dan auf sulche weis und maneir."

14. Cited by Behringer in "Erhob sich das ganze Land," 152–153: "allein dass sie dermassen wider recht und billigkeit von jedermann veracht und verworfen seyn, denen niemand schild und schutz, viel weniger Lieb und Trew hält . . . was ist es wunder, dass

sie Armuth und Noth, Trubsal und Kleinmütigkeit halben sich offt . . . dem Teufel . . . ergeben und mit Zauberey umgehen thun?"

15. Behringer, *Witchcraft Persecutions*, 161–162.

16. Ibid., 162, n. 179: "dass die Kinder allen alten Leute Unholden haissen."

17. A point first noted by Edward Bever, "Old Age and Witchcraft in Early Modern Europe," in *Old Age in Pre-Industrial Society*, ed. Peter N. Stearns (New York: Holmes and Meier, 1982), 151–157.

18. See the English translation of Weyer by George Mora, ed., *Witches, Devils, and Doctors in the Renaissance: Johann Weyer, De praestigiis daemonum* (Binghamton, NY: Medieval and Renaissance Texts and Studies, 1991), esp. 180–224. Weyer's work and influence are also discussed by H. C. Erik Midelfort, *A History of Madness in Sixteenth-Century Germany* (Stanford, CA: Stanford University Press, 1999), 196–227; and by Stuart Clark, *Thinking with Demons: The Idea of Witchcraft in Early Modern Europe* (Oxford: Oxford University Press, 1999), 198–203.

19. Mora, *Witches*, 198.

20. Cited by Clark, *Thinking with Demons*, 118.

21. Reginald Scot, *The Discoverie of Witchcraft*, repr. with an introduction by Montague Summers (New York: Dover, 1972), 4 [facsimile]. For other references by Scot to the contemporary belief that witches were old women, see 1, 2, 31, 33, 274.

22. Cited by Gaskill, "Witchcraft in Early Modern Kent," 260.

23. These skeptics can be regarded as forming part of what Stuart Clark has described as a particular genre of Protestant demonology, the central tenet of which was providentialism and the main aim of which was to try to persuade the lower orders away from belief in any sort of magic, white or black. For further details, see Stuart Clark, "Protestant Demonology: Sin, Superstition, and Society (c. 1520–c. 1630)," in *Early Modern European Witchcraft: Centres and Peripheries*, ed. Bengt Ankarloo and Gustav Henningsen (Oxford, Eng.: Clarendon Press, 1990), 45–82.

24. The misogyny of skeptical demonologists is emphasized by Stuart Clark in *Thinking with Demons*, 118. For negative contemporary comments, proverbs, and images directed against widows and old women, see Charles Carlton, "The Widow's Tale: Male Myths and Female Reality in 16th and 17th Century England," *Albion* 10 (1978): 118–129; Foyster, "Marrying the Experienced Widow," 108–124; and Lynn Botelho's chapter on the imagery of old women in early modern England in this volume.

25. Ian Bostridge, "Witchcraft Repealed," in *Witchcraft in Early Modern Europe: Studies in Culture and Belief*, ed. Jonathan Barry, et al. (Cambridge, Eng.: Cambridge University Press, 1996), 310.

26. Gaskill, "Witchcraft in Early Modern Kent," 258. See also Thomas, *Religion*; Macfarlane, *Witchcraft*. Macfarlane's book is based entirely on material from early modern Essex, with Thomas drawing on Macfarlane's research and on pamphlet and demonological literature in his work.

27. Wolfgang Behringer, "Witchcraft Studies in Austria, Germany and Switzerland," in *Witchcraft in Early Modern Europe: Studies in Culture and Belief*, ed. Jonathan Barry, et al. (Cambridge, Eng.: Cambridge University Press, 1996), 91.

28. Gaskill, "Witchcraft in Early Modern Kent," 262.

29. See Behringer in "Erhob sich das ganze Land," 152–153.

30. See Bever, "Old Age."

31. Behringer, *Witchcraft Persecutions*: "Weil auch die starcken Mannsbilder, die

reichen, die jungen, die hohen, oft umb weit geringerer Ursach willen solliches und noch grösseres Übel gethan haben."

32. For examples of those who have relied on or reproduced Macfarlane's figures, see Thomas, *Religion*, 670–672; Levack, *Witch-Hunt*, 141–142; Willis, *Malevolent Nurture*, ch. 2; Foyster, "Marrying the Experienced Widow," 109, n. 6; Pamela Sharpe, "Survival Strategies and Stories," 228, n. 33.

33. Macfarlane, *Witchcraft*, 161.

34. Macfarlane, *Witchcraft*, 166.

35. Thomas, *Religion*, 671; Macfarlane, *Witchcraft*, 162.

36. Midelfort, *Witch Hunting*, 160, 182.

37. Ibid., 101, 108, 109, 139, 142, 150, 156, 159.

38. See Ibid., 201–230, for the exceptionally detailed and lengthy list of trials Midelfort identified for southwestern Germany for this period.

39. Bever, "Old Age," 181.

40. Levack, *Witch-Hunt* (1st ed., 1987), 129; (2d ed., 1995), 142. The first edition of Levack's book went through eight impressions; the second, six by 1997.

41. Bever, "Old Age," 157, 165, 171–180. I discuss Bever's argument in depth in my forthcoming article "Witchcraft and Old Women in Early Modern Germany."

42. I have included Rebecca West in this total of 37, although she was released after acting as the Crown's chief witness; see Macfarlane, *Witchcraft*, 135.

43. Ibid., 254–309, for Macfarlane's exceptionally detailed list of abstracts of Essex witchcraft cases, 1560–1680.

44. Bever, "Old Age," 157.

45. Levack, *Witch Hunt* (2d ed.), 134.

46. Ibid., 141.

47. Macfarlane, *Witchcraft*, 135.

48. John Demos, "Underlying Themes in the Witchcraft of Seventeenth-Century New England," *American Historial Review* 75 (1970): 1314–1315.

49. Briggs, *Witches and Neighbours*, 260–261. Discussion of the gendering of witchcraft accusations is beyond the scope of this chapter; see Rowlands, *Narratives of Witchcraft*, ch. 5, for more details.

50. Demos, "Underlying Themes," 1315.

51. Bever, "Old Age," 166. Other historians suggest that menopause started later, however. For example, Sara Mendelson and Patricia Crawford argue that contemporary medical opinion thought the menopause occurred at around forty-five or fifty years; see their *Women in Early Modern England* (Oxford, Eng.: Clarendon Press, 1998), 25. Particularly useful on this issue is Lynn Botelho's excellent chapter "Old Age and Menopause in Rural Women of Early Modern Suffolk," in *Women and Ageing in British Society Since 1500*, ed. Lynn Botelho and Pat Thane (London: Longman, 2001), 43–65. Botelho argues that, while marital fertility may have ended for women by the age of around forty, menopause occurred at around fifty, and women were recognized by their contemporaries as old when they began to look old as a result of the physical changes brought about by menopause (see 52–61). Surprisingly little work exists on contemporary understanding of the experience of menopause in the early modern period.

52. Bever, "Old Age," 182–183.

53. Tables 9.3 to 9.5 are taken from Rowlands, *Narratives of Witchcraft*, Appendix I.

54. The first alleged adult witch whose age was recorded was Magdalen Dürr, aged 28 or 29, RStA Urgichtenbuch A887, 555r.

55. As an average age at first marriage for women I have used twenty-four, since this is the figure arrived at for seventeenth-century Hohenlohe (the county neighboring Rothenburg) by Thomas Robisheaux in *Rural Society and the Search for Order in Early Modern Germany* (Cambridge, Eng.: Cambridge University Press, 1989), 115–116. On the basis of general demographic information available, I have assumed that husbands were usually two or three years older than their wives, and that after a first birth, which usually followed marriage fairly rapidly, subsequent birth intervals were around two years; see Olwen Hufton, *The Prospect Before Her: A History of Women in Western Europe,* vol. 1, *1500–1800* (London: Fontana, 1997), 11, 132, 177–178, 201, 219–220; Wiesner, *Women and Gender,* 57, 63, 70; Heide Wunder, *"Er ist die Sonn, sie ist der Mond": Frauen in der Frühen Neuzeit* (Munich: C. H. Beck, 1992), 47–50, 162; Dorothy McLaren, "Marital Fertility and Lactation 1570–1720," in *Women in English Society 1500–1800,* ed. Mary Prior (London: Methuen, 1985), 22–53. Unfortunately, no demographic work has been done on these issues for Rothenburg and its rural environs.

56. The first self-confessed child witch whose age was recorded was six-year-old Hans Gackstatt, RstA Urgichtenbuch A877, 537r.

57. For examples of historians who imply this in their work, see J. A. Sharpe, "Disruption in the Well-Ordered Household: Age, Authority, and Possessed Young People," in *The Experience of Authority in Early Modern England,* ed. Paul Griffiths, Adam Fox, and Steve Hindle (London: Macmillan, 1996), 187–212; Rainer Walz, "Kinder in Hexenprozessen: Die Grafschaft Lippe 1654–1663," in *Hexenverfolgung und Regionalgeschichte: Die Grafschaft Lippe im Vergleich,* ed. Gisela Wilbertz, et al. (Bielefeld, Ger.: Verlag für Regionalgeschichte, 1994), 211–231.

58. See Rowlands, *Narratives of Witchcraft,* ch. 1 and 2, for an explanation of this reluctance on the part of Rothenburg's elites.

59. For a discussion of Rothenburg's male witches, see Rowlands, *Narratives of Witchcraft,* ch. 5.

60. For Gackstatt's age, see RstA Urgichtenbuch A877, 537r ; for Maas's, see RStA Interrogation Book A909, 278r.

61. See, for example, Midelfort, *Witch Hunting,* and Behringer, *Witchcraft.*

62. On the caution with which the inhabitants of Rothenburg and its rural hinterland approached formal accusations of witchcraft, see Rowlands, *Narratives of Witchcraft,* ch. 1.

63. On the duration of alleged witches' reputations, see Briggs, *Witches and Neighbours,* 22–23, 264; Julian Goodare, "Women and the Witch-Hunt in Scotland," *Social History* 23 (1998): 288–308; Eva Labouvie, *Zauberei und Hexenwerk: Ländlicher Hexenglaube in der frühen Neuzeit* (Frankfurt am Main: Fischer Taschenbuch, 1991), 167; Walz, *Hexenglaube und magische Kommunikation,* 300–302.

64. See Rowlands, *Narratives of Witchcraft,* Appendix I, for more details. Rothenburg's eight self-confessed female witches have been excluded from this total because no one else believed they were witches until they asserted as much themselves. It was therefore impossible for them to have reputations that predated their trials.

65. For example, Macfarlane and Bever both agree that accused women might well have been reputed as witches for lengthy periods of time before formal accusation, but they fail to incorporate the implications of this point for their emphasis on the witch-as-

old-woman stereotype; See Macfarlane, *Witchcraft in Tudor and Stuart England*, 161–162; Bever, "Old Age," 173.

66. For details, see Rowlands, "Witchcraft."

67. These themes around the issue of gaining a reputation are discussed in depth in my forthcoming article, "Witchcraft and Old Women in Early Modern Germany."

68. Macfarlane, *Witchcraft*.

69. Midelfort, *Witch Hunting*.

70. Bever, "Old Age."

71. Lyndal Roper, *Oedipus and the Devil: Witchcraft, Sexuality and Religion in Early Modern Europe* (London: Routledge, 1994), 199–225, and Roper, "Sex, Bodies and Age: Misogyny and the Witch-hunt," unpublished paper presented at the Women's History Seminar, Institute of Historical Research, London, 4 June 1999.

72. See Rowlands, "Witchcraft."

73. This case is discussed in depth in Rowlands, *Narratives of Witchcraft*, ch. 5. For full case documents, see Staatsarchiv Nürnberg, Rothenburg Repertorium 2087 fols. 1r–164r.

74. Briggs, *Witches and Neighbours*, 264; Demos, "Underlying Themes," 1315, 1317, 1318–1319.

75. The Leimbachs' twelve-year-old daughter Magdalena was also questioned formally about her own and her family's alleged witchcraft but was not jailed.

10

Naturalizing Myths of Aging: A Cautionary Tale

Kirk Combe and Kenneth Schmader

This chapter condenses and revises a fuller study wherein we combined the fields of semiotics, gerontology, geriatrics, and literary analysis in order to investigate the perception of elders and the aging process in early modern and modern Western culture.[1] That article focused on the linguistic and cultural mechanisms by which certain erroneous attitudes toward the elderly myths, if you will, are propagated. Specifically, two such myths were examined: senility and the loss of sexual activity. We began by proposing the applicability to gerontological and geriatric thinking of Roland Barthes's semiotic theory of naturalization and myth as a type of speech. We then investigated early modern stage comedy and current film comedy as powerful popular vehicles for the naturalization of such ageist stereotyping. Last, we presented an overview of the present-day clinical experience as well as gerontological and geriatric studies of cognitive and sexual function in the elderly, all of which discredit these two ageist myths. Contrary to popular belief and the comic depiction of elders, loss of mental faculties and asexuality are not typical of growing old and do not apply to all the elderly.

The present chapter highlights certain portions of our original argument. In particular, we focus on semiology as it might be applied to the study of aging and then on the depiction of elder characters from four British stage comedies of the early modern period. Our purpose here is simply to offer a word of caution to historians of aging. Namely, that the perceptions, depictions, and ways people might speak about elders and aging is often likely to be quite distinct from the reality of those things in any given historical period. As Erdman Palmore has shown in his research: "Americans have developed a set of prejudices and discriminations against our elders that may be unequaled by any other society. The prejudices range from the stereotype that most are senile to the cruel assumption that they have no need for sexual gratification." Moreover, most Americans seem quite unconscious of their own ageist views. "Ageism permeates our culture so thoroughly and conditions our attitudes and perceptions so much that most of us are unaware of most of the ageism in it."[2] If we have got so wrong our attitudes and assumptions about aging in the present, certainly we must be careful about how we read attitudes and assumptions about aging in the past. Perhaps, as Palmore suggests, late-twentieth and early-twenty-first-century America is unequaled as an ageist society. Such an assertion, however, does not mean that modern ageism is without precedent. When dealing with a human phenomenon as complex as aging, we believe one should always be mindful of the power of popular myth.

SEMIOLOGY AND AGING

Palmore surveys our language about the elderly and finds that the etymologies, meanings, and connotations of everyday words and phrases dealing with age are overwhelmingly negative.[3] Palmore's investigation, however, touches upon only what linguist Ferdinand de Saussure might classify as the *parole* of language—that is, our everyday speech manifest at a superficial linguistic level. We will take our analysis a step further, into the realm of *langue*, which is to say the deep structure of language.[4] At this deeper level—the basis of semiology itself—we observe that not merely are the signs (words) of everyday speech unfairly biased against elders. More serious still, we believe that the signifieds (generalized concepts) assigned to the signifiers (sound images) of our language dealing with the elderly constitute signs driven far more by ideology than by analogy. The intricate field of semiology and linguistics tells us that virtually all relationships among language elements are arbitrary, not absolute, ones, yet phenomena such as isology and naturalization lead us to believe that the sound utterances (again, the signifier) we make are necessarily linked to the utterable cognitions (the signified) we articulate, and that those signs themselves are necessarily linked to the material world. Semiologists assert that they are not. Instead, language is at best an approximation of the world; at worst it is our own consciousnesses projected onto the world—that is, not really the world at all.[5] What this all means for gerontology and geriatrics is that, from a semiotic point of view, social forces and time control our conceptions of the elderly, not necessarily the material facts of the aging experience. Just as language, being arbitrary, necessarily has nothing to do with the material world, our view of elders, being a construction of language, might reflect little or nothing of actual aging. In fact, such views, even though popularly taken as truths, can be wildly mistaken.

Building and expanding on Saussure's early work on the life of signs within society, Roland Barthes brings semiology more clearly into the political realm.

Calling language the domain of "articulations" and "above all a cutting-out of shapes," he asserts: "It follows that the future task of semiology is far less to establish lexicons of objects than to rediscover the articulations which men impose on reality."[6] According to Barthes, semiological analysis is the unmasking of ideology concealed in our language. In his influential work, *Mythologies* (1957), Barthes brings this undertaking to life. There Barthes categorizes myth not as an object, concept, or idea, but as a type of speech bearing a message. Myth is "a system of communication . . . it is a mode of signification, a form." As such, myth belongs within the "science of form"—that is, semiology—that "studies significations apart from their content." In other words, myths are not eternal; rather, "mythology can only have an historical foundation, for myth is a type of speech chosen by history." Myths do not happen; they are made. Myths originate in "human history which converts reality into speech."[7] Two key operations characterize Barthes's concept of myth.

The first deals with the special relationship between the first-order semiological system of language, or what Barthes terms the language-object, and the second-order semiological system of myth, what Barthes terms metalanguage. The connection between these two systems occurs at a specific point. According to Barthes, the last element of the language-object system, that is, the sign or word, serves in turn as the first element of the metalanguage system, that is, as the signifier of the myth system. Since any sign is a combination of a signifier (sound image) and a signified (generalized concept), what happens is that the finished product of language becomes the initial building block of myth. Thus, in Barthes's terms, the *meaning* of the sign at the first level of language object is transformed to the *form* of the signifier or sound image at the second level of metalanguage.[8] As such, this new signifier needs to be supplied with a new signified in order to construct a new sign at the metalinguistic or mythic level.

Here is where the linguistic and cognitive hocus-pocus takes place. In effect, the sign from the language-object system has its meaning drained from it; replacing that first-level linguistic meaning is what Barthes calls the second-level metalinguistic *signification* of the new mythic sign. For example, in our culture we value a rose far less for the historical, biological entity it is (that object represented by the first-level language sign) and associate far more with it the emotions of passion and love (which are second-level mythic significations, according to Barthes's schema). The "passionified" rose, then, is stolen and restored language. The shell or form of the object is retained, but new value is poured into it by the myth system. Specifically, new value comes by way of what generalized concept is selected to *replace* the meaning of the language-object sign. (In our current example, flowering plant that grows in dirt is *replaced* by generally amorous associations.)

Barthes identifies the motivation behind the selection of the signified of metalanguage as ideological in nature—that is, as a function of the body of doctrine, myth, symbol, and beliefs of a particular social movement, institution, class, or group.[9] By doing so, Barthes moves semiology out of the world of dry and technical linguistics and into the cultural and political realm of human power relationships. Here we encounter the second key operation of Barthes's myth system: the process of naturalization or normalization.

Naturalization is more than just the persistent and repeated expression of an idea. Naturalization is the potent phenomenon in which the consumer of myth reads, mistakenly, the signification of the metalinguistic sign not as a motive, but as a reason. Says Barthes: "everything happens as if the picture *naturally* conjured up the concept, as if the signifier *gave a foundation* to the signified."[10] If you, the reader of this chapter, were raised in the Western tradition, at some level you believe that the flower rose actually embodies and engenders human passion. You believe that rose *causes* passion. The link is an illusion of custom, not a fact of nature. In other societies, a rose is a pleasant-smelling bloom without connection to human sexuality and emotion. Even seeing through myths, however, often has little counteracting effect on their control over us. Myths aim for easy consumption and immediate impression. Rational explanation may belie the passionified rose of our cultural tradition, but you will never prevent that association from creeping into your mind. Naturalization makes us experience myth as innocent speech, not as a type of propaganda. Barthes comments: "what allows the reader to consume myth innocently is that he does not see it as a semiological system but as an inductive one. Where there is only an equivalence, he sees a kind of causal process: the signifier and the signified have, in his eyes, a natural relationship."

As a result of this naturalization, myth is fallaciously taken to be "depoliticized speech."[11] That is, a particular, historical stance is represented as universal and eternal, thereby obscuring the ideology behind the myth. Myths, then, have the power to deform and amputate the meanings of language-object signs and therefore alienate us from first-level representations of reality. Meaningful representations are supplanted with fanciful significations of an ideographic system.[12] If Barthes's theories strike you as being alarmist or even trivial, especially given the harmless example of the rose offered above, consider for a moment a more malevolent instance of mythology at work: Nazi propaganda against the Jews before and during World War II. Myth has the capacity to work actual harm on real people. Examples of this sort easily could be multiplied to include injury done to the aged. For Barthes, myth is by nature duplicitous and motivated by issues of power, and naturalization is the semiotic mechanism that allows social control to pass for conventional wisdom.

With Barthes's theories we deal with a language act of enormous force. It seems clear to us that the negative and misinformed opinions so many Americans currently hold with regard to aging (and so well documented by Palmore and others) constitute a naturalized Barthean myth system. Moreover, evidence of these same mistaken attitudes of today against the aged are visible in pre-industrial Western society as well. Both then and now, the realities of the elderly and the aging process somehow have been drained from our awareness, and replacing them are fanciful, foolish, and often panicky and harmful negative views of older people that have come to be taken as part of the natural order. Barthes advises us that in order "to gauge the political load of an object and the mythical hollow which espouses it," never look at things from the point of view of the mythical signification. Rather, study the signifier—the thing that has been robbed of its historical and political reality. Look at things from the point of view of the meaning of the language-object.[13] Such is our intent now as we consider the ageist comic tradition in the West as one of many popular myths hostile to elders in our culture.

THE ELDER IN COMEDY

No one should be surprised by the idea that ageism is institutionalized in our comic and satiric tradition. Along with sheer physical decline, dotage and aged lechery are standard shtick. Such characters prattle and bathetically intrigue everywhere in Greek and Roman comedy. In one of his fiercest satires, Satire 10, Juvenal lists in an extended passage the horrors of old age. In the scene where the elderly Polonius fruitlessly attempts to wheedle out of Hamlet the secret to his recent bizarre behavior, the young prince of Denmark toys with as well as insults the older man by referring to Juvenal's satire (see act II, scene ii). In the stage comedy and eventually the television and film comedy of our early modern and modern eras, elder characters routinely suffer similar treatment.

Surveying the span of dramatic comedy from Greek New Comedy to the middle of the twentieth century, literary critic Northrop Frye finds a genre "remarkably tenacious of its structural principles and character types."[14] At the heart of the structure of comedy is the conflict of what Frye conceives of as the new society—embodied by the young lovers ever-present in comedy—versus an old society—normally parents and the established older generation standing in the way of young love. Often this clash takes place between a son and father locked in a contest of wills. The general movement of the comic plot, moreover, is one of the eventual triumph of the emerging new society over the status quo of the old—the victory and the new order usually crystallized around the figure of the young male comic hero. This new order is intended to be regarded by the audience as the pragmatic and reality-based society of the comic hero dispelling the illusory, habit-bound, and hypocritical society of the older generation. It is not surprising that many stock character types of comedy are older people populating what Frye calls the *alazon* or imposter group—that is, the wrongheaded old society. These include parents (especially the *senex iratus* or heavy father), guardians, old bachelors, widows, older rivals to the young male lover, the older vice character, the miser, and others.[15] Comments Frye: "Thus the comic dramatist as a rule writes for the younger men in his audience, and the older members of almost any society are apt to feel that comedy has something subversive about it."[16] In gerontological terms, the literary form of comedy seems in large measure to dramatize issues of what researchers have termed age conflict and gerontocracy.[17] We find that comedy also frequently functions as a semiotic system of naturalization wherein falsehoods become infused in the popular mind as truths. In other words, according to Barthes's formula for myth, the genre of comedy is a metalanguage system that empties the signifier of the elder of its historical reality and meaning as a language object. In the place of that political reality, comedy supplies an ideological signification for the elder— a signification that more often than not has little to do with the facts of the aging process. Many kinds of ageism, some positive but most negative, are manifest in comedy. Within such a hostile myth system and literary landscape, it is inevitable, perhaps, that elders rarely are depicted well from a cognitive or from a sexual point of view.

In the early modern era comedy follows tradition with regard to its treatment of elders. Generally, a thin veneer of humor and sentimentality puts a happy and benevolent sheen over the ageist (and often sexist and classist) brutality extant at a deeper level of these dramas. The naturalization process of myth keeps our attention focused on the seemingly harmless surface charm of these productions; meanwhile, quite harmful and erroneous descriptions of the world make their way covertly into our daily outlook. A brief look at four aged characters—two men, two women—from early modern stage comedy readily reveals their depiction as people whose mental and sexual well-being has been at best compromised and at worst seriously impaired. While space allows for only a brief consideration of such characters in four plays, the negative depiction of elders is typical of the early modern era and, as we will glimpse later, standard as well in our comedy today.

Consider first the comic depiction of two elderly gentlemen. In Sir George Etherege's *The Man of Mode* (1676), the character of Old Bellair fulfills the conventional role of heavy father and blocking agent to young love—in this case, that of his son, Young Bellair. Not only has Old Bellair arranged for his son to marry a woman he does not want to marry, but the father also has cast an amorous eye on the woman with whom Young Bellair secretly is in love, Emilia, and plans to marry in spite of Old Bellair's threats of disinheritance. Even though this action forms a subplot for Etherege's play, obvious issues of generational conflict appear on stage. Rails Old Bellair of his son's reluctance to obey him: "Out a pize! youth is apt to play the fool, and 'tis not good it should be in their power" (V.ii.23–24).[18] Unfortunately for Old Bellair, it is he who plays the fool during the course of the drama and, more worrisome, in the end he who lacks the power to carry out his designs. Fundamentally, Old Bellair plays a comic butt sexually and sentiently. Both his love for Emilia and his plan to marry her are ludicrous impossibilities.

The thought of Old Bellair's advances makes Emilia shudder (e.g., II.i.22–25). For his part in the love farce, Old Bellair plays the bathetic role of spry old goat attempting to impress the younger woman with his unflagging physical energy, as when they dance (see IV.i.73–76). While his father makes a fool of himself over Emilia, Young Bellair schemes to thwart Old Bellair's every objective. Conspiring with the woman his father intends for him to marry, Young Bellair hatches a plot "to deceive the grave people!" (III.i.120–121)—meaning his elderly father and her elderly mother. As ever in comedy, the success of stratagems and counterstratagems depends on the perspicacity of the plotters. As is usual in comedy, the younger people better the older people in such mental gymnastics. At the end of the play, Young Bellair defeats Old Bellair by marrying Emilia in secret, thereby beating his father to her. Old Bellair is not only angered and betrayed, but publicly humiliated by the event:

Old Bellair: Ha! cheated! cozened! and by your contrivance, sister!

Lady Townley: What would you do with her? She's a rogue and you can't abide her.

Medley: Shall I hit her a pat for you, sir?

Old Bellair [flinging away]: A dod, you are all rogues, and I never will forgive you. (V.ii.248–254)

One implication of the Old Bellair subplot, then, seems to be the double charge against the older man that he is unfit both for the sexual and the mental contests of his society. Not only is he over the hill in these arenas but ridiculous and even hypocritical still to consider himself a player. At the same time, however, Old Bellair is by no means a villain. In fact, in his love of drink, dance, and good company he is quite a likeable fellow—if he would only behave appropriately for his age. At the very end of the play he comes around to accepting his son's marriage to Emilia, even becoming a master of the revels of sorts as he begins the final marriage dance. Thus ageism is sugarcoated with comic sentiment, making it perhaps all the more subtle and pernicious.

A century later, in *The School for Scandal* (1777), Richard Brinsley Sheridan renders a similar comic portrait of an elderly gentleman. Sir Peter Teazle, however, has actually fallen victim to the mistake of marrying a woman much younger than himself. Flirtatious and a spendthrift, Lady Teazle—far from being a comfort—has become the bane of Sir Peter's declining years (e.g., I.ii.1–5, 17–22). Once again, sexual insufficiency and mental incompetence fuel the fire of this generational conflict in the play. Clearly, Lady Teazle has little or no sexual attraction for Sir Peter. When he complains that, as her husband, he currently exercises no influence or authority over her, Lady Teazle retorts: "Authority! No, to be sure—if you wanted authority over me, you should have adopted me, and not married me; I am sure you were old enough" (II.i.11–14). With her marriage to the wealthy older gentleman, Lady Teazle escaped disagreeable economic circumstances in the country; the happiest prospect for her now would be to find herself a rich, young widow in fashionable London society. Sir Peter is well aware of these realities (see II.i.34–53, 71–84). Since their exchanges are marked by her gibes and innuendos against him, Lady Teazle readily finds occasion to belittle her husband's virility as well, as when he complains about her newfound obsession for fashion and taste.

Sir Peter: Aye—there again—taste! Zounds! madam, you had no taste when you married *me!*

Lady Teazle: That's very true, indeed, Sir Peter! And, *after* having married you, I am sure I should never pretend to taste again! (II.i.97–101)

Pitiably, Sir Peter actually enjoys her abuse: "Well, though I can't make her love me, there is a great satisfaction in quarrelling with her; and I think she never appears to such advantage as when she's doing everything in her power to plague me" (II.i.137–141). As sweet as his remarks might sound, in Sir Peter we face a portrait of an older man exiled to the margins of the sexual game: even though he enjoys the power of wealth, he commands no respect, inspires no romantic love, is capable of no real sexuality.

During the play Sir Peter shows himself as mentally incompetent as well. From the outset the audience understands the villainous nature of Joseph Surface, the arch-deceiver and sham man of sentiment of the drama. Despite the fact that Joseph simultaneously is out to get the fortune of Sir Peter's ward, Maria, through marriage *and* the honor of Lady Teazle through cuckoldry, Sir Peter steadfastly clings to his disastrous misperceptions: "I was never mistaken in my life. Joseph is indeed a model for the young men of the age. He is a man of sentiment, and acts up to the sentiments he professes" (II.i.65–69). Meanwhile, Sir Peter gravely misjudges Joseph's brother, Charles, as a wastrel in spite of reliable counsel to the contrary and the fact that Maria and Charles are in love. Thus, like Old Bellair, Sir Peter plays the role of duped blocking agent in the comedy by foolishly insisting that Maria marry Joseph. In the famous screen scene of *The School for Scandal* (4.3), Sir Peter's extreme ignorance comes suddenly and ruthlessly to his view: Joseph is a scoundrel, Lady Teazle is on the brink of adultery, Charles is a worthy fellow after all. Despite the happy and sentimentalized results of this discovery—Charles and Maria will marry; Lady Teazle, touched by the *economic* tender regard Sir Peter has shown for her, professes to see the error of her ways—Sir Peter remains a decidedly pathetic figure. The inevitable signification of his character is that Sir Peter Teazle is a sexually and mentally feeble old man.

If elderly gentlemen of position and means are portrayed negatively in comedy as being asexual and senile, then older women—and in particular widows—come in for even harsher treatment under those same imputations. Popularly judged by different and unfair standards of beauty and desirability, besides facing the bias that menopause heralds the end of sexual identity,[19] elder women in comedy are virtual pariahs on stage. Their treatment in these plays normally is extreme and often turns vicious. A perfect example of a troublesome old woman in comedy occurs in the character of Lady Wishfort in William Congreve's *The Way of the World* (1700). The primary blocking agent of the play, Lady Wishfort walks the stage both as an old coquette pathetically out of touch with the youthful mating game (the pun of her name—wish-for-it—announces her sexual plight) and as a befuddled widow at the mercy of all manner of cunning stratagems and legal maneuvers going on around her. Because she plays such a pivotal role in the comic plot, these characteristics become particular highlights of the play. Lady Wishfort suffers constant derision at the hands of the young.

Mirabell: Yes, I think the good lady would marry anything that resembled a man, though 'twere no more than what a butler could pinch out of a napkin.

Mrs. Fainall: Female frailty! We must all come to it, if we live to be old and feel the craving of a false appetite when the true is decayed.

Mirabell: An old woman's appetite is depraved like that of a girl. 'Tis the green sickness [anemia] of a second childhood; and like the faint offer of a latter spring, serves but to usher in the fall, and withers in an affected bloom. (II.i.348–359)

In these lines we find a nearly seamless combination of our two myths of aging under consideration—a kind of sexual senility portrayed by Lady Wishfort. Even more striking is the fact that these beliefs are spoken by the ostensible good guys of the comedy. Mirabell is our comic hero; Mrs. Fainall, while not the true comic heroine, was once Mirabell's lover and someone whom Mirabell will rescue (with others) from the play's comic villain, Mr. Fainall. Therefore, otherwise nice people of the drama—people with whom at a surface level we are supposed to sympathize and whom we are supposed to respect—are shown to hold extremely ageist views. More distressing still is the fact that Mrs. Fainall is Lady Wishfort's own daughter. Indeed, Mrs. Fainall seems to believe that if she, too, lives long enough (her mother is fifty-five), she will fall prey to this same carnal idiocy. The normalization of ageist and sexist mythologies described in Barthes's schema seems firmly in place in the play.

The whole of *The Way of the World*, then, revolves around Lady Wishfort's foolish attempts to find love at her advanced age compounded with her being duped at every turn by the competing schemes of Mirabell and Mr. Fainall. Both young men have the same prize in view: the money of Lady Wishfort's young niece and ward, Millamant. Mirabell is willing to marry the willful young woman; Mr. Fainall seeks to control Millamant's fortune by taking over, as son-in-law, Lady Wishfort's estate. Both hero and villain abuse Lady Wishfort terribly. Mirabell, however, inflicts considerably more mental and emotional harm on the older woman by pretending to court her himself as a way to get to Millamant and then, when that intrigue fails, by arranging for a false suitor (in fact his serving man) to propose marriage to Lady Wishfort. Through it all, due to her being "superannuated," Lady Wishfort remains an object of sexual *non*-desire as well as a widow excruciatingly confused about the way of the youthful world going on around her. At the end of the play, Mirabell saves the day via legal artifice, has his bride and cash, and keeps Lady Wishfort's estate intact for her. None of the joy of this happy ending, though, really includes Lady Wishfort. As an instrument of comic mirth, a buffoon, she has no role in the emerging new society. She is cognitively unable to keep up with it and is sexually out of touch. Lady Wishfort is placed entirely on the margin. Her poignantly accurate observation about Mirabell—"Oh, he carries poison in his tongue that would corrupt integrity itself!" (III.i.60–61)—falls on deaf ears—both those of the other characters in the play and on our own as an audience. The pleasant comic mirth of Lady Wishfort blinds us to the harmful ageist myths at the core of her character.

If Lady Wishfort is marginalized in Congreve's comedy, the widow Mrs. Malaprop of Richard Brinsley Sheridan's *Rivals* (1775) is at that play's end quite savagely rejected and humiliated by her society. Like Lady Wishfort, Mrs. Malaprop serves as a blocking agent to young love, is easily fooled by the machinations of young men, and hopelessly plays at the love game herself. In short, she, too, is portrayed as sexless and senile. The severity of the treatment Mrs. Malaprop receives, however, exceeds anything faced by her earlier counterpart. Mere ridicule becomes open callousness, even active hostility. Not only is Mrs. Malaprop an older woman trying to compete in the young person's game of courtship and marriage, but Sheridan makes her a hypocrite as well as a booby in the process. Smitten with a braggart Irish baronet named Sir Lucius O'Trigger and writing under the pastoral pen name of "Delia," Mrs. Malaprop corresponds by secret letters with her would-be lover. However, O'Trigger mistakes his correspondent for the young, wealthy, and desirable niece and ward of Mrs. Malaprop, Lydia Languish. Upon discovering this ludicrous love triangle, Lydia complains of her aunt: "Since she has discovered her own frailty she is become more suspicious of mine" (I.ii.81–82). Thus the "old tough aunt in the way" (I.i.71) perversely hinders young love while herself pursuing old love—an obvious reversal of the natural order as far as comedy is concerned as well as a heightening of the generational conflict inherent in the genre. Mrs. Malaprop does not approve of her niece's choice of a future husband, the impoverished Ensign Beverley—who is in fact the wealthy Captain Jack Absolute, wooing the flighty and overly romantic Lydia under a pseudonym in order to indulge her girlish desire to flaunt social convention. Yet here is where our own hypocrisy as an ageist audience shows through. If Mrs. Malaprop displays no awareness whatever of the fact that she indulges in the same weakness for which she persecutes Lydia, neither do we as an audience seem to discern that the same strategies for courtship we ridicule when employed by the older woman we approve when practiced by the young lovers of the play. For Lydia and Jack, the intrigue of false identity, furtive love letters, and clandestine rendezvous strike us as brisk, age-appropriate behavior. For Mrs. Malaprop, it is absurd affectation. Moreover, Mrs. Malaprop's secrecy in pursuing the affair with O'Trigger implies a certain depravity, even in her own mind, about expressions of sexual interest by the elderly—depravity that, again, in younger people is viewed as normal and healthy. Upon reflection, then, behavior that initially might appear as improper or even unprincipled on the part of Mrs. Malaprop in fact could be nothing more than bias motivated by our own preconceptions of the elderly.

The surface merriment of comedy more often than not obscures those really penetrating insights into the society made available through the drama. Mrs. Malaprop remains the primary comic butt on stage. In this role, along with her supposed hypocrisy and sexual aberration, she is portrayed not merely as mentally confused, but as downright obtuse. As her name signals, she butchers the meanings of words throughout the play (see, for example, I.ii.301–305). Worse, at one point Captain Absolute engineers the outrageous circumstance where, by reading aloud an intercepted letter to Lydia from "Ensign Beverley" (in fact himself), our comic hero is able with impunity to insult and facetiously commiserate with Mrs. Malaprop simultaneously.

Absolute: "*As for the old weather-beaten she-dragon who guards you*"—Who can he mean by that?

Mrs. Malaprop: *Me!* Sir—*me!*—he means *me!* There—what do you think now?—But go on a little further.

Absolute: Impudent scoundrel!—"*it shall go hard but I will elude her vigilance, as I am told that the same ridiculous vanity which makes her dress up her coarse features, and deck her dull chat with hard words which she don't understand*"—

Mrs. Malaprop: There, sir! an attack upon my language! What do you think of that!— an aspersion upon my parts of speech! Was ever such a brute! Sure if I reprehend anything in this world, it is the use of my oracular tongue, and a nice derangement of epitaphs!

Absolute: He deserves to be hanged and quartered! Let me see—"*same ridiculous vanity*"—

Mrs. Malaprop: You need not read it again, sir.

Absolute: I beg pardon, ma'am—"*does also lay her open to the grossest deceptions from flattery and pretended admiration*"—an impudent coxcomb!—"*so that I have a scheme to see you shortly with the old harridan's consent, and even to make her a go-between in our interviews.*"—Was ever such assurance! (III.iii.72–97)

Ever indeed, for that scheme is precisely what Jack is about during this exchange. As Captain Absolute, Jack has managed to make himself his own rival—that is, the rival to Ensign Beverley—for Lydia's hand; moreover, Mrs. Malaprop actively promotes Jack's suit to her niece. It is a brilliantly conceived comic scene, rich with mistaken identity, intricate plot turns, and witty dialogue. It is a scene played nevertheless at the extreme expense of the widow's cognitive ability.

It is in the climactic scene of *The Rivals*, however—a place in comedy traditionally reserved for the celebration of marriage and the social integration symbolized by the dance—that Mrs. Malaprop comes in for her most malign treatment. As the various plots and intrigues of the play draw to a point, Mrs. Malaprop's secret about Sir Lucius O'Trigger comes out. Suddenly, she finds herself on the open marriage market in direct competition with her niece. It is not surprising that Mrs. Malaprop discovers that she is no threat to the young and pretty (though vapid) Lydia. When O'Trigger confronts Lydia with the love letters, Mrs. Malaprop intervenes.

Mrs. Malaprop: O, he will dissolve my mystery! Sir Lucius, perhaps there's some mistake—perhaps, I can illuminate—
Sir Lucius: Pray, old gentlewoman, don't interfere where you have no business.—Miss Languish, are you my Delia, or not? (V.iii.251–256)

Clearly by his summary dismissal of Mrs. Malaprop, O'Trigger believes the older woman not only is being intrusive, but is incapable of having anything to do with the mating game. When Mrs. Malaprop reveals herself in fact to be Delia, the writer of those letters, O'Trigger is incredulous: "You Delia!—pho! pho! be easy" (V.iii.261). There ensues a cruel trading session among the young men where each attempts to fob off on the other a sexual commodity that, though it brings with it a good estate, obviously has outlived its shelf life (see V.iii.266–276). Captain Absolute's father, Sir Anthony, feigns comfort to the widow, saying: "Come, Mrs. Malaprop, don't be cast down—you are in your bloom yet." As in the case of Lady Wishfort, Mrs. Malaprop responds with an observation aptly summarizing the action of the play: "O Sir Anthony!—men are all barbarians—" (V.iii.280–283). At this point, as comedy demands, the young lovers take center stage and Mrs. Malaprop is ignored. As the father of the groom, Sir Anthony plans wedding revels at which "we single lads will drink a health to the young couples," and, in an afterthought, "and a husband to Mrs. Malaprop" (V.iii.319–320). There seems little hope, however, of Sir Anthony's toast ever being fulfilled. Mrs. Malaprop stands outside the circle of celebration that concludes the play and symbolically outside the new society whose job it is to people and to conduct the business of the world. The widow simply is old, laughable, confused, and in the way.

We can't compare representations of the elderly in early modern drama with the clinical realities of the lives of the elderly. Rather, a useful and suggestive exercise at this point would be briefly to contrast the portrayal of the elderly in today's comedy, which shares many of the stereotypes of its early modern counterpart, with the clinical reality of elders now. We believe the gap between elderly appearance and reality discernible in our own culture serves well as an object lesson for those attempting to disentangle myth from fact in cultures of the past.

THE ELDER IN POPULAR CULTURE AND CLINICAL REALITY TODAY

The comedy of our own popular culture is crowded with ill-treated elderly characters. Everywhere and to various degrees, elders in film, television, and advertising suffer, among others, the stigma of senility and asexuality.[20] Our predominantly visual and decidedly instantaneous popular media is in most ways the ideal playground for semiotic naturalization. It would be easy enough to select for examination any number of television shows or Hollywood movies openly hostile to elders. We will focus instead on two recent films that, at first glance, might seem a celebration of aging. When investigating the films *Grumpy Old Men* (1993) and its sequel, *Grumpier Old Men* (1995), one might argue that ageist stereotypes of the nature discussed in this chapter are in fact ruptured by these comedies. Elder sexuality drives both movies. Equally, witty repartee and clever intrigue—the very stuff of comedy—abounds in the exchanges and actions of the two main elderly characters, John (played by Jack Lemmon) and Max (played by Walter Matthau). Upon closer inspection, are the ageist myths of cognitive impairment and sexlessness really reversed in the films? Or in fact do these myths of aging subtly but powerfully inform the comedy, making their naturalization that much more insidious?

For one thing, the very titles of the films certainly play on ageist stereotyping. Most Americans believe, inaccurately, that the elderly live isolated, useless lives plagued by money worries; therefore, it is only natural for them to suffer from depression. Terms like "grouchy," "touchy," "cranky," and "feel sorry for themselves" commonly are applied to the elderly.[21] Both John and Max exemplify such grumpy behavior. Second, neither are strong traces of cognitive impairment absent from their characters. While neither John nor Max displays any of the overt signs normally associated with senility, both are terrible if not dangerous drivers. Both of them *always* crash into the garbage cans when trying to park at their local bait shop; it becomes a recurring if not monotonous sight gag of the films. Both movies, then, while perhaps seeming otherwise, in fact play to many of our clichés about the cerebral and emotional state of the aged. Third, in the arena of romance, what might appear initially to be an affirmation of aged sexuality in these comedies is actually little more than a cynical exercise in manipulating audience expectation in order to engineer a series of cheap laughs and sighs at the *expense* of elderly sexuality. After all, what's funnier and more pitiable to Americans, maybe the most youth-obsessed culture ever recorded in human history, than sexy old people? Far from a frank depiction of honest sexuality among the elderly, these films hand us a gross caricature of old folks getting it on. Alternately outrageous and sentimental, the comedies jab us in the ribs and tug at our heartstrings when it comes to aged sexuality. There is something inherently ludicrous and schmaltzy in the situation of John and Max, as men in their late sixties and early seventies, seeking sex. As with Old Bellair, Mrs. Wishfort, and Mrs. Malaprop, the very sexiness of these characters is dismissed not only as sexless, but as a pursuit both slightly depraved and uncomfortably amusing to behold. While certainly the open treatment of elder sexuality in these films is a healthier attitude than handling it as a forbidden topic, as is true with the great majority of popular depictions of the aged, one has to wonder if the *Grumpy Old Men* films really do much to change the public mind on this issue.

Fourth, while outwardly appearing to deal with romance among the elderly, these movies subtly give way to at least one longstanding convention of the traditional, youth-oriented comic formula. Since comedy is, at heart, a genre directed at the young men of the audience, the first order of business must be attractive heroines. The filmmakers faced a challenge on this point. Could they cast an Olympia Dukakis, Angela Lansbury, Shirley MacLaine, or any of television's "Golden Girls" opposite Jack Lemmon and Walter Matthau and elicit the same comic response from audiences? Probably not. Instead of using authentic-looking older women in these roles, they give us two aging but well-preserved sexpots, Ann-Margret and Sophia Loren. Whatever the actual ages of those two actresses, they play distinctly younger in the films—say, mid to late fifties compared to Lemmon's and Matthau's late sixties and early seventies. Their sexuality has an unmistakable youth quality about it. The filmmakers leave no doubt in our minds that both women, with their ample busts and swiveling hips, still have the power to turn the heads of *all* men, young and old alike. Sir Lucius O'Trigger would not turn either one away. Finally, despite the attempt at sharp-tongued wit in the movies, what finally defines *Grumpy Old Men* and *Grumpier Old Men* is their overweening sentimentality. Far from frank treatments of real issues facing the elderly, these are insipid Hollywood feel-good films. Their humor is based largely on ageist stereotyping; their maudlin tenderness derives from the cheap pity of older people suffering heart attacks and death—always to the same score of winsome piano music. As with all elderly characters in the youth market of comedy, John and Max do not fare well cognitively or sexually once we scratch the comic surface.

Medical facts, however, contrast markedly with the popularized fictions of senility and asexuality among the elderly. Cognition and aging has been the subject of intense interest and a number of investigations.[22] Cognition includes several areas, but most prominent are attention, memory, language, and intelligence. In general, studies show that while long–term memory tends to decrease with aging, other areas of cognition such as language, attention, and intelligence show little or no decrease. The studies also show the wide individual variability in cognitive ability in later life that is typical of so many other phenomena in geriatrics. The upshot of clinical study and experience is that disease (i.e., dementia) is the prime determinant of loss of mental faculties in late life, not aging per se. Simply growing old does not bring on mental decline. To be sure, cognitive changes may occur, but they are distinct from actual cognitive impairment and should be viewed as such.

With regard to memory, changes resulting from aging alone are not extensive. Immediate memory (perceiving and registering information within seconds) is minimally altered by age. Numerous studies of short-term memory (remembering a small amount of information over a brief period of time once registered) similarly show little to no change with age. In the area of long-term memory (reinforced short-term memories stored and remembered for long periods of time) results are mixed. Highly overlearned, important material is little lost with age. Significant age differences are found, however, in the area of free recall.

In fact, when given a large amount of new information to retain over a relatively long delay, individuals show declines in memory as early as age fifty. The important thing to note is that while a certain amount of memory loss, particularly long-term memory loss, often comes with age, that memory loss is no signal for overall mental decline or collapse.

However, impaired cognition is an important clinical problem in the elderly and has several potential medical causes. Factors that contribute to the susceptibility of older persons to cognitive impairment include age-related changes in the anatomy and function of the brain as well as the increased incidence with aging of diseases that directly or indirectly affect the brain. A reasonable summary of the data indicates that dementia occurrence is roughly 1 percent at age sixty and increases to as high as 30 to 50 percent by age eighty-five in Western societies. In the United States, scientists estimate that up to 4 million older adults currently suffer with Alzheimer's disease. The number of people with Alzheimer's disease at any one time in the United States doubles every five years beyond age sixty-five. As devastating as are the affects of dementia in the elderly, clearly the percentages show that it is not the predominant state of older persons in the West. Cognitive impairment can be a serious health problem facing the elderly; it requires careful diagnosis and treatment. Nothing, however, suggests that mental decline is normal for aging individuals. In fact, Palmore points out that "senility" is not actually a medical or a scientific term; rather, it is a vague word used by lay and medical people alike to explain away the behavior and condition of older people. Nonetheless, alarmingly, the myth of senility contributes to the current situation, in which many mental health problems among the elderly go undiagnosed and untreated in spite of the fact that mental illness is not common, inevitable, or untreatable in their population.[23] Just like their younger counterparts, elderly persons with dementia deserve to receive a proper evaluation and plan of management. They should not be dismissed as being merely "senile."

Neither should the elderly be pigeonholed as asexual nor stigmatized as perverse for maintaining an interest in sex. Unlike cognition, sexuality and aging has been the subject of a relatively small, but nonetheless important, number of investigations. Nonetheless, existing studies show some consistent results that shed light on certain realities of sexuality in late life. In general, these studies indicate that while sexual activity tends to decrease with aging, most older people engage in some form of sexual activity. The studies also show a wide individual variability in sexual activity among elders—again, a common phenomenon in geriatric study. Researchers have yet to identify the discrete boundaries between normal age-related changes in sexual function and functional impairment in the elderly. Regardless, a review of sexual interest and activity in late life as well as a brief consideration of sexual dysfunction among the elderly demonstrates that the clinical reality of older people is by no means the sexual wasteland of hackneyed comic lore.

With regard to sexual activity and interest in late life, many fewer studies of women than of men exist, but available data indicate that aging does not significantly impair intimacy, desire, arousal, or orgasm in healthy women. A significant proportion of elderly women are sexually interested and active, even past eighty. Various studies conducted since the 1950s have shown consistently that at least 30 percent (and, depending on the study, anywhere up to 70 percent) of women past the age of sixty engage in some form of sexual activity. Although studies show a decrease in sexual activity and, to a lesser extent, sexual interest in aging males, an even higher proportion of elderly men remain sexually engaged, even past the age of eighty. Studies reveal a remarkably high rate of sexuality among men over sixty, with figures normally falling within the 50–70 percent range. In short, it seems safe to conclude that a substantial amount of sexual activity as well as a considerable degree of sexual interest exists in our aged population. The recent overwhelming demand for the new potency-boosting drug Viagra serves as testimony to that assertion.

Of course, sexual dysfunction and inactivity does increase in prevalence with advancing age. However, as with cognitive impairment, disease most often accounts for functional problems. Any number of diseases and conditions may adversely affect sexual function in women.[24] With regard to sexual problems in men, studies show that with age the frequency of sexual intercourse decreases and erectile dysfunction increases. The reasons and risk factors for sexual dysfunction in men are largely the same as those for women: a combination of medical and social problems.[25] Unfortunately, the investigation and treatment of sexual dysfunction in the elderly suffers from a lack of attention in the medical community. Sexual problems often are not elicited by physicians, and most elders do not consider sexual problems abnormal for their age. Thus, they tend not to seek out treatment.[26] Palmore finds that most younger people believe that elders no longer have sexual activity or even desire, and those few who do are morally depraved or at least abnormal. Even among the elderly there may be the belief that sex is wrong in late life. Researchers find as well that adult children frequently oppose elder sexuality, and that elders often are not accorded the personal space in which to conduct sexual relations. Such attitudes and practices conflict with the fact that elders both have and need sexual intimacy, and that sex is an integral part of late life.[27]

Sexual activity and sexual satisfaction ought to be regarded as serious measures of elder well-being. Most Americans, however, including many health-care workers, assume as true the naturalized myths of popular culture against elder sexuality, making difficult a realistic approach to sexual issues and problems among older people. As in youth, sex is a fact of life for the elderly. Elder sexuality, like elder cognition, should not be the butt of cruel and uninformed jokes and attitudes that tend to inhibit the full enjoyment of life for older Americans.

AGEISM NOW AND THEN

We suspect largely the same held true for the elderly of pre-industrial Western societies; that is, both cognitively and sexually, they suffered from the stigma of similar callous myths against them. Myth works to obscure the reality of things. What we need are frank, not fanciful, assessments of the many aspects of growing older. Since myth obscures reality in our current society, it seems reasonable to believe that caution will pay off in our historical investigation of aging in pre-industrial society. Certainly unique forms of ageist belief will be found in any given historical setting. We encourage researchers always to be alert to contemporary myths of aging. In addition, we hope that with this chapter we've helped prevent the occurrence of a curiously inverse form of history repeating itself. Namely, that historians, in their study of the early modern era, should be mindful not to transport back with them our modern cultural misconceptions and prejudices against the elderly. Toward that end, we will close by theorizing four sources of ageism in America today. We offer them here first because they might well be applicable to the study of the early modern period, and second because, in fact, they might indeed *stem* from the early modern period. Causes of ageism now may very well reflect causes of ageism then.

A first source of current-day ageism might be characterized as our taking kernels of truth about the aging process and overgeneralizing them into all-inclusive descriptions of the elderly. Palmore concludes that most Americans are not gerontophobic; instead, we tend to hold a combination of milder ageist prejudices mixed with some positive stereotypes of elders.[28] Few of us then set out consciously to persecute the elderly—probably the reverse—but in our limited understanding of and experience with the actual aging process myths easily get formed.

A second factor contributing to our ageism, and one closely linked with the first, might be fear. Again, Palmore finds that we do not hate and fear older people themselves or even necessarily our own chronological aging as such; instead, we fear the "growing disabilities, senility, and approaching death" we associate with the aging process.[29] While the fear of disability itself is by no means an irrational one, projecting our fear into an unreasonable and harmful characterization of the elderly is.

A third source of ageism might arise from our economic system. Free-market capitalism, like any ideology, is not founded on recognizing social reality but rather on constructing one. Thus far in America, capitalism has tended to construct a society largely exclusive of the elderly. Liberal rather than free-market governmental policies have been put in place to alleviate this latent antipathy toward elders. Nonetheless, the cult of youth dominating our popular culture, workplace, and marketplace today is, at least in part, one result of consumer capitalism in the West gradually being adopted as our basic economic organization.[30]

A fourth reason for our ageist tendencies might be that, for young people, making fun of older people is entertaining—albeit simultaneously cruel. Given the nature of the first three sources of our ageist views, perhaps such animosity is unavoidable. Humans often make fun of what we misunderstand and fear, and the business of television, movies, print mass media, and advertising is to entertain for profit. Depictions of the elder in American popular culture, then, are almost bound to be distortions. Therefore, semiotically, Americans seem to be trapped in a vicious cycle when it comes to our perceptions about aging. Because we mix small kernels of truth about the aging process with large doses of ignorance and fear, our basic misunderstanding of growing older produces in us a deep anxiety about it. Misunderstanding and anxiety, in turn, facilitate our creation of various fabrications and misrepresentations of the elderly—myths that can even turn a profit. Those distortions then help contribute to our original misunderstanding and anxiety. In the case of comedy, the very ageist jokes we imagine we enjoy actually serve to increase our elemental dread of growing old. That dread in turn increases our need to deflect our anxiety with such jokes. In the end the joke is on us. Instead of easing our discomfort at the thought of aging, such awkward laughter and biased dramatic caricature in fact provoke it. Myths of aging backfire. They make growing older worse than it has to be.

NOTES

1. See "Naturalizing Myths of Aging: Reading Popular Culture," *Journal of Aging and Identity* 4, no. 2 (June 1999): 79–109.

2. Erdman Palmore, *Ageism: Negative and Positive* (New York: Springer, 1990), 4, 86; see also pp. 15–16.

3. Ibid., 78–81.

4. See Ferdinand de Saussure, *Course in General Linguistics*, ed. C. B. Bally and A. Sechehaye, trans. W. Baskin (New York: McGraw-Hill, 1959), 7–17 [originally published 1913].

5. See also ibid., 76.

6. Roland Barthes, *Writing Degree Zero and Elements of Semiology*, trans. A. Lavers and C. Smith (Boston: Beacon, 1970), 57; see also 92–94.

7. Roland Barthes, *Mythologies*, trans. A. Lavers (New York: Hill and Wang, 1988), 109–111.

8. See ibid., 111–117.

9. See ibid., 119–127.

10. Ibid., 129–130.

11. Ibid., 131, 143.

12. See ibid., 140–145.

13. Ibid., 144–145.

14. Northrop Frye, *Anatomy of Criticism: Four Essays* (Princeton, NJ: Princeton University Press, 1957), 163. While Frye's generic taxonomies are often reductive and thus can be limiting as a mode of literary analysis, his theories on typical comedic form nonetheless provide a sound and relevant grounding to a discussion of ageist myths in early modern plays.

15. See ibid., 163–176.

16. Ibid., 164.

17. See Palmore, *Ageism*, 14–15, 38–39.

18. Quotations from all plays are from *British Dramatists from Dryden to Sheridan*, ed. G. Nettleton and A. Case (Carbondale: Southern Illinois University Press, 1969); citations are given by act, scene, and line number.

19. See J. A. Levy, "Sexuality and Aging," in *Principles of Geriatric Medicine and Gerontology*, ed. W. Hazzard, et al. (New York: McGraw-Hill, 1994), 116, 118. See also Palmore, *Ageism*, 84, 124–125.

20. See also Palmore, *Ageism*, ch. 6.

21. Ibid., 22–24.

22. Rather than document the many studies of cognitive and sexual behavior in the elderly, we will simply summarize here the research and ask readers to refer to our original article in *Journal of Aging and Identity* for those specific references as well as for a fuller discussion of these topics.

23. See Palmore, *Ageism*, 12–13, 21–22.

24. Painful intercourse secondary to vaginal atrophy or altered anatomy from gynecological surgery are common causes. Osteoarthritis is another source of inhibiting pain. Any advanced systemic disease such as cancer, congestive heart failure, chronic obstructive pulmonary disease, or dementia will interfere with sexual activity. Medications, urinary incontinence, depression, and marital or relationship problems are other important sources of diminished sexual functioning in women.

25. Decreased physical activity, urinary incontinence, respiratory and bowel problems, sedative use, myocardial infarction, and diabetes mellitus are frequent sexual inhibitors in men. Other problems noted for inhibiting older male sexuality are fear of poor performance, erectile dysfunction, orgasmic dysfunction, not enough opportunity for sexual encounters, or a partner's pain.

26. Note the parallel to Louise Gray's chapter in this volume.

27. Palmore, *Ageism*, 20, 125–126.

28. Ibid., 29–39.

29. Ibid., 38.

30. See also ibid., chs. 5, 8, 9, 13 and D. Cowgill, *Aging and Modernization* (New York: Appleton-Century-Crofts, 1972).

Representations of Old Age and Aging

11

Aging Heroes, Buffoons, and Statesmen in Shakespeare's Plays

Janice Rossen

> We have heard the chimes at midnight, Master Shallow.
> —Falstaff, *King Henry IV Part II* (III.ii.191)

Shakespeare's aged characters are individual figures with distinct voices and particular desires. Gremio, in *The Taming of the Shrew*, burns to marry the beautiful Bianca Minola. King Lear, in the tragedy that bears his name, demands that his daughters tell him how much they love him. Queen Margaret, in *The Tragedy of Richard III*, shrieks for the entire house of York to be razed to the ground. The single-minded passions that drive each of these characters verges on obsession. Such intensity imparts a vividness to each character and reminds us that although the aging process can seem to dehumanize people because of their increasing physical weakness, they themselves will have none of this: they *desire*, therefore they are.

This individuality of character makes Shakespeare's plays salutary and startling reading. Moreover, his aged characters do not remain confined to the periphery of the action but are seen in context of the larger world—they continue to be part of humanity and are not alienated to a different status because of their age, gender, or social class. They rage, grieve, plot, and suffer with full intensity, often equal to the emotional range of their younger counterparts. At the same time, the general tendency to diminish or discount the elderly is fully recognized. The melancholy Jaques, in *As You Like It*, points to this moral in his gloomy catalog of the progress of man's brief existence, which concludes with "Last scene of all, / That ends this strange eventful history, / Is second childishness

and mere oblivion, / Sans teeth, sans eyes, sans taste, sans every thing"
(II.vii.163–66).[1] By contrast, however, the voice of an individual person within
the drama rings in a completely different register. The actual *character* in *As
You Like It* who is elderly, the servant Adam, appears in quite a different light
from the symbolic figure in Jaques's speech. To his master Oliver's contemptuous dismissal, for instance, he replies, "Is 'old dog' my reward? Most true, I
have lost my teeth in your service" (I.i.86). This has the unmistakable ring of
a unique voice, and it expresses a different kind of acute suffering than does a
philosophical pronouncement. It also demonstrates the fact that—although toothless—Adam can still bite in words. This reminds us that however much we may
distance ourselves from the phenomenon of aging, or strike a cynical pose,
people remain fully themselves as human beings, regardless of their age or
circumstances. The ultimate effect of this line of thought is to present us with
a profoundly humanist worldview.

Recent critical studies of Shakespeare's plays and the subject of aging have
tended to focus on larger paradigms that can be seen to be illustrated in the
author's works. Examples are Leslie A. Fiedler's consideration of myths about
aging and sexuality and the distinctly Freudian readings offered by Carolyn Asp
and William Kerrigan. Two essays in *Aging and Identity: A Humanities Perspective*, edited by Sara Munson Deats and Lagretta Tallent Lenker, take a sociological approach and consider the two characters of King Lear and Prospero
as models of aging. Marlene Clark's dissertation, "Aging Queens in Shakespeare's Drama," discusses the question of aging as it reflects on gender, and
William Jeffrey Phelan's "The Vale of Years: Early Modern Aging, Gender,
and Shakespearean Tragedy" broadens these categories still further, placing the
effect of aging alongside that of race, gender, and social class.[2]

While it is stimulating to apply newly devised paradigms to earlier works, I
would like to add three more generalizations about Renaissance culture to this
array of possible approaches. They each express a profound paradox at the heart
of Shakespeare's world, and as such they undermine attempts at simplification,
especially on the subject of aging. First, *memento mori* dominated much of
Elizabethan thinking, and the consciousness of wry sophistication assumed in
the face of death is evidenced by scenes like the "Yorick" speech in *Hamlet*.
Hence, Shakespeare's use of elderly characters is not surprising, as another way
of illustrating the moral that in the midst of life we are in death. Second, at the
same time that death was viewed as an integral part of the life process, the
English Renaissance was a culture essentially built on complete denial of aging
and of its consequences. For political reasons, authors such as Edmund Spenser
and Sir Philip Sidney exalted the figure of Gloriana, the virgin queen (though
not, of course, without some sense of irony verging on despair). This exaggerated idealization of Queen Elizabeth provided one way of dealing with increasing anxiety about political instability due to lack of an heir to the throne. Still,
any conclusions drawn about gender issues in works of the queen's favorite
playwright must be seen in the context of a patriarchy that was ruled—para-

doxically—by a woman. Third, the most basic generalization made by England at this time was that of Christian humanism, regarding man as the measure of all things. When Hamlet discourses: "What a piece of work is a man! How noble in reason! how infinite in faculties!" it is meant to stir us to appreciation (II.ii.310–311).

This high value for humanity informs all of Shakespeare's plays and accounts for the fascination that his characters exert over critics who seek to illustrate ideas about aging, or to use contemporary paradigms derived from sociology and history to illuminate the plays. But more important still, Shakespeare's aging characters exhibit individuality not because they are particular types, but instead because life is acknowledged in his plays to be inherently complex. This is buttressed by an amusing simplicity, as well; besides occasionally being extraordinary, his elderly characters also do what old people do, and say the kind of things that old people might be expected to say. As Justice Shallow observes in *King Henry IV, Part II*, when he meets the companion of his youth, Falstaff: "Jesu! Jesu! the mad days I have spent; and to see how many of my old acquaintance are dead!" (III.ii.29–31). This is, naturally, a pleasing reflection, filled with *Schadenfreude*—yet it is affectionately comic as well, in its nostalgia for the past: "Jesus! The days that we have seen!" Even Falstaff, pronouncing "every third word a lie" in his companion's narrative, admits, "We have heard the chimes at midnight, Master Shallow" (III.ii.194, 270, 191). At the same time that they can seem to exaggerate, in order to compensate for their present weakness, aged characters in Shakespeare's plays often match or exceed the spirit of their younger, more able counterparts—they too curse their enemies, fight against limitations or restrictions, and bewail their losses. Cardinal Wolsey's final speech in *King Henry VIII*, for example, is a meditation on personal devastation: "Farewell! a long farewell, to all my greatness!" he exclaims, after being exposed in plotting with Rome against the king. At the same time, he seeks to make the best of his plight, observing: "I know myself now; and I feel within me / A peace above all earthly dignities, / A still and quiet conscience" (III.ii.414, 445–447).

This marks a determined attempt to deal with a reversal of circumstance. Still, older characters in Shakespeare remain interesting, whether they change substantially or not. They exhibit a logical continuity with the past, not only in historical, linear terms, but temperamentally. Their reactions make sense, from what we know of them before the action of the play begins—Lear's rage, Falstaff's resilience, Queen Margaret's venom. (As Kirk Combe, Kenneth Schmader, and Sara Munson Deats have all observed, Prospero in *The Tempest* shows himself capable of change, and in a way which suggests personal nobility, but also a consistency in what we know of his essential character.) In each of these cases, individuality is crucial: David Van Tassel observes cogently that old age "is a function of the life that the person has lived."[3] This fact makes Shakespeare's plays an exhilarating source for the study of aging, as he presents us with a wide array of aging kings, ministers of state, buffoons, hostesses of brothels, dethroned queens, cranky hermits, and faithful servants. While they might be representative of certain social types, individual people in the plays age differently—and often in a way that transcends traditional notions of "successful" aging. This is Shakespeare's great contribution to our understanding. When William Kerrigan points out that many aged characters in these plays find conformity anathema—that they are, on occasion, "not always subdued or quiescent in spirit, but enraged, and some of them sublimely," he has given us a valuable insight.[4]

In short, while it can be useful to discuss various paradigms as they relate to Shakespeare's plays, it is also appropriate to consider the sheer breadth and complexity of possible ways of feeling that he dramatizes.

With this as my main focus, I want to consider the individual—even eccentric—nature of Shakespeare's aged characters as they appear within the context of the literary notions of genre and plot. Since he wrote in three genres—comedy, history plays, and tragedy—the means of this emotional expressiveness varies among these larger categories. Still, the throb of passion remains authentic in each of his characters. Furthermore, the seeming paradox of elderly people who continue to feel strongly, to make brave and heroic choices (as well as rash and self-destructive ones) adds a deeper dimension to his plays.

> Let me be your servant.
> Though I look old, yet I am strong and lusty;
> For in my youth I never did apply
> Hot and rebellious liquors in my blood,
> Nor did not with unabashful forehead woo
> The means of weakness and debility.
> Therefore my age is as a lusty winter,
> Frosty but kindly. Let me go with you;
> I'll do the service of a younger man
> In all your business and necessities. (II.iii.49–58)

Adam bears out Van Tassel's observation that one's previous choices in life affect one's later years; Adam is proud to offer his services to Orlando, with the quiet boast that he has preserved his strength for just such an occasion. His youthful abstention from strong drink is perhaps less meaningful than Adam's firm belief that it has made him able to take on such a challenge, thus expressing his consistent character as one who desires above all to be a truly worthy servant.

Further, he exhibits an independence of spirit by attempting to preserve his strength for as long as possible, and also to save enough to support himself when strength has finally failed: he tells Orlando, "I have five hundred crowns, / The thrifty hire I saved under your father, / Which I did store to be my foster nurse / When service should in my old limbs lie lame / And unregarded age in corners thrown" (41–45). By sacrificing his means of support to Orlando, he is able to give him the means of escaping death, by revealing Oliver's plan to murder him, advising him not to enter the house, and fleeing with him to the Forest of Arden.

Adam becomes, in fact, a crucial hinge of the plot—and he does so by show-ing extraordinary willingness to set out on an adventure:

> Master, go on and I will follow thee
> To the last gasp with truth and loyalty.
> From seventeen years till now almost fourscore
> Here lived I; but now live here no more.
> At seventeen years, many their fortunes seek,
> But at fourscore it is too late a week.
> Yet Fortune cannot recompense me better
> Than to die well, and not my master's debtor. (72–79)

He does receive this reward, and in a way that preserves both his own integrity and the rightful state of authority. When he faints for lack of food in the forest, Orlando cares for him, nurturing the aged, faithful family retainer, and replacing the money or "thrifty hire" that Adam has saved with the warmth of affection. This honor is fully deserved on Adam's part: in their flight away from danger, he has made the ultimate self-sacrifice and laid down his life for his young master. It also demonstrates the irony of Adam's desire for independence; though he can hold weakness and age at bay for an extraordinary length of time, he cannot altogether overcome its erosion. His collapse lends a melancholy cast to the comedy, which at times verges on the bitter—Jaques as a commentator and moralizer strikes this note just before Adam's entrance to the duke's circle in the forest. Whether Adam is actually intended to have died at this moment or not (the text does not make this clear), he certainly has no more voice in the play. Moreover, if he has died, his will not be one of the merry and wondering faces among the wedding guests at the close of the drama. In some sense, he has simply removed to another place, in a similar way to two other characters, the "hermit" in the forest (who never appears onstage) and the usurping duke, who chooses to retire into contemplation with the hermit at the end of the play. Through this resolution of the plot—and the distinct conversion in character that it is predicated upon—As You Like It offers the spectacle of age as a means of retreating from worldly affairs, in order to attain peace and to acquire a measure of wisdom. Jaques himself becomes so intrigued by this possibility that he de-cides to quit the duke's company and join the two hermits.

Old age asserts a powerful hold on the imagination in this play. While the dénouement of the drama delights the audience with its traditional comic reso-lution of marriage (no less than three couples are united at the end) and rightful restoration of power (the usurping duke cedes his place to the rightful one), a strong current of the ever-present theme of aging acts as an undertow to the plot. The linear view of time is stressed repeatedly: seven ages of man, and an inexorable progression to nihilism, arriving at a state of being "sans everything."

As Jaques gleefully reports the Fool's moralizing on this subject: "from hour to hour we ripe and ripe, / And then from hour to hour we rot and rot. / And thereby hangs a tale" (II.vii.26–28).

At the same time, while evoking this paradigm of relentless, progressive decay, Shakespeare subverts this notion repeatedly (not least in the peaceful death of faithful Adam). When Rosalind first approaches Orlando in her disguise as Ganymede, she hits upon the ruse of asking him for the time, as an excuse for accosting him in conversation. His reply is incredulous and humorous: "You should ask me what time o' day. There's no clock in the forest" (II.ii.278–279). As in all truly magical places, both things are true at once. Time is relative; as twentieth-century writers Henri Bergson and Marcel Proust have pointed out, the way in which it appears to us may be widely different from its linear measurement. Similarly, when Rosalind pines away for Orlando to appear, she appeals to the tyranny of the clock, which makes waiting unbearable because she is in love (a phenomenon outside of chronological time): "Break an hour's promise in love?" she chides him (IV.i.39). The agony engendered by a succession of minutes in this context lies on a different scale altogether.

In the end, what exerts the most power over the characters is neither the clock, ticking away industriously, nor passions of the heart, but the seasons. These constitute a deeper rhythm, underlying both forest and town, shepherds and court. With this paradigm, Shakespeare aligns aging with winter, a natural process that leads to death—but in a redemptive way as well as a poignant one. Adam's death is not tragic in this setting—it occurs quietly, and surrounded by the glow of a noble action and true affection from his young master. Furthermore, it works for good because it has the ring of truth: as the exiled duke discourses, to be close to nature's rhythms has a kind of integrity allied to it.

> Are not these woods
> More free from peril than the envious court?
> Here feel we not the penalty of Adam,
> The seasons' difference?—as, the icy fang
> And churlish chiding of the winter's wind
> Which when it bites and blows upon my body
> E'en till I shrink with cold, I smile and say:
> "This is no flattery; these are counselors
> That feelingly persuade me what I am." (II.i.3–11)

It is tempting to read these lines ironically, and as redolent of self-deception—at the least, they can sound like making the best of a bad job. At the same time, they also express a deeper truth, and one that is close to the heart of the play. To be, or to fully become, what one *is* has high merit in Shakespeare's world.

Resignation and contemplation are not the only responses of the elderly to their world in the comedies. The discomforts of aging are also felt—and felt keenly (as the biting of the wind is perceived by the duke). Antonio and Leonato in *Much Ado About Nothing*, for instance, chafe furiously at the impotence of old age to revenge itself properly upon the younger men who have insulted Leonato's daughter, Hero. Again, a major point here is the fierceness of passion that grips the sufferer; where Antonio counsels patience and self-control, Leonato replies:

> I pray thee, peace! I will be flesh and blood;
> For there was never yet philosopher
> That could endure the toothache patiently,
> However they have writ the style of gods
> And made a push at chance and sufferance. (V.i.35–39)

He is also keenly alive to the denigration that others might cast on him because of his age, and he turns this recognition back upon his opponents. When the two brothers accost Claudio and the Prince, he tells them:

> Tush, tush, man! never fleer and jest at me:
> I speak not like a dotard nor a fool,
> As, under privilege of age, to brag
> What I have done being young, or what would do,
> Were I not old. (V.i.63–67)

At the same time, however, he is shown to be powerless to revenge himself on the younger soldiers. Although the conventions of the plot (and the revelation of the deception that has been practiced) will right the wrong, the injury of such a disgrace is felt to be terrible. Accordingly, Leonato and Antonio are allowed dignity and yet also appear pathetic in their plight. The irreverence of the young is cruel in its contempt: Claudio tells Benedick, after this confrontation: "We had like to have had our two noses snapped off with two old men without teeth" (V.i.125–126).

Since no one is exempt from Shakespeare's brilliant wit, aged characters can also be portrayed as wholly ridiculous. Where they appear in the tragedies, they can act as dramatic contrast to the weighty action going forward by appearing ludicrous: everyone remembers the chattering nurse in *Romeo and Juliet*. In the comedies, of course, examples of self-deceived and self-important characters abound. Old Gobbo, in *The Merchant of Venice*, is clearly a figure of fun—and so, for that matter, is the elder statesman Polonius in *Hamlet*. ("This counsellor / Is now most still, most secret, and most grave, / Who was in life a foolish prating knave," says his murderer, in a wry tone [III.iv.232–234].) The hapless constables Dogberry and Verges in *Much Ado About Nothing* derive much of their humor from reference to aging as a sign of infirm mind—and indeed, Dogberry's deficiencies have serious consequences for the plot, as the two men discourse tediously with Leonato:

Dogberry: Goodman Verges, sir, speaks a little off the matter: an old man, sir, and his wits are not so blunt, as, God help, I would desire they were; but, in faith, honest as the skin between his brows.

Verges: Yes, I thank God, I am as honest as any man living, that is an old man and no honester than I. (IV.v.8–13)

One of the most entertaining elderly figures on Shakespeare's stage is Gremio in *The Taming of the Shrew*. He is clearly a type which Fiedler labels as the *Senex* of Roman comedy, the old man doomed to romantic disappointment; and yet he is not wholly ridiculous.[5] In putting himself forward as a suitor for Bianca, along with several other (younger) men, Gremio deliberately flouts the stigma of age. Is this enlightened self-interest or disgusting pretentiousness? Something definitely seems to be blinding him to what is possible or reasonable—as far as the lady herself is concerned, he is utterly rejected in favor of a younger man. At the same time, her father has determined to accept the highest bidder for her hand in marriage. Therefore his hopes seem to be well founded, on purely mercenary grounds, and except for his shortage of wealth in comparison with his rival, he might have attained his goal. Age is nevertheless deemed unsuitable for the role of romantic lover: "Greybeard, thy love doth freeze," sniffs Tranio (to which Gremio replies defensively, "thine doth fry" [II.i.361–362]). Still, what makes Gremio ridiculous is not so much age in itself, but the inappropriateness of his desire for a much younger woman—who moreover has given no sign of desiring him in return. While he is very much a stock character, he also appears to feel genuine emotion; and this in itself is not derided as ludicrous.[6] He takes his place with the other unsuccessful suitors at the end of the play, who "shot and miss'd" (V.i.54).

Moreover, in the case of a licensed buffoon, such as Falstaff, his genuine powers of attraction remain in full play. *The Merry Wives of Windsor* casts him in a different mode, of course, as the "fairies" pinch and pull him, burning him with their tapers for his presumption in approaching the "honest" wives. On the other hand, in *King Henry IV Part II*, Falstaff illustrates both the fickleness of love and yet its power to command emotion, taking Doll Tearsheet on his knee: "I am old, I am old," he declaims. Her reply assures him, though, "I love thee better than I love e'er a scurvy young boy of them all" (II.iv.238–240). This exchange hints at the persistence of sexual desire, yet also the nostalgic affection of longtime friends.

A major danger inherent in aging, as Gremio's plight illustrates, is self-deception (and, perhaps, selfishness). Certainly, older characters (even Falstaff included) are not expected to have *unregulated* sexual desires—though this is often simplified to a demand that they feel none at all. Queen Gertrude in *Hamlet* is an object of disgust to her son because of her sexual appetite for the usurping Claudius—though Hamlet challenges her on the grounds of her age and lack of discretion: "You cannot call it love, for at your age / The heyday in the blood is tame, it's humble, / And waits upon the judgment," he avers (III.iv.76–78).

It is not so much aging that seems inherently ridiculous in these contexts as it is willful persistence in desire for an unsuitable object. I will hasten to add that Shakespeare's plays are full of this sort of mismatched romantic yearning— Malvolio's self-aggrandizing love for Olivia in *Twelfth Night*, for instance, is a case in point, and self-deception is not predicated on aging alone. As *Love's Labour's Lost* makes plain, the disease of romantic love makes fools of anyone who is so brazen as to discount it. Moreover, what Shakespeare dramatizes for us again and again is the complexity of hidden motives and devious desires, which the characters often cannot even fathom themselves.

What this conflict of passions engenders is a fundamental sense in Shakespeare's plays that selfish desire in any character of any age or station in life is potentially shocking and harmful. A straightforward illustration of this occurs when both the king of Morocco and the Prince of Arragon in *The Merchant of Venice* choose the wrong caskets in search of Portia's hand in marriage. They are blinded to the necessity that Bassanio intuits, which is that one must not seek rewards or consequence in love, but rather "*give and hazard all he hath*" (II.ix.21).[7] Thus aging, as a phenomenon, constitutes a kind of extension of life and human values that does not alter in any substantial way the difference between selfishness and generosity, greed and self-sacrifice. That is, old age does not exempt Shakespeare's characters from being bound to play by the same rules as everyone else on stage; the elderly are neither sentimentalized as being needier, nor are they portrayed as being wiser, nobler, or more self-disciplined.

At the same time, neither are they denied the dignity of *having* desires— sexual, familial, or domestic. Whereas Gremio in *Taming of the Shrew* is made to appear ludicrous through lusting for a younger woman, older characters who have chosen and won wives in a suitable way are treated with respect and honor. In the later comedies, for instance, there is often a reunion (beyond all reasonable hope) of families who have been separated for years. Family members who have been recovered constitute a literal fulfillment of dashed hopes for a royal lineage: in *The Winter's Tale*, the restoration of Perdita to the kingdom of Sicilia is crucial to the prosperous fortunes of the state as a whole—and constitutes the only hope for the king to produce an heir to the throne. Similarly, in *Cymbeline*, the king recovers his two lost sons, as well as his daughter, at the end of the play. In *Pericles*, the hero recovers his daughter, Marina. Nor is it only children who are deemed irreplaceable as individuals; wives are infinitely precious as well. It forms a key part of the plays' resolutions that such reunions occur: Hermione is restored to Leontes, Thaisa to Pericles, and Imogen to Posthumous.

This restoration of a lost spouse occasionally takes on almost purely comic proportions in similar happy endings. The resolution of Shakespeare's *Comedy of Errors* involves the reunion of Aegeon with his spouse Aemilia, now an abbess at Ephesus, whom he had lost in a shipwreck several decades earlier. Still, the symbolism of these reunions satisfies the audience's desire for closure. The importance of these reunion scenes reflects profoundly on the subject of aging, since the grief and loss that can be attendant upon aging hinges on the restoration of a particular person. No one else will do, and a lost lover is irreplaceable. In *The Winter's Tale*, Leontes, still encouraged in his grieving by Paulina, is sternly urged to meditate on the virtues of his long-lost queen: "If one by one you wedded all the world, / Or from the all that are took something good, / To make a perfect woman, she you kill'd / Would be unparallel'd" (V.i.15–18). This may seem excessive idealization of the heroine as a woman— and yet, the penance that the king owes to his wronged queen does justify this observation. Though we can argue that an incomplete grieving process is taking place here, the play also suggests simply that individual people are unique and worth mourning as such. Though his courtiers urge him to take another wife in order to produce children who would assume the succession of the state, Leontes is urged by Paulina to cling to the memory of the uniqueness of his former wife. This suggests that even if one is a king, and with a state duty to perform, it cannot be performed except at the expense of dehumanizing the particular woman whom he has formerly loved and wronged.

Similarly, Pericles, king of Tyre, becomes so overwhelmed by his grief at the loss of his wife and daughter that he becomes a recluse and will speak to no one. The reunion with his daughter stresses the agony of this loss, which time has not lessened; yet it also affirms the common humanity of everyone in the matter of suffering. Marina, his daughter, seeks to make him respond to her, and as she does so, she recounts her own losses (equal to, and as grievous as his). Aged people alone do not suffer; fate is not a respecter of persons.

It is part of the business of a comedy to set things right in the end, and to some extent characters in these dramas are ruled by this convention. The predominate myth is one of springtime, renewal, and redemption—more elaborately so in Shakespeare's late comedies. There is a marked difference in views of aging, by contrast, in Shakespeare's history plays and tragedies. Although they share the same basic worldview, they reformulate it from a more complex and darker perspective. The history plays are generally concerned with the proper use of authority in government, and therefore the greatest issue for elder statesmen is the handing on of power in a more or less gracious manner. Again, as in the comedies, aging courtiers (and even monarchs) are no different from anyone else in their essential humanity—and vulnerability. To be at court is, in itself, a hazard fraught with peril, and the arrest of the duke of Buckingham at the beginning of *King Henry VIII* for treason is as likely to occur without warning, as is the murder of Duke Humphrey in his bed in *King Henry VI Part II* or the confinement of Edmund Mortimer in his prison in *Part I*.

> This royal throne of kings, this scept'red isle,
> This earth of majesty, this seat of Mars,
> This other Eden, demiparadise,
> This fortress built by Nature for herself.
> Against infection and the hand of war,
> This happy breed of men, this little world,

This precious stone set in the silver sea,
Which serves it in the office of a wall
Or as a moat defensive to a house
Against the envy of less happier lands;
This blessed plot, this earth, this realm, this England. (II.i.40–50)

For an aging woman, the situation is often desolate indeed. The duchess of York in *Richard III* has lost everything in the death of her family members, leaving her almost without speech: "So many miseries have craz'd my voice, / That my woe-wearied tongue is still and mute" (IV.iv.17–18). Queen Katherine, in *King Henry VIII*, pleads to retain her rights as a wife and queen by appealing to her years of patient servitude toward the king—though she too has lost all except her remaining dignities: "Alas! Has banished me his bed already, / His love too long ago! I am old, my lords, / And all the fellowship I hold now with him / Is only my obedience. What can happen / To me above this wretchedness?" (III.i.133–137).

In the history plays, the dehumanization—and disinheritance—of the aging man or woman is made much more vivid a possibility because of the power struggle in which *everyone* engages—elderly and young children alike, all of whom are at risk. This is not to say that older characters do not instinctively meet their troubles in a different way, from long being inured to them. John of Gaunt counsels patience to his exiled son, Bolingbroke—though he also sets the power of kings as naught in respect to the progress of time. When King Richard politely observes that Gaunt will have many years in which to live, he replies:

But not a minute, king, that thou canst give.
Shorten my days thou canst with sullen sorrow
And pluck nights from me, but not lend a morrow.
Thou canst help time to furrow me with age,
But stop no wrinkle in his pilgrimage.
Thy word is current with him for my death,
But dead, thy kingdom cannot buy my breath. (II.i.28–34)

The pain that elderly characters suffer—and upon which they discourse with eloquence—marks them as being as human as everyone else embroiled in the ongoing turmoil. This being so, it is not surprising that the most famous rejection of a former favored companion is cast in exactly these terms: that of being negated as an individual. When King Henry V assumes the throne, in *King Henry IV Part II*, he disowns Falstaff with the withering phrase, "I know thee not, old man: fall to thy prayers; / How ill white hairs become a fool and jester!" (V.v.47–48).

Whereas the history plays subvert all questions of age to the larger struggle for power, and seem at times to deal out disgrace and misfortune with cruel impartiality, it is the business of comedy to redeem what might otherwise be devalued or lost. Although Antonio in *The Merchant of Venice* protests to Bassanio that the fatal "pound of flesh" exacted by Shylock is something to be shrugged off because he himself is relatively valueless, this judgment does not stand. He claims that "I am a tainted wether of the flock, / Meetest for death: the weakest kind of fruit / Drops earliest to the ground, and so let me" (IV.i.116–118). In a true, redemptive comedy, however, the life of each person is deemed worthy to be preserved.[8]

It is not surprising that in the history plays, the most important feature of an elderly character is that of memory—above all, a recollection of particular people. This can drive home a point, as when Queen Margaret in *Richard III* teaches her younger counterparts to mourn in acutely personal terms, telling the other bereaved women onstage: "I had an Edward, till a Richard killed him; / I had a husband, till a Richard kill'd him: / Thou hadst an Edward, till a Richard kill'd him; / Thou hadst a Richard, till a Richard kill'd him" (IV.iv.40–43). While younger, inexperienced courtiers squabble over political alliances and power, strewing sugar on the bottled spider Richard of Gloucester, the single-minded former queen retells the past with accuracy.

> Old men forget; yet all shall be forgot,
> But he'll remember with advantages
> What feats he did that day. Then shall our names,
> Familiar in his mouth as household words—
> Harry the King, Bedford and Exeter,
> Warwick and Talbot, Salisbury and Gloucester—
> Be in their flowing cups freshly rememb'red. (IV.iii.52–58)

The history plays, in the most literal sense, tell the history of a nation. They do so, moreover, through the medium of heroic strivings, disappointments, and collective memories—not least in the naming of individual names. The infinitely more complex genre of tragedy shares many of the characteristics of the history plays, but it focuses on internal change as well as outward events. Its concern is with suffering, and in particular with an agony that leads to insight or resolution in its main characters. It is possible, of course, for a character to end his life in bitterness, and without significant knowledge of his own heart. The clearest example of this is Timon in *Timon of Athens*, who ends his life as a misanthropic hermit, bitterly disillusioned with the world. At the same time, though it is facile to say that he brought such tragedy upon himself, there is a definite sense in which his earlier persistence in ignoring the advice of his faithful steward, Flavius, leads directly to his poverty and exile.

The most powerful example of Shakespeare's exploration of the theme of aging and inner transformation is *King Lear*, whose tragic hero expresses perhaps the most profound fear attached to aging: that he will lose his mind under the load of griefs and shocks that overtake him. Madness poses the greatest threat, as it seems to disintegrate the personhood of the king and to effect his ultimate dehumanization. As a counterpart to this, the main problem is formulated in his fundamental lack of self-knowledge, which is seen as having been of long standing. His daughter Regan conflates this handicap with that of increasing ill judgment: " 'Tis the infirmity of his age. / Yet he hath ever but slenderly known himself" (I.ii.314–315).

Abandonment is, perhaps, the most deeply rooted fear harbored by aging characters. King Lear is refused entrance to his son-in-law's castle, turned out onto the heath, and into a raging storm—but it is the rejection of his two eldest daughters that occupies his mind incessantly: "In such a night as this! O Regan, Goneril! / Your old kind father, whose frank heart gave you all,— / O, that way madness lies; let me shun that! / No more of that!" (III.iv.21–24). As a tragedy, *King Lear* takes up all these issues of time, aging, and loss of personal power in the world that appear in the comedies and history plays and creates a terrible crisis of identity. If the play is to be seen as redemptive—in other words, with Lear becoming a tragic hero instead of a deserving victim of his own stubbornness—it is because he does attain a measure of self-knowledge. His admission to Cordelia that he fears he is not "in [his] perfect mind" shows humility, and he characterizes himself in a completely new way to her when he says: "I am a very foolish, fond old man" (IV.vii.73, 70).

Aging in itself is not the central point in this drama, as it is not the *cause* of the tragedy that occurs. What lies behind the skewed series of events that unfold in rapid succession is the folly of Lear throughout his life, and it is this that the Fool points out: "Thou shouldst not have been old till thou hadst been wise" (I.v.39–40). The king has hardened in his insistence on a certain pattern being maintained, and on being reassured that his daughters love him (which he also demands must be expressed in certain terms). That is the real danger: rigidity based on unacknowledged fear. That Shakespeare can show his character breaking down under the disintegration of everything that he *has* believed heretofore, and at the end becoming a man who can crave forgiveness, is extraordinary.

In light of these challenges to Lear's character, it is appropriate to ask whether Shakespeare's aged characters can change. The classical humanist tradition holds that a man's character is fixed from birth inalterably. All the same, in a world where man is the measure of all things, it is important to explore not only his essential nature, but his capacity to transcend himself and to act differently. By placing elderly characters in extreme crisis situations, Shakespeare explores this question at its most sensitive point—not in the tradition of the deathbed conversion (a distinctly medieval convention), but with kingdoms in the balance, and finally encompassing even unspeakable tragedy, as in the death of Lear's beloved daughter Cordelia.

The point is not so much what the answer to this question about possible transformation is, in various individual cases, as it is that Shakespeare implicitly poses it for every character in his plays. Neither aging—even extreme age— nor youth guarantee any immunity from trouble in the world. The same trials, shocks, tribulations, and potential losses are as immediate and personal for everyone on the stage. If we consider what this says about the values of Shakespeare's culture, it speaks compellingly about nobility of spirit, integrity, and the call to those in authority to show compassion toward those beneath them in the structure.

What the plays seem to suggest as a model for dealing with an elderly person is the respect accorded to Nestor in *Troilus and Cressida*; no matter how much he might speak, or seem to boast, no one ever openly laughs at him. His enemy, Hector, greets him in the Greek camp with courtesy: "Let me embrace thee, good old chronicle, / That has so long walk'd hand in hand with time" (IV.v.221–222). There is a certain irony in Nestor's boasts of his own prowess, which verge on the ridiculous; yet he is not excluded from his fellows but remains an integral part of the council of soldiers. Ulysses includes Nestor in his plots to spur Achilles from his languor. Above all, courtesy is seen as being due to Nestor, for his courage and his years. Caught up in great events, eager to maintain his honor as a soldier, he asserts both claims in his reply to Hector: "By this white beard, I'd fight with thee tomorrow. / Well, welcome, welcome. I have seen the time" (227–229).

Literature is primarily concerned with a representation of possible events and of experience on an intuitive level. Shakespeare's characters, accordingly, do not stop feeling, thinking, desiring, and—somewhat surprisingly—having the power to affect things, because they continue to be part of the human community. While never oversimplifying his representation of human nature, Shakespeare also nudges us toward goodness, free from priggishness or pedantry. As King Henry V tells his intended bride, on the subject of aging: "A good leg will fall, a straight back will stoop, a black beard will turn white, a curl'd pate will grow bald, a fair face will wither, a full eye will wax hollow. But a good heart, Kate, is the sun and the moon, or rather the sun and not the moon, for it shines bright and never changes, but keeps his course truly. If thou wilt have such a one, take me" (V.ii.155–161).

Shakespeare's plays suggest the extraordinary capacity of his audience (whom he helped to educate) to see everyone as an individual who could choose—to a large extent—his or her own destiny. In an age when the humanist value of "man" as the "measure of all things" was being promoted, this seems fitting. This also is the contribution that his work continues to make to our own study of such a universal phenomenon. The aging person remains a *person*. How we as an audience handle this realization is left to us—but the recognition of it remains inescapable.

NOTES

I am especially grateful to Beverly Bardsley, Tony Howe, William Rossen, Joan Morgan, and the late Gareth Morgan for contributing to my familiarity with—and above all, enjoyment of—these plays. I also express my thanks to my excellent editors, especially Susannah Ottaway.

1. All references are taken from *The Yale Shakespeare: The Complete Works*, ed. Wilbur L. Cross and Tucker Brooke (New Haven, CT: Yale University Press, 1993).

2. See Leslie Fiedler, "Eros and Thanatos: Old Age in Love," in *Aging, Death and the Completion of Being*, ed. David D. Van Tassel (Philadelphia: University of Pennsylvania Press, 1979), 235–254; Carolyn Asp, " 'The Clamor of Eros': Freud, Aging, and King Lear," and William Kerrigan, "Life's Iamb: The Scansion of Late Creativity in the Culture of the Renaissance," both in *Memory and Desire: Aging—Literature—Psychoanalysis*, ed. Kathleen Woodward and Murray M. Schwartz (Bloomington: Indiana University Press, 1986), 192–204 and 168–191 respectively; Kirk Combe and Kenneth Schmader, "Shakespeare Teaching Geriatrics: Lear and Prospero As Case Studies in Aged Heterogeneity," and Sara Munson Deats, "The Dialectic of Aging in Shakespeare's *King Lear* and *The Tempest*," both in *Aging and Identity: A Humanities Perspective*, ed. Sara Munson Deats and Lagretta Tallent Lenker (Westport, CT: Praeger, 1999), 33–46 and 23–32 respectively; Marlene Clark, "Aging Queens in Shakespeare's Drama," Ph.D. diss., University of Michigan, 1998; and William Jeffrey Phelan, "The Vale of Years: Early Modern Aging, Gender and Shakespearean Tragedy," Ph.D. diss., University of California at Los Angeles, 1998.

3. David D. Van Tassel, Introduction to *Aging, Death and the Completion of Being*, ed. David D. Van Tassel (Philadelphia: University of Pennsylvania Press, 1979), x.

4. Kerrigan, "Life's Iamb," 180.

5. In delineating myths about aging, he astutely characterizes the elderly figure's task (assumed by society) as that of renunciation: "older generations [are expected to] withdraw from sexual competition and prepare for death, learn, in short, to be *properly old*." The function of comedy is to dramatize this, often by ridiculing sexual desire in elderly characters (Fiedler, "Eros and Thanatos," 236).

6. Shakespeare inverts this notion of aging as anti-romantic in the amusing exchange which King Henry has with Princess Katherine in *Henry V*, where part of the persuasion he uses in wooing her is to stress that aging cannot diminish such a plain countenance as he already possesses: "My comfort is that old age, that ill layer-up of beauty, can do no more spoil upon my face. Thou hast me, if thou hast me," he tells her, "at the worst" (V.ii.217–219).

7. Another irony in this play is that Portia's dead father—who has insisted upon the test of the caskets for her suitors—is proven to be vindicated by the choices that these men make. In his case, age equals wisdom (perhaps even cunning), and Nerissa's observation that men may have holy inspirations on their deathbeds finds full support.

8. It must be noted here that Fiedler strenuously disagrees with this view of a satisfactory resolution for the play, assuming that Antonio's loss of Bassanio to Portia is compounded by his inability to make a heroic gesture in response to it. He remains, in Fiedler's view, "closed out by the Happy Endings of everyone else, and abandoned on the empty stage without lines" (Fiedler, "Eros and Thanatos," 243).

12

Images of Old Age in Early Modern Cheap Print: Women, Witches, and the Poisonous Female Body

L. A. Botelho

Images, symbols, and signs: they are a shorthand means of communication. They can convey volumes of information in a word, phrase, or picture, or they can oversimplify, distort, mislead, and even deceive. Are images descriptive, a visual accounting of daily life? Or are they prescriptive, a representation of how society thought life should be? The answer is debatable, changeable, and context-sensitive.[1]

The visual world of early modern England, both urban and rural, was certainly not undernourished. Churches, even if after the Reformation they did not always have whole Bible stories laid out in reds, blues, and blacks, still provided a whole range of images. Misericordes, pew ends, baptismal fonts, capitals, stained glass, stonework, and roof bosses continued to tell their late-medieval Christian tales.[2] Post-Reformation church art did not merely substitute text for image, the Ten Commandments for Christ on the cross. Text could also be accompanied by traditional images, as in Exeter Cathedral, where Moses and Aaron flank the Tablets of the Law.[3] English churches, therefore, remained a source of visual nourishment at least through the end of the seventeenth century, and the "visual anorexia" of English religious culture has probably been over-stated by Patrick Collinson.[4]

The secular sphere of early modern life was equally rich in its array of images and symbols. The alehouse, tavern, and inn were similar to the church in many ways: they served the important function of gathering space for the local community, and they, too, were filled with images. The walls themselves would have been painted, or hung with painted cloths, and even wallpapered with ballads telling a variety of stories, such as Susanna, Dives and Lazarus, the prodigal son, the advance of time, the dance of death, "the History of Iudeth," and "Daniel in the Lyons Den."[5] Private homes and cottages, too, would have been decorated with both wall paintings and painted cloths but would also have had ballads, broadsides, and Godly Tables pasted to the walls, pinned to cloths, and lining lids of trunks. Even the poorest laborers would have had access to visual images, if not in their own homes, then in those of their neighbors, their alehouse, and their church.

Early modern England, which witnessed the introduction and widespread acceptance and accessibility of printed materials, was characterized by an intermingling of literate and oral traditions. Popular culture was never purely oral, nor had it been for centuries; neither was it purely literate, as mass literacy was achieved in England only at the end of the nineteenth century.[6] The penny chapbook, small pamphlet, and broadside, with their combination of both printed words and images, were in many ways a representative artifact of a popular culture that could read more than it could write but was still able to speak with ease "the complex language of . . . emblems and pictorial conventions . . . which the medieval audience had learnt to read."[7]

This chapter singles out one aspect of England's rich visual tradition, the inexpensive printed image, and uses it to explore one stage of the life cycle, old age. It seeks to gain some understanding of the popular perception of old age among the humble and does not necessarily represent the realities the elderly faced. This distinction is important. The reality of old age in pre-industrial England was significantly more complex than it was in the woodcut world of cheap print. Images of the elderly people in the popular culture, as projected by cheap print, indicate a sharp division along gender lines: male old age may have been a time of poverty as well as wealth, but it was always dignified and conveyed authority. Female old age, conversely, was portrayed as physically unpleasant, never truly wise, and often purely evil. The key question, therefore, is *why* was the old woman vilified, and why did she terrify? The answer brings us to the heart of gender politics and to the most basic assumptions of early modern society: she no longer fulfilled her appointed roles as housewife and mother; her own biological state as an aged woman conspired against her. The social norms that she violated by living outside the virtuous female roles were the same areas transgressed by witches, and in strikingly similar ways.

IMAGES AS HISTORICAL SOURCES

The use of images as a historical source poses a particular set of methodological concerns and problems. The first consideration is to construct a representative sample. The nature of the source itself makes selection particularly problematic. Printed on lightweight paper that did not wear well, ballads and chapbooks were cheap in more ways than just their purchase price; they were not designed for long-term use or survival. Few woodcuts pasted above the cottage fire or upon an alehouse wall survived because of their daily exposure to smoke, the dirty fingers of careful readers, and the passing of time. Their attrition was aided by their use in the early modern privy, both as reading material and as toilet paper.[8] Known to scholars of the period as ephemera, the likelihood of their survival was slight. Tessa Watt estimates that, at best, they stood only a 0.013 percent chance of survival.[9] Fortunately, Samuel Pepys, the noted diarist of seventeenth-century London, was also a consistent collector of cheap print, and his collection is considered representative of the mid-seventeenth century.[10]

The second methodological consideration is whether the image can be analyzed separately from the text of the penny chapbook or broadsheet. Such a separation is valid, even for the later seventeenth century, especially as the image seldom matched the text.[11] The most famous such example is "the picture of a noisy, drunken company of animals, among which the boar is vomiting, that accompanies the farewell dialogue of two lovers."[12] Indeed, most of the woodcuts used in the sixteenth century were not produced in England, since the quality of the English woodcut was quite poor, but were recycled images from the continent, especially from the Low Countries.[13] In the early seventeenth century, England began producing crude images in order to more closely align text with image.[14] Still, contemporaries often viewed the image separately from the text, quite literally. In the late eighteenth century, the poet John Clare recounted his rural childhood and "recalled the attraction of the woodcut prints at the start of each poem that his father used to read haltingly to them—the boy cut out the prints and burned the rest of the book to avoid detection."[15] In this culture of marginal literacy and culturally embedded iconographic skills, the image remained important enough to stand alone, despite the publishers' seventeenth-century efforts at multimedia.

The final methodological consideration, and perhaps the most important, is whether ballads and their images reflected popular taste. There are two questions we must ask ourselves about the images presented below before we can speak in terms of national stereotypes: (1) how wide was the geographic circulation of such pictures and (2) which levels of the social order did they reach?

Most images were dispersed by itinerant chapmen: "Starting out with his arms and his pack full of broadsides, the singer," in the time-honored tradition of selling through song, "would go to the doors of theaters, to markets, fairs, bear baitings, taverns, alehouses, wakes, or any other place where a crowd could gather, and begin his song" and by the early seventeenth century it was safe to assume that even the most isolated villages had at least occasional access to cheap printed pictures.[16] This distribution system allowed the humble sort at least potential access to cheap printed images, but in itself it does not demonstrate that penny chapbooks and broadsides actually made it into the hands of the humble or were viewed by the eyes of the poor.

Their price was set deliberately low by the ballad publishers—two pence for a chapbook and a penny for a single sheet—so that even the poorest could buy them.[17] Their intended market of the poorer purchaser is also demonstrated in the nature of the printed text, which was clear, straightforward, and devoid of the trappings of elite culture.[18] The issues addressed in these books were traditional ones, such as courtship and marriage, and the gender roles they projected were conventional.[19] The lead players in these stories were familiar characters, often from the lower orders. While there certainly was a popular print genre of adventurous young men, there were far more stories of the courtship of "Honest John and Loving Kate," shepherds and alewives, and the many other stock village figures. In other words, country villagers purchased songs and stories about people very similar to themselves.

In this world of mixed written and visual media, literacy levels, at least as calculated by historians, would not have been a bar to purchasing ballads. In this period, people learned to read before they learned to write, with vast numbers learning the first skill but not the second.[20] Therefore, literacy levels based on the ability to sign one's name did not reflect one's ability to read. Besides, for those who did not learn to read, others would read out loud to them.[21]

Among the indicators of the successful penetration of the humbler levels of society was the success of cheap print as a publishing concern. Fleet Street printers, like all business people, printed principally for profit, and ballads and chapbooks were profitable.[22] In short order, people such as "Widow Sherleaker who lived by printing pictures" specialized in images and related stencils. These pictorial templates appeared in profusion as decorations for the insides of chests, the lids of trunks, and nursery walls.[23] However, it was the alehouse that may have been most responsible for the accessibility of ballads, broadsides, and chapbooks at the humblest level of society, for even the smallest establishments were expected to provide decoration for their clients. The alehouse served not only as a place of rest for the poorer sort of traveler, but its main function seems to have been social and informational, becoming the preferred meeting place for members of a rural community or an urban neighborhood.[24] Many people, therefore, may have seen the newest Fleet Street publication pasted on the wall of their local pub.

In fact, "woodcut pictures may have reached a wider public through use as patterns by craftsmen in other media," facilitating the spread of these images into areas not normally associated with printed matter and onto surfaces far more durable and hardier than bottom-of-the-line paper.[25] The poor man's picture was the painted wall hanging, which was both ornamental and practical, pleasing to the eye and a deterrent to cold drafts. Wall paintings reached their peak of popularity in the mid-sixteenth century and were later replaced by stained cloths and pasted-up ballads.[26]

Images of the elderly were among those reproduced on both walls and hangings. *A Pleasant New Ballad of Tobias*, for example, contains two images of old men and was particularly popular in poorer alehouses. The woodcut accompanying this ballad, with its "strong black lines and stunted figures," looks very similar to the painted scenes, complete with accompanying text in black letter style, from the Old Testament apocryphal Book of Tobit found on the walls of a former tavern in Stratford-on-Avon, now the White Swan Hotel.[27] The same story and images also appeared in private homes. A 1575 inventory specifically mentioned the image of Tobias, and in 1584 an Essex mercer's testate records list his ownership of "a little story of Tobias with other stained clothes."[28] The very ubiquity of cheap print and its images of the elderly, viewed both at home and in public, strongly suggests that they were seen and known by all members of society, but especially among the lowest orders, toward whom they were directed.

IMAGES OF OLD AGE

This chapter examines 103 individual images of old women and men collected primarily from ballads, of which 86 were drawn from the Pepys Collection, and all were in English circulation.[29] Nearly all the images date from the seventeenth century.[30] Twelve images were repeated more than once; for example, the same king appeared in five ballads. In all, 31 images of old people were repeated in one form or another.[31] The "repeats" were removed from the sample, leaving 72 distinct pictures of elderly people to form the core of our analysis.

The first thing we are struck by is how few elderly women were visually represented in popular print. Only 17 of the 72 prints contained old women.[32] Furthermore, elderly women were primarily assigned to just one stereotype. They were typically depicted as witchlike, if not as actual witches.[33] In fact, in just under half (7/17) of the images, aged females were clearly identifiable as witches, complete with their brooms and familiars, their large noses and chins, and their toothless and shrunken mouths.[34] The Lancashire witches of 1612 provided the craftsmen with fresh inspiration and a template for others to follow, which featured old women flying high on brooms, accompanied by the very devil himself.[35] In this woodcut, the old woman calls upon her broom-straddling colleagues: a hatted old witch, the black devil, and even a flying male companion. The witch of Newbury, whose story was retold in *A Most Certain, Strange and True Discovery of a Witch* (1643), as well as the image of Margaret Flower, one of the witches of Leicestershire (1619), reinforces the notion that witches were women well advanced in years, while adding additional details to the composite image: wrinkles, staffs, and a host of familiars. Another woodcut, this time of a bawd leading a young woman away from a life of chastity, modesty, and purity, is also tightly linked to the idea of satanic intervention. She is seen following Nicticorix, one of the devil's imps.[36] Even the famous Mother Shipton, who prophesied doom and gloom for England in general and Wolsey in particular, looks very witchlike.[37] (See Figure 12.1.) She holds a staff that is identical to the witch of Newbury's and to the oldest of the three witches of Leicestershire. Again, like the witch of Newbury, Mother Shipton's skin is wrinkled, and she has a toothless and shrunken mouth. Indeed, female prophets and witches were at times difficult to distinguish, as a number of "wise women" learned in the witch hunts of England and Scotland.

Figure 12.1
The Prophecies of Mother Shipton. Ursula Shipton. *Mother Shiptons Prophesie*. 1685 (title page). This item is reproduced by permission of The Huntington Library, San Marino, California.

Mother *SHIPTONS*

PROPHESIE:

WITH

Three and XX more, all moſt Terrible and Wonderful, Predicting ſtrange Alterations to befall this Climate of *ENGLAND*.

VIZ.

1. Of *Richard* the III^d.
2. Mr. *Truſwal* Recorder of Lincoln.
3. *Lilly's* Predictions.
4. A Propheſie alluding to the *Scots* laſt Invaſion.
5. *Ignatius* his Proph ſie.
6. Mrs. *Whites* Propheſie.
7. Old *Sybilla's* Propheſie.
8. *Merlin's* Prophesies.
9. Mr. *Bright man's*.
10. Old *Oswel Bins*.
11. *Paulus Grebnerus* Proph.
12. A Propheſie in old *Engliſh* meeter.
13. Another ancient Proph.
14. Another ſhort, but pithy.
15. Another very obſure.
16. *Saltmarſh* his Predict.
17. A ſtrange Propheſie of an old Welch-woman.
18. St. *Bede's* Propheſie.
19. *William Ambroſe*.
20. *Toa's* Propheſie.
21. *Thomas* of *Aſtledown*.
22. *Saunders* his predi[c]tions.

23. A Propheſie of *David*, Cardinal of *France*, &c.

Wolſey.

Mother Shipton.

Yorke.

LONDON,
Printed for *W. Thackeray*, at the Sign of the Angel in *Duck-Lane*, neer *Weſt-ſmithfield*, 1685.

Even if old women were not viewed specifically as witches, they were portrayed as sharing many of their physical features. Few, if any, of these woodcut women were beautiful in old age. In fact, most were decidedly ugly, making a nice visual contrast, for example, to the young lass who populated a large part of this ballad world such as that in the ballad of *The Country Lass, Who Left Her Spinning-Wheel for a More Pleasant Employment.* Two women, one old, one young, serve as foils to each other: youth and smooth skin opposes old age and a craggy face.[38]

Toothlessness was ubiquitous in old women of cheap print.[39] Characterized by an overextended nose and chin, and visually reinforced by a recessed and shrunken mouth, old women were consistently portrayed without teeth.[40] They were also often depicted in profile, their facial features in relief, serving only to exaggerate an already exaggerated form. Given the limitations of early modern woodcuts and the less advanced state of English woodcut production, it is not surprising to have old women pictured from the side, where this iconographic convention of toothlessness could be quickly conveyed. The old woman in *The Country Lass*, who stands opposite the bonny girl in search of better employment, possesses a wonderfully puckered face and serves as a forceful example of the toothless state associated with old age.

The lack of teeth may have been more than just an iconographic device and in fact may have been a fact of life for most older women in early modern society. Women of the lower social orders may have lost their teeth from their notoriously monotonous poor diet of bread and beer, and its decided lack of calcium and vitamins, all of which would have been exacerbated by childbirth, breast feeding, and menopause.[41] It is surprising that only three old women were pictured as stooped and bent with old age, despite the effects of osteoporosis that would have resulted from their calcium-deficient diet.[42] Only four were pictured with a supporting stick or staff, which is in sharp contrast to their male counterparts.[43]

Old women, at least in this format, were not depicted with the same breadth of emotion and reflection of reality as they were in the artistic medium of the elites. Visually, old women were given the smallest range of stereotypes, fewer than they would receive in the ballads' texts, and fewer still than men were to have in the same visual arena. The early modern villager was presented with a visual archetype—an artistic convention—of female old age, one that certainly did not fully reflect the reality they saw around them, which would have included grandmothers by their fires, wise and respected midwives, and vigorously active old women. The depiction of the toothless woman, whether as a witch or merely as old, must have served a storytelling function, acting as a reminder of the physical decline to come, as well as the threat of witchcraft accusation that could ambush females in old age.

Male old age was refracted visually into a much wider spectrum of image and stereotype. Old men could be wise.[44] They could be kings, seated on a throne, their faces framed by crowns on top and beards beneath, a scepter in hand, and a regal look in their eye.[45] The advanced years of the king who graces the ballad *A Most Sorrowfull Song* are nicely contrasted against the smooth-faced younger man who approaches the throne.[46] In fact, several images of wise old men closely resemble that of the old king. For example, the wise judge in the woodcut from *Newes from Scotland* who is seated in judgment of the four kneeling and suspected witches is strikingly similar in appearance to the king in *A Most Sorrowfull Song*, complete with throne and facial hair.

While old men tended to be presented as wise and respected more often than as foolish and fooled, another set of paired characteristics—wealth and poverty—were more evenly balanced in the world of early modern woodcuts and prints. Four old men were clearly portrayed as rich, with their fancy collars, elegant robes, and dignified expressions, as shown in the well-worn and partially worm-eaten woodcut used in *A Friends Advice*.[47] Six elderly men were obviously poor, as was the beggar in *The Golden Age*, with their bare feet and bare heads, their hands, hats, and begging bowls out and ready to accept the offered dole.[48]

Old men tended to keep their teeth (only 9 are clearly toothless)[49] and their money, but they could not seem to do without their beards. Forty-five out of the 55 images of old men have their faces, or at least their chins, covered in facial hair of various lengths and conditions, sometimes neat and trimmed, other times long and unkempt, a few discreetly forked in the middle, and a handful of beards, such as that accompanying *A Most Excellent Ballad of an Old Man and His Wife*, which reached truly venerable proportions.[50] Beards were commonly associated with both age and wisdom, and the lack of beard with youth and rashness. Frances Quarles wrote of "rash, and beardless counsel," and Shakespeare commented critically on the untested military mettle of a "beardless boy."[51] A contemporary Quaker pamphlet controversy of the 1650s between young James Parnell and Thomas Drayton pivots on Parnell's youthful beardless state and Moses' requirement in Leviticus 19:32 that "thou shalt rise up before the hoary head, and honour the face of the old man, and fear thy god." This, according to Drayton, should have prohibited Parnell from attempting to instruct "ancients" such as himself. Parnell's response likens Drayton's spiritual "confusion" to the "profusion" of hairs which covered his face.[52] Beards were universally seen as a mark of maturity and male authority, and both were traits that were particularly desirable in old men of early modern society.

Beards might disguise a toothless head, but the aged man in popular print was more often (6) stooped or disfigured than old women, and still more often (14) pictured with a stick or cane.[53] A stick was the mark of frail old age, illustrated in Spenser's *Faerie Queene* as the "old old man that on a staffe his feeble steps did frame."[54] An older man's reliance upon a staff symbolizes the aftereffects of a lifetime of physical labor, as well as being a token of man's greater mobility. At the same time the staff, in and of itself, is an important iconographic symbol. In classical literature the staff was traditionally associated with old age and particular gods, thus Tempus and Thanatos were usually pic-

tured as old men with a staff or crutch.[55] Later it was linked directly to Christian pilgrims and missionary saints, but more generally it is associated with dignity, royal authority, and power.[56] The crozier denotes a bishop's pastoral dignity, the scepter symbolizes a monarch's royal authority, and the wand represents the power of the magician. All three are found in this collection of images. As used in cheap print, the staff clearly functions as a visual reinforcement of the axiom that male old age resulted in wisdom and carried with it respect.

Women with staffs, particularly in the gnarled hands of the elderly, carried a much more menacing meaning. Staffs in these hands certainly denoted power and possibly respect, but not the power of office nor the respect of old age. Instead, these staffs represented the power of the witch in an unholy union with the devil, and only the respect born of fear. They resemble the magician's wand, but without the respectability of his learning; the staffs of witches and old women were clearly visual clues to the unsavory character of the people who held them.

Visually, old men did not have the competing negative and evil image that was so much the mark of the elderly woman. The closest this particular artistic genre comes to presenting old men in such a light is the early modern convention of depicting Time, often in the company of Death, as a bearded old man, Father Time.[57] Apart from his ominous hourglass, and in some cases his scythe, Father Time differs very little from woodcut images of kings and counselors; all have serious countenances, wise looks in their eyes, and stately beards. Time runs out for everyone; Death comes to all. *The Daunce and Song of Death* is a graphic example of how death claims fools and the wise alike, now linked for an eternity, as they hold each other's hands and follow Death into the open grave. In such images, the child and the old man are also hand-in-hand, as are the beggar and the king, both sets meekly following Death's lead.

In spite of Father Time's close association with the skeletal figure of Death, it is arguable that the old man, Time, was much less of a threatening figure than was the witch.[58] Time's passing could not be stopped, nor could death. The very certainty of these related facts probably made them less fearful than the unpredictable *maleficium* of the witch.[59] The witch was malicious and personal. Her acts were directed against a specific individual. She did not strike against all in the equalizing manner of Death. The very personal nature of the attack would have produced a great deal of anxiety, which was undoubtedly compounded by the knowledge that people might be able to stop the witch through their own efforts at countermagic, thus increasing an individual's level of fear. Father Time, then, served as a nonpersonalized warning and reminder of the temporary nature of life on earth and was not a devilish and individualized threat.

Old men had beards; women no teeth. That was the visual representation of the elderly in England's popular press. It was in fact more complicated. While neither gender was represented with much visual variation, old men seem to have been held in better, and more positive, regard. They could be rich as well as poor, healthy as well as sick. They could be wise but seldom fools. They could be good, but never truly bad. Old women, conversely, were never rich, but could be poor. They were never regal but were occasionally cunning and overwhelmingly evil. Visually, old women were either simply old and ugly or they were old, ugly, and evil.[60]

WOMEN, WITCHES, AND THE POISONOUS FEMALE BODY

Deeply embedded in the popular mind, vividly and widely projected in the images of cheap print, seems to be the understanding of old women as particularly loathsome. Critical to understanding this was the societally approved role for women of all social orders as housewives and mothers, and the older woman's redundancy because of old age and menopause. Seventeenth-century European society had yet to develop the societal role of "grandmother"; although they certainly did exist, there was no established position for older women.[61] In some cases old, and always poor, women who were especially esteemed by the community were awarded the honorific title of "mother" and thus were granted an honorary continuation of their prescribed role. Clearly, the woman's duty as mother and housewife was paramount in the construction of her identify, and the elderly woman, therefore, was in violation of the social code. The fear with which the aged woman was commonly held was in direct relationship to her state of antihousewife/antimother that she shared with the witch.

The role of woman was narrowly defined in early modern society: she was to bear and raise children while organizing and maintaining the household economy. The good housewife, as instructed by a plethora of advice and conduct books, was to feed, clothe, and care for her charges by the transformation of raw materials into usable goods, such as wool to thread and cream to butter. She was to oversee their distribution in such as way as to ensure the continued good health of the household, and, ideally, to create a back stock of goods and wealth to move her family ahead in the world.[62]

The old woman, by virtue of being old, violated this good order. At best, her children were grown and established in households of their own and her servants were dismissed as part of her own declining responsibilities. Her social significance as goodwife was severely diminished under such circumstances, that is, if it existed at all. In all likelihood, the aged woman was a widow, without spouse and therefore without function, outside the proper ordering of society.[63] Furthermore, in the event of her coresidence within the household of an adult child, she was seen as a potential threat to the authority of her female offspring or daughter-in-law. The fear that she could usurp the younger woman's housewifely authority and upset the order of their household was ever present.[64] The old woman was a housewife without a household, a woman out of place.[65]

She was also a woman who could no longer be a mother. With age came menopause and with the cessation of the menses came the end of fertility, and the end of woman's most hallowed function. Protestant and Catholic Europe were in close agreement on women's role as ordained by God: to bear and raise children. "Women are created," wrote Martin Luther, "for no other purpose than to serve men and be their helpers. If women grow weary or even die while bearing children, that doesn't harm anything. Let them bear children to death; they are created for that."[66] An aged woman, one past childbearing, had outlived her usefulness, was once again "out of order," and consequently entered into a transgressive category.[67]

Maleness, however, was defined by measures not necessarily diminished by their aged bodies—status, authority, and wealth, as well as heading a household—and even their ability to procreate was not curtailed at old age. Fertility problems, regardless of their actual cause, were assigned to female malfunctioning and not male inability. Men therefore could retain their prescribed functions in society, even throughout old age, while women could not.[68]

Still, the redundant housewife and childless mother, and the nature of those disorders, were not enough to inspire fear, let alone terror, in the hearts of early modern society. Horror and dread arise in the presence of a clear and certain danger, and the source of that danger was in the very nature of the aged female body. Her biological condition magnified her disorderly state and unequivocally marked her as a cause of disorder and the source of harm.

The postmenopausal woman became, in many ways, a female beyond the control of males. Women, by custom and law, were to be under the authority of men. Married women, for example, could not normally enter into legal contracts, control the profits of their labors, or make a last will and testament. Unmarried women faced the same restraints, as they were typically under the authority of their father or male guardian. Women, therefore, were in the same legal category as "children, wards, lunatics, idiots, and outlaws." [69] Indeed, even her very body was controlled by men, not just in terms of social action, but at the most fundamental biological level. Men could make women pregnant and quite visibly cause her body to swell and change shape. After menopause, men could no longer impregnate a woman, and control of her body, at least at this level, was lost to them.[70]

Sexual control was further lost to the "merry widow," whose stereotype as a sexual predator is perhaps the most enduring of the period. Beyond pregnancy, free of its fear, this aged woman appeared in plays, jests, masks, and song as overdressed and oversexed. She shamed herself by her wantonness and her wanton pursuit of sex.[71] Her dominating sex drive was largely viewed as a medical condition. The womb was thought of as an entity in its own right, capable of movement, and in need of constant supervision, care, and feeding. Sexual intercourse, on a timely and regular basis, and firmly within the confines of marriage, was considered crucial to the good health of the womb and by extension the woman. According to Aristotle, one of early modern England's venerated authorities, "the action of the semen in the male in 'setting' the female's secretions in the uterus is similar to that of rennet upon milk."[72] The widow, it was thought, was suffering from the lack of sex and driven purposefully forward by her womb in pursuit of it. The nature of that sex, however, without the chance of procreation, was in direct violation of the church's teaching that intercourse should lead to offspring, making the widow's behavior both "inappropriate and illicit."[73] Society was afraid of widows, for they violated the period's "concept of a hierarchical cosmic order. Being without a man to guide them they were a weak link in the great chain of being."[74] The widow was the epitome of the disorderly woman and the unavoidable end product of woman removed from male headship.

Medical authorities and the wisdom of the ancients did nothing to reassure patriarchal England about the disorderly condition of the aged woman. In accordance with humoral theory, the nonmenstruating old woman, by virtue of her stopped menses, had become more male, as her body became hotter and drier, and generally much harder. Concomitantly, the elderly woman could also assume other male characteristics, such as greater authority and wisdom. This more male version of womanhood was resistant to male domination and consequently more threatening to England's patriarchal society.[75]

As presented in contemporary woodcuts, the harder and drier female body was a withered body, an ugly body.[76] Her skin was wrinkled and her teeth missing. She was the antithesis of the desired female body, the maternal body, the controlled body. In the visually significant world of early modern England where external beauty was equated with internal grace, old women were loathed for their looks and feared for their features.[77]

The post menopausal woman was a dangerous woman. Her menstrual blood, which had previously flowed out of her on a regular basis, was "bad blood" in the literal sense, and its ejection from her system was necessary for her good health.[78] Menstrual blood itself—as attested by a variety of religious taboos[79]—was considered poisonous, and to call someone or something a menstrous rag was the foulest slur. The blood featured in a wide range of magic potions, from bewitching a lover to assisting in conception.[80] It was thought inherently evil enough for the vicar of Great Totham, Essex, to refuse communion to menstruating parishioners.[81] Aristotle, meanwhile, assured the learned reader that the gaze of a menstruating woman would tarnish a mirror, and Pliny remarked that "nothing could easily be found that is more remarkable than the monthly flux of woman," which could, by mere proximity, "blunt knives, turn new wine sour, wither crops, dry up seeds, drive dogs mad," and the like.[82] It could even kill the man with whom she had intercourse.[83] With menopause, this poisonous blood remained in the body, collecting and magnifying its malignancy. The spirits of old women, according to the *Malleus Maleficarum*, were particularly "inflamed with malice or rage" and "their disturbed spirit looks through their eyes, for their countenances are most evil and harmful."[84] Old women, consequently, threatened more than just England's social order, but could attack the very health of its inhabitants.

Witches, of any age, shared these traits: they attacked the same areas of the social order and manifested the same dangerous physical characteristics. The witch was the quintessential antihousewife: she caused food to spoil, milk to curdle, cows to dry up, and households to run riot. It is the witch "who causes pollution where there should be order, who disrupts food supplies which must be ordered and preserved, who wastes what is necessary."[85] So, too, was she the epitome of the antimother.[86] Whereas the good mother bears children according to God's commandments, the witch was barren, surrounded by her familiars who served as devilish surrogate children. Consequently, according to the *Malleus*, witches were thought to cause stillbirths and deformities, as well as being able to

directly prevent the erection of the member which is accommodated to fructification. And this need not seem impossible, when it is considered that they are able to vitiate the natural use of any member. Secondly, . . . they prevent the flow of the vital essences to the members in which resides the motive force, closing up the seminal ducts so that it does not reach the generative vessels, or so that it cannot be ejaculated, or is fruitlessly spilled.[87]

Witches did this when they were not taking "away the male organ, not indeed by actually despoiling the human body of it, but by concealing it with some glamour."[88]

Whereas the good mother transforms her potentially poisonous blood into the clean and white milk of the breast, the source of nourishment and life for her child, the witch offers only her cold, devil's mark, a teat near her anus, upon which her familiars suck. Indeed, the witch's inability or willful refusal to turn her blood into milk was understood to explain why witches typically attacked a household's milk reserve by "directing milk supplies to their own ends, of demanding milk from householders, of stealing the breast milk of women or animals, and (most significantly of all) of turning milk into blood, that is, turning it back into pollution."[89]

Unlike the normal and younger female body, which was thought to be overflowing with "humors or liquids, resembling a bag full of potentially polluting substances," the witch's body was "unnaturally hard and dry, especially for a woman," resembling instead the withered body of the aged female.[90] If one could scratch a witch, causing her to break open and bleed, one could therefore undo a bewitchment. The hard and dry body of the witch also stood in direct opposition to the good mother, as Dianne Purkiss explains:

The hard-bodied witch recalls the bad mother, who refuses to yield to the infant's needs and to be pliant to his wishes. She is beyond maternity, partly because her hardness and dryness are the results of age, and partly because they are the antithesis of the desired maternal body, flowing with clean nourishment.

Furthermore, the witch was ugly, often with a beard, moles, and warts. She was anything but beautiful. She was "a figure who refuses to be controlled or managed as a soft or yielding object of desire."[91] Her briefest glance, the cast of her hard eyes, could destroy all that was held dear.

It is at this point that several powerful cultural forces come together in the popular fear of old women. As we have seen, women were identified closely with the biological processes of fertility and sex, in addition to the well-being of their families and households. Through the process of aging, old women were in violation of the moral and social code. They became a potential fountain of disorder, delinquents outside of male authority, and creatures of malevolence. These, too, were the hallmarks of the witch. The extrapolation from one to the other would not have been difficult, flowing effortlessly between the waters of both popular and elite culture.[92]

CONCLUSION

Images are an apt artifact for this world where popular and elite cultures were separated by a permeable membrane, with ideas and symbols being shared by rich as well as poor, where people could read more often than they could write; indeed, where cheap print for the poor survived because a rich man like Samuel Pepys read it and kept it. This world of early modern England was also experiencing a significant transformation of its communication infrastructure. Propelled by the demands of a nascent capitalist economy, traders now consistently reached all parts of England, and in this instance, brought with them cheaply printed pictures and thereby ensured the place of such stereotypes in the country's popular culture.

These images were produced for and mainly about the humbler sort. They projected a truncated range of old-age attributes and far fewer than we find in items directed to wealthier audiences. This narrowing of scope as one moved down the social hierarchy undoubtedly reflected a very real constriction in lifestyles. What stands out is not the limited number of aged females, but the virtually myopic stereotype that portrays old women as witches or witchlike. This stands in sharp contrast to their actual lived experience. Few old women were actually prosecuted as witches, even of those who "looked" like them. People, then as now, were capable of reading past the stereotype when it came to the particulars of their own experience, while nonetheless simultaneously subscribing to the validity of the stereotype more generally. "It is apparent from court records," writes Bob Scribner, "that although villagers were influenced by the simple witchcraft imagery belonging to the oral tradition, and sustained by cheap print, they were clearly not restricted by it regarding whom they accused at law." Instead, the witch stereotypes "came to have a cultural life of their own among both the learned and the unlearned [who] could both believe in the broad stereotype of witchcraft, while being wholly sceptical of its particular application to their own circumstances."[93] Images of old women as witches or as witchlike could be, and in fact were, projected across the breadth of early modern society without anyone believing that all old women were witches.[94]

The idea of the witch went far beyond the localized fear of her harmful actions. It served a significant iconographic function in early modern society, signaling moments of fear and concern. For example, Europe's deep unease after encounters with the Amerindians was also projected onto the visual image of the witch as cannibal. Theodore de Bry (1590–1620) depicted the ritual cannibalism of the Brazilian Tupinamba as a new world version of the witches' sabbath, complete with grill and the roasting of dismembered bodies.[95] Earlier, in 1585, Jean Lery set the tone by describing these Brazilian natives with words borrowed directly from French demonological texts and explicitly linking their practices to those of witches.[96] The visual image of the witch, as well as the language of witchcraft, represented more than the actual threat of the witch. She was summoned by artist and author alike to express the fear and cultural anxiety experienced by a Europe obsessed with order and stability. The portrayal of old women as witches was therefore axiomatic, especially given their shared status as antihousewives, antimothers, and vectors of evil.

NOTES

I would like to thank the participants of the Aging in Pre-Industrial Societies Conference for their insights and suggestions. In addition, I would like to thank especially Theresa Smith and Alison Rowlands for their gracious sharing of their knowledge and expertise.

1. Since the 1980s, the analyses of images and their place in society has grown steadily in significance. For example, see Lynn Hunt, *The French Revolution and Culture* (Berkeley: University of California Press, 1989); and Frances E. Dolan, *Dangerous Familiars: Representations of Domestic Crime in England 1550–1700* (Ithaca, NY: Cornell University Press, 1994).

2. T. Watt, *Cheap Print and Popular Piety, 1550–1640* (Cambridge, Eng.: Cambridge University Press, 1991), 161, 165, 172–174, 246–248. See also E. Duffy, *The Stripping of the Altars: Traditional Religion in England, 1400–1580* (New Haven, CT: Yale University Press, 1992); J. Phillips, *The Reformation of Images: Destruction of Art in England, 1535–1660* (Berkeley: University of California Press, 1973), esp. 10–29; and M. Aston, *England's Iconoclasts*, vol. 1, *Laws Against Images* (Oxford, Eng.: Clarendon Press, 1988), esp. 20–34. For the mid-seventeenth-century destruction of surviving pre-Reformation art, see Trevor Cooper, ed., *The Journal of William Dowsing: Inconclasm in East Anglia during the English Civil War* (Woodbridge, Eng.: The Ecclesiological Society with Boydell, 2001).

3. Watt, *Cheap Print*, 173.

4. P. Collinson, *The Birthpangs of Protestant England* (New York: St. Martin's Press, 1988), 19. See also Watt, *Cheap Print*, 136.

5. D. Lupton, *London and the Countrey Carbonadoed and Quartred into Severall Characters* (London, 1632), 127. See also P. Clark, *The English Alehouse: A Social History 1200–1830* (London: Longman, 1983), 67, and Watt, *Cheap Print*, 178–256.

6. B. Reay, *Popular Culture in England, 1550–1750* (London: Addison Wesley Longman, 1998), 39.

7. Watt, *Cheap Print*, 131. See also Kirk Combe and Kenneth Schmader, "Natural-

izing uralizing Myths of Aging: A Cautionary Tale," in this volume for an exceptionally lucid explanation of reading the signifier and signified as a method of understanding the visual image.

8. This practice continued until the 1920s and was practiced by a wide variety of social sorts. Cheap printed paper was used for a variety of other tasks, including the lighting of tobacco, the lining of pie tins, and the wrapping of spice. See M. Spufford, *Small Books and Pleasant Histories: Popular Fiction and Its Readership in Seventeenth-Century England* (Athens: University of Georgia Press, 1981), 48–50.

9. Watt, *Cheap Print*, 141. See also S. Achinstein, "Audiences and Authors: Ballads and the Making of English Renaissance Literary Culture," *Journal of Medieval and Renaissance Studies* 22 (1992): 320.

10. A brief introduction to the Pepys Collection and a reprinting of a selection from the Pepys Collection can be found in Samuel Pepys, *Penny Merriments*, ed. Roger Thompson (New York: Columbia University Press, 1977). See 11 for the composition of the four volumes of the collection. See Spufford, *Small Books*, 131–135, for a demonstration of the representative nature of the Pepys Collection. While the Pepys Collection may be the best English example of cheap print, it pales considerably when compared to the number and thoroughness of the German and French collections. See also Spufford, *Small Books*, 147, and Watt, *Cheap Print*, 141.

11. N. Wurzbach, *The Rise of the English Street Ballad, 1550–1650*, trans. Gayna Walls (Cambridge, Eng.: Cambridge University Press, 1990), 9.

12. Watt, *Cheap Print*, 148, and Wurzbach, *Rise of the English Street Ballad*, 13, 288, n. 44; quote from n. 45.

13. One possible reason that so many women were depicted as witches may have been that woodcuts were routinely recycled. The potential force of this augment is diminished, however, when one considers that ten of the seventeen images of old women were not in fact witches but were decidedly witchlike. For the recycling of woodcuts in early modern England, see Roger Thompson's introduction to Pepys, *Penny Merriments*, 11. *The Illustrated London News* was still recycling images in the nineteenth century. Jennifer McLerran, "Saved by the Hand That Is Not Stretched Out: The Aged Poor in Hurbert von Herkomer's *Eventine: A Scene in the Westminster Union*," *Gerontologist* 33 (1993): 768; Watt, *Cheap Print*, 147–148. Roger Thompson speculates that the poor quality of the printed ballad, complete with editorial errors, was a result of assigning this work to apprentices. The presence of a young and growing indigenous woodcut tradition is confirmed by a Jacobean "upsurge" in the use of such printed images, particularly as part of the ballad, which was itself experiencing rapid growth. This period witnessed the consolidation of copyrights into the hands of a group of printers known as "the ballad partners" and a concomitant emphasis on their part on a "market strategy" whose "most striking" aspect was the institution of the woodcut as a "standard feature."

14. Reay, *Popular Culture*, 36.

15. As quoted in Wurzbach, *Rise of the English Street Ballad*, 13. The specifics of this early modern distribution network, and the roll of chapman within it, are thoroughly discussed in Spufford, *Small Books*, 111–128.

16. Spufford, *Small Books*, 188–189.

17. Wurzbach, *Rise of the English Street Ballad*, 17.

18. John Walter, "The Commons and Their Mental World," in *The Oxford Illustrated History of Tudor and Stuart Britain*, ed. John Morrill (Oxford, Eng.: Oxford University Press, 1996), 210.

19. Spufford, *Small Books*, 21–37.

20. As quoted in Spufford, *Small Books*, 28–29.

21. Wurzbach, *Rise of the English Street Ballad*, 13, 17.

22. Spufford, *Small Books*, 81–91.

23. Watt, *Cheap Print*, 146–149, 221–222.

24. Watt, *Cheap Print*, 195. Peter Clark suggests that part of the mid-sixteenth-century rise in the victualing trade may be explained by the decline of the church as a communal gathering spot. As he notes, "the picture is more complex than a simple transfer of functions from church to alehouse." Clark, *English Alehouse*, 33, 50, 152, 160. Also quoted in Watt, *Cheap Print*, 196, n. 83. Watt suggests that a similar transfer from church to alehouse may have taken place in access to visual images (196).

25. Watt, *Cheap Print*, 189. Many wall painters appear to have been stenciled according to a pattern and then filled with color.

26. Near this same turning point, a slide began down the "ladder of sanctity" from New to Old Testament figures, and by the time of Queen Elizabeth I's death, wall paintings were primarily of allegorical subjects and portraits, and by the end of the seventeenth century paintings drawn from the Gospels were "positively grounds for suspicion." This change in subject matter and the secularization of painted and printed images is clearly part of England's complex and at times antagonistic relationship with religious images as they chose to follow a different path from the Germans during England's extended religious reformation. The Germans, meanwhile, had very cleverly exploited the appeal of woodcuts and sought to create a core of Protestant popular ballads. Watt, *Cheap Print*, 131–132, 201–202. See also Aston, *England's Iconoclasts,* and R. Scribner, *For the Sake of Simple Folks* (Cambridge, Eng.: Cambridge University Press, 1981).

27. The central character of this book is Tobit, a pious Jew, who nonetheless was blinded by sparrows while he was still unclean after burying another Jew found strangled on the streets. Tobit's son, Tobias, was able to cure his father's blindness with the help of the angel Raphael. The wall paintings date between 1570 and 1580 (Watt, *Cheap Print*, 209–210).

28. Watt, *Cheap Print*, 210.

29. Most of these illustrations are woodcuts (94), a few are engravings (5), and 4 are drawings. Two of the illustrations are from German sources, 2 from French, and 1 from an Italian book.

30. The print used with Pepys I: 492 was first dated as being from 1596. The often-copied old man with a staff and no teeth printed alongside Pepys II: 88 was first used in 1595. Another woodcut has been dated as early as 1568 and shows Time as an old man with a scythe, hourglass, wings, and a long beard who accompanies the skeleton Death: Pepys II: 62.

31. Sometimes only part of a woodcut was reused. For example, a rich old man is seen giving money to a poor man in Pepys I: 152 but appears alone in Pepys I: 50.

32. Their visual scarcity was not a product of recycling and economic printing practices: only 7 of the 31 duplicated images were of old women.

33. Pat Thane argues that Western art reflected a variety of old-age experiences for men and women, including both the negative and the positive as well as the satirical and the idealistic (P. Thane, "The Cultural History of Old Age," *Australian Cultural History* 14 [1995]: 23–39). The medieval tradition of representations of the aged body were largely negative, but clearly gendered. Shulamith Shahar, "The Old Body in Medieval

Culture," in *Framing Medieval Bodies*, ed. Sarah Kay and Miri Rubin (Manchester, Eng.: Manchester University Press, 1994), 160–186. Victorian imagery, however, could sometimes cast the elderly as beacons of "the morally and spiritually uplifting virtues," especially those images of the aged found in England's seafaring communities (Andrew Blaikie, "Beside the Sea: Visual Imagery, Ageing and Heritage," *Ageing and Society* 17 [1997]: 629–648). See, too, Mike Featherstone and Andrew Wernick, eds., *Images of Ageing: Cultural Representations of Later Life* (London: Routledge, 1995), which offers a wide range of essays on the subject.

34. For images of witches as old women, see *Witches Apprehended, Examined and Executed*, 1613; Ralph Gardiner, *England's Grievance Discovered*, 1655; Thomas Potts, *The Wonderfull Discoveries of Witches in the Countie of Lancaster*, 1613; three contemporary impressions of witches and their familiars, 1621 (British Museum Add. Ms 32496); *A Most Certain, Strange and True Discovery of a Witch*, 1643; *The Wonderful Discoverie of Margaret and Philip Flower*, 1619; Matthew Hopkins, *Discoverie of Witches*, 1647; and "An English witch and her toad imps," 1630 (reprinted in C. Larner, "Witch Beliefs & Witch-Hunting in England & Scotland," *History Today* (February 1981: 32).

35. Thomas Potts, *The Wonderfull Discoveries of Witches in the Countie of Lancaster* (London, 1613).

36. Other details in the picture include a goat, which symbolizes lechery, and a young woman representing whoredom.

37. *Mother Shiptons Prophesie* (London, for W. Thackeray, 1685), Wing Short Title Catalogue (hereafter Wing STC) S349. For further discussion of Mother Shipton and related tales, see Spufford, *Small Books*, 3–4, 146.

38. See Shahar, "Old Body," 166–167.

39. Fifteen of the 17 images of old women were of individuals without teeth: "Three Contemporary Impressions of Witches and Their Familiars, 1621" (British Museum Add. MS 32496); *The Wonderful Discoverie of the Witchcrafts of Margaret and Philip Flower*, 1619; Thomas Potts, *The Wonderfull Discoveries of Witches in the Countie of Lancaster*, 1613; *A Most Certain, Strange and True Discovery of a Witch*, 1643; Matthew Hopkins, *Discoverie of Witches*, 1647; "An English witch and her toad imps"; "Bawd"; *Mother Shiptons Prophesie;* Pepys I: 365; Pepys II: 83; Pepys III: 183; Pepys III: 253; Pepys III: 290.

40. For more physically flattering visual images of elderly women, see Rembrandt's mother, Bernhard Keil's seventeenth-century painting "The Lacemaker" (Ashmolean Museum, Oxford), and scores of private portraits of the gentry and nobility.

41. L. Botelho, "Old Age and Menopause in Rural Women of Early Modern Suffolk," in *Women and Ageing in Britain Since 1500*, ed. Lynn Botelho and Pat Thane (London: Longman, 2001), 43–65.

42. The three stooped old women are found in contemporary drawings (British Museum Additional Manuscripts [hereafter Add. MS] 32496).

43. "Bawd"; "Three Contemporary Impressions of Witches and Their Familiars," 1621 (British Museum Add. MS 32496); *A Most Certain, Strange and True Discovery of a Witch*, 1643; and *The Wonderful Discoverie of the Witchcrafts of Margaret and Philip Flower*, 1619.

44. For old men as wise, see Pepys II: 92, Pepys IV: 301, Pepys IV: 370; Michael Sparke, *Truth Brought to Light and Discovered by Time* (London, 1651) Wing S4818;

and *Newes from Scotland* (London, 1591). For an old man as a prophet, see Pepys II: 61.

45. For examples of old men as kings, see Pepys I: 50, Pepys I: 64, Pepys I: 76–77, Pepys I: 145, Pepys I: 352, Pepys II: 230, and Pepys II: 246.

46. Pepys I: 64.

47. Pepys I: 55.

48. For examples of rich old men, see *An Answer to the Forc'd Marriage* Wing A3409 (two figures), Pepys I: 55, and Pepys II: 246. For examples of poor old men, see Pepys I: 43, Pepys I: 152, Pepys I: 160, Pepys I: 218–219, Pepys II: 88, and "Beggar" by Jacques Callot, Paris, 1629.

49. For toothless old men, see "Beggar" by Jacques Callot. Paris, 1629, Pepys I: 152, Pepys I: 164, Pepys II: 37, Pepys II: 88, Pepys IV: 8, Pepys IV: 300, Pepys IV: 311, and Pepys IV: 370.

50. For examples of bearded old men, see Pepys I: 16–17; Pepys I: 43; Pepys I: 64; Pepys I: 69; Pepys I: 76–77; Pepys I: 137; Pepys I: 145; Pepys I: 152; Pepys I: 160; Pepys I: 162; Pepys I: 164; Pepys I: 218–219; Pepys I: 268; Pepys I: 352; Pepys I: 438; Pepys I: 488–489; Pepys I: 490–491; Pepys I: 492; Pepys II: 175; Pepys II: 230; Pepys II: 246; Pepys II: 32; Pepys II: 36; Pepys II: 55; Pepys II: 61; Pepys II: 62; Pepys II: 76; Pepys II: 92; Pepys II: 332; Pepys IV: 104; Pepys IV: 116; Pepys IV: 295; Pepys IV: 299; Pepys IV: 301; Pepys IV: 370; "Beggar" by Jacques Callot; *The Old Man's Complaint*, Wing F35; Michael Sparke, *Truth Brought to Light and Discovered by Time* (London: by Richard Cotes, 1651) Wing S4818; Francis Quarles, *Hieroglyphikes of the Life of Man* (London, 1638) STC20548; *Passion and Discretion, in Youth, and Age* (London: T. & R. Cotes, 1641); and *Newes from Scotland*, 1591.

51. F. Quarles, *Esther* (London, 1638), and William Shakespeare, *The Life and Death of King John*, ed. Henry M. Belden (New York: Macmillan, 1912), V.i.69.

52. I would like to thank M. Kate Peters for this reference. James Parnell, *Goliaths Head Cut Off with His Own Sword* (London, 1655), 12 (Wing STC P538); and Thomas Drayton, *An Answer According to Truth, That Trembles Not nor Quakes, nor Quayleth, Bound with Certain Counter Queries Propounded by James Parnel and His Associates the New and Former Sectaries* (n.d.), 2–3.

53. For stooped or lame old men, see Pepys I: 162, Pepys I: 218, Pepys I: 490–491, Pepys II: 32, Pepys II: 332, and "Beggars" by Jacques Callot. For old men with staffs, see Pepys I: 76, Pepys I: 152, Pepys I: 268, Pepys I: 438, Pepys I: 488, Pepys I: 490–491, Pepys II: 32, Pepys II: 61, Pepys II: 62, Pepys II: 88, Pepys IV: 8, Pepys IV: 300, and Pepys IV: 301.

54. Pepys I: 43, Pepys II: 332, Edmund Spenser, *The Faerie Queene* (London, 1590), I.viii.30.

55. P. Preston, *A Dictionary of Pictorial Subjects from Classical Literature* (New York: Charles Scribner's Sons, 1983), 82, 248.

56. For the association of the staff and particular saints, see J. Hall, *Dictionary of Subjects and Symbolism in Art* (London: J. Murray, 1974), 289.

57. "Father" was an honorific title given to some poor elderly men as a sign of respect, generally in their sixties. For a discussion of honorific titles among the elderly poor of both sexes, see Botelho, "Old Age," 49–51.

58. For the secularization of death in early modern England, see Spufford, *Small Books,* 138, 143.

59. According to P. Aries, before the modern age death was not feared but accepted

as part of the natural course of events. While he overstated the lack of fear, death was undeniably more public and arguably less anxiety-producing than at other periods of history (*The Hour of Our Death*, trans. H. Weaver [New York: Vintage Books, 1981]).

60. If one were to weigh more heavily repeated images as particularly representative of the popular mindset, there would be an even stronger gender divide with more female witches and more royal men.

61. The socially recognized and valued role of grandmother has only recently begun to be studied. Preliminary results suggest that it first developed among the aristocracy during the eighteenth century. See Jean-Pierre Bois, "L'Art d'être grand-mère, XVIIe–XIXe siècle," *Annales de démographie historique* (1991): 7–19; and Vincent Gourdon, "Les Grands-parents dans la littérature française au XIXe siècle," *Annales de Démographie historique* (1991): 77–89.

62. Much has been written of the role of women in early modern society, and its focus upon the domestic sphere of household and motherhood, including S. Mendelson and P. Crawford, *Women in Early Modern England* (Oxford, Eng.: Clarendon Press, 1998), and M. Wiesner, *Women and Gender in Early Modern Europe* (Cambridge, Eng.: Cambridge University Press, 1993), 9–35. For an insightful guide to the vast quantity of advice literature for women, the standard remains Suzanne W. Hull's *Chaste, Silent & Obedient: English Books for Women, 1475–1640* (San Marino, CA: Huntington Library, 1982).

63. Richard Wall offers a long chronological view, from the sixteenth to the close of the twentieth century, of the households of elderly women, concluding that then, as well as now, most elderly women lived alone. R. Wall, "The Residence Patterns of Elderly English Women in Comparative Perspective," in *Women and Ageing in British Society Since 1500*, ed. L. Botelho and P. Thane (London: Longman, 2001), 139–165. See also Susannah Ottaway, "The Old Woman's Home in Eighteenth-Century England," in *Women and Ageing in British Society Since 1500*, ed. L. Botelho and P. Thane (London: Longman, 2001), 111–138.

64. Diane Purkiss, *The Witch in History: Early Modern and Twentieth-Century Representations* (London: Routledge, 1996), 97, 120–121.

65. E.M.W. Tillyard, *The Elizabethan World Picture* (London: Chatto and Windus, 1943), is an old but excellent and concise introduction to the Great Chain of Being, and Susan Dwyer Amussen, *An Ordered Society* (New York: Columbia University Press, 1988), is a valuable study of the role and function of gender and class in early modern England. Freud, too, had difficulty placing the aged woman into his scheme. Mike Featherstone and Andrew Wernick, Introduction to *Images of Ageing: Cultural Representations of Later Life*, ed. M. Featherstone and A. Wernick (London: Routledge, 1995), 9.

66. As quoted in Wiesner, *Women and Gender*, 9. See also 21–25.

67. Shahar, "Old Body," 167.

68. Shahar, "Old Body," 170, 171–172.

69. Sara Mendelson and Patricia Crawford, *Women in Early Modern England, 1550–1720* (Oxford, Eng.: Clarendon Press, 1998), 34–48.

70. See also C. Larner, *Enemies of God: The Witch-Hunt in Scotland* (Baltimore, MD: Johns Hopkins University Press, 1981), 93.

71. The oversexed old woman, and elderly widows in particular, was thought by some to be unable to be satisfied by "mere mortal men" and could only be sated by demon lovers. Anne Llewellyn Barstow, *Witchcraze: A New History of the European Witchhunts* (San Francisco: Pandora, 1994), 137. See also the chapter by Katharine Kittredge in this

volume. Cf. Carol Everest, "Sex and Old Age in Chaucer's *Reeve's Prologue*," *Chaucer Review* 31 (1996): 99–114, for a look at elderly male sexuality in an earlier period.

72. As quoted in Purkiss, *Witch*, 121.

73. Barstow, *Witchcraze*, 137. The medieval commentator Gerald of Wales was stinging in his wonder at those willing to have sex with an old woman: "The female body is so easily destroyed by sickness or old age. . . . Who could, for purposes of carnal intercourse, of licentious kisses so wantonly desire this skin (however much it was formerly desired) withered by sickness or shriveled into an old woman's wrinkled by age" (Quoted in Shahar, "Old Body," 166).

74. Charles Carlton, "The Widow's Tale: Male Myths and Female Reality in 16th and 17th Century England," *Albion* 10 (1978): 126.

75. Botelho, "Old Age," 52; V. L. Bullough, "Medieval Medical and Scientific Views of Women," *Victor* 4 (1973): 485–501; Lesley Ann Dean-Jones, *Women's Bodies in Classical Greek Science* (Oxford, Eng.: Clarendon Press, 1994), 107; Mendelson and Crawford, *Women in Early Modern England*, 23; and P. Thane, *Old Age in English History: Past Experiences, Present Issues* (Oxford, Eng.: Oxford University Press, 2000), 22.

76. Purkiss, *Witch*, 127.

77. Barstow, *Witchcraze*, 137, and Shahar, "Old Body," 164.

78. An earlier, yet still fundamental, study of menstruation is P. Crawford, "Attitudes to Menstruation in Seventeenth-Century England," *Past and Present* 91 (1981): 47–73. See also Mendelson and Crawford, *Women in Early Modern England*, 21–26, 28–29.

79. Dean-Jones, *Women's Bodies*, 236–240.

80. Barstow, *Witchcraze*, 136.

81. Keith Thomas, *Religion and the Decline of Magic* (New York: Charles Scribner's Sons, 1971), 38, 438. Some women voluntarily did not go to church at such times having internalized "the theory of pollution to such an extent that it was easier to go without the comfort of communion than to enter the presence of the divine" (Dean-Jones, *Women's Bodies*, 239).

82. Dean-Jones, *Women's Bodies*, 249.

83. Barstow, *Witchcraze,* 136.

84. Heinrich Kramer and James Sprenger, *The Malleus Maleficarum*, trans. M. Summers (New York: Dover, 1971), 17.

85. Purkiss, *Witch*, 97.

86. See also Wiesner, *Women and Gender*, 29, for witches as "an inversion of the normal order."

87. *Malleus Maleficarum*, 117–118.

88. *Malleus Maleficarum*, 118. See too Lyndal Roper's "Stealing Manhood: Capitalism and Magic in Early Modern Germany," in *Oedipus and the Devil: Witchcraft, Sexuality and Religion in Early Modern Europe*, ed. Lyndal Roper (London: Routledge, 1994), 125–144. This form of witchcraft was less frequent in England than on the Continent, although its possibility was recognized (Thomas, *Religion and the Decline of Magic*, 437, fn.).

89. Purkiss, *Witch*, 134. See Jim Sharpe, "Women, Witchcraft and the Legal Process," in *Women, Crime and the Courts in Early Modern England*, ed. J. Kermode and G. Walker (London: University College London, 1994), 106–124. The emphasis on blood in the transgression of witches is strikingly similar to the medieval blood libels against

Europe's Jews (Jeremy Cohen, *The Friars and the Jews*: *The Evolution of Medieval Anti-Judaism* [Ithaca, NY: Cornell University Press, 1982], 44–45).

90. Purkiss, *Witch*, 119, 125.

91. Purkiss, *Witch*, 127. Barstow, *Witchcraze*, 129, writes of the witch and her suckling familiar as "an inversion of a natural female function, a parody turned into deadly jest."

92. See also Larner (*Enemies of God*, 93), where she links women, but not specifically aged women, to the "stereotype of witchcraft."

93. As quoted in Malcolm Gaskill, "Witchcraft in Early Modern Kent: Stereotypes and the Background to Accusations," in *Witchcraft in Early Modern Europe: Studies in Culture and* Belief, ed. Jonathan Barry, et al. (Cambridge, Eng.: Cambridge University Press, 1996), 258.

94. See Alison Rowlands, "Some Thoughts on Connections Between Old Age and Witchcraft in Early Modern Germany," *Past and Present* 174 (2002): 50–89, for the "varied and complex" circumstances behind witchcraft prosecution, such as the hard-to-quantify characteristics of reputation and "unusual" economic success, and a correspondingly decreased emphasis on old age. I would like to thank Dr. Rowlands for access to this paper.

95. For an insightful examination of the mirrorlike function of the witch figure, see Charles Zika, "Cannibalism and Witchcraft in Early Modern Europe: Reading the Visual Images," *History Workshop Journal* 44 (1997): 77–105, esp. pp. 88–89. See Purkiss, *Witch*, passim, for an examination of witches on the English stage and their use as "interpretative challenges leading to moral homilies; the effect was to give the witch public meaning in defining . . . the notion of good order in the political and social realms," 179–275, quote p. 3.

96. Wiesner, *Women and Gender*, 229–230.

13

"The Ag'd Dame to Venery Inclin'd": Images of Sexual Older Women in Eighteenth-Century Britain

Katharine Kittredge

In the conclusion to her book, *Writing a Woman's Life*, Carolyn Heilbrun quotes an Isak Dinesen character: "Women, when they are old enough to have done with the business of being women, and can let loose their strength, must be the most powerful creatures in the world."[1] This quotation reveals the twentieth-century expectation that appropriate gender performance will be defined differently at various stages of a woman's life, and that the performance of traditional feminine gender—"the business of being women"—will have a negative impact on the amount of power that they wield. The relationship between age-related norms for gender performance and the social power available to mature individuals reveals much about a society's configuration of sex roles, biological status, economic class, and parameters of individual expression. This chapter examines the cultural context for women's aging in one very specific setting—the world of middle- and upper-class women in England during the eighteenth century. The focus will be on those women who are "no longer young" (over the age of thirty), but who are still physically strong and have the potential to wield considerable power within their families and their social circles. It will examine the views of the aging women as they are presented in contemporary written texts—literary works of fiction, popular writing, and didactic texts. It is necessary to use this wide range of texts because each genre offers different insights: (1) novels present some of the most fully developed and culturally visible embodiments of aging, (2) the (usually anonymous) popular ballads and tracts tend to be harsher in their depictions of aging women, and (3) didactic or "conduct" literature is more explicit about the social codes in effect. I will also be turning to the personal writings of contemporary women to see how their views and experiences echo or contradict the written texts.

An analysis of the contemporary texts indicates that mature women were encouraged to believe that they could never "have done with the business of being women"; a wide range of media (paintings, prints, ballads, fiction, pamphlets, drama, and medical texts) assured women that their heterosexual status would continue to form the core of their identity, even though contemporary standards of sexual desirability meant that older women would be judged inadequate and inferior. Although there are some images in which mature women were physically (and sexually) powerful, the majority of the available depictions represent the process of aging as rendering older woman pathetic or grotesque. This is especially true of the extremely negative images of spinsters and widows that proliferated during this period.[2] The virulence of these portrayals seems to indicate a cultural uneasiness with the role of mature women and a preoccupation with those women who were outside the direct male control of father, husband, or son. These examples offer us a fascinating case study of how negative images of aging and divergent female sexuality functioned as a mechanism for both constraining and erasing forms of female power that fell outside the socially acceptable/male-defined stages of the appropriate female life cycle: youth as the attractive mistress, maturity as the dutiful wife, and an old age of self-effacing widowhood. The pervasive nature of these images does more than give us insight into the nature of contemporary misogyny; it also indicates the presence and visibility of mature women who were existing outside acceptable social roles and engaging in alternative (nonfeminine) ways of performing gender.

It was through these monitory images—specifically those of grotesque spinsters and widows—that eighteenth-century women were conditioned to think of their mature years—a life phase that modern women cherish as a time of new opportunities—as a time of social invisibility and personal despair. As a result of this sexist, ageist environment, even women whose fame rested on their wits rather than their beauty exhibited an obsessive concern with the physical effects of aging. At thirty-two Mary Wortley Montagu, noted poet and correspondent and one of the premier wits of her day, called herself an "old beauty" and lamented: 'I should not fail to amuse myself tolerably enough but for the damned, damned quality of growing older every day, and my present joys are made imperfect by fears of the future."[3] Hester Thrale Piozzi, a published author and one of the acknowledged leaders of the intellectual group of women known as the "Bluestockings," tried to make a distinction between the effect of aging on women of different intellectual capacities: there is the "Old Coquette who never had any Merit but Beauty to boast—when Age attacks *that* Qualification, nothing is left, and she looks sad and sullen . . . [by contrast] Mrs. [Elizabeth Robinson] Montagu or Queen Elizabeth rather gain than lose Admiration when their heads are white as is Snowdonia's now."[4] Ironically, the personal writing of Elizabeth Robinson Montagu, Thrale's friend and "Queen of the Bluestockings," showed no such sense of security; Mrs. Montagu wrote personal letters lamenting her status as "old" at thirty-six. When a male correspondent chided her upon her dissatisfaction with growing older, she responded: "You despise, you say, all the old women who wish to be young; your contempt is very comprehensive, it takes in all the old women that ever were or will be, from before the flood to the dissolution of our globe."[5] It is clear that even a woman as universally admired for her intelligence as Mrs. Montagu was not able to overcome the predominant views that a woman should be judged according to her appearance; furthermore, her comments reveal that antiage sentiments were so deeply embedded in the cultural norms that they were viewed as an eternal concomitant of human nature ("from before the flood to the dissolution of our globe") rather than a socially constructed prejudice.

The ubiquity of the negative depictions of female aging must have made it seem inevitable that older women would lead a bleak life. An appalling variety of contemporary sources indicated that a woman's social status "naturally" deteriorated once she was beyond the age of twenty-five; it was widely understood that only beautiful young women were entitled to social approbation. Older women who insisted on continuing to live a socially visible existence could be depicted as pathetic or grotesque. Mary Astell's proto-feminist manifesto, *A Serious Proposal to the Ladies* (1695), bluntly describes how a woman who is "no longer young" will grow "every day more and more sensible, that the respect which us'd to be paid her decays as fast as her Beauty."[6] The same sentiments are echoed in the popular midcentury conduct book, *Sermons to Young Women* (1766), in which James Fordyce wrote that a woman "past her prime" could expect to "tread the beaten round, unpraised, neglected, forlorn!"[7] At the end of the eighteenth century, the anonymous author of the tract *The Female Aegis* (1798) draws a stark picture of the passing of youthful beauty:

As youth and beauty wear away, the homage which had been paid to them is gradually withdrawn. They who had heretofore been treated as idols of public and private circles, and had forgotten to anticipate the termination of their empire, are suddenly awakened from their dream, and constrained to rest satisfied with the common notice shewn to their station, and the respect which they have acquired by their virtues.[8]

All these sources may be seen as positive in their urging women to cultivate inner rather than external worth, but the nature of female education—aimed at enhancing a young woman's charms and fashioning them into a suitable ornament to grace a husband's drawing room and table—gave them few inner resources from which to draw. In Fanny Burney's late-century novel, *The Wanderer*, an elderly gentleman speaks of how unprepared many gently raised young women are for the role they will play later in their lives:

In maturity—ah! there's the test of sense and temper in the waning beauty!—in maturity, shocked and amazed to find herself supplanted by the rising bloomers; to find that she might be forgotten or left out, if not assiduous to come forward; to be consulted only upon grave and dull matters, out of reach of her knowledge and resources, alternately mortified by involuntary negligence, and affronted by reverential respect![9]

Here, Burney (whose novels Hester Thrale Piozzi praised as "an exact and perfect Copy of those Manners which at this Moment prevail in this Nation,"[10]) emphasizes that girls raised to be beauties are not given the "knowledge and resources" to cope with the everyday concerns of living. Thus, the mature years, which should be a time of increased freedom and the exploration of new forms of self-expression, are merely a time of impotence and regret.

When sources dealt with aging women who had married at an appropriately young age, less time was devoted to describing the physical effects of aging, and more emphasis was placed on their properly performing their roles as wives and mothers. According to Amanda Vickery, upon marriage, women "settled down to a period of self-conscious retirement." In addition to containing the young matrons' sexuality, Vickery points out that these retirements served the purpose of conserving domestic resources, since "below a certain financial threshold it was simply not possible to pursue a public life in the polite sense of the word.[11] A married woman was subject to criticism if she continued to favor public diversions over private duties. *The Spectator* describes with scorn the wife who is "an Old Coquet, that is always hankering after the Diversions of the Town" and thus is thought by her sons to be "no better than she should be."[12]

It is interesting that the specter of physical aging is most explicitly raised when a woman is perceived to be drifting back into the role of an autonomous, potentially attractive younger woman. This is most evident in the criticisms leveled at the mother who refuses to perform her prescribed role of chaperone in favor of retaining her own coquetteries. *The Female Aegis* describes the inappropriate older woman who is

unwilling to permit her daughters to accompany her in public, lest their native bloom should expose by contrast the purchased complexion of their mother . . . disgracing herself, and disgusting even those who deem it civility to flatter and deceive her.[13]

It is significant that this criticism casts mothers and daughters as rivals for male affection—playing on the misogynist belief that even the most nurturing of women's relationships are ultimately subordinate to female competition for the attention of men. Its message about female aging is equally pernicious. This tract implies that any attractiveness that an older woman possesses is essentially fraudulent—"purchased" rather than "native"—and indicates that any positive attention that she receives hides the instinctive revulsion of all her social acquaintance. In the same section, *The Female Aegis* explicitly condemns the "spectacle" of the woman "in the wane of beauty" who is seen "shutting her eyes against those alterations in countenance and figure which are visible to every other person on the slightest glance."[14] Both these criticisms are designed to encourage a kind of pervasive female paranoia—it assures the older woman that at a certain age she would become a figure of ridicule and disgust, although outwardly social response would seem as warm and supportive as ever. In addition to creating intense insecurity, these "warnings" require women to view all positive social interactions as hypocritical, cutting them off from potential sources of support and affirmation. Such "wisdom" was at the heart of the fear of aging that so many contemporary women exhibited—how could you ever know for sure that they were *not* laughing behind your back? Small wonder that so many women chose the security of a "self-conscious retirement."

Although matrons who deviated from their prescribed role as nurturing wife and mother were subject to criticism, the most explicitly vicious depictions of female aging were always of unmarried women—both widows and spinsters. From medieval times to the eighteenth century, widows and spinsters shared the space just outside "normal" womanhood. While they were equally "manless," though, their status, social roles, and aging characteristics were profoundly different. In her discussion of the status of "singlewomen" in medieval Europe, Ruth Mazo Karras discusses the relative social positions of widows and unmarried women during the middle ages:

The widow was not as problematic as the singlewoman; medieval society recognized her existence and allowed her space . . . Whereas singlewomen were out of place for not marrying, widows had performed that obligation. . . . Their independence and morals might be suspect like those of singlewomen, but they were not as anomalous.[15]

No doubt it is this anomalousness that is at the root of the graphic—and malicious—images of female aging which characterized the depictions of "old maids" in the prose of eighteenth-century Britain. These images were so unremittingly grotesque in their depiction of female aging that they acted as a universal monitory symbol, hastening young women into marriage. In 1707 Lady Mary Pierrepont (later Lady Mary Wortley Montagu) wrote in a letter: "I have a mortal aversion to be an old maid; and a decaying oak before my window leafless, half rotten, and shaking its withered top, puts me in mind every morning of an antiquated virgin, bald, with rotten teeth, and shaking of palsy."[16] The fictional portraits of old maids during this period are equally minute in their physical descriptions. In Mrs. Skinn's novel, *The Old Maid*, the heroine's maiden aunt is described by an arrogant young man as "a pretty tall woman, extremely thin—nay, in short the best description I can give you of her, is to suppose two deal boards before you nailed together, with a death's head on top." This same youth again uses images of death and decay when Aunt Patty defends her virtue against him: "Ravish you, ha! ha! ha! says I; why I'd as soon ravish my grandmother, who has been dead these twenty years—why my sweet Madame, you are fitter for a charnel house than a young fellow's bed."[17]

Prominent in these descriptions of older women are images of mortality and decay. Both the "decaying oak" and the charnel house images conflate aging and decrepitude unto death. In spite of the ongoing debate about a woman's sexual and social position, it is clear that in the stylized depiction of the old maid there is no middle ground and no middle age. In some ways, the old maid has become the repository for all the physical changes brought about by female aging. Against all logic, aging is presented as the punishment that women receive for failing to attract a man. Specifically, the qualities of aging that are emphasized in these images—shrinking bosom, hollowing of the cheeks brought about by declining body fat and dental disasters, thinning hair—are qualities that make the old maid into a masculine (or at least androgynous) figure.

One of the things that makes the images of old maids so jarring is the way that they juxtapose the desexualizing aspects of physical aging with the old maid's persistence in participating in the forms of feminine gender construction: clothing, physical display, and flirtatious behavior. The fictional spinsters are frequently mocked for the energy they expend on personal adornment and for the ultimate failure of their attempts to appear to be desirable females. Tabitha Bramble, the quintessential spinster from Smollett's *Humphry Clinker*, is described in a letter by her niece: with "her rumpt gown and petticoat, her scanty curls, her lappet-head, deep triple ruffles, and high stays . . . she was twenty good years behind the fashion." Like most aging women, Tabitha was as unable to see that the fashions of her youth had changed as she was incapable of seeing that her own youth had passed. Her behavior is equally undignified and inappropriate: "she laughed and romped, and danced, and sang, and sighed, and ogled, and lisped, and fluttered, and flattered."[18] Tabitha is being pilloried equally for her inability to comprehend contemporary forms of female desirability and for the spectacle of a nonfeminine woman adopting hyperfeminine behaviors.

Alternately, unmarried women were as subject to criticism if they successfully adopted fashions that were in vogue with contemporary youth. The anonymous author of *Amusements in the Highlife* (1786) mercilessly vilifies "Lady Harriet Pastime" for the ridiculous figure she makes in "the dress of a girl of eighteen, displayed upon a woman where the hand of time had made its ravages."[19] Later in the century, we find the even more restrictive statements of William Hayley directed at spinsters:

I advise them [old maids] to avoid every kind of personal decoration, which custom has in any degree appropriated to youth, above all, the use of pink ribbons, to which they have a particular propensity. A wag of my acquaintance declares, that he looks upon every old maid, who arrays herself in ornaments of this colour, as a vessel displaying signs of distress, and inviting every bold adventurer to hasten to her relief.[20]

At the root of these rules about dress and comportment is the insistence that older women capitulate in their social erasure by eschewing all forms used by other women to project an appropriately feminine image. The "wag's" humorous remarks indicate that the penalty for refusing to vanish goes beyond the threat of social ostracism—that transgressive women will lose the rights and privileges accorded "decent" women. If they persist in presenting themselves as sexual beings concerned with the attracting of males, they will run the lewd woman's risk of being taken by any "bold adventurer" who may decide to board her.

Underlying many of the negative portraits of old maids is the criticism of the spinster's unwillingness to adhere to the social rules for women. Kate Willow is a spinster described by *The Spectator* as having remained single because "She was so flippant with her answers to all the honest Fellows that came near her, and so vain of her Beauty, that she has valued herself upon her Charms till they are ceased."[21] A young woman might also find herself left a spinster after she erred in the opposite direction. Smollett's Tabitha Bramble is still unmarried because she "had gone some lengths in the way of flirting with a recruiting officer" in her youth so that "her reputation was a little singed."[22] There were many practical reasons for remaining unmarried—physical isolation, engrossing family obligations, lack of a dowry, physical disability—but in popular publications, spinsterhood was most frequently depicted as the result of poor choices or inappropriate values. Both Kate Willow and Tabitha Bramble are assumed to be driven by an arrogance that placed personal worth or satisfaction above adherence to contemporary codes of conduct.

Because she was viewed as having already turned irrevocably away from the socially acceptable role for young women (wife and mother), the spinster was inevitably regarded as outside the sexual norm for "mature" women. This left her without a clearly defined sexual identity and no explicit code for appropriate behavior. If she relaxed the rigid restrictions placed on young virgins too soon, her reputation would be irrevocably damaged and she was liable to be considered a fallen woman. If she adhered rigidly to these codes during the years when she was considered to be past sexual desirability (and thus beyond the danger of seduction), she was still subject to criticism. When Aunt Patty, the maiden aunt of the heroine of *The Old Maid*, is inadvertently kidnapped by one of her niece's suitors, she responds with Pamela-like horror. Her potential ravisher describes her behavior: "Pretending she was fainting for want of breath, she sank into my arms . . . she faintly exclam'd . . . I hope, Sir, you won't hurt me! Nor thus meanly take advantage of my disorder to compleat any wicked design upon my virtue." The kidnapper finds this "amorous" behavior amusing but restrains his laughter because of his "apprehension of being ravish'd in my turn by this reverend piece of antiquity."[23] This situation illustrates the difficulties of an unmarried woman in this stage of her life; one wonders whether there is any possible behavior available to her that would not have been read as sexual.

In contemporary texts, it is not uncommon to find spinster characters adamantly denying that they have any heterosexual desires—they proclaim their hatred for men and their abhorrence of marriage and romance. It was understood that these spinsters' prudish postures were hypocritical and that they were certainly finding deviant ways of satisfying their sexual needs. In the course of their respective narratives, both the previously mentioned Aunt Patty and Lady Harriet Pastime are surprised while in bed with their butlers. Both encounters feature the breakage or spilling of a full chamber pot whose contents smear the lovers. The application of excrement is meant as broad, slapstick comedy but may also have some psychosexual significance. The spinster has given into her bodily desires at a time when she will not exhibit to the public the "natural" outcome of sexual activity—a visibly pregnant body—instead, she must exhibit and claim as her own the only products her postmenopausal body generates (excrement). In this way the freedom that attends a woman (like Henry Fielding's character, Slipslop) when she has "arrived at an age when she might indulge herself in any liberties with a man, without the danger of bringing a third person into the world to betray them" is portrayed as revolting.[24] A spinster's sexuality is presented as a perverted form of "normal" desire that, given her lack of social position and physical charms, makes her the least powerful and most thwarted of creatures.

Herein lies the root of much of this explicit information on the deportment and presentation of aging female bodies: the social mandate that older women cease to present themselves as sexual beings is undercut by the certainty that an adult human being *is* a sexual being. In spite of the medical context, which increasingly denied female desire, the literary conventions that erased mature female bodies, and the sartorial and behavioral customs that denied them social visibility, it was understood that women continued to be sexual (and sometimes sexy) beings well beyond their reign as nubile "beauties."

Historians such as Roy Porter maintain that during the eighteenth century there was still a predominant belief that sexual appetite in both sexes was "an essential part of Nature. As integral to human nature, it was an important component to happiness."[25] Sexual relations were viewed as being a social act as much as they were viewed as being an act of procreation. Regular sexual intercourse was thought to be an essential part of a happy marriage; in *Conjugal Lewdness and Matrimonial Whoredom*, Defoe sanctions a number of motives for marital sex: "a desire of Children, or to avoid Fornication, or to lighten and ease the cares and sadnesses of Household-affairs, or to endear each other."[26]

Although much of the fiction of the day is concerned with the young woman's preservation of her virginity (as in Richardson's *Pamela* or *Clarissa*), there are still a wide range of sources that depict women as sexual beyond their childbearing years. Lemuel Gulliver's amusing *Pleasures and Felicities of Marriage* contains the following account of a husband and wife whose blood had been fired at a neighborhood card party:

they no sooner got Home, but they were both of 'em seized with such an amorous fit, that they could not stay to undress, but went at it with all the Spirit and Eagerness of their first Embrace. I can't say, adds she, that I was ever so delighted in my Life; and altho' I was not then young, nor had been with Child for six years past, yet that Day nine months I was deliver'd of my son Bob.[27]

Although *Pleasures* is unusual in its graphic celebration of hot postmenopausal sex (and its ability to restore the capacity to bear children), even the most misogynistic writings from this period exhibit a certain amount of respect for the sexual abilities of older women. This is especially true of depictions of widows. Whereas old maids were frequently presented as androgynous or masculine, widows could be shown to embody a hypersexualized form of female potency. In the anonymous tract "The Folly, Sin, and Danger of Marrying Widows, and Old Women in General," the author, "A True Penitent," claims that "It is seldom or never seen, that a Man marrieth with a Widow for her Beauty nor for her Personage, but only for her Wealth and Riches," but he also finds it necessary to warn: "if she be Rich and Beautiful withal, then thou matches thy self to a She Devil."[28] The male discussants in Defoe's *Conjugal Lewdness* also leave open the possibility of attraction:

Jack: I think I may have a Woman past Child-bearing, and not have an old Hag, I hope.

Tom: Prithee, tell me, what will please you; and then a Body may look out for you.

Jack: Why, a good jolly handsome well-bred Woman, about Forty-eight to Fifty.[29]

Here, we have a concept of aging that approaches our contemporary concept of "middle age"—a time when one is no longer young, but neither is one explicitly old. It is interesting that this window of extended attractiveness is applied only to previously married women. Still, even in the descriptions of attractive widows, the author carefully stipulates that their beauty is not to be confused with the "real" beauty, which can be possessed only by young women. The bitter "True Penitent" takes some pains to make this distinction clear:

The Widow may happen to be Mistress of Female Accomplishments, and may therefore make some worthy necessitous Youth happy, but let her not think herself good enough for a man of Fortune. The Old Woman may also have her peculiar native Endowments still about her, and flourishing in an uncommon Degree tho' in the autumn, or Winter of her Days; and these wither'd Beauties may possibly strike the Heart of some honest dull Fellow, whose Taste is not over delicate.[30]

Such statements indicate that the possibility of sexually attractive mature women was present in the culture, but that these images inevitably clashed with the powerful taboos against mature female sexuality. The paradoxical juxtaposition of these opposing beliefs posed a particular problem for nonfictional, living, breathing older women who had to negotiate conventional mores in the course of their own pursuit of sexual happiness. The quandaries were myriad: Are one's charms a potent snare for unwary youths or a grotesque parody of female appeal? Should one's social conduct reflect one's status as a sexless androgyne or an insatiable sex goddess? And how does one dress for either role?

A rich source of reflections on aging, attraction, and sexual power is *The Thraliana,* which Hester Thrale Piozzi began to write as a personal journal when she was thirty-five. She records the following conversation with Samuel Johnson:

And yet says Johnson a Woman has such power between the Ages of twenty five and forty five, that She may tye a Man to a post and whip him if She will. I thought they must begin earlier & leave off sooner, but he says that 'tis not Girls but Women who inspire violent and lasting passions—Cleopatra was Forty three Years old when Anthony lost the World for her.

Reflecting on these observations later in the journal, Thrale remarks, "The power of one Sex over the other does certainly begin sooner & end later than one should think . . . Old Scrase has a sentimental Attachment to a Widow of fifty-seven Years old & I should not have the same Power over Johnson's Spirits or Sir Philip Clerke's, if I were not a Woman."[31] Unlike didactic writers and novelists, Thrale examines sexual attraction as distinct from physical beauty: "I have observed that Female Beauty does not excite proportionate Passion. Qualities which do cause Passion may certainly be annex'd to Beauty & often are so, but they do not necessarily belong to it." She speculates:

Those women seem to have most Empire over Men who boldest claim it: Mrs. Fitzherbert, Mrs. Greatheed, Mrs. Cramer: all moderate as to Beauty, and limited as to Talents, hold in their Chairs three very handsome and sensible men . . . all Men younger than themselves, and infinitely superior to their Tyrants in every natural Gift & acquired Knowledge.[32]

Mrs. Thrale's personal study of the subject, however, and her conclusions upon it were largely disproven when she tried to put them into practice. Upon her widowhood at age thirty-nine, Mrs. Thrale records: "I am sullen with the Town, for fancying me such an amorous Ideot that I am dying to enjoy every filthy fellow."[33] When she later made her intentions to marry Gabriel Piozzi known among her friends, she received this reply from Fanny Burney:

the Mother of 5 children, 3 of them as Tall as herself, will never be forgiven for shewing so great an ascendence of passion over Reason. . . . all is at stake—& for what? a gratification that no one can *esteem*, not even he for whom you feel it. . . . We were not Born for ourselves & I have regularly practiced, as far as occasion has offered, the forbearance I recommend.[34]

Clearly, the images of power and passion she had herself observed were reduced to nothing more than a dismal choice between Burney's comfortless "forbearance" and the role of "amorous Ideot" to the town.

When she expresses the desire for remarriage, Hester Thrale places herself in the problematic category of the mature woman who is heterosexually active while being both outside of the control of a man and under the scrutiny of the public eye. Older women who chose to marry were regarded as being so driven by their unsatisfied sexual desire that they were unable to correctly evaluate prospective husbands. This was thought to be especially true of spinsters, who were depicted as being willing to disregard all consideration of class, economic stability, or physical fitness in pursuit of sexual satisfaction. As Ned Ward describes the scenario: "So, at last the haughty madam . . . having an absolute aversion to leading Apes in Hell [dying a spinster], resolves to lay fast Hold of the next Offer; which in all Probability proves an unbenefic'd Curate, in Hopes of a Living, or some tottering Apothecary."[35]

In a similar vein, Defoe discusses the likely outcome of unequal marriages in which the woman has an advantage in birth or fortune. In this dialogue, "the Lady" widow's cousin counsels her against her proposed match:

Well, Cousin, says the Lady . . . I am resolved to take a young Man, that has his Dependence upon me, and I am sure to preserve my Authority over him. I take him with nothing; I shall make a Gentleman of him. Ay, Madam, though you do, says the Cousin, I have known so many underling Fellows turn Tyrants, and domineer and insult their Benefactresses, that I can never think of anything, but of being betrayed and ill treated, when I hear of such Matches.[36]

In Defoe's narrative, the cousin proves to be correct, and after she has asserted her authority over a man (and gratified her physical desires) the widow finds herself with a broken heart and a ne'er-do-well brute for a husband. Other popular tales tell of fortune-hunting rogues who marry the widow, take her fortune, and vanish, leaving her and her children to starve on the streets. All these stories contribute another element to the antiaging mythos that permeated the culture: whereas spinsters and matrons were assured that men never admired them for their physical charms—and any apparent admiration masked contempt—widows were taught to view any male attention as rising out of man's desire to exploit an unprotected woman.

Even in these cautionary tales in which the older women are presented as foolish or naïve, there is still an underlying fear that the lust of mature women, especially those who are outside male control, poses a threat to both physical and social constructions of masculine dominance. The remarriage of widows was viewed as a woman's taking the initiative in procuring the man she finds most worthy or enticing. It is assumed that these widows would not be likely to abandon their autonomy after marriage and will not be as easily governed as would a young woman. Ned Ward writes in *Female Policy Detected*, "Widows are so froward, so waspish, and so stubbord, that thou canst not wrest them from their wills; and if thou think to make her good by stripes, thou must beat her to death."[37] The "True Penitent" makes the usual remarks about the folly of marrying for money and the status of the widow as a "second-hand Commodity, and certainly in some Respects the worse for Wear,"[38] but he introduces a new element in his focus on "the Wiles of the Widow":

Her deep Dissimulation, her artful Appearances, are by far an Over-match for all the Wisdom and Policy of Man; who may as well pretend to Fathom and discern the Depth and the Bottom of the Ocean, as to Form a right Judgment of the true Character of a Widow.[39]

The Penitent explains that the widow's ability to outwit her husband is derived from her membership in a female community in which "Great Numbers of married Women and Widows, when in company with those of their own Sex and Class, give such a Loose to their Thoughts and Words, as greatly tends to the Corruption of each other; rendering their Conceptions gross, their Deportment masculine and immodest." In these groups, older women discuss managing a husband, eating, drinking, and their "receipts for Washes, Cordials, Abortion, Fainting-Fits, Paint &c &c."[40] These images of a female cabal present an alternative, "underground" society open only to older women in which all aspects of life—from the most basic acts of sustenance and reproduction to the most frivolous conventions of social adornment—are brought under total control. The control exerted by these mature women is all the more threatening because in this narrative, at least, older women are presented as creatures driven by a prodigious sexual appetite. The "True Penitent" laments: "My Wife, tho' Sixty-five Years old, still preserved a lusty, warm and vigorous Constitution, and had not the least aversion to the Pleasures of Youth . . . the Fretting and Vexation which I Daily endured, from the termagant Behavior of my Wife, had worn me to a Skeleton."[41] The "wearing away" of the younger husband creates a size disparity that completely inverts the differences created by sexual dimorphism. It seems here that men are diminished by sexual activity, while women are enlarged by it.

The long-term physical effects of voracious sexuality are shown in the mid-century depictions of brothel-keeping prostitutes who are made physically larger by their intemperance and "gross habit."[42] An excellent example of the mature woman's depiction as enlarged or engorged can be found in the first brothel keeper described in John Cleland's *Memoirs of a Woman of Pleasure* (1749), "Mrs. Brown," who is a "clumsy fat figure," "squab-fat, red-faced and at least fifty." The most intimate aspects of her anatomy are discussed in excruciating detail as the young Fanny Hill watches a sexual encounter between Mrs. Brown and her young paramour. Cleland minutely describes her enormous, discolored, "flagging soft" breasts and the "greasy landscape" visible where "her fat brawny thighs hung down."[43] Lois Banner considers the depiction of Mrs. Brown as part of the pornographic novel's desire to titillate by breaking taboos: "Even the presumed ugliness of aging had to it an erotic quality of being beyond the ordinary, of stretching the limits of the visible beyond the socially acceptable, of indicating new realms of vice."[44] At the same time, the physical description that Cleland supplies is very similar to the monitory figure of Mrs. Sinclair, the procuress in the avowedly didactic *Clarissa* (1748), whose dying body is vilified with such gusto by Richardson:

Her misfortune has not at all sunk but rather . . . increased her flesh; rage and violence perhaps swelled her muscly features. Behold her then, spreading the whole tumbled bed with her quaggy carcase . . . mill-post arms . . . broad hands clenched with violence . . . big eyes goggled and flaming-red . . . matted grizzly hair . . . fat ears and brawny neck . . . her wide mouth . . . splitting her face, as it were in two parts; and her huge tongue hideously rolling in it; heaving, puffing as if for breath, her bellows-shaped and various-coloured breasts ascending by turns to her chin and descending out of sight with the violence of her gaspings.

Cleland's Mrs. Brown had been made large by her hearty physical appetites; Mrs. Sinclair seems to be distended by her evil deeds—Richardson describes her immoral corruption of others as her "intemperance" and "diffusive wick-edness." Her death-bed lamentations are mixed with less articulate forms of communication; she is described as: "crying, scolding, cursing," "howling more like a wolf than a human creature," and making a sound "more like that of a bull than a woman." The expansion of Sinclair's body has not only erased her femininity; it has made her less than human. In these images, the choice of older women to move away from socially/morally acceptable sexuality seems to bring with it a physical price—a physical metamorphosis into monstrosity.[45] In spite of their participation in the male prerogative of trafficking in female flesh, nei-ther of these brothel keepers has any real autonomy. It is clear that Lovelace is the real master in Sinclair's house, and she is little more than a tool employed to achieve his will. Mrs. Brown, in turn, is mastered by the "tall, brawny horse-grenadier" who performs sexual favors for her in return for access to her em-ployees and direct payment. Not only does she "maintain" him, but Mrs. Brown is "under too much subjection to him" and cannot have her fill of him sexually—"the old lady only now and then got her turn."[46] These brothel keepers have become creatures encased in uncontrollable bodies, and, as a result, are ulti-mately more vulnerable to male control. Like the flirtatious spinsters, and the widows who marry fortunehunters, sexual desire makes these "fallen women" powerless even though they are legally/economically/socially outside male con-trol.

> The ag'd dame to venery inclin'd
> With a dry body and a salacious mind
> Whose swimming eyes distil eternal brine
> Whose india teeth the burnish'd jett outshine;
> A thousand lovers court, to win her gold,
> Whose youthful veins at sight of her grow cold,
> And, from the twinkling of her letchrous eyes
> Presage, whose fortune waits the golden prize.[47]

Although the prerogative of upper-class males to purchase female attention was well established in this culture, women who exhibited the same behaviors were subject to unparalleled scorn. One of the nastier portraits of aristocratic appetite is that of "Iantha" in Delariviere Manley's New Atalantis (1709), whose first lover finds her "Generous, Amorous Temper, extreamly Commodious to his Necessity for Money." Iantha's great sexual appetite and considerable fortune ensure that she has a steady stream of lovers who are able to make love to her only by covering her ugly face with a handkerchief, "lest something less charming than her Body, shou'd pall their Ardors and abate their Excess."[48]

Though these images were clearly intended to humiliate their subjects, they still convey a subversive impression of female sexuality. In both these cases, women are violating the "natural order" of the sexual hierarchy. As was true of the Butler-boffing spinsters, these rich older women are using their social status as a means of compelling male sexual compliance; thus, they are inverting the standard sexual hierarchy that declares that working-class women are the natural sexual prey of their male employers. These aristocratic women also overturn convention by placing men in the subordinate, "female" role in which their sexual status becomes their single defining feature.

The prevalence of these images of man-hungry spinsters, gigolo-hunting crones, and sex-crazed widows is strange if we are to consider the demographics of the period. Demographers and social historians consider the eighteenth century to be a time of virtually "universal" marriage when unmarried women made up a relatively minute part of the population[49] as a whole and remarrying widows as a group actually declined during the century.[50] In spite of these images of the wealthy single woman abusing the power conferred by her class and financial status, unmarried women—even those of gentle birth—were far more likely to be poverty-bound than husband-hunting. This may be at the root of the construction of the virulently negative stereotypes of single women. Such images may have served to free the more comfortable members of society from having any sense of moral obligation to help these socially and economically disadvantaged individuals. For economic, social, and psychological reasons it was more comfortable for society to erase the existence of older women, and to stigmatize those who continued to be visible. Clearly, since the stereotypes of the sexually dominant spinsters and widows have little basis in historical reality, these images must have addressed some deeply held prejudice or facilitated the development of some newly emerging social construct.

As a powerless minority, the unmarried older woman may have served as a scapegoat for many of the fears that society harbored about women's sexual power. This seems to be indicated by the extremely wide range of physical types and behaviors that were subject to criticism by these negative depictions: skinny spinsters, obese procuresses; withered crones, unnaturally nubile widows; women who paint too much, women who hide too little; women who persist in inappropriately decorous forms of femininity, women who leave all humanity behind and become monstrous. The message communicated by these varied images is that the female body beyond the age of twenty-five must be grotesque, and that any form of mature female sexuality that is not employed to placate a husband must be corrupt. The juxtaposition of the texts' unremitting focus on the unappealing physical characteristics of aging with images featuring feats of female sexual potency and male domination emphasizes that this is not sexual activity to be celebrated or desired. The images of primping hags who are unaware of their physical repellence discourage older women from pursuing sexual pleasure, by depicting them as unwitting dupes of fortune hunters rather than as sexually autonomous lovers. The written texts of this period demonstrate that older women are unfit for sexual activity outside the marriage bed from every standpoint: aesthetically, emotionally, socially, and economically. Still, in spite of these venomous warnings, in the "real world" as it is represented in the writings of Hester Thrale Piozzi, the "business of being a woman" and the mysteries of attraction are not so comprehensible or controllable as the conduct writers would have us believe.

The literature from the eighteenth century offers clear examples of the intertwining of sexism and "ageism" that has been discussed in our own century by feminist critics such as Gloria Steinem, Naomi Wolfe, Susan Faludi, and Germaine Greer. The wealth of images of female aging include frank depictions of some aspects of aging that continue to be issues in modern American society—physical changes brought about by menopause, older women's sexuality, and the indefinite social role of the older woman. Studying eighteenth-century attitudes toward aging women allows us to see these aspects of aging outside our own more consumer-driven society and hints at some of the deeper causes of ageism within pre-industrial Western society.[51]

It seems that there is something deeply threatening about the image of the aging woman. In the popular imagination, older women continued to be defined in heterosexual terms that excluded them from the predominant tropes of feminine value. This meant that they were either erased by what Margaret Doody has called "the coercive social lie that a woman ought to be sexually dead at forty"[52] or made monstrous by a caricature that presented the sexually alive older woman as "a very odd sort of an Animal."[53] Whether she was married, widowed, or single, none of these older women exhibit the passivity necessary to conform to the eighteenth century's "feminine ideal." The older woman may be blameless, but she knows too much to ever again be innocent. At the same time, unlike her younger sisters, she may be saddened by social disapproval, but her life can no longer be destroyed by it. Their knowledge and social autonomy meant that older women had a very unfeminine capacity to move beyond the gender lines being imposed upon them and to assert their identities as individuals with their own needs and desires. The negative images of pathetic or grotesque older women in thrall to their deviant sexuality are clearly an effort to deny their potency and to contain their disruptive capabilities.

NOTES

1. Carolyn Heilbrun, *Writing a Woman's Life* (New York: W. W. Norton, 1988), 128.

2. I am choosing to use the word *spinster* to refer to "never-married women" because the eighteenth-century employment of the term was purely descriptive and did not have

any of the negative connotations that it would acquire in later centuries. I will also employ the term *old maid* when I am discussing the depiction of the negative stereotype of unmarried women that was prevalent in eighteenth-century Britain. Although I am appreciative of the reasoning behind Amy Froide's employment of the term *singlewomen*, I prefer to use language that is consistent with eighteenth-century usage. See A. Froide and J. Bennett, Introduction to *Singlewomen in the European Past 1250–1800*, ed. A. Froide and J. Bennett (Philadelphia: University of Pennsylvania Press, 1999), 2.

3. Robert Halsband, ed., *The Selected Letters of Lady Mary Wortley Montagu* (New York: St. Martin's Press, 1970), 135.

4. Hester Thrale Piozzi, *The Thraliana*, vol. 2, ed. Katharine Balderston (Oxford, Eng.: Clarendon Press, 1951), 971.

5. Matthew Montagu, ed., *The Letters of Mrs. Elizabeth Montagu* (London: T. Cadell and W. Davies, 1809), 178.

6. Mary Astell, *A Serious Proposal to the Ladies* (London: R. Wilkin, 1695), 132.

7. James Fordyce, *Sermons to Young Women* (London, 1766), 112.

8. *The Female Aegis* (New York: Garland, 1974), 164–165. Originally published in 1798.

9. Frances Burney, *The Wanderer* (New York: Oxford University Press, 1991), 542–543. Originally published in 1814.

10. Piozzi, *Thraliana*, vol. 2, 695.

11. Amanda Vickery, *The Gentleman's Daughter: Women's Lives in Georgian England* (New Haven, CT: Yale University Press, 1998), 265, 270.

12. Joseph Addison, *The Spectator*, no. 128, vol. 1, ed. C. Gregory Smith (London: J. M. Dent and Sons, 1964), 390.

13. *Female Aegis*, 165.

14. Ibid.

15. Ruth Mazzo Karras, "Sex and the Singlewoman," in *Singlewomen in the European Past 1250–1800*, ed. Judith Bennett and Amy M. Froide (Philadelphia: University of Pennsylvania Press, 1999), 132.

16. Montagu, *The Letters*, 36.

17. Ann Skinn, *The Old Maid*, vol. 3 (London, 1771), 49, 50.

18. Tobias Smollett, *The Expedition of Humphry Clinker* (New York: Oxford University Press, 1984), 94, 262. Originally published in 1771.

19. *Amusements in High Life* (London, 1786), 84.

20. William Hayley, *A Philosophical, Historical, and Moral Essay on Old Maids*, vol. 1 (London, 1786), 56.

21. Steele, *Spectator*, vol. 1, 360.

22. Smollett, *Humphry Clinker*, 60.

23. Skinn, *Old Maid*, vol. 1, 56, 57.

24. Henry Fielding, *Joseph Andrews* (New York: Penguin, 1988), 71. Originally published in 1742.

25. Roy Porter, *Sexual Underworlds of the Enlightenment* (Manchester, Eng.: Manchester University Press, 1987), 8.

26. Daniel Defoe, *Conjugal Lewdness and Matrimonial Whoredom* (London, 1727), 54.

27. Lemuel Gulliver, *The Pleasures and Felicities of Marriage* (London, 1745), 62.

28. A True Penitent, "The Folly, Sin, and Danger of Marrying Widows and Old Women in General" (London: J. Robinson, 1750), 66.

29. Defoe, *Conjugal Lewdness*, 245–246.

30. Penitent, "Folly, Sin and Danger," 25.

31. Piozzi, *Thraliana*, vol. 1, 386, 423.

32. Ibid., vol. 1, 737, 760.

33. Ibid., vol. 1, 531.

34. Margaret Doody, *Frances Burney* (New Brunswick, NJ: Rutgers University Press, 1988), 162.

35. Ned Ward, *The Modern World Disrob'd* (London, 1708), 77.

36. Defoe, *Conjugal Lewdness*, 223–224.

37. Ned Ward, "Female Policy Detected" (London, 1716), 65.

38. Penitent, "Folly, Sin, and Danger," 13.

39. Ibid., 14.

40. Ibid., 20–21.

41. Ibid., 21.

42. Samuel Richardson, *Clarissa* (New York: Viking Penguin, 1985), 1390. Originally published in 1747–1748.

43. John Clelend, *Memoirs of a Woman of Pleasure* (New York: Signet Books, 1965), 41, 21, 41. Originally published in 1748–1749.

44. Lois Banner, *In Full Flower: Aging Women, Power and Sexuality* (New York: Vintage Books, 1992), 174.

45. Richardson, *Clarissa*, 1388, 1389, 1387.

46. Cleland, *Memoirs*, 40, 43.

47. *The Joys of Hymen* (London, 1768), 21.

48. Delariviere Manley, *Secret Memoirs . . . from the New Atalantis*, vol. 2 (London, 1709), 205, 206.

49. E. A. Wrigley, et al., *English Population History from Family Reconstitution* (Cambridge, Eng.: Cambridge University Press, 1997), 195. Wrigley et al. indicate that the proportion of women never marrying reached its peak (20 percent) in the mid-seventeenth century. It remains at less than 10 percent from the end of the seventeenth century through the middle of the nineteenth.

50. Barbara Todd, "The Remarrying Widow," in *Women in English Society*, ed. Mary Prior (London: Methuen, 1985), 83; Richard Grassby, *Kinship and Capitalism: Marriage, Family and Business in the English-Speaking World, 1580–1740* (Cambridge, Eng.: Cambridge University Press, 2001), 125.

51. For a related conclusion see the chapter by Combe and Schmader in this volume.

52. Doody, *Frances Burney*, 163.

53. Joseph Addison, quoted in Germaine Greer, *The Change: Women, Aging and the Menopause* (New York: Alfred A. Knopf, 1992), 282.

Appendix: Citations from the Pepys Ballad Collection, Madgalene College, Cambridge

The Ballads are arranged in alphabetical order by title as recorded, with the Pepys citation (volume and item number) at the end.

The Bashfull-Maidens No, No, No, Turn'd to I, I, I. Or, The Down-Right Wooing of Tom and Doll. London, 1680. [Pepys III: 183].

Brittains Triumph. London, 1685. [Pepys II: 230].

A Caveat for Young-Men. London, 1680–1682. [Pepys II: 36].

The Country Lass, Who Left her Spinning-Wheel for a More Pleasant Employment. London, 1690. [Pepys III: 290].

[Hill, T.] *The Doleful Dance, and Song of Death; Intituled, Dance After my Pipe*. London, 1655. [Pepys II: 62].

England's New Bell-Men Ringing into All Peoples Ears, God's Dreadful Judgement to this Land and Kingdom. London, 1690. [Pepys II: 61].

The Extravagant Youth; or, An Emblem of Prodigality. London, 1684–1685. [Pepys II: 92].

Fancy, P. *The Age and Life of Man. Here you ma [sic] See the Fraility that in Men, Till they have Run the Years Threescore and Ten*. Tune of Jane Shore. London, 1675. [Pepys II: 32].

The Father's Wholesome Admonition; or, A Lumping Pennyworth of Good Counsel for Bad Husbands. London, 1685–1691. [Pepys II: 83].

[Campion, T.] *A Friends Advice: In an Excellent Ditty, Concerning the Variable Changes in this World*. London, 1650–1658. [Pepys I: 55].

The Golden Age; or, An Age of Plaine-Dealing. London, 1698. [Pepys I: 152].

Good Admonition; or, To Al Sorts of People this counsell I Sing, That in Each Ones Affaire, To Take Heed's a Faire Thing. London, n.d. [Pepys I: 50].

A Goodfellowes Complaint Against Strong Beere; or, Take Heed Goodfellowes for Heere

You May See How it is Strong Beere that Hath Undone Me. London, 1630. [Pepys
I: 438].

The Good Shepherds Sorrow for the Death of his Beloved Sonne. London, n.d. [Pepys
I: 352].

*The Lamentable Burning of the Citty of Corke (in the Province of Munster in Ireland)
by Lightning*. London, n.d. [Pepys I: 69].

The Lamentable Ditty of Little Mousgrove, and the Lady Barnet. London, 1658. [Pepys
I: 365].

*Mans Amazement: It being a True Relation of one Thomas Cox, a Hackney-Coach-Man,
to Whom the Devil Appeared on Friday Night*. . . . London, 1684. [Pepys II: 175].

A Merry New Catch of All Trades. London, 1656. [Pepys I: 164].

*A Most Excellent Ballad, of an Old Man and his Wife, Who in their Great Want and
Misery Sought to Children for Succour, by Whom they were Disdained, and Scor-
nefully Sent Away Succourlesse, and Gods Vengeance Shewed upon them for the
Same*. London, 1658–1664. [Pepys I: 43].

A Most Notable and Worthy Example of an Ingratious Sonne. London, 1658–1664.
[Pepys II: 180–181].

*A Most Sorrowfull Song, Setting Forth the Miserable End of Banister, Who Betraied the
Duke of Buckingham, his Lord and Master*. London, n.d. [Pepys I: 64].

*A Mournful Caral; or, An Elegy Lamenting the Tragical Ends of Two Unfortunate Faith-
ful Lovers, Frankin and Cordelius, He being Slain, She Slew herself with her
Dagger*. London, 1680–1682. [Pepys II: 76].

A New Ballad Intituled, The Old Mans Complaint Against his Wretched Sonne. London,
n.d. [Pepys I: 137].

*Oh Gramercy Penny: Being a Lancashire Ditty, and Chiefly Penn'd, to Prove that a
Penny is a Mans Best Friend*. London, n.d. [Pepys I: 218–219].

The Old Mans Advice to Batchellors, About the Choice of their Wives. London, n.d.
[Pepys IV: 104].

The Old Mans Sayings Concerning the Alteration of the Times. London, n.d. [Pepys IV:
301].

[Pope, W.] *Old Mans Wish*. London, 1684. [Pepys IV: 370].

The Old Miser Slighted. London, 1685–1692. [Pepys IV: 8].

The Old Woman's Resolution. London, 1688–1692. [Pepys III: 186].

Pitties Lamenation for the Cruelty of this Age. London, n.d. [Pepys I: 162].

A Pleasant New Ballad of Tobias. London, 1655–1658. [Pepys I: 488–489].

The Poor Folks Complaint; or, a Hint of the Hard Times. London, 1668. [Pepys IV:
340].

The Poor Man put to a Pinch; or, A Declaration of these Hard Times. London, n.d.
[Pepys IV: 299].

*The Poor Man's Complaint; or, The Sorrowful Lamentation of Poor Plain-Dealing, at
this Time of Distress and Trouble*. London, 1690–1700. [Pepys IV: 300].

The Poor Peoples Complaint of the Unconscionable Brokers and Talley-Men. London,
1667–1689. [Pepys IV: 353].

Poor Robins Dream: Commonly Called Poor Charity. London, 1673? [Pepys IV: 295].

*The Protestants Great Misery in Ireland, Relating the Inhumane Cruelties that are Daily
Committed There by the French and Irish Papists*. London, 1691. [Pepys II: 332].

The Rarest Ballad that Ever was Seen, Of the Blind Beggers Daughter of Bednal-Green.
London, 1658–1664. [Pepys I: 490–491].

The Second Part of the Jewes Crueltie, Setting Forth the Mercifulnesse of the Judge Towardes the Marchant. London, n.d. [Pepys I: 145].

The Shepheard and The King, and of Gillian The Shepherds Wife, with Her Churlish Answers: Being Full of Mirth and Merry Pastime. London, 1650? [Pepys I: 76–77].

The Sorrowful Wife; or, Love in a Tub. London, 1683–1700. [Pepys IV: 116].

The Subtil Miss of London; or, The Ranting Hector Well Fitted by this Cunning Miss. London, n.d. [Pepys III: 253].

A Third Touch of the Times. London, 1688. [Pepys IV: 311].

Times Alteration; or, the Old Mans Rehearsall, What Brane [sic] Dayes he Knew, A Great While Agone, When this Old Cap was New. London, 1641. [Pepys I: 160].

The Western-Triumph; or, The Royal Progress of Our Gracious King James the II, into the West of England. London, 1688. [Pepys II: 246].

A Worthy Example of a Vertuous Wife, Who Fed her Father with her Own Milk, Being Condemned to be Starved to Death. London, 1658–1664. [Pepys I: 492].

The Young-Mans Repentance. London, 1685–1688. [Pepys II: 37].

Selected Bibliography

We list here only sources that are focused primarily on old age in preindustrial Western societies, rather than including publications from such highly relevant fields as the history of poverty and poor relief. This is not meant to be an exhaustive listing of the published work on old age, but it is designed to be a helpful starting point for readers and to acknowledge those works that have been most widely cited in this volume.

Achenbaum, W. A. *Old Age in the New Land: The American Experience Since 1790.* Baltimore, MD: Johns Hopkins University Press, 1978.

Arco y Garay, Ricardo del. "La Ínfima levadura social en las obras de Cervantes." In *Estudios de historia social de España*, vol. 2, edited by Carmelo Viñas y Mey, 209–290. Madrid: Consejo Superior de Investigaciones Científicas, 1952.

Asp, C. " 'The Clamor of Eros': Freud, Aging, and King Lear." In *Memory and Desire: Aging—Literature—Psychoanalysis*, edited by Kathleen Woodward and Murray M. Schwartz, 192–204. Bloomington: Indiana University Press, 1986.

Barker-Read, M. "The Treatment of the Aged Poor in Five Selected West Kent Parishes from Settlement to Speenhamland (1662–1797)." Unpublished Ph.D. diss., Open University, 1988.

Bever, E. "Old Age and Witchcraft in Early Modern Europe." In *Old Age in Preindustrial Society*, edited by P. Stearns, 150–190. New York: Holmes and Meier, 1982.

Bois, Jean-Pierre. *Les Vieux: de Montaigne aux premières retraites*. Paris: Fayard, 1989.

Bonfield, L. "Was There a Third Age in the Pre-industrial Past? Some Evidence from the Law." In *An Aging World: Dilemmas and Challenges for Law and Social Policy*, edited by J. Eekelaar and D. Pearl, 37–53. Oxford, Eng.: Oxford University Press, 1989.

Borscheid, P. "Der alte Mensch in der Vergangenheit." In *Zukunft des Alterns und ge-*

sellschaftliche Entwicklung, edited by Paul B. Bates and Jürgen Mittelstrass, 35–61. Berlin, Ger.: de Gruyter, 1992.

———. *Geschichte des Alters. Vom Spätmittelalter zum 18. Jahrhundert.* Münster: Deutscher Taschenbuch, 1987.

Botelho, L. "Aged and Impotent: Parish Relief of the Aged Poor in Early Modern Suffolk." In *Charity, Self-Interest and Welfare in the English Past*, edited by M. Daunton, 91–111. New York: St. Martin's Press, 1996.

———. "Old Age and Menopause in Rural Women of Early Modern Suffolk." In *Women and Ageing in British Society Since 1500*, edited by L. Botelho and P. Thane, 43–65. London: Longman, 2001.

———. "The Old Woman's Wish: Widows by the Family Fire? Widows' Old Age Provisions in Rural England." *History of the Family* 7 (2002): 1–20.

Botelho, L., and P. Thane, eds. *Women and Ageing in British Society Since 1500*. London: Longman, 2001.

Bourdelais, P. *Le Nouvel âge de la vieillesse: Histoire du vieillissement de la population*. Paris: Éditions O. Jacob, 1993.

Cavallo, S. "Family Obligations and Inequalities in Access to Care in Northern Italy, Seventeenth to Eighteenth Centuries." In *The Locus of Care: Family, Community, Institutions and the Provision of Welfare Since Antiquity*, edited by P. Horden and R. M. Smith, 90–110. London: Routledge, 1998.

Cavallo, S., and L. Warner, eds. *Widowhood in Medieval and Early Modern Europe*. London: Longman, 1999.

Clark, M. "Aging Queens in Shakespeare's Drama." Unpublished Ph.D. diss., University of Michigan, 1998.

Cole, T. *The Journey of Life: A Cultural History of Aging in America*. Cambridge, Eng.: Cambridge University Press, 1992.

Combe, K., and K. Schmader. "Shakespeare Teaching Geriatrics: Lear and Prospero As Case Studies in Aged Heterogeneity." In *Aging and Identity: A Humanities Perspective*, edited by S. Munson Deats and L. Tallent Lenker, 33–46. Westport, CT: Praeger, 1999.

Conrad, C., and H.-J.von Kondratowitz, eds. *Zur Kulturgeschichte des Alterns*. Berlin, Ger.: Deutsches Zentrum für Altersfragen, 1993.

Deats, S. Munson. "The Dialectic of Aging in Shakespeare's *King Lear* and *The Tempest*." In *Aging and Identity: A Humanities Perspective*, edited by S. Munson Deats and L. Tallent Lenker, 23–32. Westport, CT: Praeger, 1999.

Demos, J. "Old Age in Early New England." In *Past, Present and Personal: The Family and the Life Course in American History*. Oxford, Eng.: Oxford University Press, 1986.

Dinges, M. "Self-Help and Reciprocity in Parish Assistance: Bordeaux in the 16th & 17th Centuries." In *The Locus of Care: Family, Community, Institutions and the Provision of Welfare Since Antiquity*, edited by P. Horden, and R. M. Smith, 111–124. London: Routledge, 1998.

Engelhardt, D. von. "Altern zwischen Natur und Kultur. Kulturgeschichte des Alters." In *Alter und Gesellschaft*, edited by Peter Borscheid, 13–24. Stuttgart: Hirzel, 1995.

Fauve-Chamoux, A. "Aging in a Never-Empty Nest: The Elasticity of the Stem Family." In *Aging and Generational Relations over the Life Course: A Historical and*

Cross-Cultural Perspective, edited by Tamara K. Hareven, 75–99. Berlin, Ger.: Walter de Gruyter, 1996.

Featherstone, M., and A. Wernick, eds. *Images of Ageing: Cultural Representations of Later Life*. London: Routledge, 1995.

Fiedler, L. "Eros and Thanatos: Old Age in Love." In *Aging, Death and the Completion of Being*, edited by David D. Van Tassel, 235–254. Philadelphia: University of Pennsylvania Press, 1979.

Finlay, R. "The Venetian Republic As a Gerontocracy: Age and Politics in the Renaissance." *Journal of Medieval and Renaissance Studies* 8 (1978): 157–178.

Fischer, D. Hackett. *Growing Old in America*. New York: Oxford University Press, 1978.

Froide, A. "Old Maids: The Lifecycle of Single Women in Early Modern England." In *Women and Ageing in British Society Since 1500*, edited by L. Botelho and P. Thane, 89–110. London: Longman, 2001.

Gilbert, C. "When Did a Man in the Renaissance Grow Old?" *Studies in the Renaissance* 14 (1967): 7–32.

Granjel, L. S. *Los ancianos en la Españade los Austria*. Salamanca, Sp.: Universidad Pontificia, 1996.

Gunnlaugsson, G., and L. Guttormsson. "Transition into Old Age. Poverty and Retirement Possibilities in Late Eighteenth- and Nineteenth-Century Iceland." In *Poor Women and Children in the European Past*, edited by J. Henderson and R. Wall, 251–268. London: Routledge, 1994.

Gutton, J. *Naissance du vieillard: Essai sur l'histoire des rapports entre les vieillards et la société en France*. Paris: Aubier, 1988.

Hammel, E. A. "The Elderly in the Bosom of the Family: La Famille Souche and Hardship Reincorporation." In *Aging in the Past: Demography, Society and Old Age*, edited by D. Kertzer and P. Laslett, 107–128. Berkeley: University of California Press, 1995.

Hemphill, D. "Age Relations and the Social Order in Early New England: Evidence for Manners." *Journal of Social History* 28, no. 2 (Winter 1994): 271–290.

Johansen, H. "Growing Old in an Urban Environment." *Continuity and Change* 2, no. 2 (1987): 297–305.

Johnson, P., and P. Thane. *Old Age from Antiquity to Post-Modernity*. London: Routledge, 1998.

Jütte, R. "Aging and Body Image in the Sixteenth Century: Hermann Weinsberg's (1518–1597) Perception of the Aging Body." *European History Quarterly* 18 (1987): 259–290.

Kerrigan, W. "Life's Iamb: The Scansion of Late Creativity in the Culture of the Renaissance." In *Memory and Desire: Aging—Literature—Psychoanalysis*, edited by K. Woodward and M. Schwartz, 168–191. Bloomington: Indiana University Press, 1986.

Kertzer, D. "Toward a Historical Demography of Aging." In *Aging in the Past: Demography, Society and Old Age*, edited by D. Kertzer and P. Laslett, 363–383. Berkeley: University of California Press, 1995.

Kertzer, D., and P. Laslett, eds. *Aging in the Past: Demography, Society and Old Age*. Berkeley: University of California Press, 1995.

Klassen, S. "Aging Gracefully in the Eighteenth Century: A Study of Elderly Women in Old Regime Toulouse." Unpublished Ph.D diss., Syracuse University, 1996.

———. "Greying in the Cloister: The Ursuline Life Course in Eighteenth-Century France." *Journal of Women's History* 12, no. 4 (2001): 87–112.

———. "Old and Cared for: Place of Residence for Elderly Women in Eighteenth-Century Toulouse." *Journal of Family History* 24, no. 1 (1999): 35–52.

Kondratowitz, H.-J. von. "The Medicalisation of Old Age: Continuity and Change in Germany from the 18th to the Early 20th Century." In *Life, Death and the Elderly: Historical Perspectives*, edited by M. Pelling and R. M. Smith, 134–164. London: Routledge, 1991.

Kugler, A. " 'I Feel Myself Decay Apace': Old Age in the Diary of Lady Sarah Cowper (1644–1720)." In *Women and Ageing in British Society Since 1500*, edited by L. Botelho and P. Thane, 66–88. London: Longman, 2001.

Laslett, P. "Family, Kinship and Collectivity as Systems of Support in Pre-industrial Europe: A Consideration of the 'Nuclear-Hardship' Hypothesis." *Continuity and Change* 3, no. 2 (1988): 153–175.

———. *Family Life and Illicit Love in Earlier Generations: Essays in Historical Sociology.* Cambridge, Eng.: Cambridge University Press, 1977.

———. "Necessary Knowledge: Age and Aging in the Societies of the Past." In *Aging in the Past: Demography, Society and Old Age*, edited by D. Kertzer and Idem, 3–77. Berkeley: University of California Press, 1995.

———. "The Traditional English Family and the Aged in Our Society." In *Aging, Death and the Completion of Being*, edited by D. Van Tassel, 97–113. Philadelphia: University of Pennsylvania Press, 1979.

Minois, G. *History of Old Age: From Antiquity to the Renaissance.* Cambridge, Eng.: Polity Press, 1989.

Ottaway, S. "The Old Woman's Home in Eighteenth-Century England." In *Women and Ageing in Britain Since 1500*, edited by L. Botelho and P. Thane, 111–138. London: Longman, 2001.

———. "Providing for the Elderly in Eighteenth-Century England." *Continuity and Change* 13, no. 3 (1998): 391–418.

Pelling, M. "Old Age and Poverty in an Early Modern Town." *Bulletin of the Social History of Medicine* 34 (1984): 42–47.

———. "Old Age, Poverty and Disability in Early Modern Norwich: Work, Remarriage and Other Expedients." In *The Common Lot: Sickness, Medical Occupations and the Urban Poor in Early Modern England*, 134–54. London: Longman, 1998.

———. "Older Women: Household, Caring and Other Occupations in the Late Sixteenth-Century Town." In *The Common Lot: Sickness, Medical Occupations and the Urban Poor in Early Modern England*, 155–75. London: Longman, 1998.

———. "Thoroughly Resented? Older Women and the Medical Role in Early Modern London." In *Women, Science and Medicine 1500–1700*, edited by L. Hunter and S. Hutton, 63–88. Gloucester, Eng.: Sutton, 1997.

———. " 'Who Needs to Marry?' Ageing and Inequality Among Women and Men in Early Modern Norwich." In *Women and Ageing in British Society Since 1500*, edited by L. Botelho and P. Thane, 31–41. London: Longman, 2001.

Pelling, M., and R. M. Smith, eds. *Life, Death and the Elderly: Historical Perspectives.* London: Routledge, 1991.

Phelan, W. J. "The Vale of Years: Early Modern Aging, Gender and Shakespearean Tragedy." Unpublished Ph.D. diss., University of California at Los Angeles, 1998.

Philibert, M. "Le Statut de la personne âgée dans les sociétés antiques et préindustrielles." *Sociologie et sociétés* 16, no. 2 (1984): 15–27.

Plakans, A. "Stepping Down in Former Times: A Comparative Assessment of 'Retirement' in Traditional Europe." In *Age Structuring in Comparative Perspective*, edited by D. I. Kertzer and W. K. Schaie, 175–195. Hillsdale, NJ: L. Erlbaum Associates, 1989.

Pollet, G., and B. Dumons. *L'État et les retraites: genèse d'une politique*. Paris: Belin, 1994.

Premo, T. *Winter Friends: Women Growing Old in the New Republic 1785–1835*. Urbana: University of Illinois Press, 1990.

Rodríguez Grajera, A. *La Alta Extremadura en el siglo XVII. Evolución demográfica y estructura agraria*. Cáceres: Universidad de Extremadura, 1990.

Roebuck, J. "When Does Old Age Begin?: The Evolution of the English Definition." *Journal of Social History* 12 (1979): 416–429.

Salomon, N. *Lo villano en el teatro del Siglo de Oro*, translated by Beatriz Chenot. Madrid: Editorial Castalia, 1985. [First published as *Recherches sur le thème paysan dans la "comedia" au temps de Lope de Vega* (Bordeaux: Feret et Fils, 1965).]

Schen, C. S. "Strategies of Poor Aged Women and Widows in Sixteenth-Century London." In *Women and Ageing in British Society Since 1500*, edited by L. Botelho and P. Thane, 13–30. London: Longman, 2001.

Smith, D. S. "The Demography of Widowhood in Preindustrial New Hampshire." In *Aging in the Past: Demography, Society and Old Age*, edited by D. Kertzer and P. Laslett, 249–272. Berkeley: University of California Press, 1995.

Smith, J. E. "Widowhood and Ageing in Traditional English Society." *Ageing and Society* 4 (1984): 429–449.

Smith, R. M. "Ageing and Well-being in Early Modern England: Pension Trends and Gender Preferences Under the English Old Poor Law, c. 1650–1800." In *Old Age from Antiquity to Post-Modernity*, edited by P. Johnson and P. Thane, 64–95. London: Routledge, 1998.

———. "The Structured Dependency of the Elderly As a Recent Development: Some Sceptical Historical Thoughts." *Ageing and Society* 4 (1984): 409–428.

Sokoll, T. "The Household Position of Elderly Widows in Poverty: Evidence from Two English Communities in the Late Eighteenth and Early Nineteenth Centuries." In *Poor Women and Children in the European Past*, edited by J. Henderson and R. Wall, 207–224. London: Routledge, 1994.

———. "Old Age in Poverty: The Records of Essex Pauper Letters, 1780–1834." In *Chronicling Poverty: The Voices and Strategies of the English Poor, 1640–1840*, edited by T. Hitchcock, P. King, and P. Sharpe, 127–154. Basingstoke, Eng.: Macmillan, 1997.

Spicker, S. F., and K. Woodward, eds. *Aging and the Elderly: Humanistic Perspectives in Gerontology*. Atlantic Highlands, NJ: Humanities Press, 1978.

Stavenuiter, M., et al., eds. *Lange Levens, stille getuigen: Oudre vrouwen in het verleden*. Zuthpen, Neth.: Walburg Pers, 1995.

Stearns, P., ed. *Old Age in Pre-industrial Society*. London: Holmes and Meier, 1982.

Thane, P. "Aging in the West." In *Handbook of the Humanities and Aging*, edited by T. Cole, R. Kastenbaum, and R. Ray. New York: Springer, 2000.

———. "The Cultural History of Old Age." *Australian Cultural History* 14 (1995): 23–29.

———. *Old Age in English History: Past Experiences, Present Issues*. Oxford, Eng.: Oxford University Press, 2000.

———. "Old People and Their Families in the English Past." In *Charity, Self-Interest and Welfare in the English Past*, edited by M. Daunton, 113–138. New York: St. Martin's Press, 1996.

Thomas, K. "Age and Authority in Early Modern England." *Proceedings of the British Academy* 62 (1976): 205–248.

Thomson, D. "The Welfare of the Elderly in the Past: A Family or Community Responsibility?" In *Life, Death, and the Elderly: Historical Perspectives*, edited by M. Pelling and R. M. Smith, 194–221. London: Routledge, 1991.

Troyansky, D. G. "Balancing Social and Cultural Approaches to the History of Old Age and Ageing in Europe: A Review and an Example from Post-Revolutionary France." In *Old Age from Antiquity to Post-Modernity*, edited by P. Johnson and P. Thane, 96–109. London: Routledge, 1998.

———. "Historical Research into Ageing, Old Age and Older People." In *Critical Approaches to Ageing and Later Life*, edited by A. Jamieson, S. Harper, and C. Victor, 49–61. Buckingham, Eng.: Open University Press, 1997.

———. *Old Age in the Old Regime: Image and Experience in Eighteenth-Century France*. Ithaca, NY: Cornell University Press, 1989.

Van Tassel, D. *Aging, Death and the Completion of Being*. Philadelphia: University of Pennsylvania Press, 1979.

Van Tassel, D., and P. Stearns, eds. *Old Age in a Bureaucratic Society*. Westport, CT: Greenwood Press, 1986.

Vinovskis, M. "Stepping Down in Former Times: The View from Colonial and 19th Century America." In *Age Structuring in Comparative Perspective*, edited by D. I. Kertzer and W. K. Schaie, 215–225. Hillsdale, NJ: L. Erlbaum Associates, 1989.

Wales, T. "Poverty, Poor Relief and the Life-Cycle: Some Evidence from Seventeenth-Century Norfolk." In *Land, Kinship and Life-Cycle*, edited by R. M. Smith, 351–404. Cambridge, Eng.: Cambridge University Press, 1985.

Wall, R. "Elderly Persons and Members of Their Households in England and Wales from Preindustrial Times to the Present." In *Aging in the Past: Demography, Society and Old Age*, edited by D. Kertzer and P. Laslett, 81–106. Berkeley: University of California Press, 1995.

———. "Les Relations entre générations en Europe autrefois." *Annales de Démographie Historique* (1991): 133–154.

———. "The Residence Pattern of Elderly English Women in Comparative Perspective." In *Women and Ageing in Britain Since 1500*, edited by L. Botelho and P. Thane, 139–165. London: Longman, 2001.

Welte, M. "Das Alter im Mittelalter und in der Frühen Neuzeit." *Schweizerische Zeitschrift für Geschichte* 37 (1987): 1–32.

Wright, S. J. "The Elderly and Bereaved in Eighteenth-Century Ludlow." In *Life, Death and the Elderly: Historical Perspectives*, edited by M. Pelling and R. M. Smith, 102–133. London: Routledge, 1991.

Index

About the Contributors

L. A. BOTELHO is associate professor of history at Indiana University of Pennsylvania. She has published essays on older women and the aged poor, as well as *Women and Ageing in Britain Since 1500*, with P. Thane (2001), *The Churchwardens' Accounts of Cratfield, Suffolk, During the 1640s and 1650s* (1999), and *John Winthrop's Worlds: England and New England, 1588–1649*, with F. Bremer (forthcoming). She is currently revising for publication *Old Age and the Dole: Provisions for the Elderly in Early Modern England*.

KIRK COMBE has published *A Martyr for Sin: Rochester's Critique of Polity, Sexuality, and Society* (1998) and coedited *Theorizing Satire: Essays in Literary Criticism* (1995). His articles on satire, drama, literary history, popular culture, education, and aging have been published in such journals as *Modern Philology*; *Texas Studies in Literature and Language*; *Restoration: Studies in English Literary Culture, 1600–1700*; *Notes and Queries*; *Pretexts: Studies in Writing and Culture*; and *Journal of Aging and Identity*. He has also edited Restoration drama and contributed a chapter entitled "The Sentimental and the Satirical" to *The Blackwell Companion to Restoration Drama*.

LOUISE GRAY is currently a Wellcome Trust researcher at the Wellcome Trust Centre for the History of Medicine at the University of East Anglia. Her Ph.D. dissertation, "The Self-Perception of Physical Afflictions Among the Labouring Poor. Pauper Petitions and Territorial Hospitals in Early Modern Rural Hesse,

Germany," was recently completed at the Wellcome Trust Centre for the History of Medicine at University College, London.

ANGELA GROPPI is early modern history researcher at University of Roma "La Sapienza." She was one of the founders and editors of the review *Memoria, rivista di storia delle donne*. Her recent publications include *Il dilemma della cittadinanza. Diritti e doveri delle donne*, edited in collaboration with G. Bonacchi (1993); *I conservatori della virtù: Donne recluse nella Roma dei papi* (1994); and the edited volume *Il lavoro delle donne* (1996).

KATHARINE KITTREDGE is an associate professor of English at Ithaca College, where she teaches courses in eighteenth-century British literature, women's writing, and science fiction. She is the editor of a collection of essays entitled *Lewd and Notorious: Female Transgression in the Eighteenth Century* (forthcoming) and is currently working on a series of autobiographical essays drawn from her experiences as a woman playing ice hockey in men's recreational leagues in Binghamton, New York.

SHERRI KLASSEN is a visiting scholar at the Institute for Human Development, Life Course and Aging at the University of Toronto. Her publications include "Life and Death in an Eighteenth-Century Convent: The Life Course of Religious Women in Old Regime Toulouse" in the *Journal of Women's History* (January 2001), "Old and Cared for: The Place of Residence of Elderly Women in Eighteenth-Century Toulouse" in the *Journal of Family History* (January 1999), and "The Domestic Virtues of Old Age in the French Revolutionary Festival" in *Canadian Journal of History* (December 1997).

ANNE KUGLER is assistant professor of history at John Carroll University. She is the author of *Errant Plagiary and Its Uses: The Writing Life of Sarah, Lady Cowper (1644–1720)* (forthcoming). Her work on aging, women, and prescriptive literature has appeared in the collection *Women and Ageing in British Society Since 1500* (2001) and the *Journal of British Studies*.

SUSANNAH R. OTTAWAY is assistant professor of history at Carleton College. Her book *The Decline of Life: Old Age in Eighteenth-Century England* is forthcoming. Her articles have appeared in *Continuity and Change, Archives,* and the collection *Women and Ageing in British Society Since 1500* (2001).

JANE PEARSON finished her dissertation, "The Rural Middle Sort in an Eighteenth-Century Essex Village: Great Tey, 1660–1830," at Essex University in 1997 and has published in the journal *Rural History* and "Figures in a Landscape: The County of Essex through the Eyes of Its Clergy" in the collection *Essex Harvest* (forthcoming). She works as a lecturer at Essex University and is engaged in research on the social and economic history of Essex.

JACK RESCH is professor of history at the University of New Hampshire at Manchester. He has received fellowships from the National Endowment for the Humanities and was a Fulbright lecturer at the Institute of English and American Studies, Debrecen University, Hungary. He is the author of numerous articles and a book, *Suffering Soldiers: Revolutionary War Veterans, Moral Sentiment, and Political Culture in the Early Republic* (1999). He is currently researching the impact of the market economy on Peterborough, New Hampshire, 1790–1860.

JANICE ROSSEN is a senior research fellow at the Harry Ransom Humanities Research Center, the University of Texas at Austin. She has published extensively on British literature, including *The World of Barbara Pym, Philip Larkin: His Life's Work*, and *The University in Modern Fiction*. She has recently completed a biography of critic and novelist Philip Toynbee, and her study of contemporary British women novelists, *Beyond Gender*, is forthcoming.

ALISON ROWLANDS is a lecturer in European history at the University of Essex, Colchester, England. Her publications on early modern German gender and witchcraft history include "In Great Secrecy: The Crime of Infanticide in Rothenburg ob der Tauber, 1501–1618," in *German History* (1997) and "Witchcraft and Popular Religion in Early Modern Rothenburg ob der Tauber," in *Popular Religion in Germany and Central Europe, 1400–1800*, edited by Bob Scribner and Trevor Johnson (1996). Her book on Rothenburg's witch trials, titled *Narratives of Witchcraft in Early Modern Germany*, is forthcoming.

KENNETH SCHMADER is an associate professor of Medicine-Geriatrics at Duke University Medical Center, Durham, NC. He is also a Senior Fellow, Duke Center for the Study of Aging and Human Development, Medical Director of the Duke Geriatric Evaluation and Treatment Clinic, and Staff Physician and Investigator at the Durham Veterans Affairs Medical Center. He has numerous publications and has received many fellowships. His publications in the field of aging include the article he co-authored with Kirk Combe in *The Journal of Aging and Identity*.

DAVID G. TROYANSKY is associate professor of history at Texas Tech University. He is the author of *Old Age in the Old Regime: Image and Experience in Eighteenth-Century France* (1989) and the principal editor of *The French Revolution in Culture and Society* (Greenwood Press, 1991). More recently he has written "Memorializing Saint-Quentin: Monuments, Inaugurations and History in the Third Republic," in *French History* (1999), "Alsatian Knowledge and European Culture: Jérémie-Jacques Oberlin, Language, and the Protestant Gymnase in Revolutionary Strasbourg," in *Francia* (2000), and the essays "Death" and "The Elderly" for the *Encyclopedia of European Social History*, edited by Peter N. Stearns (2001). His current book projects include "Entitlement and Complaint: Ending Careers and Reviewing Lives in the French Magistracy, 1814–1853" and "French Provincial: Historical Excursions on the Cognitive Map of France."

DAVID VASSBERG is emeritus professor at the University of Texas, Pan American, and has published *The Village and the Outside World* (1996), *Land and Society in Golden Age Castile* (1984), and *La venta de tierras baldias: el comunitarismo agrario y la corona de Castilla durante el siglo XVI* (1983). He has also written numerous articles on early modern Spain, which have appeared in journals such as *History of the Family*, *Agricultural History*, the *Journal of Peasant Studies*, the *Journal of Modern History*, and *Estudios Geograficos*.